DICTIONARY
JOHNSON

Gough Square as it might have looked in Johnson's time. Ceiling painting by Felix Kelly.

DICTIONARY
JOHNSON

———◄◦►———

Samuel Johnson's
Middle Years

BY

JAMES L. CLIFFORD

HEINEMANN: LONDON

Textual Note

Spelling, capitalization, and punctuation of prose quotations have been changed to twentieth-century British practice, but poetry has been left as it first appeared.

1 2 3 4 5 6 7 8 9 0 D O D O 7 8 3 2 1 0 9

LIBRARY OF CONGRESS CATALOGING IN PUBLICATION DATA
Clifford, James Lowry
    Dictionary Johnson.
    Includes bibliographical references and index.
    1. Johnson, Samuel, 1709-1784—Biography.
2. Authors, English—18th century—Biography.
3. Lexicographers—England—Biography.   I. Title.
PR3533.C58   828'.6'09[B]   79-13497
ISBN 0-07-011378-5

Book design by Christine Aulicino.

William Heinemann Ltd
10, Upper Grosvenor Street, WIX 9PA
London   Melbourne   Toronto
Johannesburg   Auckland

First published in Great Britain 1980

SBN 434 13805 3

CONTENTS

PREFACE

SAMUEL JOHNSON'S MIDDLE YEARS, from 1749 to 1763, were the most productive in his career as a writer. During the 1750's he composed his best-known essays—*Ramblers, Adventurers,* and *Idlers*—and produced *The Dictionary of the English Language,* which brought him his familiar nickname. His miscellaneous political contributions to *The Literary Magazine* and his most remarkable piece of fiction, *Rasselas,* were written during these years. These were the works which established Johnson's lasting reputation. Yet not much has been written about his character and daily life during this period.

Although these years represented a fifth of Johnson's life, they occupy only about a tenth of the space in Boswell's memorable biography. He discusses Johnson's writings at this time, but gives few clues to his private life. As he had with the earlier years, Boswell moved speedily through the 1750's, preferring to give more space to Johnson's later life for which he possessed masses of accurate, first-hand material. Yet few readers are troubled by the fact that almost half of Boswell's account concentrates on Johnson's last eight years. Almost everyone would agree that Boswell's own accounts are superior to any he might have received from Johnson's early friends. Boswell's records of his subject's conversation give us a unique view of a colorful personality. Without them we would have a less adequate understanding of the great man's keen mind and moral convictions.

But Samuel Johnson was much more than a witty and eccentric talker. He was a challenging writer and profound thinker. In his published works, especially in his little-known journalism of the 1750s, his attitude is refreshingly relevant for twentieth-century readers. We find him wrestling with such problems as the treatment of blacks, the dangers of colonial expansion, and the evils of war. In clear, forceful terms he expresses his moral judgment on international affairs, corruption in high places, and the threat of big business. He said uncommonly well much that we still need to express. During the recent Watergate scandal a pertinent quotation from Johnson found a prominent place in a discussion of "executive privilege" in the *New Yorker* magazine.

Each new generation finds stimulating and controversial ideas in Johnson's works. Thus there will always be new interpretations and fresh revaluations of his basic ideas. Yet these studies must depend upon what can be known about Johnson's life and background. To understand the basic motivations of any writer it is necessary to know something about his physical surroundings, the characters of his close associates, and the intellectual, political, and social currents of the day.

And so we need to examine in greater depth the productive years when Johnson did his most characteristic writing, to bring together the isolated pieces of evidence which have come to light since the eighteenth century. The devoted researches of scholars like Aleyn Lyell Reade, who turned up masses of material, formed the basis for my previous study of Johnson's early life. Similarly his mature years can be illustrated with new insights drawn from a wealth of hitherto unknown manuscripts.

There are interesting surprises. From court records one finds that when providing bail for the wife of one of his amanuenses, Samuel Johnson encountered Henry Fielding in his quarters in Bow Street. It had been uncertain that the two writers ever met. The minutes kept at the Foundling Hospital make it evident that Johnson narrowly escaped being brought into court to defend himself against charges of defamation—an incident unknown until recently. Records kept by a group of artists describe Johnson's help in planning their first exhibitions. The unpublished letters of the Warton family tell us more about the authorship of *The Adventurer* essays; and in the correspondence of Thomas Birch we are offered shrewd comments on Johnson's works and plans. Diaries like those of Thomas Hollis and Thomas Percy, as well as daily newspapers, yield new information about his social and professional activity.

In the following pages I have tried to put into narrative form what is known about Johnson's middle years—not only how and with whom he spent his days and the sequence of events, but his reactions to them— evidence of the ambiguity of his feelings toward his wife and mother, his failure to conquer bad habits or to obtain financial security, and his fears of insanity. If there are still gaps in our knowledge, that is inevitable. But this account will at least give some idea of the personal life of a great writer during the years in which his remarkable talents found their fullest expression.

JAMES L. CLIFFORD
New York City
April, 1978

ILLUSTRATIONS

The frontispiece reproduces a ceiling painting from the Donald Hyde Rooms in the Houghton Library, Harvard University. We are grateful to the artist, Felix Kelly, and to the Houghton Library for this view of Gough Square as it might have looked in Johnson's time.

The picture of Cave and his assistants at St. John's Gate, standing before Fame (p. 10), was designed by S. Wale and used as an emblematical frontispiece, together with "The Vision: a Poem," for the 1747 yearly volume of the *Gentleman's Magazine*. Over a hundred years later, in the March 1857 number, pp. 283–84, Cave's attendants, to the right, were identified as "Hawkesworth, Johnson, and others of his friends." One of the ladies may have been Elizabeth Carter. This could have been the first imaginary picture of Johnson ever to appear. This print is from a photograph made by Warren Mild from a copy of the *Gentleman's Magazine* in the Sterling Library, Yale University.

The present owner of the portrait of Hawkesworth by Reynolds (p. 30) is unknown. The portrait of Hawkins by James Roberts (p. 30) is in the Music Room at Oxford University. The Reynolds portrait of Samuel Dyer (p. 38) is reproduced with permission of the Courtauld Institute. These three men were members of the Ivy League Club.

The only surviving portrait of Tetty (p. 94), the letter to Strahan on November 1, 1751 (p. 58), and the only known manuscript page of the *Dictionary* (p. 49), now in the Hyde Collection in Somerville, New Jersey, are used with the kind permission of Mrs. Donald F. Hyde.

The portrait of Miss Williams (p. 94) was provided by Miss Margaret Eliot of the Gough Square Johnson House Museum.

The Reynolds portrait of Johnson (p. 178), traditionally known as the 1756 portrait, was begun by Reynolds shortly after the appearance of the *Dictionary*. It was used by Boswell for his *Life of Johnson* in 1791. In 1977, during cleaning at the National Portrait Gallery, several layers of paint, believed to have been added at various times, were removed, exposing an earlier version (p. 179). See London *Sunday Times*, May 15, 1977.

Both versions are reproduced with permission of the National Portrait Gallery.

Johnson's letter to Tonson, asking help in paying his debts (p. 193), is now in the Johnson Birthplace Museum. It is reproduced here by kind permission of the Lichfield District Council.

Dr. John Edgcumbe of Exmouth, Devon, has graciously provided a print of his portrait of the Reynolds sisters (p. 287), painted by Frances Reynolds just three years before Johnson visited with them in Devon. She is shown seated, and at the left is her sister Mary, Mrs. Palmer.

We are indebted to Mr. W. S. Lewis for the use of the two satirical prints (pp. 269 and 276) from the Lewis Walpole Library in Farmington, Connecticut.

List of Illustrations

Acknowledgment

During my research I was helped by consultation with John Abbott, Bertram H. Davis, David Fleeman, Mary Hyde, the late James M. Osborn, Frederick A. Pottle, and the Late L. F. Powell. Others who have given general advice and criticism of the manuscript are: Mary Dobbie, Donald Greene, Frances Hanson, the late Allen T. Hazen, John H. Middendorf, and John Riely. Recognition of the help I have received on specific problems will be found in the notes. I am grateful for the careful textual editing of J. A. Cochrane. Always, as with the preceding volume, my chief helper and advisor has been my wife, Virginia.

Editor's note

James Clifford completed the manuscript before his death in April 1978, but his wife and his editor made the final selection of illustrations.

Mrs. Clifford wishes to thank Donald Greene for preparing the index and John Middendorf and Richard Rabicoff for editorial assistance. She acknowledges also the help of Ronald and Barbara Paulson and Pamela Thomas. She has appreciated the help and cooperation of the editor, Thomas Quinn.

CHAPTER I

The New Playwright

EARLY IN THE EVENING of Monday, February 6, 1749, a noisy crowd was gathering at the Theatre Royal in Drury Lane. At six o'clock a new play was to be performed, and no one quite knew what to expect. The morning newspapers provided the bare details, all, that is, except for the author's name. That day, it was announced, His Majesty's Company of Comedians would present for the first time a new tragedy entitled *Mahomet and Irene*,[1] with a stellar cast including the popular young actor-manager David Garrick, his rival the "silver toned" Spranger Barry, and their two leading ladies, Mrs. Pritchard and Mrs. Cibber.

Patrons were reminded of other practical details: a place in a box cost five shillings; in the pit, three; the first gallery, two; and the upper gallery, one. Places for the boxes were to be secured from Mr. Hobson at the stage door of the theater; and notice was given of a recent ruling aimed at increasing efficiency: " 'Tis hoped no gentleman will take it ill they can't be admitted behind the scenes." But if anyone was curious enough to wonder who had written the play, such information had to come by word of mouth. After all, the name Samuel Johnson meant nothing to the ordinary theatergoer.

In London that evening there was much to attract a seeker for entertainment.[2] One might go to see Theophilus Cibber and Peg Woffington in their old standby, *The Careless Husband,* at Covent Garden, to the Haymarket to see Samuel Foote's *Auction of Pictures,* or hear a concert of vocal and instrumental music by Mr. Balincourt at the Devil Tavern. At the Haymarket later in the evening was scheduled the last ball of the season. But for most of the intelligent fashionable world the center of interest was Drury Lane. The ubiquitous scholar-clergyman Thomas Birch, after dining with his patron, the Honorable Philip Yorke, his wife, the Marchioness Grey, and the poet Richard Owen Cambridge, went with them to the opening.[3] Tom Davies, the bookseller, was there with his pretty wife, as was Dr. Adams from Pembroke College, Oxford.[4] An obscure music master named Charles Burney had come down from King's Lynn in Norfolk to be on hand. Fortunately they either kept diaries or, years later, told Boswell. Doubtless the packed house that night also included the usual number of posing wits eager to show off: glib critics seeking fresh targets on which to sharpen their claws, handsome ladies in new gowns, anxious to see and to be seen, and as many of the author's personal friends as could squeeze in.

Conspicuously seated in one of the side boxes was the author himself, the object of curiosity and witty repartee. For Samuel Johnson this was a new experience, and properly to play his part he had bought a scarlet waistcoat, with rich gold lace, and a gold-laced hat.[5] But no amount of finery could hide the huge, lumbering frame, the pock-marked face, and the strange nervous twitchings of the fierce Grub Street journalist, for once stepping out of obscurity into the full light of the social arena.

A casual onlooker could have had little inkling of what was going on behind that stern countenance. This night represented the culmination of twelve years of struggle and frustration. The poor bookseller's boy from the midlands, a brilliant, erratic scholar forced to leave Oxford after only thirteen months, a failure as a teacher and in almost everything else he tried, had finally in his fortieth year reached the pinnacle of success, with a play produced in Drury Lane. The difficult years as an impoverished hack journalist, at times without even a roof over his head, wandering the streets all night with that strange pretender, Richard Savage, or climbing dirty stairs to some bare garret room; the separations forced by illness and poverty from his much older, ailing wife; the shifts and subterfuges of the insecure ghostwriter, ever seeking some means to acquire even temporary security—all this could for the moment be pushed to the back of his mind as he watched his own creation materialize on the stage.

For over a decade all Johnson's writings had been anonymous—some political satires in the late 1730s, his poem *London,* and the reports of parliamentary debates and biographies in the *Gentleman's Magazine.* His identity and talents were recognized only within an inner circle of publishers and close friends. Then a few weeks before the opening of *Irene,* the publication of his remarkable satirical poem *The Vanity of Human Wishes,* the first of his works which carried his name on the title page, had ended his days as an unknown.

The poem epitomized his ripened philosophy of life—a belief in the inability of mankind to create a new world. It was, however, realism without cynicism, lack of hope without despondency, an attitude which recognized the grandeur of life's struggle and the value of its pleasures. Johnson has been called a "pessimist with an enormous zest for living." He could put aside the pain and insecurity of his own recent years and enjoy the opening night of his new play produced at Drury Lane.

The play itself had been a long, cruel struggle, for there had been one disappointment after another. The idea of a tragedy molded out of the story of a Greek slave, Irene, captured at the fall of Constantinople and the plaything of Mahomet II, had first struck Johnson on reading an old history of the Turks some thirteen years before.[6] He had had three acts sketched out as far back as 1737 when first he came to London. Nothing came of that, and even after all five acts were complete and he had the backing of his employer, Edward Cave of the *Gentleman's Magazine*, no producer was willing to take a risk.

It was only when the impossible happened, when his former pupil, young Davy Garrick, had become the toast of London as the most exciting actor of the day, and then became manager of Drury Lane as well, that the worn manuscript could be brought out again. Davy had followed the fortunes of his master's ill-fated tragedy with fierce loyalty. No matter what strains there may have been between the two as persons, he was determined to arrange somehow to secure a fair hearing for the work.

The relations between former master and pupil, between the unsuccessful pedagogue and the most popular actor of the day, have often been discussed. How can one explain their seeming incompatibility and yet strange attraction? Between them there was respect and disrespect at the same time. Johnson's sneering remarks about actors and his careless slurs about Garrick's facility in stimulating emotion yet feeling none are well known. Nevertheless, he was always ready to defend his former pupil against attacks by others. And Garrick, well aware of Johnson's weaknesses and ready to make cruel sport of his eccentricities while hilariously mimicking his physical infirmities, still retained deep admiration for the older man's intelligence. If the two inevitably quarreled and disagreed, if they now moved largely in different social circles, the basic attachment remained firm.

At the opening of Drury Lane in the autumn of 1747, Garrick had proudly recited a noble prologue which Johnson had provided, and he immediately afterward set in motion a production of the tragedy of *Irene*. At first scheduled for the 1748 season, the production had to be delayed for various reasons. Although Johnson might chafe and rumble, Garrick did not allow other arguments from better-known writers to divert him from his goal. Aaron Hill, already the successful author of numerous plays, thought his *Merope* should have precedence, and Samuel Richardson had to explain to him about Garrick's prior commitment to his old schoolmaster.[7] One must be fair to the new manager. If he seemed to be in no hurry, he was under severe and conflicting pressures.

Once he had made the decision, Garrick was determined to do everything he could to ensure the success of the production. Eventually he offered the showy name part of Mahomet to the popular Spranger Barry and kept the livelier part of Demetrius for himself.[8] He cast his best-known tragic actress, Mrs. Pritchard, as Irene, and Mrs. Cibber as Aspasia. No expense was spared in providing gorgeous costumes and splendid scenery, to give the effect of a Turkish seraglio, with a view of elegant Eastern gardens. Indeed, it may be suspected that some patrons found the scenic effects more gratifying than the noble sentiments. In an attempt to enlist support in high government circles, Garrick asked Sir William Yonge, then Secretary at War, to write the Epilogue.

But Garrick's chief problem lay elsewhere. He saw from the start that in order to render Johnson's poetic tragedy palatable to the ordinary London playgoer, certain changes were vitally necessary. Here he was up against an immovable object. It was the everlasting struggle between director and author, with opposite points of view. Joseph Cradock, who later knew Garrick well, believed that it was Johnson who had insisted on Garrick's playing Demetrius, "merely on account of speaking some favourite passages in the first act," and that later, when Garrick was vainly trying to find ways of making the play more successful, he proposed "that he should act Mahomet, instead of Demetrius," and that Johnson "should write for him a mad scene, which might very well be introduced, and he would exert himself to the best of his abilities." But this proposal, according to Cradock, "was only met by the rudest reply possible."[9]

When the impasse appeared insurmountable, Garrick had the good sense to enlist the help of Johnson's other old friends. But even Dr. Taylor of Ashbourne, a crony from his Lichfield days, could make no impression. "Sir," exploded Johnson, "the fellow wants me to make Mahomet run mad, that he may have an opportunity of tossing his hands and kicking his heels." It was with the greatest difficulty that Johnson was at last prevailed upon to allow certain cuts and to make some textual changes.[10]

Throughout January, we may imagine, rehearsals progressed steadily, enlivened by constant bickerings between author and performers. Somehow, compromises were effected, though we may never know just what they were since no copy of the acting version has apparently survived. All that is certain is that Johnson was never fully satisfied. More than one observer on the opening night heard him muttering protests in the prominent side box as the performance progressed—objections to his own lines and what had been made of them.[11]

As rehearsals progressed and the opening night drew near, Garrick saw to it that the coming play was widely publicized. The first actual published criticism, two weeks after the opening, began by pointing out that for some months before its appearance the play "engrossed" the conversation of the town, and "every one was big with expectation of seeing a piece planned and wrote up to the highest pitch of a dramatic performance."[12] There is no doubt that through talk in the coffeehouses and taverns, and in the drawing rooms, a certain amount of curiosity had been stirred up about the coming production. Who was this man whose first play was about to be produced? What had he done to deserve such favor? Some people, indeed, even suspected that the publication on January 9 of Johnson's majestic Juvenalian satire, *The Vanity of Human Wishes,* was partly an advertising trick to make his name better known. John Blair wrote on January 19 to his friend John Douglas, who was that winter in Leipzig, giving him all the latest news of the theatrical season. After telling of Lord Lyttelton's strenuous efforts to pack the benefit nights at Covent Garden of *Coriolanus* for the benefit of the family of his late friend, James Thomson, and of Garrick's success with a farce called *Lethe,* he mentioned a new play being prepared at Drury Lane by a man called Johnson. Then he added that "Johnson in order to make the world a little acquainted with his name before hand has published a satire in imitation of the tenth of Juvenal's in which there is both good poetry and judgment."[13] By whatever means, curiosity had been widely stimulated by the evening of February 6.

It was a somewhat unruly audience that first night, so Dr. Adams later reported, with a few catcalls and hisses even before the play began, perhaps from noisy partisans of other playwrights who had been passed over in favor of the new dramatist.[14] But Johnson's manly prologue, spoken by Barry, soon calmed the crowd.

> Be this at least his praise; be this his pride;
> To force applause no modern arts are try'd.
> Shou'd partial cat-calls all his hopes confound;
> He bids no trumpet quell the fatal sound.
> Shou'd welcome sleep relieve the weary wit,
> He rolls no thunders o'er the drowsy pit.
> No snares to captivate the judgment spreads;
> Nor bribes your eyes to prejudice your heads.
> Unmov'd, tho' witlings sneer, and rivals rail,
> Studious to please, yet not asham'd to fail.
> He scorns the meek address, the suppliant strain,

With merit needless, and without it vain.
In reason, nature, truth he dares to trust:
Ye fops be silent! and ye wits be just![15]

Challenged thus to give the play a fair hearing, the audience was for the most part appreciative. Charles Burney, indeed, insisted that on that first night the scenes were "much applauded," particularly Garrick's brilliant rendering of Demetrius's speech on "tomorrow" in the third act.[16] "There was not the least opposition," Burney insisted, until very near the end, when the plot demanded the death of the heroine. When preparing this scene someone had had a clever idea about how to bring more violent action into a slow-moving plot. Why not have Irene strangled before the viewer's very eyes, using the proverbial Turkish device of a bow string? In the original brutal story in Knolles's *General History of the Turks,* Mahomet slices off Irene's head with one stroke of his gleaming scimitar. But such realism could only be achieved on a modern stage by adopting one of the well-known tricks of the pantomime magicians, and for a serious tragedy this would be out of the question. Merely to have used a dagger or short sword would have been too routine. Cradock insists that the decision to use the more exotic device was originally Johnson's, though it is difficult to believe he would have favored such a flagrant violation of classical practice. Certainly London theatergoers would not be a party to such refined cruelty, and a general cry of "Murder, Murder" went up from the pit. Shakespeare might leave any number of corpses strewn about the stage, but in a classical drama the amenities must be followed. So the audience kept shouting, refusing to let the play proceed. At last Mrs. Pritchard was led off the stage, presumably to be dispatched out of sight, and the performance was allowed to continue.

According to Burney and Tom Davies this offending piece of action was removed after the first night, and from then on all was placid. On the other hand, an anonymous diary of someone at Drury Lane shows that there was still some hissing at the second performance, perhaps merely a survival of protest rather than reaction to the tardy correction.[17] To be sure, the anonymous author of *A Criticism of Mahomet and Irene,* which appeared two weeks later, might wittily remark that one advantage of having the heroine's head "cut off in good earnest," as the original story plainly called for, would have been the added pleasure of seeing a new Irene every night, but most viewers apparently accepted as suitable the offstage execution.

Having survived this major crisis of the opening night, and some random hissing on the second, the production was off to a reasonable run. During Lent the London theaters were closed on Wednesdays and Fridays.

Mahomet and Irene, then, ran continuously for nine nights, February 6, 7, 9, 11, 13, 14, 16, 18, 20, and Johnson attended every performance. Every third night, according to contemporary practice, was reserved for the benefit of the author, when, after basic expenses were subtracted, the profits went directly into the author's pocket. These were the days when a man's supporters rallied round and when strenuous efforts were made to pack the house.

The figures show that Johnson's friends were effective and on the third night the place was jammed. One patron whom they were not able to secure, if indeed they made any serious effort to do so, was the King. The night before, when *Mahomet and Irene* was given its second performance, George II went instead to Covent Garden to see Quin and Peg Woffington in *Jane Shore,* and the *General Advertiser* reported that His Majesty had been particularly diverted by the afterpiece of "Harlequin's Escape into the Bottle."[18] The Prince of Wales viewed this ingenious spectacle the next night. But none of the Hanoverian royal family apparently were interested in a new play by someone who was reputed to have Jacobite leanings.

Attendance evidently held up well through Johnson's second benefit on the fourteenth, but by this time Garrick saw the need of other expedients to lure additional customers. For safety, on the seventh night, he added a farce, *The Anatomist; Or, The Sham Doctor,* and some Scottish dancing; on the eighth the dancing was repeated along with Garrick's own farce, *The Lying Valet;* and on the ninth there was "the Savoyard Dance by Mr. Matthews, Mr. Addison, etc." and Henry Fielding's farce, *The Virgin Unmasked.* What Johnson thought of clinging to Fielding's risqué situations for support does not appear. What is certain is that an acceptable run was easily achieved and that everyone in the theater was happy about the result.

If by twentieth-century standards a run of nine nights does not appear very remarkable, it must be remembered that in those days scarcely any new plays did much better. Addison's *Cato,* the most successful tragedy of the age, had run for only twenty nights. James Thomson's *Tancred and Sigismunda* in 1745 had run nine, and his posthumous *Coriolanus* in January 1749, with all of Lord Lyttelton's support, only ten. Aaron Hill's *Merope,* which followed *Irene* later in the spring, had a normal run of nine, with two more later, one by royal command. Johnson's play, then, was a definite success by contemporary standards. Financially Johnson obviously had no reason to complain. The total receipts for the three benefit nights came to £384 17s., allowing him a clear gain of £195 17s., to which was added £100 from the publisher Dodsley for the copyright of the published version, which came out on February 16.[19] It would be a long time before Johnson would again have so much ready cash available. Materially, then, his foray into the theater could be considered a great success.

Considered as a work of art, the play is more difficult to assess. Apparently it aroused varying degrees of enthusiasm in the spectators, and the reason is not difficult to explain. In order to expand into five acts the simple dramatic story which he had found in Knolles's history, or in the Abbé Vertot's version, Johnson found it necessary to make a number of changes. The original is merely an account of an infatuated military leader's return to normal, after a long period of relaxation in the arms of his mistress, and his final willingness to have her murdered to impress his generals. If earlier plays using the same plot had begun the process of complication, Johnson altered the whole radically.[20] What had been a tale of passion and cruelty became in his hands a moral study of temptation. Irene is clearly mistress of her own fate. She has freedom of choice, and in order to make clear the contrast Johnson added a new character, Aspasia, who represents strict virtue. In the end Aspasia escapes with her virtuous lover, while Irene, who has yielded to ambition, pays the ultimate penalty. Thus the tragic ending comes as a just punishment for weakness; but to make this moral clear to all observers required more talk than dramatic action. The result was that many contemporary critics found the play too static, with not enough gripping action—a vast heap of noble sentiments and poetic lines, with little compelling plot.

One of those in the pit for the opening night later insisted that the audience had been "more disposed to admire the author than to be affected by his scenes." As the spectator looked around, "he saw nobody using their handkerchief; but the whisper was strong and prevalent, that the *poet was a prodigy of learning.*"[21]

As an irritated rival dramatist, Aaron Hill can scarcely be ruled an impartial critic, but undoubtedly his initial reaction was not uncommon.

> I was in town [he wrote to David Mallet] at the *Anamolous* [*sic*] Mr. Johnson's benefit, and found the play his proper representative, strong sense, ungraced by sweetness, or decorum: Mr. Garrick made the most of a detached and almost independent character. He was elegantly dressed, and charmed me infinitely by an unexampled silent force of painted action; and by a peculiar touchingness, in cadency of voice, from exclamation, sinking into pensive lownesses, that both surprised, and interested! Mrs. Cibber, too, was beautifully dressed, and did the utmost justice to her part. But I was sorry to see Mahomet (in Mr. B—y) lose the influence of an attractive figure and degrade the awfulness of an imperious Sultan, the impressive menace of

a martial conqueror, and the beseeching tendernesses of an
amorous solicitor, by an unpointed restlessness of leaping levity,
that neither carried weight to suit his dignity, nor struck out
purpose to express his passions.[22]

At the second performance on the fourteenth there was another spectator from out of town, who reported in detail what he experienced in a
letter to the *General Advertiser* on February 18. The inconsistent reports
he had been hearing of the new play, he began, had made him eager to see
for himself. Why was there so much difference of opinion?

I took my station in the centre of the pit, that I might hear the
opinion of the critics before the curtain drew up. I had not been
long seated, before I heard a voice pronounce, with a kind of
pert assurance, *Demme! there is not one line in it worth hearing;* I turned about, and perceived the speaker to be a tall
well-dressed young man, with *a round unthinking face,* and
that he finished his sentence by taking a pinch of snuff, with
an air of great importance. At that instant, a person on my right
hand told his companion, that the three first acts were very fine,
but that the author had been scandalously negligent in the
fourth and fifth, which he intended to write over again, and
bring his play on the stage the next winter. . . . This gentleman,
perceiving me to be attentive to what he delivered, asked me if
I had seen *Irene* before; upon my answering him in the negative, he told me, with an air of confidence, that if I had not
come that night I should not have seen it at all; for that it
would be performed no more, and he even doubted whether
the players would be suffered to go on; he further told me that
the hero of the piece was one *Demetrius,* who undertook the
delivery of his country from no other principle than the love of
a woman who was a captive in the Turk's seraglio; that there
was no change of fortune in the play; that the plot was too
simple, and that the whole piece had no moral.[23]

Another gentleman sitting directly before him was then consulted, who
said he had been so crowded at an earlier performance as not to be able
to hear all the lines, and so had come again, but that he thought the piece
had great merit. The curtain then went up and the writer had an opportunity to check for himself.

In less than five minutes, I was convinced that the critic, whose
sentiments I first heard, formed his judgment of *good lines,* by
rules very different from my own; the first three acts confirmed
the opinion of the second observator, but the fourth and fifth

Edward Cave and his assistants at St. John's Gate, home of the Gentleman's Magazine, *1747.*

made me strongly suspect that he had been misinformed concerning the author's intention of new-writing them; the falsehood of his prediction, that the play would be no more acted, appeared by its being given out for *Thursday;* this was received with universal approbation; upon which I turned about, and he, perceiving me smile in his face, instantly sneaked from his seat, with a look that convinced me he had more modesty than I before thought consistent with his criticism. Upon the whole, I dare affirm that the judgment of posterity will concur with me in distinguishing *Irene* as the best tragedy which this age has produced, for sublimity of thought, harmony of numbers, strength of expression, a scrupulous observation of dramatic rules, the sudden turn of events, the tender and generous distress, the unexpected catastrophe, and the extensive and important moral.

In struggling further to explain the great difference of opinion about the new play, the writer had to admit that the people who could genuinely appreciate true poetry were very few. Yet despite this fact, "all who admire *Irene* pay a compliment to their own judgment, and it is with the utmost pleasure that I tell the world, in honour of the ladies of Great Britain, that I scarce ever saw so shining an assembly in the boxes."

Obviously, the town was severely split. Whereas Lady Luxborough, writing to thank the poet Shenstone for sending her a copy of the printed version, which had the original title, *Irene,* commented, "I hear it is not much liked at London,"[24] the February issue of the *London Magazine* reported that the play was received "with great applause."[25] Moreover, Tom Davies in his later life of Garrick insisted that no tragedy since Addison's *Cato* had been so admired for "beauty of diction, energy of sentiment, harmony of versification, and purity of moral."[26] The published reviews showed the same dichotomy. Before the end of the run there appeared a pamphlet called *A Criticism on Mahomet and Irene in a Letter to the Author,* printed for W. Reeve in Fleet Street, in which the anonymous writer questioned the setting, attacked the drawing of character, and amusingly spoofed much of the action of the play.[27] Another anonymous pamphlet, with the title *An Essay on Tragedy, with a Critical Examen of Mahomet and Irene,* published by Ralph Griffiths on March 8, continued the attack.[28] On the other side, Johnson's employer Cave saw to it that the February *Gentleman's Magazine* contained a highly favorable analysis of the plot and much praise for many of the lines. Cave even included, doubtless because of pressure from Johnson, some lines which Garrick had left out of the acting version.[29] And in the *General Advertiser* for February 18 there was the fulsome laudatory letter quoted above.

In some ways the most judicious verdict came in a later report by John Blair, again passing on London gossip to his friend John Douglas. Writing on March 30, over a month after performances had ended, and after making some general comments on Elizabethan times, Blair commented:

> We have got nothing nowadays ourselves to compare with the productions of that time. Both Thomson's and Johnson's plays are poor enough; the last has got a warm fancy but little or nothing of the pathetic for his piece is more overrun with metaphor than even Rowe himself would have done if possible, so that his talent does not seem to fit him for the stage. He published by way of ushering in his play a very good imitation of Juvenal's tenth satire, which gave a very favourable expectation of his play, but there was a dreadful falling off. But if we seem to sink our genius for play writing the scale certainly rises in other things. The three last volumes of Clarissa are inimitably well and Fielding's new piece of Tom Jones reads not badly.[30]

It was in the novel that the genius of the mid-eighteenth century found its clearest voice. Although new tragedies continued to be written, they tended to be literary exercises rather than dramatic expressions of the life of the time.

Years later the clergyman George Gleig, in a letter to George Monck Berkeley, summed up the general impression of what was wrong with Johnson's tragedy. "The common objection to *Irene* is that it represents characters and manners to which the greater part of every audience must be strangers, and exhibits distresses arising from circumstances in which the inhabitants of Britain can never be involved."[31] Another objection was that Johnson did not have a real feeling for stage presentation of tragic themes.

> To be a dramatic writer a man ought to devote his time to the theatre and the reading of the best works of the great masters both ancient and modern. I do not think it probable (possible no doubt it is) that brightest genius by *solitary* study could write a *great* tragedy; because a work when read may make *impressions very different* from *what* it will do when acted.

Johnson may well have sensed this fact and bowed to the inevitable. He certainly never again tried his hand at poetic drama.

Nevertheless, it is a mistake to assume that Johnson himself felt that the attempt had been a complete failure. Even though the tragedy was never revived and did not become a staple in Garrick's repertoire, it was much read in the printed version. There are various well-known anecdotes of Johnson's own later reactions—the time when he left a room where the play was being read out loud, commenting sadly, "I thought it had been better"—and the honest comment when told that a man named Pot thought it the best tragedy of the age: "If Pot says so, Pot lies." And his stoical acceptance of what had happened is illustrated by his reply when asked how he felt about the ill success of his tragedy. He answered, "Like the Monument."[32]

Mrs. Thrale insists that he did retain a sneaking feeling of loyalty to his early work. Although she never heard him complain about the verdict of the public, she could see that *Irene* was still "a violent favourite with him."[33] He was much offended, she added,

> when having asked me once what single scene afforded me most pleasure of all our tragic drama, I, little thinking of *his* play's existence, named, perhaps with hasty impropriety, the dialogue between Syphax and Juba in Addison's Cato. "Nay, nay," replied he, "if you are for declamation, I hope my two ladies have the better of them all."

But these anecdotes all are based on later evidence, after Johnson had become known as an essayist, lexicographer, and literary critic. At the time he had no such doubts about the play.

In the spring of 1749 Johnson was not considering giving up writing for the stage. Others before him had improved on early mistakes. Despite all the worries and troubles of a stage production, it must have been pleasant for a few weeks to be the talk of the town. It was flattering to be thought of as a rising new dramatist. Although he was aware of adverse criticism, he also knew that his creation had been widely praised. It was gratifying to have one's work called in print "the best tragedy which this age has produced."[34]

When the final performance was over in late February, Johnson must have found it difficult to return to his old rhythms. For two months he had been living in a dream world of dramatic unreality and excitement. He was accepted in the green room of the theater and backstage as an important person. The wenches dropped him curtsies as he passed, and the actresses listened to his remarks.[35] He mixed easily in the sprightly chit-chat of that entirely new world. To be sure, he later humorously observed to his friend Bennet Langton that when he was all dressed up in his gold-laced waistcoat and hat he found it more difficult to treat people with quite the same ease than when in his usual plain clothes, and gradually the finery was put aside.[36] Much later, when describing his finery and his backstage visits, Johnson commented, "I soon laid aside my gold-laced hat, lest it should make me proud."[37] And the scarlet waistcoat with rich gold lace was also discarded, except perhaps for special occasions.

Of course, with the closing of *Mahomet and Irene* he did not give up his theatergoing. For some years he continued to find entertainment and distraction there, and temporarily as a successful, practicing dramatist he had an entrée backstage. But by April in the spring of 1749 he was able to write to James Elphinston of his "recluse kind of life."[38] The excitement of the winter had passed, his wife was probably away, and nothing remained but the drudgery of steady work on the dictionary of the English language.

CHAPTER II

Life in Gough Square in 1749

I N THE SPRING OF 1749 Johnson was living at 17 Gough Square, off
Fleet Street, in a house which he had first leased in 1747 shortly after beginning his lexicographical work.¹ Occupying part of the western side of the
square, it was a dignified edifice built early in the century. Today a well-kept
museum, it is the only one of Johnson's many London dwellings to survive.

A symmetrical building of dark red brick, with a twin-pointed roof,
it probably looked in Johnson's time very much as it does now. There are
two entrances, one in the center of the front, and the other at the side
leading to a small garden. However small, it was a place where Johnson
could walk when he needed exercise. Carlyle, when he visited the house in
1832, called the garden "somewhat larger than a bed-quilt."²

The front door is reached by a short flight of steps with iron railings
on each side, leading to a carved doorway supposedly put up shortly before
Johnson's time. The heavy door opens into a small paneled hall, and as
protection against burglary there are strong bolts.

Immediately facing the door is the staircase with a pine balustrade,
built around a center well, which goes up to the attic. The two rooms on
the ground floor are both paneled in pine without decoration. Although
the original chimneypieces are gone, they have been replaced by mantel-
shelves of the same style as the front door. To the left as one enters is the
dining room, which has a cupboard in the wall, with space for plates and
other table equipment. Across the hall is the parlor, which has seats under
the windows and shutters in recesses on the sides. Between the window and
the fireplace, where now there is a double-doored cupboard, there was
originally a recess, or alcove, where there could have been a wig-stand.

Here, too, there might have been space enough for a commode. In the paneling near the bottom on the staircase there is a small cupboard, probably used for storing bedroom candles.

On the floor above on either side there is a large room, the inner wall of which is built like a partition, with two hinged double doors. These could be easily swung around, leaving access to the staircase through the doors. It is not clear how they could ever have been thrown together to make one large salon while still using both doors. In Johnson's day it is doubtful that they were so used. One chamber would have been used as a bedroom and the other as a dressing room. The one with southern exposure, now labeled "Miss Williams' Room," may have been where Tetty and her maid slept whenever they were in town, for it would have been warmer and lighter than the one opposite, now called "the withdrawing room," probably used to receive visitors who came to see her when she was bedridden.

On the floor above there is a seat under the window with a hinged top, under which chamber pots and other utensils could have been stored. Johnson probably slept in the south room on this floor, just under the garret, and Dr. Levet or some other friend may have occupied the one to the north. None of the rooms on the upper floors has full-sized closets, though in the garret there were shallow alcoves where furniture could have been placed. Unfortunately, none of the furniture there in 1749—beds, chests, screens, and commodes—has survived.

At the top of the house the large garret has massive oak beams. It was at the time fitted up like a counting house, with desks for Johnson's amanuenses who were helping with the *Dictionary*. From all accounts it was a shambles, with piles of books, papers, and rickety furniture.[3] This was one part of the house to which Johnson could retire free from the possibility of annoyance from his wife or other members of the household. Tetty never came to the attic. Above was a "cock loft" which could have been used for storage.

On the ground floor, at the back of the hall, a door leads to another stairway down to the basement. Here was the kitchen, with two large open-hearth fireplaces, one used for cooking joints on a roasting jack or spit, and the other with chains to hold pots and kettles. Roasts, baked food, and bread would all have been purchased from nearby shops. There may have been a shallow stone sink, and in 1749 probably a cistern or tank for storing water and possibly a cess pit where waste water could have been thrown. The kitchen has heavy oak beams, which may have survived from an earlier house, and also a door leading into two arched cellars which extended out under the pavement of the square, where provisions and coal and wood could be stored (these may not have been there in Johnson's time). Somewhere in the basement there would have been a bed for a servant. Windows facing the square allowed light to enter, and there was a door on the north side.

As for heating, each room of Johnson's house including the attic had a small fireplace, where coal fires would have been kept burning during cold weather. At night one of these might have been banked with ashes so that there would be live coals ready to use in starting fires the next morning, with some help from a hand bellows. To start from scratch with flint and tinder was not as easy as using live coals. Although firewood in London in those days was not plentiful, it would be purchased in bundles and stored in the cellar or in a woodshed in the garden. Coal was carried around the street in bags.

Although his house is not too difficult to describe, any attempt to portray Johnson's daily life in Gough Square must take into consideration the deteriorating relations with his wife, Tetty. When they were married in 1735 he was twenty-five, and she was a widow of forty-six, with three grown children—two sons who refused to accept their mother's choice, and a teenaged daughter who did.[4] The motivations for the marriage have always puzzled readers. Why did he choose someone almost twice his age? And why did this reasonably attractive widow with money decide to marry this nervous, half-blind young man with convulsive starts, with no settled occupation and a depressed state of mind? We will never know. There must have been strong physical and mental attractions on both sides.

After their marriage, using her money, Johnson had set up a school at Edial, near Lichfield. When this obviously was not a success, he had drifted to London, doing odd jobs and writing for the *Gentleman's Magazine*. When Tetty joined him their existence apparently was precarious, and they moved about from one dismal lodging to another. Only after he began his great lexicographical project, a dictionary of the English language, were they able to secure a comfortable house at 17 Gough Square. But even then, Tetty preferred to spend as much time as she could outside London.

She may well have been away in February 1749 and never have seen *Mahomet and Irene*. In all the surviving accounts of Johnson's brief period of fame as a new dramatist there is never any mention of his wife. The autumn before she had been staying in Hampstead for her health, and Johnson saw her, and that not too happily, only when he made the long trek out of the city. It was there in Hampstead that he had written down most of *The Vanity of Human Wishes*. Was Tetty still there in February? Of course, there may be another explanation. She may have been in Gough Square too ill to keep up with the exciting theatrical adventures of her husband.

But now back to Johnson's everyday life in the simple but commodious house in Gough Square. One may easily guess where Johnson and Tetty slept, but more perplexing problems have to do with sanitation and cleanliness. When Johnson wanted to wash his face, where did he find the water? And what happened to the dirty water after he was through? When he took a bath, if he ever did, where was the tub? In the bedroom? Or in the basement kitchen near one of the large fireplaces? And what happened to the contents of his chamber pots? There are no references to such mundane matters in surviving diary entries or letters. All we can do is speculate, using such evidence as has come to light.

In 1749 in Gough Square there were certainly no bathrooms or running water.[5] No ordinary London house at that time had bathrooms, and hardly any nobleman's. When Johnson and Tetty washed it was undoubtedly in a china bowl, with water from a nearby pitcher. By mid-century most houses on major streets did have leaden pipes bearing water from conduits coming into the basement or kitchen, but the water was turned on for short periods only three times a week.[6] Thus the householder had to have a cistern or tank in the basement where water could be stored. For those without pipes the contents could be replenished by rainwater from gutters on the roof. And there were water carriers in most parts of London. Since Johnson did not live directly on a major street, it is unlikely that his house was supplied with pipes from the outside. In any case, water had to be carried upstairs by servants in pitchers or buckets, one explanation of the small size of portable tubs and the infrequency of bathing.

What happened to used water no one can tell. And even more problematical is the disposal of the contents of chamber pots. Hogarth's well-known prints would indicate that they were thrown out of the window into the streets.[7] It was considered good manners, at least in Scotland, for those up above to cry "Gardy-loo" (*Gardez l'eau*) before throwing. Those walking below would yell up "Haud yer han' " with other expletives, but it was a dangerous business. All pedestrians were advised to keep in the middle of the street.

There is no doubt that this practice of throwing waste materials out of the window did sometimes occur in London, as well as in Scotland. In 1721 the Grand Jury of the City of London warned constables and watchmen of the "quantities of soil cast into the streets in the night time," and in 1755 in Marylebone there was a local act forbidding "night soil" to be thrown in or near the streets.[8] But by this time most decent households took care of the problem in other ways. Jonathan Swift's advice to chamber maids to empty pots out of the window was obviously meant as satire, recommending the exact opposite of what he thought proper.[9]

In most houses off the main streets, in courts and side alleys, there would have been neither open sewers nor sewer pipes entering the houses. When a law-abiding citizen obeyed the calls of nature he did so in various ways. Often London houses had a privy, or "place of convenience," at the bottom of the garden, sometimes called a "Jericho," or "jakes," or "house of easement," which stood apart over a cesspit dug in the ground.[10]

Apparently Joshua Reynolds at his house in Leicester Fields had an outside privy, and hating to waste time going to and fro, he built a private staircase at the back of his house leading from the studio to the garden. James Northcote later described to Benjamin Haydon how in the course of a day one could hear Reynolds "dart down and up again striding over 5 or 6 stairs at a time—anxious not to lose a moment."[11]

For houses with no backyards, where structures abutted each other, the cesspits were dug directly under the basement floor, and it was here that the waste products would have been thrown. It was customary to have the vaults, or cesspits, periodically cleaned out, and there were special workmen called "night men" who came with their wagons at night to do the job. Unfortunately the contents had to be carried in buckets, often through the house, not a very sanitary or fragrant procedure.

At 17 Gough Square there is no surviving evidence to show where the privy or Jericho stood, or where the cesspool was located. It might have been outside in the very small garden south of the house, but more likely it was north of the house in a space below the level of the next street, Pemberton Row. Here is sufficient room for a cesspit (or a privy) accessible through a door opening out from the basement. Today this space is surrounded by an iron fence, and there are stairs leading down from the sidewalk, through an iron gate. In Johnson's day there might have been stone steps. This would have been the most convenient place to have the privy, the easiest to clean from outside and the least likely to produce unpleasant odors inside.

Of course, it is possible that, like Pepys, Johnson did have a cesspit in the basement.[12] In some houses in Johnson's time there were privies over open cesspools at the foot of the basement stairs. And there may have been other seats on the upper floors. In some better homes there may have been drain pipes leading down to basement pits, but hardly in Gough Square. For the most part, reliance was placed on pots kept under the beds or hidden behind screens in commodes. As one later critic describes the situation, "any dark hole, corner, cupboard, place or recess next a living room or bedroom" was considered a fit place to hide a "close stool."[13] Obviously having one available in a main room of the house did occasionally result in embarrassing moments, as when Pepys came home and surprised Lady Sandwich, who had come to see him, "doing something upon the pot" in his dining room.[14] Presumably the contents of the pots were later carried downstairs and emptied into the cesspit.

The custom of having pots easily available in downstairs rooms, often inside cupboards or sideboards, may have been related to the general social practice of ladies leaving the dining room after dinner, while the men remained to talk. Visitors from the Continent, indeed, were sometimes shocked by what occurred. The Duc de la Rochefoucauld, in describing one dinner he attended while in London, commented: "The sideboard too is furnished with a number of chamber pots and it is a common practice to relieve oneself whilst the rest are drinking; one has no kind of concealment and the practice strikes me as most indecent."[15]

And another French visitor, Pierre-Jean Grosley, referring to what happened after dinner in London in 1765, wrote: "The women having retired, and the room being furnished with a certain necessary utensil, they [the men] lean upon the table with their elbows, drink about, and settle the affairs of the nation."[16]

Very likely Johnson and his male friends on occasions used pots hidden somewhere on the ground floor, and at other times visited the privy or close stool. There must have been a wide variation in style and decoration for these "necessary houses." When Johnson and Boswell were in the Hebrides in 1773, on the island of Coll, they talked about "little houses" and the fact that at the new castle, just as at Raasay, there was none, though there had been one in the old castle.[17] This led to further discussion, Johnson remarking that "if ever a man thinks at all, it is there. He generally thinks then with great intentness. He sets himself down as quite alone, in the first place." When Boswell insisted that a man is "always happy" under these circumstances, Johnson refused to agree. And when Boswell described an elegant quilted seat he had seen at the Dutch Ambassador's in Paris, Johnson insisted, "Sir, that is Dutch; quilted seats retain a bad smell. No, Sir, there is nothing so good as the plain board." Thus we may assume that somewhere at 17 Gough Square Johnson had what used to be called a "one-holer" with a plain board.

Sitting in the privy was generally accepted as a time for thinking and reading. When talking to Johnson in the Hebrides, Boswell argued for having books and prints easily available, and Johnson mentioned a gentleman who had a "set of the *Spectator* in that place." Lord Chesterfield, giving advice to his son, once mentioned a man he knew who was so good a manager of his time "that he would not even lose that small portion of it which the calls of nature obliged him to pass in the necessary-house." Chesterfield's acquaintance gradually went through all the Latin poets while on the seat. Having purchased a cheap edition of Horace, "he tore off gradually a couple of pages, carried them with him to that necessary place, read them first, and then sent them down as a sacrifice to Cloacina."[18] Johnson may have preferred instead to think about his next essay or piece of journalism. Paper was not the only method employed. In Samuel Rolleston's anonymous *Philosophical Dialogue Concerning Decency*, published in 1751, after complaining about the over-delicacy of English ladies, he added: "Whereas I have known an old woman in Holland set herself on the next hole to a gentleman, and civilly offer him her muscle shell by way of scraper after she had done with it herself."[19]

Even without modern plumbing and sanitary equipment or central heating, 17 Gough Square must have been a comfortable home, much better than anything Johnson occupied until then in London. What rent he paid his landlord, Sir Harry Gough, is not clear.[20] No receipts or specific accounts have survived. To be sure, we can gain some idea of the amount from the records of land tax assessments now in the Guildhall Library.[21] In 1750, for example, Johnson paid £3 12s. on "Rents," which the tenant was supposed to pay and later reclaim from the landlord, and 11s. for "personal estate," meaning probably his own belongings. From other sources we know that at that time the rate normally used was four shillings in the pound. This would suggest that Johnson was paying about £18 rent, and almost £3 on his personal property. In later years the amounts varied. By 1758 he was paying £4 16s. on "Rents" and 16s. on "personal estate." The sum of £26 later used in other records to indicate the general amount of his payments as compared to that assigned to other householders in the square may have included also special taxes, parish tithes, and other charges. The sum may thus have been an overall estimate of his total liabilities.

If Johnson's paying 11s. on personal property might be considered quite low, only one other householder in his part of the square paid more. Could this suggest what old, ramshackle furniture he was using and his lack of anything valuable? From all accounts he had only necessary furniture, and much of that was broken down.[22] When moving into the larger house, Johnson must have merely picked up whatever he could secure cheaply. Never did he have sufficient money to buy handsome new household belongings.

As a householder in the New Street Precinct in the ward of Farringdon Without, and in the parish of St. Bride's, Johnson had various other fixed payments in addition to taxes and rent. Again the surviving records at the Guildhall Library provide much evidence, though there are still problems, since some of the ledgers are missing, and one year Johnson is called "Henry" instead of "Samuel." Nevertheless, it is possible to put together some kind of general estimate of what he was paying.

Living in St. Bride's parish, Johnson was subject to regular assessments for "impropriate tythes" and "augmentation" dues. In 1750 he paid twice yearly—on Michaelmas and Lady Day, 7s. 7d. for the tithes and 1s. 4½d. for the dues. Johnson also had to pay assessments for street lighting, the watch, the poor-rate, and special claims such as the support of orphans. In 1755 he paid 2s. 8d. to help raise £1200 for orphans, as the result of an Act of the Council the year before. In 1756 he paid 17s. 4d. for "cleaning repairing and beautifying the Church."

From the Guildhall records it is also possible to discover who were Johnson's near neighbors, though the names mean little to us today. In Gough Square there were Peter Kinsey, Thomas Millicent, Eleanor Remmington, and Leuyns Boldero, all of whom paid slightly higher rent than Johnson, and James Patterson, who paid less. Apparently there was a good deal of mobility in the neighborhood, with some houses empty part of the time. During the 1750s Johnson remained in one place longer than any of his neighbors. The house in the square having the lowest rent had a succession of tenants—James Patterson, James Dodd, Isaac Isaaks, John Roman, John King—and by 1756 all the better houses had new tenants. These were now John Raynor, John Hilditch, and Richard Landcake.

We have no way of knowing how well Johnson knew his neighbors. One neighbor who was fairly close Johnson did see often, the printer William Strahan. Reputedly Johnson had chosen the Gough Square area originally to be near Strahan's establishment in New Street, where type for the *Dictionary* was to be set. It would have taken not more than five minutes to carry copy and proofs through the maze of back alleys and crooked lanes between the square and Strahan's shop in Gunpowder Alley.[23]

The records also reveal something about other local matters. One of the surviving account books is the "Lamp Ledger."[24] In 1755–1756 Johnson is listed as owing 4s. 4d. each six months for street lighting. Apparently he did not pay during the year, and unfortunately there is then a ten-year gap in the old records. But even if he did not pay his assessment, Johnson would have enjoyed the advantages of well-lighted streets, for London in that respect was the most advanced large city in Europe. None of the streets and squares of Continental capitals were so well-illuminated as those in London. Indeed, a visiting German prince, arriving in London at night, jumped to the conclusion that it must have been especially illuminated in his honor.[25] As is evident from the various Acts of Common Council, much thought had been given to street lighting. By 1739 there were supposed to be 4,825 lamps in twenty-six wards, which were maintained at a cost of £9,698 14s. 5d. by seventeen contractors. They were responsible for obtaining and repairing lamps, for supplying wicks and oil, and for lighting them at sunset and extinguishing them at dawn.[26]

One lamp was usually thought sufficient for five houses. Gough

Square would thus have probably been entitled to two or three lamps.[27] And according to contemporary maps of the area the courts leading into Gough Square were well-populated and paved, so that they, too, would have been adequately lighted. The lamps, using whale oil, may not have shone as brilliantly as our modern light bulbs, but they were quite effective. When Johnson came home from a nearby tavern in the early hours of the morning he did not have to feel his way along in pitch darkness.

Johnson also paid regular fees for police protection and for "scavengers." In the "Ledger for the Watch and Scavengers" from December 25, 1755, to December 25, 1756, for example, Johnson paid 3s. 6d. quarterly for the watch and 5s. annually for scavengers.[28]

In several statutes passed during the reign of George I it was stipulated that scavengers should bring their carts into the streets every day except Sunday and holidays, give notice by ringing a bell or some other signal, stay a convenient time, and bring away all dirt and rubbish. Those who did not obey these rules were subject to a fine of 40s.[29] The same statutes ordered the inhabitants to follow definite rules—to sweep their streets every Wednesday and Saturday, not to dump ashes or dirt in the streets before their houses, and other mandates—or to pay a fine of 10s. In addition, householders were required to keep streets, lanes, and alleys before their doors paved to the middle of the street.

These statutes were not generally obeyed. The scavengers certainly did not come every day, nor were they very efficient in removing filth. Some years earlier, in the April 1742 issue of the *Gentleman's Magazine*, in one of the parliamentary debates which Johnson put together from details secured from others and his own imagination (ostensibly debates in the Senate of Lilliput, they were assumed to follow closely actual parliamentary debates the year before) a speaker, Lord Tyrconnel, brought forward a motion for the better cleaning and paving of the streets.[30] This is the way he launches his proposal:

> The filth, sir, of some parts of the town, and the inequality and ruggedness of others, cannot but in the eyes of foreigners disgrace our nation, and incline them to imagine us a people, not only without delicacy, but without government, a herd of barbarians, or a colony of hottentots.
>
> The most disgusting part of the character given by travellers of the most savage nations is their neglect of cleanliness, of which, perhaps, no part of the world affords more proofs than the streets of the British capital; a city famous for wealth, and commerce, and plenty, and for every other kind of civility and politeness, but which abounds with such heaps of filth, as a savage would look on with amazement.

The putrefaction and stench, the speaker continued, causes of pestilential distempers, must be corrected. There seems little doubt that the obvious outrage which pervades this speech echoes Johnson's own observations of the streets and alleys in his own part of the city.

By midcentury conditions were so bad that some citizens of London and Westminster were moved to apply to Parliament for new laws which would provide better cleaning of the streets, along with other improvements. This drew a reply from someone who signed himself "W. W." in the *Daily Advertiser* for October 22, 1753, in which he pointed out that laws already on the books, if properly obeyed, would render new laws unnecessary.

What Johnson and others paid for watch, or police protection, as we would call it, was hardly worth it. One has only to browse about in the daily newspapers to see that walking on the streets of London in the mid-eighteenth century was not safe. Mugging and robbery were common. In January 1749 the *Whitehall Evening Post* complained that "the frequency of audacious street robberies repeated every night in this great metropolis call aloud on our magistrates to think of some redress."[31] After remarking on the hazard of sustaining a fractured skull, the writer continued, "The villains now go in bodies, armed in such a manner, that our watchmen, who are generally of the super-annuated sort, absolutely declare they dare not oppose them." The papers were full of schemes for reducing thievery and crime.

In the *Penny London Post* there was an account of a gentleman who, coming down the Strand, was met "by three fellows armed, who tripped up his heels, one of whom picked his pocket of 27s, the second took his shoe and knee buckles, the third his hat and wig, and all used him very ill because he had no watch in his pocket."[32] And there was an account of a man attacked by three men, "who robbed him of six shillings, and beat him unmercifully because he had no more for them."[33]

In April 1750 the celebrated sculptor Roubiliac "was robbed of his watch and money in Dean Street, Soho, by three fellows: one presented a pistol to him, and swore he would blow out his brains if he made any noise; and while he was giving him his money, a second came behind and took out his watch."[34] When another man was robbed also near Soho Square, "as one of the rogues was taking the buckles out of his shoes, a pistol went off which was held to his ear, by which a slug went through the corner of his hat"—which frightened the robbers and they fled.[35]

There is one difference from the accounts in our day. Often the onlookers actively took the side of the one being robbed, and themselves punished the criminals. "Tuesday night last two women were detected in Covent Garden, as they were endeavouring to steal the cushion seats out of a gentleman's coach which stood near the play-house door; for which they were dragged to the pump in the market place and severely treated by the populace before they were set at liberty."[36]

With his huge bulk and ragged clothes, Johnson was obviously not a target for muggers. Anyone could see that he carried little money or valuables. If attacked, he probably would have put up a vigorous defense.

It is impossible to be certain about Johnson's daily routine. He was not a man of exact habits. Later in life he reputedly stayed in bed until nearly noon, but while at work on the *Dictionary* he may well have been up with his amanuenses in the garret by the middle of the morning. Certainly he was no early riser.

In London in the mid-eighteenth century common laborers were often up at sunrise and in summer would begin work by six o'clock. A grocer's shop might be open by seven, and an assistant in a haberdasher's shop would begin work by eight. "Quality hours" were, of course, a very different matter. At Bath the usual hour for breakfast was nine-thirty to ten o'clock, after bathing or a "constitutional." Horace Walpole, who usually rose about eight and breakfasted at nine, tells us that his friend Lady Upper Ossory did not get up until one o'clock.[37] Country gentlefolk in midcentury usually followed some such routine as Fanny Burney described in her early Norfolk diary: "We live here, generally speaking, in a very regular way—we breakfast always at 10, and rise as much before as we please—we dine precisely at 2, drink tea about 6—and sup exactly at 9."[38] The dinner hour was gradually moving later. In 1749 many were still holding to two o'clock, but it was steadily moving on to 3 or 4 P.M. Tea and cold supper also came later.

As for Johnson, in 1749 he probably rose in the midmorning, breakfasted on bread and butter, or rolls and tea, with perhaps some fruit if he could afford it, or perhaps instead had a "nunchion" (defined in the *Dictionary* as "a piece of victuals eaten between meals"), then worked for a while in the attic, came down to the ground floor for a hearty dinner about two or three, and returned to the top floor for more work in the late afternoon. We know that Johnson liked heavy, rich food for dinner, perhaps boiled or roasted beef or mutton, cabbage done in a floury sauce, and a sweet pudding or tarts. The hot food would have been brought up from the basement to the ground-floor dining room by one of the maids, or the cook, probably in covered dishes. During the evening hours there would be more tea and cold dishes.

How many servants there were at 17 Gough Square at this time depended upon whether Tetty was away in Hampstead, or visiting some friend outside the city, or was ill in her bedroom. As described in my account of Johnson's earlier years, when Tetty was living in Hampstead she had as her maid, or companion, Mrs. Desmoulins, who quite likely was also a member of the Gough Square household at other times. There probably was always a cook and perhaps another maid, who would have done household chores and helped with the cooking.

In the spring of 1749 life for Johnson had become increasingly dull. Regular work in the attic with his copyists was hardly exhilarating. After the excitement of the production of *Irene* in February, he slipped back into an almost barren existence. On April 20, in his letter to a Scottish friend, James Elphinston, already referred to, Johnson explained that he had not answered Elphinston's earlier letter because in his kind of life he was "not likely to have much more to say at one time than at another."[39]

When Tetty was in Gough Square she was usually in ill health, most of the time in her bedroom. Theirs could hardly have been a very happy household. On July 12, 1749, Johnson wrote to his stepdaughter, Lucy Porter, in Lichfield, mentioning his own recent illness, "I have been often out of order of late, and have very much neglected my affairs," and ending, "Your poor Mamma is come home but very weak, yet I hope she will grow better, else she shall go into the country. She is now upstairs and knows not of my writing."[40]

Rarely did Tetty entertain any of Johnson's close associates. Apparently during these years Johnson did not bring close friends home for tea, as he did in later years when Anna Williams acted as his hostess. From various accounts Tetty spent much of the time in bed, drinking and reading romances. Perhaps on doctor's orders, she also indulged in drugs.[41]

Some inkling of what life must have been like comes from a story later passed on by Miss Williams to Lady Knight.[42] When Johnson and Tetty were married, the widow's sons vigorously opposed the match— "perhaps because they, being struggling to get advanced in life, were mortified to think she had allied herself to a man who had not any visible means of being useful to them." Fortunately, Lucy, Tetty's daughter, was amenable, and later lived with Johnson's mother in Lichfield helping with the bookshop. Lucy's two brothers refused to keep any contact with their mother. Only once, so far as we know, did Jervis Henry Porter, the elder son, who later became a captain in the Navy, show the least interest in what happened to his mother. Sometime during her residence in Gough Square he came and knocked at the door, and asked the maid if her mistress was at home. The maid answered:

> "Yes, Sir, but she is sick in bed." "O!" says he, "if it is so, tell her that her son Jervas [*sic*] called to know how she did"; and was going away. The maid begged she might run up to tell her mistress, and, without attending his answer, left him. Mrs. Johnson, enraptured to hear her son was below, desired the

maid to tell him she longed to embrace him. When the maid descended, the gentleman was gone, and poor Mrs. Johnson was much agitated by the adventure: it was the only time he ever made an effort to see her.

When Johnson heard what had happened he did everything he could to console his wife. The only explanation he could later give to Miss Williams to account for the visitor's strange actions was: "Her son is uniformly undutiful; so I conclude, like many other sober men, he might once in his life be drunk, and in that fit nature got the better of his pride."

As pointed out earlier, Tetty spent long periods out of the city, either in Hampstead or visiting friends like the Hawkesworths in Kent.[43] Her obvious excuse was to better her health, but perhaps an even more basic reason was to get away from her husband. It seems clear from various evidence that she found his amorous desires increasingly difficult to accept.

The most explicit evidence we have as to Johnson's sexual drives and restraints comes from a remarkable conversation which Boswell and the painter Mauritius Lowe had much later with Mrs. Desmoulins on Easter Day, April 20, 1783.[44] While Johnson was having a nap, and Miss Williams was elsewhere, Boswell and Lowe decided to quiz her about rumors they had heard of Johnson's impotence. Had he ever had sexual relations with his wife, Tetty? Or was their union merely platonic? To this Mrs. Desmoulins replied that there had never been a man with stronger amorous inclinations, but for the most part he conquered them. As to various rumors that there had been a "criminal connection" between Johnson and blind Miss Williams, that suspicion had no possible basis in fact. But when Boswell continued to press her for specific evidence that Johnson and Tetty had made love, she cited Garrick's dramatic account of what he saw through the keyhole at Edial. Garrick at least claimed to have seen them preparing for intercourse. To be sure, she herself had no way of knowing what occurred during the early years of the marriage. She had known Tetty best during her later years, when Tetty would not allow her husband to sleep with her. This had been wholly her decision. During these years when she was a steady drinker and ill much of the time, Tetty had insisted that she could not "bear a bed-fellow."

Mrs. Desmoulins then recalled an incident which happened while she was Tetty's companion out in Hampstead. Another young woman came for a visit and there were only two beds. Tetty agreed to let the visitor have the smaller one and to allow Mrs. Desmoulins to sleep with her, only if she would promise never to tell Johnson. If his wife could endure sharing her bed with Mrs. Desmoulins, why not with him? When Lowe waggishly suggested that Johnson may have been such a poor bed-fellow, with no passion, Mrs. Desmoulins again insisted that this could not have been true, for no man had stronger sexual desires. When eagerly asked how she could be sure, Mrs. Desmoulins described what had happened when Johnson came out from the city to Hampstead, sometimes two or three days a week. For a while Dr. Bathurst was living nearby and Johnson would go over to visit him and talk till two or three in the morning. The maid and Tetty would go to sleep long before then, but Mrs. Desmoulins would wait up for Johnson's return to see that his bed was warmed with a pan of coals. Often the younger woman would sit on his bed, after he undressed, for talk and some caressing—even at times laying her head on his pillow. When Boswell excitedly asked if Johnson really showed strong signs of passion, Mrs. Desmoulins admitted that he had, even confessing that he fondled and kissed her, not with any fatherly kind of approach. But when Lowe suggested that he had even played with her breasts, she insisted that nothing had been done "beyond the limits of decency." Nevertheless, she could see clearly his strong sexual desires combined with a firm determination to curb them. Sometimes he would be so aroused that he would push her away and tell her to leave the room. She could see his struggle and moral determination not to give in. She even admitted that their failure to make love was wholly his decision. She had had so much "awe" and admiration for him that she might have given in had he really attempted to seduce her. Though he was constantly tempted, it was Johnson's moral resolve not to commit adultery which was the controlling factor.

Why then, one might wonder, in his later prayers did Johnson harp so much on his former sins, on the "sensuality" of his thoughts, and on his need for repentance? If he completely refrained from sexual intercourse after the death of Tetty, as seems likely, perhaps "sensual thoughts" replaced actions, and this generated a deep sense of guilt. Or he may have substituted other means of releasing pent-up passions. Even while Tetty was alive and reluctant to accept his amorous advances, he may have resorted to masturbation after fondling Mrs. Desmoulins. The letter "M" occasionally inserted in his later diaries has been thus interpreted by George Irwin and others.[45] It is possible that such release was stirred up through erotic dreams. We know that he later confessed to Mrs. Thrale that his first sexual inclinations came in a dream. Such normal activity, by some considered to be sinful, is a more likely explanation for Johnson's later feelings of guilt than other suspicions that Johnson had indeed succumbed to the temptations of prostitutes during his early years in London.

For one with his deep moral sense, the mere fact that he was plagued by sexual fantasies, and that he sometimes found ways to release tensions, would have resulted in the feelings of guilt he showed in later years.

CHAPTER III

The Ivy Lane Club
and a Few Old Friends

WITH SUCH A TROUBLED HOME LIFE, Johnson very much needed out-side diversion. So, during the winter of 1749, he helped organize a small group to meet once a week for informal talk; later it became known as the Ivy Lane Club. Though he may have been thinking of such a possibility for a long time, nothing had materialized. But now, with *Irene* out of the way, the time seemed propitious.

For many modern readers the Ivy Lane Club is no more than a name. Boswell devotes only two sentences to it in his life of Johnson.[1] The later Club, with all its famous members and long history, he thought deserved more coverage, and undoubtedly he was right. Certainly Johnson's first club was not a prestigious group. Almost everything we know about it comes from Sir John Hawkins, who was one of the original members. In his life of Johnson, commissioned by the booksellers after Johnson's death, Hawkins gives many details about the members and some of the topics they discussed, though he leaves some unanswered questions.[2]

According to his account, during the winter of 1749 a group of friends began meeting every Tuesday evening at the King's Head, Horseman's well-known beefsteak house in Ivy Lane, between Paternoster Row and Newgate Street near St. Paul's. Here they would begin with supper, which included wine, and would then talk for the rest of the evening, stopping about eleven o'clock, the accepted time to break up. The cost of supper and wine was apparently equally divided among those who attended.

Hawkins tells us that there were ten members in all: three physicians, one lawyer, one bookseller, one merchant, one elderly church dignitary,

Sir John Hawkins by James Roberts, 1786. (detail)

John Hawkesworth by Sir Joshua Reynolds, 1773.

and a youthful theologian intending to enter the nonconformist ministry, one practicing journalist, and one hack writer who aspired to be a dramatist and lexicographer (Johnson himself). The group was certainly heterogeneous, for the most part young men of whom few ever achieved renown. Modern readers will recognize no member equal to Reynolds, Burke, or Goldsmith. Indeed, aside from Johnson himself, only Hawkins and Hawkesworth are known to twentieth-century scholars. The rest are merely names, remembered, if at all, because of their connection with Johnson.

Nevertheless, it was an interesting company, and it contributed in many ways to the development of its founder. So far as we can learn, Johnson took the initiative in forming the group and was responsible for the choice of most of the members. The majority were his friends, and the others were acquaintances who had impressed him with their willingness to talk, or at least to hear him talk. And so, after some negotiations, they agreed to form a club which continued to meet for the next six or seven years, until about 1756 or 1757.

Why was the club limited to ten members? From an anecdote in the Fitzherbert papers it is clear that Johnson had strong feelings about the necessity for confining groups of this kind to manageable numbers.[3] A lady whose daughter about this time attended a school run by Mrs. John Hawkesworth at Bromley in Kent met Johnson, who with his wife used to visit the Hawkesworths. Later another daughter heard her mother tell about one occasion when in a numerous company someone brought up the subject of "the most eligible number to form an agreeable society." When Johnson kept silent, one of the company asked for his opinion, "upon which he gravely replied, 'between The Muses and the Graces.' " That is, between a maximum of nine and a minimum of three. For the Ivy Lane Club Johnson perhaps thought it possible to have nine Muses in addition to himself. Amusingly enough, at the beginning of the successor Club in 1764, membership was originally intended to be limited to nine, but it, too, soon went up to ten, and gradually to forty.

Who, then, were the ten founding members of the Ivy Lane Club? In 1749 John Hawkins was an articled clerk, working for an attorney and solicitor, still unmarried and financially insecure. He had known Johnson for at least eight or nine years, having first met him through Cave and the *Gentleman's Magazine*.[4] Hawkins had published poems, moral essays, and an extended dramatic criticism and was a music enthusiast. Many years later Fanny Burney recorded a conversation she heard between Johnson and Mrs. Thrale when Hawkins's name was mentioned as one of Johnson's friends whom, like Garrick, he would never allow others to abuse.[5] Only Johnson could provide a fair balance between his friend's good and bad traits. Hawkins, Johnson insisted, was basically an honest man, though

penurious and sometimes mean and brutal. Then he described how
Hawkins and he had

> once belonged to the same club, but that as he ate no supper
> after the first night of his admission, he desired to be excused
> paying his share.
>   "And was he excused?"
>   "Oh yes, for no man is angry at another for being inferior
> to himself! We all scorned him, and admitted his plea. For my
> part I was such a fool as to pay my share for wine, though I
> never tasted any."

As Johnson had to admit, Hawkins was "a most *unclubable* man!"

Although we cannot be certain that the club Johnson referred to
in this anecdote was that at Ivy Lane, the evidence points that way. During
those years Hawkins had been elected to the Madrigal Society, whose records show he never paid his dues.[6] Later, after he married a well-to-do wife,
Hawkins became more generous. It is to be noted that in this period Johnson refused to drink any wine, although by 1764, when the successor Club
began, Johnson's attitude toward the grape had somewhat relaxed.

John Hawkesworth, another associate of Johnson's at the *Gentleman's Magazine,* by this time had become one of his best friends. Apparently Hawkesworth had taken over most, if not all, of Johnson's duties at
St. John's Gate where the magazine was produced. In a print used as an
introduction to the collected issues of 1747, Johnson and Hawkesworth are
shown as Cave's principal helpers (see p. 10).[7] Although by 1749 Johnson
was ostensibly giving all his time to work on the *Dictionary,* he probably
was frequently consulted by Cave and Hawkesworth. Born a Londoner,
Hawkesworth had worked in his youth as a goldsmith and watchmaker,
later entering an attorney's office.[8] Not a scholar in the academic sense,
Hawkesworth proved to be an excellent journalist, demonstrating a keen
mind and wide interests. No one else could better imitate Johnson's style,
a fact which makes the identification of Johnson's later work for the magazine extremely difficult. Doubtless Hawkesworth brought to the Ivy Lane
Club news of current books and recent events to be written up for the
magazine, as well as problems of all sorts.

John Ryland, who was married to Hawkesworth's sister, had started
out as a lawyer, but by this time was an active West Indian merchant and
businessman. At times he had contributed to the *Gentleman's Magazine*
and once briefly took over Hawkesworth's duties at St. John's Gate.[9]
Ryland was a devout dissenter in religion and a firm supporter of the
Hanoverians in politics. Indeed, Johnson used to attack him as a "republi-
can and a roundhead." But at the same time Ryland had an abhorrence

of those radicals who kept talking about "liberty and equality." He was, as John Nichols later called him, a "Whig of the old school." Although disagreeing with many of his positions, Johnson undoubtedly respected Ryland's "strict integrity" and "forcible manner."

Another member whom Johnson probably first met through Cave and the magazine was John Payne, who had started as an accountant in 1746 but about the time of the founding of the Ivy Lane Club had moved into publishing.[10] Later he was the publisher of Johnson's *Rambler* and *Idler* essays and of Hawkesworth's *Adventurer*. Later still he changed professions and finally became Chief Accountant of the Bank of England. Once near the end of 1749 Payne actually brought proofs of a volume he was publishing to a club meeting to ask the members' advice.[11] Undoubtedly he was a valuable connection for various club members.

Of the younger physicians, none of whom ever became eminent, Johnson's favorite was Richard Bathurst. As Arthur Murphy expressed it, "Dr. Bathurst was the person on whom Johnson fixed his affection. He hardly ever spoke of him without tears in his eyes."[12] And Mrs. Thrale records that he once spoke of him as "my *dear dear* Bathurst, whom I loved better than ever I loved any human creature."[13] Another time he said to Mrs. Thrale: "Dear Bathurst . . . was a man to my very heart's content: he hated a fool, and he hated a rogue, and he hated a *whig*; he was a very good *hater*," though to suggest that it was Bathurst's politics which endeared him to Johnson would be an oversimplification. To be sure, his Tory inclinations may have been one part of his attraction, but Johnson evidently had other personal reasons for his admiration for Bathurst.

Another of Johnson's favorites was William McGhie; indeed Hawkins suggests that Johnson "may almost be said to have loved him." He was a Scot, "one of those few of his country whom Johnson could endure." He had gained a doctor's degree in Scotland, but when he came to London found that London was already "overstocked with Scotch physicians." Later he became attached to Guy's Hospital.[14] "A learned, ingenious, and modest man," McGhie was always treated with civility by Johnson; but McGhie could never move ahead in his profession and died young in poverty, buried by contributions of his friends. According to his good friend Tobias Smollett, he was a poet as well as a physician.

The third physician, Edmund Barker, was a very different sort. As a dissenter, he had studied physic in Leyden, where he had been a fellow student with another member, Samuel Dyer, and had returned to England just about the time the Ivy Lane Club was formed. Although very intelligent, Barker was, as Hawkins described him, "a thoughtless young man, and in all his habits of dress and appearance so slovenly as made him the jest of all his companions." But it was not careless dress which irritated

Johnson. He was slovenly enough himself. Although Barker was an excellent classical scholar who had read widely in the Italian poets (skills which probably had led to his election), he had other traits which did not endear him to Johnson. It was Barker's religious and philosophical position which constantly stirred up antagonism. A professed Unitarian, Barker was an enthusiastic follower of Shaftesbury. For the orthodox Johnson this was cause enough for constant argument. Consequently, Johnson "so often snubbed him" that Barker's attendance at the club "became less and less frequent."

The other two members were both theologians—one an elderly Church of England dignitary, the other a young prospective nonconformist minister.

Samuel Salter was a very tall man, a Cambridge divine who had held a number of positions in the church.[15] According to Hawkins, a dispute with his children had driven him from his home in Norwich to come to live in London. Over seventy years old, he was not a remarkable scholar, but he was "well-bred, courteous, and affable, and enlivened conversation by the relation of a variety of curious facts, of which his memory was the only register." Evidently Salter was a natural target for Johnson's tendency to needle minor representatives of the establishment. Although a Church of England man himself, Johnson loved to argue with church dignitaries lower than a bishop, even at times being a bit "splenetic and pertinacious" and "wanting in civility." With the much older Salter, Johnson "took delight in contradicting, and bringing his learning, his judgment, and sometimes his veracity to the test." Despite the efforts of other members of the club to calm the waters, Johnson refused to be diverted. Why? One can only guess, but Hawkins's own explanation does appear to have some validity.

As someone who because of poverty had been forced after only thirteen months to leave the university without a degree, Johnson was jealous of those who had been more fortunate and who had led a softer, easier life. When a person with what he regarded as lesser intellectual endowments treated him as an inferior because of his lack of a degree, Johnson naturally boiled. Even when the dignitary was as polite and unruffled as Salter, Johnson could not resist probing his remarks with insistent skepticism. Fortunately, as Hawkins adds,

> Dr. Salter was too much a man of the world to resent this behaviour: "Study to be quiet" seemed to be his rule; and he might possibly think, that a victory over Johnson in any matter of dispute, could it have been obtained, would have been dearly purchased at the price of peace. It was nevertheless a

temerarious act of him to venture into a society, of which such
a man was the head.

Somehow Johnson and Salter remained on friendly terms until the latter's
death in 1756.[16]

Perhaps the most controversial member was young Samuel Dyer,
who together with Hawkins also belonged to the later Club. There is sharp
disagreement over some of Dyer's qualities. Percy, Malone, Boswell, and
other members of the later group praised him highly and defended his
character against what they thought were Hawkins's unjust slurs.[17] Nevertheless, even if Hawkins was prejudiced, his account must be used, if
skeptically, as a basis for any description of Dyer.

The son of a London jeweler who was a dissenter, Dyer was educated
first at a private school near Moorfields, then at an academy at Northampton, and at Glasgow, where he studied ethics and metaphysics under
Francis Hutcheson, the well-known philosopher. Intended by his father
for the dissenting ministry, he was sent to complete his "learned education" in Leyden in the Netherlands, to study Hebrew literature under
Albert Schultens, a celebrated professor at the university there.[18] After
two years he returned to London eminently qualified, so his father must
have thought, for his projected calling. Hawkins called him "an excellent
classical scholar, a great mathematician and natural philosopher, well
versed in the Hebrew, and master of the Latin, French and Italian languages." His character, moreover, was very appealing. "He was of a temper
so mild, and in his conversation and demeanour so modest and unassum-
ing, that he engaged the attention and affection of all around him. In all
questions of science, Johnson looked up to him." By now Dyer was attending a course in chemistry given by Henry Pemberton at Gresham College,
and would sometimes entertain the other members of the group by describing various chemical processes, while Johnson listened attentively.

But when his friends pressed young Samuel Dyer to begin preaching
and teaching so that his talents could be put to some valuable use, he
demurred. Apparently he was not yet ready to decide on a profession. At
first his friends thought the reason was basically that he was too modest,
unwilling to get up and speak before large audiences. Later, as the years
wore on, they began to suspect another reason. Instead of devoting himself
to self-sacrificing Christian duties, he found the "pleasures and enjoy-
ments" of life more appealing.

> His company, though he was rather a silent than a talkative
> man, was courted by many, and he had frequent invitations
> to dinners, to suppers, and card-parties. By these means he be-

came insensibly a votary of pleasure, and to justify this choice, had reasoned himself into a persuasion that, not only in the moral government of the world but in human manners, through all the changes and fluctuations of fashion and caprice, whatever is, is right.

As a result, he began "to grow indifferent to the strict practice of religion," and gladly accepted more and more invitations to Sunday parties. To quote Hawkins,

> He had an exquisite palate, and had improved his relish for meats and drinks up to such a degree of refinement, that I once found him in a fit of melancholy occasioned by a discovery that he had lost his taste for olives!

Hawkins further describes what happened to this young man destined for the ministry:

> Having admitted these principles into his mind, he settled into a sober sensualist; in a perfect consistency with which character, he was content to eat the bread of idleness, laying himself open to the invitations of those that kept the best tables, and contracting intimacies with men not only of opposite parties, but with some who seemed to have abandoned all principle, whether religious, political or moral. The houses of many such in succession were his home; and for the gratifications of a well-spread table, choice wines, variety of company, card-parties, and a participation in all domestic amusements and recreations, the owners thought themselves recompensed by his conversation and the readiness with which he accommodated himself to all about him.

Hawkins's description, written long after Dyer's death, was, to be sure, based on observation of his later years. At the time of the founding of the Ivy Lane Club, when Dyer was only twenty-four years old, many of these traits may not have been evident. Most of the members of the club may still have assumed that Dyer was headed for the ministry, though, according to Hawkins, "Johnson suspected that his religious principles, for which at first he honoured him, were giving way, and it was whispered to me by one who seemed pleased that he was in the secret, that Mr. Dyer's religion was that of Socrates."

When his father died, most of his estate went to the widow and to an older brother and sister, leaving very little to Samuel. Could this have been one way of expressing disapproval of his son's shift of interest? Certainly Dyer did not have sufficient funds to live as sumptuously as he would have liked. To earn more, he was urged by Johnson and Hawkins to write the life of Erasmus, a suggestion he refused. Finally he was prevailed on to do a less arduous task, a revision of the old translation of Plutarch's *Lives,* and after "heavy complaints of the labour of his task" it was completed and published in 1758. According to one account, after the death of his mother and brother, when Samuel inherited the bulk of their estates, he speculated on Johnson's advice in annuities on Lord Verney's estate, and lost the whole of his fortune.[19] When Dyer died suddenly at the age of forty-seven in 1772, it was rumored that he had committed suicide, leaving insufficient money even to pay for his funeral.[20]

During his later years, he became a favorite of Edmund Burke, Thomas Percy, and others. His keen intelligence was so much admired that it was even suspected that he was the author of the anonymous letters of Junius in 1769–1772.[21] Reynolds painted his portrait and later Johnson secured a mezzotint of it, along with those of Burke and Goldsmith, to hang on his wall.[22] Burke, in a piece written for the newspaper after Dyer's sudden death, described him as

> a man of profound and general erudition, and his sagacity and judgment were fully equal to the extent of his learning. His mind was candid, sincere, and benevolent, his friendship disinterested and unalterable. The modesty, simplicity, and sweetness of his manners rendered his conversation as amiable as it was instructive, and endeared him to those few who had the happiness of knowing intimately that valuable and unostentatious man.[23]

Balancing Hawkins's and Burke's opinions, one can see clearly that Samuel Dyer was a delightful and interesting person. Notwithstanding his weaknesses and lack of purpose, and his delight in sensual pleasures and an easy existence which rendered his life largely one of unfulfilled promise, his modesty and polite behavior, together with his great learning and wide knowledge, clearly made him a valuable club member.

What did they talk about on those Tuesday evenings at the King's Head in Ivy Lane? According to Hawkins's and other accounts, some of the topics were scarcely controversial—recent scientific experiments, new inventions, medical treatments, and similar subjects. When these were brought up Johnson was probably willing merely to sit back and learn. Literature may even have been the source of many long discussions, and occasionally they may have moved into the other arts, though Johnson was largely insensible in this area. As Hawkins makes clear, Johnson had practically no interest in music in general. He was once heard to say that

Samuel Dyer by Sir Joshua Reynolds, 1770.

"it excites in my mind no ideas, and hinders me from contemplating my own." Of one fine performer, he remarked that he had "the merit of a canary-bird."

Moreover, in the visual arts, because of his limited sight in one eye and almost complete blindness in the other, Johnson showed little interest. Of course, Hawkins may give a somewhat one-sided summing up of Johnson's deficiencies in this area when he says that he had little respect for "symmetry, and harmony of parts and proportions." For Johnson a "statue was an unshapen mass, and a sumptuous edifice a quarry of stone." One evening at the club Hawkins brought with him a small roll of prints (possibly landscapes by Gabriel Perelle), which he had acquired that afternoon. When Johnson's curiosity made him examine each print with great attention, he asked Hawkins what sort of pleasure such things could give him.[24] When Hawkins tried to explain how views or rural scenes and landscapes stirred up his imagination, Johnson confessed that he was unable to experience the same reaction, for "in his whole life he was never capable of discerning the least resemblance of any kind between a picture and the subject it was intended to represent."

For the most part the talk very likely concentrated on matters where he could see at least two sides, where there could be sharp disagreement. Let the conversation touch on religion, or philosophy, or politics, and his combative spirit was aroused. Then there could be trouble, or at least excitement. Since Johnson, the founding father, was a Tory and reputed to be a Jacobite sympathizer, while the majority of the Ivy Lane Club were Whigs and a good many were nonconformists, some restraint was required on the part of younger members who thought of themselves as Johnson's disciples, yet disagreed with what they thought were his prejudices. "We all saw the prudence of avoiding to call the then late adventurer in Scotland, or his adherents, by those names which others hesitated not to give them." For the most part, then, one suspects that the club kept off political arguments.

What occupied much of their time would have been philosophical matters. When anyone brought up ideas associated with moral obligation, Johnson "was uniformly tenacious." He was suspicious of most of the modern "sects or classes of writers on morality," though he did admire Samuel Clarke. But most of the others drew his withering scorn, among them Shaftesbury with his too facile equation of individual happiness with general welfare. According to Hawkins, "Little as Johnson liked the notions of Lord Shaftesbury, he still less approved those of some later writers, who have pursued the same train of thinking and reasoning, namely, Hutcheson, Dr. Nettleton, and Mr. Harris of Salisbury." Since Dyer had been Hutcheson's student, he apparently came to his defense,

and others of the group might have been called Shaftesburians. Topics
connected with these writers "were, not unfrequently, the subjects of
altercation between Johnson and Dyer." As Hawkins pointed out, it might
be observed of these contests, as Johnson himself once said of two dis-
putants, "that the one had ball without powder, and the other powder,
without ball." Hawkins continues:

> For Dyer, though best skilled in the controversy, was inferior to
> his adversary in the power of reasoning, and Johnson, who was
> not always master of the question, was seldom at a loss of such
> sophistical arguments as the other was unable to answer.

Hawkins could not resist pointing out that in these discussions

> Johnson made it a rule to talk his best, but that on many sub-
> jects he was not uniform in his opinions, contending as often
> for victory as for truth: at one time *good,* at another *evil,* was
> predominant in the moral constitution of the world. Upon one
> occasion he would deplore the non-observance of Good-Friday,
> and on another deny that among us of the present age there is
> any decline of public worship. He would sometimes contradict
> self-evident propositions, such as, that the luxury of this coun-
> try has increased with its riches; and that the practice of card-
> playing is more general than heretofore. At this versatility of
> temper, none, however, took offense; as Alexander and Caesar
> were born for conquest, so was Johnson for the office of sym-
> posiarch, to preside in all conversations; and I never yet saw
> the man who would venture to contest his right.
>   Let it not, however, be imagined that the members of this
> our club met together with the temper of gladiators, or that
> there was wanting among us a disposition to yield to each other
> in all diversities of opinion.

Nor should it be inferred that serious disputation was the chief purpose
of their meetings. No effort was made to keep discussion to particular
topics, and much of the talk was mixed with humor. Johnson himself "was
a great contributor to the mirth of conversation, by the many witty sayings
he uttered, and the many excellent stories which his memory had treasured
up, and he would on occasion relate."
    The Ivy Lane Club undoubtedly was a major source of relaxation
for Johnson. After he had eaten his supper, so "solid and substantial" that
Hawkins suspected he had had no dinner, Johnson would open up and
become the center of the evening's entertainment. Then, with no other

incentive to hilarity than lemonade, Johnson was, in a short time after our assembling, transformed into a new creature: his habitual melancholy and lassitude of spirit gave way; his countenance brightened; his mind was made to expand, and his wit to sparkle; he told excellent stories; and in his didactic style of conversation, both instructed and delighted us.[25]

One special meeting which has often been described occurred when Johnson persuaded the members to hold an all-night party to honor his protégée, a young writer named Charlotte Lennox. Born in 1729, she was the daughter of Captain James Ramsay, a Scottish army officer who had served at Gibraltar.[26] When about ten years old, she accompanied her parents to Albany, in the colony of New York, where Ramsay was commander of frontier troops. When he died in 1742 Charlotte spent a few months in New York City before being sent back to England to be cared for by a prosperous Essex family named Luckyns. By this time she had become known as a poet, was patronized by two noble ladies, and even promised a place at court. Such prospects were dissipated when in October 1747 she married a poor and shiftless Scot named Alexander Lennox, "whose fortune, like that of the object of his regards, consisted wholly in hopes and expectations."[27] Lennox may possibly have worked for the printer William Strahan, though to keep alive, Charlotte became a strolling player and a slave to the booksellers.[28] If Horace Walpole thought her acting "deplorable," still her poetry was admired.[29]

It is uncertain just when or where Johnson and Charlotte Lennox first met. Fanny Burney implies that Charlotte "waited on" Johnson in order to solicit his patronage.[30] Or they may have been introduced by one of their mutual acquaintances—Strahan, Cave, Birch, or Samuel Paterson, who had published her *Poems on Several Occasions* in 1747. There is one dubious anecdote describing their first meeting, where Johnson is supposed to have treated her like a child, taken her on his knee, carried her in his arms to see his library, and even sent out his servant to purchase some cakes.[31] Although almost thirty years old when this was supposed to have occurred, Charlotte was small and youthful in appearance. Still, most of the other details are probably pure fabrication. Of one thing we can be certain: Johnson was greatly struck by Charlotte's intelligence and verve, and he tried to help her in every way he could.

By October 1750 Johnson was actively furthering her career, and he probably played an important part in successful negotiations with Cave and Payne. In October Payne issued *Proposals* for a subscription edition of her poems and, with Joseph Bouquet, in December published her first novel, *The Life of Harriot Stuart,* based on her earlier American experiences. At various times Cave publicized the two ventures in the *Gentleman's Magazine* by printing two of her own poems and two others praising her work and including a brief notice of the novel when it appeared.[32] Thus the Ivy Lane all-night party may well have been part of a well-planned campaign to build up the reputation of a talented young writer who had captured Johnson's admiration.

Hawkins describes the celebration with more than his usual gusto, although unfortunately not all the details seem to fit.

> Mrs. Lennox, a lady now well known in the literary world, had written a novel entitled *The Life of Harriot Stuart,* which in the spring of 1751 was ready for publication. One evening at the club, Johnson proposed to us the celebrating the birth of Mrs. Lennox's first literary child, as he called her book, by a whole night spent in festivity. Upon his mentioning it to me, I told him I had never sat up a whole night in my life, but he continuing to press me, and saying that I should find great delight in it, I, as did all the rest of our company, consented. The place appointed was the Devil tavern, and there, about the hour of eight, Mrs. Lennox and her husband, and a lady of her acquaintance, now living, as also the club, and friends to the number of near twenty, assembled. Our supper was elegant, and Johnson had directed that a magnificent hot apple-pie should make a part of it, and this he would have stuck with bay leaves, because, forsooth, Mrs. Lennox was an authoress, and had written verses; and further, he had prepared for her a crown of laurel, with which, but not till he had invoked the muses by some ceremonies of his own invention, he encircled her brows. The night passed, as must be imagined, in pleasant conversation, and harmless mirth, intermingled at different periods with the refreshments of coffee and tea. About five, Johnson's face shone with meridian splendour, though his drink had been only lemonade; but the far greater part of us had deserted the colours of Bacchus, and were with difficulty rallied to partake of a second refreshment of coffee, which was scarcely ended when the day began to dawn. This phenomenon began to put us in mind of our reckoning, but the waiters were all so overcome with sleep, that it was two hours before we could get a bill, and it was not till near eight that the creaking of the street-door gave the signal for our departure.[33]

Hawkins himself had been troubled all evening with a bad toothache, which Dr. Bathurst had tried to alleviate "by all the topical remedies and palliatives he could think of." Hawkins later remembered that his conscience troubled him by the resemblance their gathering had to a debauch, but once he had taken a few turns through the Temple grounds and had had breakfast in a neighboring coffeehouse he felt better. While Johnson may have been delighted by this unusual celebration, most of the other members were probably determined not to make it a regular occurrence.

This is the story. But how accurate is it? For one thing, why did they pick the Devil Tavern? It was certainly famous for all-night debauches. In this old eating house between Temple Bar and the Middle Temple Gate, nearly opposite St. Dunstan's church, Ben Jonson and his cronies early in the seventeenth century used to dine and make a night of it. Was Johnson merely following the example of his namesake? The sign outside had St. Dunstan pulling the devil by the nose, and naturally the place came to be called the Devil Tavern. It was a resort of booksellers as well as writers.

More important, what work of Charlotte Lennox was really being celebrated? And exactly when did the celebration occur? Hawkins says that it was *The Life of Harriot Stuart,* which was brought out on December 13, 1750, certainly her first published work of fiction. Yet in London in December the dawn would not, as Hawkins recorded, have come shortly after five o'clock. Mrs. Lennox's second work, *The Female Quixote,* her first real success, does not seem to have been the one celebrated and could not have been called her "first literary child," though it was her first good one. Could the celebration have been arranged when Mrs. Lennox finished writing the first draft of *Harriot Stuart,* or when it was accepted for publication, perhaps around the beginning of May, or August, 1750? Sunrise in early May would have been about 5:30. There is even the possibility that Johnson's motive was to stir up John Payne's interest in publishing the work. The fact that Payne is never mentioned in Hawkins's account might be thought a bit strange if the gathering had been planned to mark the actual appearance in print of Mrs. Lennox's first novel. But really it makes little difference which of Charlotte Lennox's works was being celebrated, or whether the gathering occurred in the summer or winter. What is important is the evidence this account gives us of Johnson's dominance over the Ivy Lane group, of his early enthusiasm for the work of Charlotte Lennox, and of his typical behavior on such occasions. Even if other club members were never again willing to sit up all night while Johnson imbibed huge quantities of lemonade and placed crowns of laurel on the brows of young authors, it undoubtedly happened once and was worth remembering.

There can be no doubt of the importance of the Ivy Lane Club to Johnson during this difficult period. What it meant to another of the members is summed up in a later account of the career of John Hawkesworth. During the early 1750s he "generally attended the Rambler's weekly club, from which if any man departed without being wiser or better it certainly must have been his own fault."[34] For all concerned, the Tuesday gatherings must have been a rewarding experience.

During these years Johnson's social relationships were not centered wholly in the Ivy Lane Club. He still kept closely in touch with his old employer Cave, and through him with others he had first known at St. John's Gate, Thomas Birch, Elizabeth Carter, Mrs. Masters, the poet, and others. Apart from acquaintances made through the *Gentleman's Magazine*, he occasionally saw John Taylor of Ashbourne, whom he had known since grammar school in Lichfield. At first planning to be a lawyer like his father, Taylor had later decided to enter the church, where his "desire for preferments was insatiable."[35] He became a pluralist, purchasing some positions with money inherited from his father, and had hopes of moving even further up in the hierarchy. In 1746 he became prebendary of Westminster, and preached in the Broadway chapel in Westminster.

In the late 1740s Taylor regularly spent some time each year in London, where he and Johnson saw each other fairly often. Whenever Taylor needed a sermon for a special occasion, he would come to his old schoolfriend for help. As Baretti later put it, "in the earlier part of Taylor's priesthood, Johnson wrote many sermons for Taylor's use," for which he paid "two guineas a piece."[36] It was Johnson's regular practice when ghostwriting sermons to make his recipient copy the sermon in his own handwriting, after which Johnson would destroy any notes or early versions in his own. He did not wish evidence of his authorship to survive.

In 1747 Taylor had been accidentally involved in Lord Chesterfield's seeing an early copy of Johnson's *Plan* for the *Dictionary* and apparently was in close touch with his friend's project. From 1750 Taylor and his second wife had a house in Little Dean's Yard, in the Cloisters, Westminster. Here Johnson would occasionally see them. Not that he and Taylor were perfectly attuned. Johnson once remarked to Daniel Astle that Taylor had "never relished a book in his earlier days."[37] But, even so, they remained close friends.

Another friend from Lichfield days was Dr. Robert James. In 1741–1742 Johnson had helped James with his *Medicinal Dictionary*, writing a good many of the pieces in it. Perhaps remembered better for his famous "fever powders," which were marketed by Newbery and reputed later to have been partly responsible for the death of Oliver Goldsmith, James had a wide practice, though not in fashionable circles. Once, so we are told, someone observed in a large gathering that "Dr. James was little known by people of rank, fashion, or talents." Johnson admitted the truth of the remark and added, "His company, Sir, was like his conversation, coarse.—James and gentlemen were never seen together."[38]

In addition to being a heavy drinker, James was also a notorious rake. The story was widely told that once when he was driving along in a coach with his whore, they picked up Johnson and carried him to his destination. It was not until later that Johnson heard who the lady was. When next he met James he sternly reproached him for carrying an old friend around in such company. "James apologized by saying that he always took a swelling in his stones if he abstained a month etc.—Damn the rascal, says Johnson, he is past sixty; the swelling would have gone no farther."[39] But, as with Taylor, Johnson never allowed dislike of personal weakness to force a break with childhood connections. And when the sexual habits of a close friend were at issue, Johnson was usually able to remain friends even when he did not approve of the other's actions.

Since he did little traveling outside London, he apparently did not keep up with other earlier friends like Edmund Hector in Birmingham. For the time being, Johnson was firmly centered in London.

CHAPTER IV

Lexicographer at Work

DURING THESE YEARS Johnson spent much of his time in the garret at Gough Square. When he could drag himself out of bed in the late morning and have breakfast, he would climb up to supervise the work of his helpers. Seated on his old three-legged chair, amidst battered furniture and piles of books, he did what he could to move ahead with his project.

The need for an English dictionary had been obvious for a long time. There had been numerous proposals and plans, and by 1736 there was available a huge *Dictionarium Britannicum* by Nathan Bailey. But Bailey and the others left much to be desired. None really tried to define all the words or to provide the kind of grammatical advice twentieth-century readers have come to expect in a dictionary. Finally, the publisher Robert Dodsley, greatly impressed by Johnson's erudition and mastery of the language, suggested that he produce what was needed. After some hesitation, Johnson decided to accept the suggestion, and on June 18, 1746, he signed an agreement with a group of booksellers including Dodsley, Andrew Millar, John and Paul Knapton, and others. For the overall sum of £1,575 Johnson agreed to prepare a full dictionary of the English language, hoping to have it completed in three years' time. This was supposed to occupy all his time for these years. But the work proved more complex and arduous than expected, and progress was slow. From the start he had the help of a number of amanuenses, the first one Francis Stewart, and later at least five others. They were supposed to do much of the mechanical work of copying quotations and other details. At the start there was the long, laborious task of finding useful quotations from earlier writers, largely from the seventeenth century, showing the proper usage of words.[1]

Then he had to have those quotations copied, sorted out, and alphabetized. The next step was to provide definitions, separating various types of meanings, and adding meager etymologies. Finally, all the material had to be assembled on sheets of paper to be carried to the printer. Recently much new information about the methods used has been discovered, largely through the exhaustive work of Eugene Thomas.[2] After careful examination of all the surviving marked books and manuscript slips, Thomas is now able to explain more accurately than before just what took place.

Johnson's procedure can briefly be described this way: Having chosen a writer whom he admired, he selected a volume of the man's works, either from his own shabby collection or borrowed from a friend who obviously did not care what happened to it, and then read through it carefully. When he found some word which he thought correctly used, he would underline the word in pencil, then put vertical lines at the beginning and end of the passage to be copied, the first letter of the word in the outer margin. Sometimes more than one word was underlined in the same passage. After he had gone through the volume, marking what he thought he needed, he passed it over to his assistants.

After transcribing each passage, the copyist struck through the letter which Johnson had placed in the margin. It seems that each amanuensis had his own peculiar type of cross-out stroke—multiple horizontal, single vertical, single diagonal, double diagonal, single horizontal, or double horizontal. Johnson had his own mark for use in the margins. Since all the copyists used straight lines, he devised a circular mark—a distinctive, compact swirl stroke—which he used whenever he happened to change his mind, or chanced to discover repetitions, or decided to use a better example.

It may well be that the six recognizable cross-out strokes correspond to the six amanuenses named by Boswell as working at one time or another with Johnson on the *Dictionary*, though so far it has not been possible to identify each one completely. Interestingly enough, there appears to be a correlation between one copyist's cross strokes and some mistakes which later scholars have found in the *Dictionary*. Misattribution of quotations for which Johnson has been blamed, as when the wrong play of Shakespeare is cited, may have resulted from the carelessness of that particular transcriber, whose errors were not caught by his employer. After long hours of handling a volume of Shakespeare, the helper might easily have been confused as to which play he was using.

One theory is that in some cases the copyists worked in pairs, seated side by side before a desk, going through books from beginning to end.[3] Evidence from the markings would seem to confirm that at times this occurred, but also that a large part of the work was done by a single copyist working alone. Crossing out Johnson's marginal letter with a pencil, he copied quotations on sheets of paper or in blank books. These were then cut out (or "clipped," to use Johnson's term) into separate slips, which were deposited in nearby bins. It would thus have been possible, from the number of slips in each box, for Johnson to keep an accurate tab on the productivity of each amanuensis.

Many more slips were made than were used. Perhaps some were omitted for practical reasons of space, or because they turned out to be repetitions. But a great number may accidentally have been lost. Indeed, most of the quotations transcribed by "Copyist 2" never appeared in the printed text (of some 6,714 passages he marked in the surviving volumes, only 290 were actually used). Might they somehow have been lost along the way? Or had there been some quarrel with this particular amanuensis which made Johnson decide not to use his slips? Since some duplicate passages have survived, the likelihood is that the loss was accidental, possibly occurring when the project was being moved from earlier quarters to Gough Square.

The next step would have been to alphabetize the huge stacks of slips, sorting out the quotations for each separate word, after which Johnson, rejecting those that were repetitious or superfluous, would decide which ones to use. Then he would revise the quotations to suit his immediate purpose, a process which probably took more time than one might suppose.

From the start Johnson took liberties with his sources. In his later Preface he warned readers that some quotations had been compressed and others modified.[4] In other words, citations did not exactly reproduce the original text. Some, of course, were precisely as he found them, but others were changed, with opening words or conclusions deleted, and sometimes with major changes in phraseology. In some instances Johnson deleted or recast substantial portions of the material he had marked for transcription. One reason must have been the saving of space, but often, one suspects, it was also a question of taste. When Johnson disliked the style of an author, he did not hesitate to improve it. After all, he was using earlier authors merely as a means of providing evidence of the proper usage of words, and it was the later readers he was serving.

As Gwin and Ruth Kolb describe the process, Johnson's alterations "usually consist of extensive, artfully devised omissions."[5] As an example of the use of the word "perpetuity," Johnson marked this passage from South's *Sermons:* "It is indeed a real trepan upon it; feeding it with colours, and appearances, instead of arguments, and driving the very same bargain, which *Jacob* did with *Esau*: a mess of pottage for a birth-right; a

Page from the Preface to the Dictionary *in Johnson's handwriting.*

present repast for a perpetuity." This he reduced to: "A mess of pottage for a birth-right, a present repast for a *perpetuity*." And illustrating the word "economical," he marked a passage in Watts's *Logick*: "in *moral, political, economical* affairs, having proposed the *government of self*, a *family*, a *society* or a *nation*, in order to their best interest, we consider and search out what are the *proper laws, rules* and *means* to effect it." This was trimmed down to read: "In *economical* affairs, having proposed the government of a family, we consider the proper means to effect it." He allowed himself the liberty of a little rewriting: a passage from Watts illustrating the word "plenary"—"The method of treating a subject should be *plenary* or *full, so that nothing may be wanting;* nothing which is necessary or proper should be omitted"—appears in the *Dictionary* as follows: "A treatise on a subject should be *plenary* or full, so that nothing may be wanting, nothing which is proper omitted."

Perhaps an even better example might be a quotation from Brian Duppa's *Holy Rules* (1675).[6] On page 45 of this work Johnson underlined the word "tempter" in this sentence: "Prayer hath the nature (of a charm) to keep temptations from you, so when by humane weakness and the arts of the *tempter* you are led in to them, prayer is as the thread to bring you out of this labyrinth." But in the *Dictionary* Johnson used the quotation for another word, "temptation," and condensed the quotation to read: "When by human weakness, and the arts of the tempter, you are led into *temptations*, prayer is the thread to bring you out of this labyrinth." By removing "charm," which might suggest the power of magic, not faith, he makes the quotation center on "prayer." It was the precept of piety which he wanted to stress.[7]

Of course, the changes were usually not so extensive, and his versions are basically faithful to the original purposes of his authority. In manipulating another man's prose, Johnson showed his own skill at pithy, epigrammatic phrasing. He saved space, and at the same time made his volumes more readable.

All this editing necessarily meant much recopying by the amanuenses. It was probably in the final transcription of the passages that the necessity for careful cutting became apparent. Once when copy was going to the printer and there had been complaints concerning the waste of space because of faulty cutting, Johnson wrote to Strahan explaining the cause of the trouble.

It proceeds from the haste of the amanuensis to get to the end of his day's work. I have desired the passages to be clipped close, and then perhaps for two or three leaves it is done. But since poor Stuart's time I could never get that part of the work into regularity, and perhaps never shall. I will try to take some more care but can promise nothing; when I am told there is a sheet or two I order it away. You will find it sometimes close; when I make up any myself, which never happens but when I have nobody with me, I generally clip it close, but one cannot always be on the watch.[8]

As soon as he had all his slips of illustrative quotations before him— and the major work of copying must have been over by the late summer of 1750—Johnson began the laborious process of definition, trying to divide words under various uses, and finally providing short etymologies. Study of surviving evidence shows clearly that his definitions are closely related to the quotations he was using from earlier writers. The final step was a kind of paste-up job, or recopying for the printer, putting all the material in final sequence.

According to a later recollection by someone who had either himself been actively involved in the printing of the *Dictionary,* or who had talked to someone who had, and who signed himself merely "W. N." (perhaps one of the Nichols family), copy was produced on "4to post, and in two columns each page."[9] Johnson himself wrote

in his own hand, the words and their explanation, and generally two or three words in each column, leaving a space between each for the authorities, which were pasted on as they were collected by the different clerks or amanuenses employed: and in this mode the MS. was so regular, that the sheets of MS. which made a sheet of print could be very exactly ascertained.

But this would have been the final technique. In the early stages there were numerous mistakes. From the start Johnson was not too clear in his mind just how copy should be prepared for the printer. Never an efficient manager, he and his helpers at various times tried a number of impractical methods and were forced to change techniques in midstream, apparently having to learn from experience. Boswell, many years later, recorded in his notebook that Johnson had told him that at first final copy had been written in eighty large blank books, using both sides of the pages, and when it was found that this was unacceptable to the printer it cost him twenty pounds for paper and labor in order to have it all recopied on one side.[10]

Although our knowledge of Johnson's helpers is fragmentary, we can identify some of them fairly well. The first to be hired was probably a Scot named Francis Stewart. On the very day that Johnson and the book-sellers signed the contract, June 18, 1746, Stewart signed a receipt which read: "I received by way of advance three pounds three shillings, to be repaid out of twelve shillings a week for which I contract to assist in compiling the work, and which is to begin to be paid from midsummer next."[11]

The son of an Edinburgh bookseller, Stewart may have been working for one of the proprietors involved in Johnson's project and have been transferred to work on the *Dictionary* at this time. Johnson had already begun the long process of marking passages even before the contract was officially signed, so that Stewart could begin at once the job of transcribing them. Since this was well before Johnson had found a house in Gough Square, Stewart started his work in his own home. Later, we know, Johnson hired other helpers, but Stewart, because of his seniority and his former connections, appears to have served as a liaison with the booksellers.[12]

During the early years of the project "Frank" Stewart was employed in many ways. Not only did he help in the collection of authorities to be used, but he managed most of the affairs between Johnson, "his booksellers, and his creditors who were then often very troublesome." Indeed, much of the outside business was handled by Stewart. As one later commentator put it, Stewart was better qualified for this than his employer, "as he had been more accustomed to common business, and more conversant in the ways of men." To be sure, Stewart was reputed to have been a "porter-drinking man," who was sometimes drunk in the evenings, but his convivial connections were useful for the dictionary work. For low cant phrases and gambling and card-playing terms he became Johnson's chief authority.

How much help Johnson had from outsiders who were not involved in the project cannot be documented. It is likely that he was constantly hearing technical terms or slang phrases which he had to consider. He must have had much debatable advice. One story has it that when working on this project Johnson once sent a note to the *Gentleman's Magazine* asking for advice as to the origin of the word "curmudgeon." He received an anonymous letter, which he used as his authority for the *Dictionary* definition: "It is a vicious manner of pronouncing *coeur méchant*."[13] If this actually occurred, Johnson's query to the magazine has never been found.

Of the other amanuenses, we know that Alexander and William Macbean, Robert Shiels, V. J. Peyton and a man named Maitland worked on the *Dictionary*. Possibly the second to be hired was Alexander Macbean, whom Johnson once described as "a man of great learning," though hardly one of great discernment. Macbean had for years been helping with Ephraim Chambers's *Cyclopaedia*, the fifth edition of which appeared in 1746. When this was completed, Macbean may have come to work for Johnson. His experience working with Chambers would have been invaluable, and the number of times that Chambers was used in the completed *Dictionary* may be the result of Macbean's experience.[14]

Years later, at Johnson's suggestion, Macbean started work on a geographical dictionary. There are various versions of what happened when he showed his former employer what he had done. According to Mrs. Piozzi, Johnson commented to Macbean that

> he had dwelt too little on the article *Athens*. "Ah Doctor!" says
> the man, "but if I make so much writing about *Athens*, what
> room will be left for me to talk about Abingdon?" After this
> conversation, cries Johnson, you may be sure we talked no more
> of work.[15]

Little is known about Alexander Macbean's younger brother William, who was the only one to survive Johnson, and who spent his later years working on another lexicographical project.[16] This was intended as a supplement to Johnson's *Dictionary*, adding new words and interpretations. But though he worked at the project for many years, it was never published.

About another Scot, Robert Shiels, who had begun as a journeyman printer, we do know more. Johnson certainly thought highly of him even if he did find his devotion to the blank verse of James Thomson amusing, and he called him a man of very "acute understanding." In 1749, probably while Johnson's amanuensis, Shiels wrote in blank verse a poem, "Marriage," in praise of *Irene*. After ending his work on the *Dictionary*, Shiels produced a first valuable collection of lives of English poets, apparently with Johnson's help, but gained little acclaim since the publishers insisted on ascribing it to Theophilus Cibber, who was better known. When working for Johnson he may have been in bad health, for he died of consumption on December 27, 1753.[17]

Little is known about Peyton, the only Englishman of the group, though his wife caused some trouble for Johnson. On March 12, 1750, Johnson apparently went over to Bow Street to stand bond for the sum of £20 in behalf of Mary Peyton (presumably the wife of his helper), guaranteeing that she would appear at the next General Quarter Sessions to answer charges that had been brought against her, and meantime would keep the peace, especially toward someone named Mary Humphreys.[18] But just who the latter was, or what caused the rumpus between the two women, is a mystery. An interesting fact brought out by the court record which gives us these details is that it was signed by Henry Fielding, then Justice of the Peace for Westminster. Even though the later records add nothing further about Mary Peyton and her difficulties, at least they show that Johnson and the novelist, whom he later described to Boswell as a "barren rascal," were once in the same room and doubtless talked to each other.

It is likely that Peyton and at least one other amanuensis were working in Gough Square after Stewart's death and the departure of some of the others. It was Peyton and one of the Macbeans who helped Johnson prepare the revised fourth edition published in 1773.

The number of copyists working in the attic in Gough Square varied. On August 6, 1748, Thomas Birch wrote to his patron Philip Yorke that Johnson had four still working for him (possibly Stewart, Maitland, Alexander Macbean, and Shiels), but that their work of transcribing the quotations was almost over.[19] But this, like Johnson's own early estimate of the time needed to do the work, was unrealistic. Merely to sort out and put together nearly 114,000 quotations used in the *Dictionary* was a huge task, and the final paste-up job with etymologies and definitions would take longer. In the spring of 1749 Johnson apparently still had at least two copyists working for him, and perhaps three.

Nevertheless, there was a general feeling that the great project was nearing completion. In the February 1749 number of the *Gentleman's Magazine* there is a letter, signed "W. S.," on the significance of words, which ends with the sentence:

> However, it is hoped that our language will be more fixed and better established when the public is favoured with a new dictionary, undertaken with that view, and adapted to answer several other valuable purposes; a work now in great forwardness.[20]

If, as seems likely, "W. S." was William Strahan, or someone writing for him, it looks as if the proprietors thought some preliminary advertising might be useful. If Johnson helped to compose the letter—later he used portions of it in his Preface—he must himself have approved. Strahan's basic purpose, however, might have been to prod Johnson into greater productivity.

That this optimism was widespread is shown in a letter of Joseph Ames to Sir Peter Thomson in the autumn of 1749 where he told of meeting Johnson and Cave, and commented that Johnson's lexicographical work was "ready for the press." Of course, he may have meant that the first sheets were ready.[21] Actually the final phase was to take much longer than anyone realized.

One of his constant problems was financial—how to keep himself alive and also pay regular wages to his amanuenses. One anecdote describes how, while working on the *Dictionary* in Gough Square, Johnson "was in debt to a milkman, who attempted to arrest him."[22] His reaction was to bring down his bed, barricade the door, and harangue the milkman and the bailiffs—"Depend upon it, I will defend this my little citadel to the utmost."

Possibly as early as late 1749, before he began to write *Rambler* essays, he wrote to Strahan, pointing out his difficulty in paying his assistants 23s. a week, without receiving much help from them, and promising to be more efficient, the chief point being to get two guineas for himself. Such phrases as "I know not how to manage" and "fall better in method" show clearly his uncertainty at the time.[23] If he was paying only 23s. a week to his amanuenses, that would mean that he probably had only two working at the time (one receiving 12s. and the other 11s.), or possibly three, with lower wages (9, 7, 7). Though eventually they did begin to get copy to the printer, there continued to be difficulties, sometimes practical, and sometimes editorial.

Although some early biographers offer conflicting evidence, we know that Johnson was, at some point, supposed to receive a guinea for carefully prepared copy which would make a printed sheet. This was paid on delivery, and every guinea parcel was then tied up at the printers and "put upon a shelf in the collector's room till wanted." Printed sheets were sent back to Gough Square for revision. But there were always problems. Once Johnson wrote to Strahan:

> What you tell me I am ashamed never to have thought on—
> I wish I had known it sooner—Send me back the last sheet; and
> the last copy for correction. If you will promise me hence-
> forward to print a sheet a day, I will promise you to endeavour
> that you shall have every day a sheet to print, beginning next
> Tuesday.[24]

No matter how well-meaning his promises were, there continued to be difficulties. One mixup, either from Johnson's own carelessness or the cheating of one of his helpers, occurred when the printers were setting type for letters D, G, and L, all at the same time, and Johnson for once had "received more money than he had produced MS. for."[25] Johnson had "supplied copy faster than the printers called for it; and in one of the heaps of copy it happened that, upon giving it out to the compositors, some sheets of the old MS. that had been printed off were found among the new MS. paid for." The story got out, and in some circles Johnson was blamed. But "W. N.," in his later account, how dependable it is impossible to tell, defended him and insisted that in the circumstances Johnson could hardly have been driven to such lengths as to "make use of this shabby trick to get three or four guineas." Instead what happened was probably due to Johnson's practice of "keeping the old copy, which was always returned him with the proof, in a disorderly manner." But at the printing house there were other theories, based on suspicion of at least one of Johnson's helpers, "not of the best characters." One of these had lately been discharged for other reasons though for some time he had been kindly treated by Johnson, "notwithstanding all his loose and idle tricks." Many suspected that it was this man who tried the expedient of "picking up the old MS. to raise a few guineas, finding the money so readily paid on the MS. as he delivered it." When it was discovered what had happened, Francis Stewart, then largely in charge of such matters, immediately supplied the proper amount of other copy, which fortunately was ready, and thus, "in the course of an hour or two," he "set every thing to rights." Thus the later suspicions of critics like Francis Grose were unfounded.[26] "W. N." concluded that Johnson must be acquitted of any complicity, for he had "rather too little thoughts about money matters."

Being ahead of the game was for Johnson a very rare condition. Usually the situation was entirely reversed and the printers had legitimate cause for complaint. Once, the situation became so bad that the proprietors even had the unrealistic idea of threatening to cut off all of Johnson's supplies and payments. This so infuriated Johnson that he dashed off one of the most strident, combative letters of his whole career. On November 1, 1751, he wrote to Strahan:

> The message which you sent me by Mr. Stewart I do not consider as at all your own, but if you were contented to be the deliverer of it to me, you must favour me so far as to return my answer, which I have written down to spare you the unpleasing office of doing it in your own words. You advise me to write, I know with very kind intentions, nor do I intend to treat your counsel with any disregard when I declare that in the present state of the matter "I shall *not* write"—otherwise than the words following—
>
> "That my resolution has long been, and is *not* now altered, and is now *less* likely to be altered, that I shall *not* see the gentlemen partners till the first volume is in the press which they may forward or retard by dispensing or not dispensing with the last message."
>
> Be pleased to lay this my determination before them this morning, for I shall think of taking my measures accordingly tomorrow evening, only this that I mean no harm, but that my citadel shall not be taken by storm while I can defend it, and

that if a blockade is intended, the country is under the command of my batteries. I shall think of laying it under contribution tomorrow evening.[27]

With this ultimatum Johnson made clear who really was the master. He would fight to the end to keep his project going the way he wanted. Evidently Strahan was able to calm down the two sides, and secure some kind of peace. Work went on as usual with copy sent to the printers, if not regularly, at least without too great delays. Presumably, too, Johnson was able to keep paying his staff every Saturday. But it was not until April 1753, almost seven years after the start of the project, that the first volume was completed and he could begin the second.[28]

DURING 1749 AND 1750 Johnson's connections with the *Gentleman's Magazine,* which had been his chief means of support in the early 1740s, were, at best, tenuous. Although he kept in close touch with what was going on through Hawkesworth and other friends, it is unlikely that he did much regular writing for Cave. It must be admitted that Donald Greene and other modern scholars have made persuasive attempts to identify Johnson's hand in some dramatic criticism, as well as in other reviews.[29] But Hawkesworth had learned to imitate Johnson's style so perfectly that it is risky to use stylistic evidence, or internal details of any sort, as conclusive proof of authorship. Nevertheless Johnson may have helped Hawkesworth with some of the pieces and may well have been responsible for many of the ideas. Still, we know that during these years Hawkesworth was Cave's chief helper at St. John's Gate, and it is safer to assume that he was responsible for most decisions in the fields of liberal arts.

One such set of decisions, however, became the prelude to an important episode in Johnson's life, one which has come to be known as the "Lauder affair."[30] It is necessary first to look back a few years. For readers of Boswell and for students of Milton it all began early in 1747 when there appeared in the *Gentleman's Magazine* a letter signed "W. L." suggesting that at times Milton in *Paradise Lost* was not wholly original, but instead was imitating certain little-known modern authors. But readers more interested in basic causes or psychological approaches might say that it all started years earlier when a young Scot, watching a golf match on Bruntisfield Links near Edinburgh, was hit in the knee by a wild shot. The young man was named William Lauder, and after neglect, or faulty treatment, he had to have his leg amputated three inches above the knee and be fitted with a wooden leg.[31] As a result, he became a bitter, resentful cripple

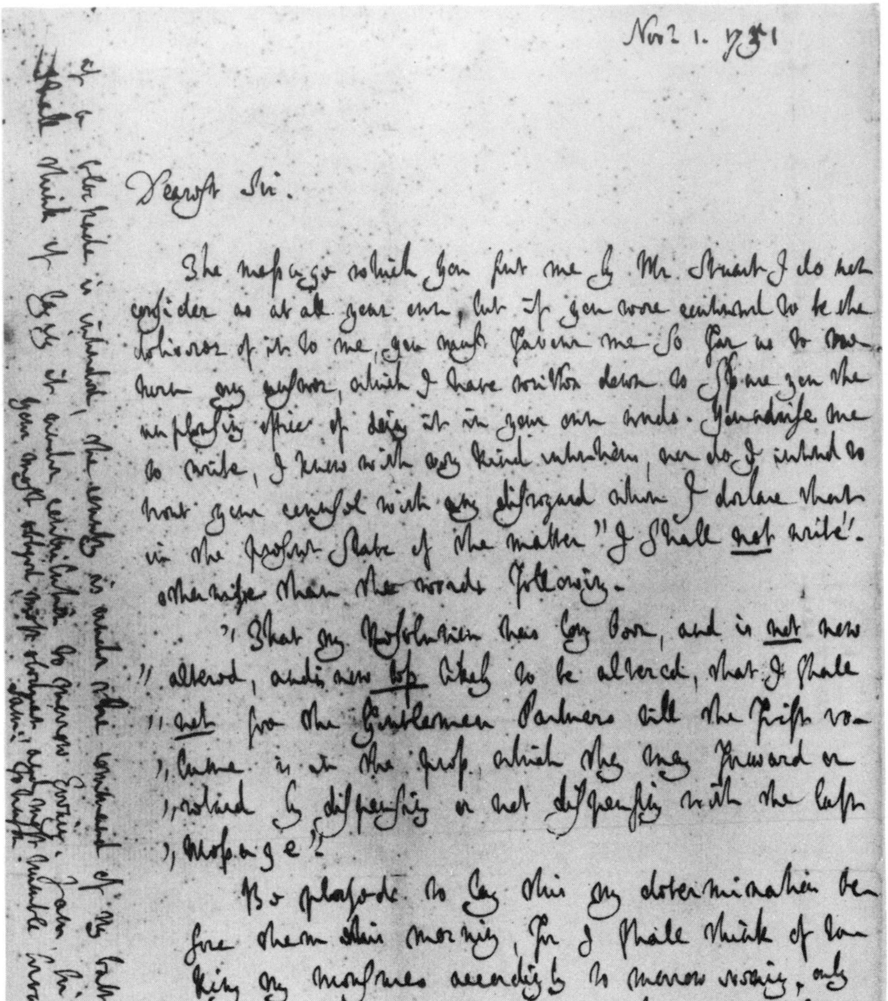

Nov. 1. 1751

Letter by Johnson to William Strahan.

for the rest of his life. Although an excellent classical scholar, he failed in various attempts to secure permanent teaching and library posts.

Sometime in 1746, perhaps shortly after the defeat of Bonnie Prince Charlie at Culloden, William Lauder made his way to London, no doubt hoping that his talents would be more highly regarded there than they had been in Edinburgh and Dundee. At first he lived "at the corner-house, the bottom of Ayre-street, Piccadilly," making his living as a Latin tutor, and at the same time investigating other possible ways of getting ahead. He is described as a man of ordinary height, with "a white complexion, large rolling fiery eyes, and a thundering voice," his temper naturally explosive, and "his turn of mind very sanguine and fierce."[32] Deeply resentful of mankind, he apparently sought revenge in various ways, one of them blackening the character of one of England's greatest writers, John Milton.

Clearly Lauder's original impulse while still in Scotland was political —hatred of the Commonwealth and loyalty to the Stuarts—and only later did he move into scholarly and literary areas. Just when he made his first connection with the *Gentleman's Magazine* is not clear, nor exactly when he met Johnson. It is tempting to suspect that Johnson may have had something to do with the inclusion in the October and December 1746 numbers of the magazine of some Latin translations of the beginning of *Paradise Lost*. This might have been intended as a kind of introduction to what the editors knew was coming early the next year. In any event, in the January 1747 number, which appeared early in February, there appeared W. L.'s "Essay on Milton's Imitation of the Moderns," which started a lengthy argument.

About this time Johnson may have met Lauder personally, have been impressed by his classical attainments and moved by his misfortunes. Here was a first-rate scholar, an ardent Jacobite, crippled through no fault of his own, a deserving man who had failed to attain proper recognition in his own country perhaps because of his physical disabilities, who now proposed a promising piece of research, studying major and minor analogues to *Paradise Lost* (what some modern scholars have been doing with great success).[33] Even if Lauder may have appeared overexcitable and a bit mad, Johnson could forgive all that in the light of what he had heard about his past. He could have had no suspicion of dishonesty on the part of the poor Scot.

In the February number W. L.'s contribution was continued. In these discussions he did not take a firm stand against Milton. All he suggested was that the author of *Paradise Lost* had been influenced by his reading of modern Latin authors like Jacobus Masenius and Hugo Grotius, as well as by the classics. On the surface it sounded like a worthwhile piece of scholarly research.

True, in the April 1747 number of the *Gentleman's Magazine* W. L. made more serious "charges" against Milton, though he did not suggest plagiarism. For Johnson and those at St. John's Gate it may still have appeared to be a valuable project. Others, too, were favorably inclined, and in the June number, where further passages were cited, there was a letter signed "W. B." (William Brakenridge), praising Lauder. It was not until the July number that the first major objection appeared, in a letter signed "R. R." (Richard Richardson). This, however, was answered in what might have appeared to be a convincing manner in the August number by Lauder, here, for the first time, signing his full name. Consequently, Johnson was easily prevailed upon to write some *Proposals* for publishing by subscription a new edition of Grotius's *Adamus Exsul,* to be edited by Lauder, with an English translation and notes. The advertisement for this appeared in the August number, issued early in September.³⁴

Sir John Hawkins's later claim that Johnson's support of Lauder was the result of his own personal antipathy to Milton may have some validity.³⁵ Having grown up in Lichfield, which had been partly demolished during the Puritan Revolution, Johnson had a strong prejudice against Milton's political allegiance, and he could hardly be considered completely objective about Milton the man. Nevertheless, Johnson's early support of Lauder was probably even more influenced by his sympathy for a poor, crippled scholar who deserved help.

Through the remainder of 1747, 1748, and early 1749, Lauder's claims were discussed in the magazine, with various reactions, some of high praise and others stoutly defending Milton. One letter, signed "Philo-Miltonus" and dated October 17, 1747, supporting Richardson, was held up by Cave and Hawkesworth, perhaps with Johnson's approval, and was finally printed in the February 1748 number. There were pamphlets such as Richardson's *Zoilomastix,* letters from other readers, numerous verses, and in August 1748 there appeared a strange biographical account of Lauder with the title *Furius: Or, a Modest Attempt towards a History of the Famous W.L.*³⁶ In some London circles the wild Scot's arguments were the subject of constant discussion. Johnson obviously knew of the appalled reactions of Milton's supporters, but was still largely on Lauder's side.

Then on December 14, 1749, was published Lauder's *Essay on Milton's Use and Imitation of the Moderns in His Paradise Lost,* in which he printed as a Preface what Johnson had written for the Grotius *Proposals* over two years before, adding two more paragraphs, perhaps with Johnson's permission. At the end was a Postscript also written by Johnson, urging support for Milton's surviving granddaughter, who was in financial difficulties. Obviously this was one way of showing that the whole matter was not merely personal bias against Milton and his family.

The *Essay* was essentially an expansion of Lauder's articles in the *Gentleman's Magazine*. Preceding the main argument were extracts from four letters written by other scholars supporting his position, which had appeared in the same periodical, the one by "W. B." having been expanded by the interpolation of six passages. Lauder's chief claim was that *Paradise Lost* was a work which had been much influenced by various modern writers, most of them largely unknown except to a few experts. The beginning of the epic, for example, was derived from Masenius, Grotius, Andrew Ramsay, Buchanan, Du Bartas, and Molinaeus, and in later books Milton drew on other writers such as Staphorstius, Taubmannus, Barlaeus. Lauder blamed Milton for not acknowledging publicly these sources. Instead of being a completely original poet, as so many readers supposed, Milton was essentially an "unlicensed" plagiarist.

There are many unanswered questions connected with the publication of Lauder's sensational essay. How much was Johnson involved in preparing the final text? Who wrote the last two paragraphs of the Preface? Did Johnson help Lauder secure a publisher? Was it at a meeting of the Ivy Lane Club, perhaps on Tuesday, December 5, described by Hawkins, that the publisher John Payne brought proofs of Lauder's work to be discussed by the members?[37] Was it there that Johnson indicated his approval of what Lauder was doing? And most crucial of all, did Johnson have any suspicions at all about the legitimacy of the added quotations which Lauder had inserted to prove his point?

During the early part of 1750 the angry revulsion to Lauder's shocking assertions steadily mounted. But Johnson was himself too busy with other matters—attempting to prepare copy for the printers of the *Dictionary* and beginning a new periodical, *The Rambler*—to give any time to controversy. It is doubtful that he did much to help with Lauder's published *Proposals* for printing in four volumes the works of twenty-six authors used by Milton, which appeared in July.[38] For the time being the whole affair was merely something for casual conversation at the Ivy Lane Club or when Johnson happened to meet Milton supporters at social gatherings. The real explosion did not come until late in 1750.

A number of well-known clergymen tried to check carefully Lauder's acknowledged sources, though they were often hard to find, with a growing conviction that the wily Scot must have fabricated some of his evidence. John Bowle of Oxford and Richard Richardson of Cambridge almost simultaneously discovered several falsifications in Lauder's work, but it was John Douglas, later to become the Bishop of Salisbury, who finally pulled the evidence together.[39] Although unable to find many of the texts cited by Lauder, Douglas sensed what Lauder had been doing.

Some details may even this early have been shown to Johnson. There

is convincing evidence that Johnson was in touch with the Milton supporters and always ready to argue with them about specific points. In a
letter from Richard Richardson to the *Gentleman's Magazine* dated January 28, 1749 (1750), but not published until almost a year later, Richardson discussed a passage which Lauder claimed Milton had translated from
Masenius. This particular passage, he added, "so struck Mr. J—n that the
last time I had the pleasure of seeing him, he said he would venture the
merits of the cause that Milton had seen *Masenius*, since it is rendered
almost *verbum verbo*."[40]

Douglas planned to publish a pamphlet containing all the evidence
he could find and wished to dedicate it to his patron, Lord Bath. For a
while during the autumn the authorship of the exposé was not widely
known, and Birch suspected that Thomas Newton was involved. But by
November 17 Birch could write to Yorke:

> Mr. Douglas's piece against Lauder was committed to the press,
> but some new discoveries of the forgeries of that modern Zoilus
> occasioned him to take back his manuscript for its improve-
> ment. And this, with a new living, to which Lord Bath, who is
> just come from Paris, has collated him, will a little retard the
> publication of his pamphlet. I saw a letter of his written in the
> beginning of this book, in which he says that Lauder pleads
> guilty. But that he is resolved to expose the imposter in a man-
> ner that he shall never be able to show his face again to man-
> kind.[41]

The pamphlet finally appeared on November 26 with the title *Milton
Vindicated from the Charge of Plagiarism Brought Against Him by Mr.
Lauder and Lauder Himself Convicted of Several Forgeries and Gross
Impositions on the Public.*[42] It became the talk of the town immediately—
at least in literary circles—and was generally received with delight.

Although he had not been able to see some of the texts which were
central to Lauder's claims, Douglas cited a number of passages which had
obviously been interpolated. Therefore he insisted that Lauder at once
produce the originals to prove his case. Throughout, the implication is
that if some of Lauder's claims were based upon forgeries, the likelihood
was that most of the others were also illegitimate.

To Johnson and to Lauder's publishers it must have been obvious
that something had to be done at once to save their own reputations.
Douglas, indeed, suggested as much. Those who had been helping Lauder,
Douglas wrote, must have implicitly taken for granted that the evidence
which was brought forward was to be depended upon. No sensible person

would ever have suspected such gross frauds. Then alluding to Johnson personally, he added:

> 'Tis to be hoped, nay 'tis *expected,* that the elegant and nervous writer, whose judicious sentiments and inimitable style point out the author of Lauder's Preface and Postscript, will no longer allow one to *plume himself with his feathers* who appears so little to have deserved his assistance: an assistance which, I am persuaded, would never have been communicated had there been the least suspicion of those facts, which I have been the instrument of conveying to the world in these sheets.[43]

This was clear enough, and Johnson caught the message, if indeed he had not been aware of it much earlier. Something more than a mere admission of guilt in a few instances must be given to the public.

So, two days after the appearance of Douglas's pamphlet, on November 28, in the *London Gazeteer* and presumably other papers, the booksellers John Payne and Joseph Bouquet published this advertisement:

> Upon the publication of the Rev. Mr. Douglas's Defence of Milton, in answer to Lauder, we immediately sent to Lauder and insisted upon his clearing himself from the charge of forgery which Mr. Douglas has brought against him, by producing the books in question. *He has this day admitted the charge,* but with great insensibility. We therefore disclaim all connection with him, and shall for the future sell his book only as a masterpiece of fraud, which the public may be supplied with at 1s. 6d. stitched.[44]

In addition, Johnson wrote for the publishers "A New Preface," dated December 1, 1750, in which they apologized for the imposition and tried to explain how they had been deceived. Lauder's original discoveries had come to them recommended only by "novelty and singularity" and a false impression of his honesty, "at least of his want of capacity to contrive and execute a fraud."

> But the inferences which he draws from his doctrine, in impeachment of Milton's *moral* character, produced an opinion of his integrity; for though these inferences were not likely to extend their influence, as they appear at first sight to be the decisions of a weak and distempered judgment, yet they are made with great indignation and bitterness; and it was not possible to conceive that a man could even think of supporting

so bold a charge of dishonesty and secret dealing, by actual
fraud and the violation of every duty which an authour in his
circumstances was obliged to practise.[45]

There followed a repetition of the contents of the advertisement, together
with the booksellers' demands and Lauder's acknowledgement of his
interpolations, made with "great confidence," and apparent wonder "at
the folly of mankind, *in making such an extravagant rout about eighteen
or twenty lines.*"

Also, the publishers later provided a new Postscript, to be inserted,
like the Preface, in copies of Lauder's *Essay* now being sold at half-
price as a rarity. The last page of the "New Postscript" was ostensibly
an apology of "W. B." (William Brakenridge, the Rector of St. Michael
Bassishaw, and librarian at Sion College, a Fellow of the Royal and Antiquarian Societies), who had written "Extract III" in the original *Essay*
and now wanted to explain why. It is quite possible that this was written
by Johnson and represents substantially an explanation of his own involvement in the affair. In 1747, the writer insisted, when he had first written for Lauder he did so because he was convinced of the genuineness of
the quotations cited, and "from a generous motive to favour Mr. Lauder
and his family, who were then in distress." He wrote long before the later
controversial book appeared, "having then only seen that simile of a ship
from Ramsay in a printed copy, which struck him much, and a few others
from Grotius and Masenius in M.S., which it never entered into his heart
to suspect." When the book was in progress, he advised the author to be
candid, and clear from all "reflections on Milton's political character."
Then when he was later shown the manuscript, "those forgeries detected
by Mr. Douglas were not in it, so far as he remembers, nor was it in the
form in which it now appears." In other words, he had been completely
deceived, just as had so many others.

But while Johnson, Payne, and Bouquet were strenuously trying to
defend themselves, the general reading public was greatly enjoying the
disclosures. Douglas's persuasive presentation of the evidence had won
almost complete acceptance of his conclusions. As a sample of what an
intelligent lady of fashion thought, there is a letter written by Lady Anson
from the Admiralty to her brother-in-law, Thomas Anson, M.P., on
December 1. Doubtless she had been hearing all sorts of rumors and welcomed what she thought was a proper conclusion to a shocking piece of
skullduggery.

I hope you have heard of and rejoiced at the detection of
Lauder's wickedness (the man who pretended to prove Milton

a plagiary from a parcel of stupid, modern German, Latin Poets); he has been proved to have falsified his quotations from those authors, and inserted into them lines from a Latin translation of Milton; nay and has forged one line and a half for Milton, as a translation of a thought in one of his authors: this worthy wight, who has got money for the lying Essay in which all these forgeries are cited, and also subscriptions from all sorts of great men for new editions of these favourites of his, has confessed the charge, upon his booksellers insisting on his depositing with them his editions; and owned it with a great deal of impudence. I want to devise some grievous punishment for Lauder, for surely it is hard that the laws should not reach so atrocious a crime. Caligula's decree about bad authors is this minute come into my mind, and I think the making him lick out all his lies and forgeries would be no severe, and a proper kind of penalty for him.[46]

And Catherine Talbot wrote to Elizabeth Carter on December 17: "Do not you rejoice in the public infamy of that villainous forger Lauder?"[47]

Reviews in the periodicals were just as one-sided. Ralph Griffiths gave nine pages to a full account of the whole affair in the December issue of the *Monthly Review*;[48] and the *Scots Magazine* for February 1751 devoted some six columns to extracts from Douglas's pamphlet, ending with his strong statement:

Compassion I think should be also out of the case here. There is something so invidious in our author's [Lauder's] scheme; he prosecutes it with such a spirit of rancour and malice; he appears so well pleased to rob his country of the glory of having a poem, equal at least, if not superior to the noblest productions of antiquity; and, which is chiefly to be considered, he has recourse to such vile arts, such glaring impostures in the prosecution of his design, that it is the duty of every one who has had opportunities of detecting him, to expose him to public censure, to brand him what that infamy he deserves.[49]

The *Gentleman's Magazine* in its December number did not include a review, but did offer full apologies, perhaps written by Johnson, for its support of Lauder in the past.[50] The editors admitted Douglas's charges, passed on word that Lauder was about to confess everything in a letter to Douglas, explained the new Preface provided by the booksellers for Lauder's pamphlet, apologized for not paying proper regard to Richard Richardson who had tried unsuccessfully to show them the truth in earlier letters, and attempted somewhat lamely to explain the magazine's failure to publish his later communications. They had, they admitted, refused to keep the controversy going in their pages because "it was become tedious to our readers," and "we could not admit a suspicion of so gross a forgery."[51] To make amends they included Richardson's earlier letter after holding it for almost a year.

Lauder's formal confession, alluded to by the *Gentleman's Magazine* editors as something which was about to appear, actually must have come out about the same time as their apologies.[52] Dated December 20, it occupied the first pages of Lauder's *Letter to the Reverend Mr. Douglas Occasioned by His Vindication of Milton*. There has never been the slightest doubt that it was written, or dictated, by Johnson, and it is always included in his complete works. Certainly it is a forthright admission of guilt on Lauder's part, with his "offense" admitted with "candour" and specific interpolated passages fully quoted. The last paragraph is expressed in Johnson's most forceful style:

> But for the violation of truth I offer no excuse, because I well know that nothing can excuse it. Nor will I aggravate my crime by disingenuous palliations. I confess it, I repent it, and resolve that my first offence shall be my last. More I cannot perform, and more, therefore, cannot be required. I entreat the pardon of all men whom I have by any means induced to support, to countenance, or patronize my frauds, of which I think myself obliged to declare that not one of my friends was conscious.

But there still remain numerous questions. When was this confession obtained? And how?

Boswell, in his *Life of Johnson,* relying for his facts on material supplied by friends, including Douglas, who remembered the affair, merely tells of the detection of the "gross forgery" and then adds that Johnson "now dictated a letter for Lauder, addressed to Dr. Douglas, acknowledging his fraud in terms of suitable contrition."[53] Sir John Hawkins says that after the publication of Douglas's pamphlet, *Milton Vindicated,* Lauder's booksellers

> called on Lauder for a justification of themselves, and a confirmation of the charge; but he, with a degree of impudence not to be exceeded, acknowledged the interpolation of the books by him cited, and seemed to wonder at "the folly of mankind in making such a rout about eighteen or twenty lines." However, being a short time after convinced by Johnson and others, that it would be more for his interest to make an ample confession of his guilt, than to set mankind at defiance, and stigmatize them with folly; he did so in a letter addressed to Mr. Douglas.[54]

There can be little doubt that Douglas early in November knew that Lauder had confessed to some forgeries. Perhaps he knew as early as October, although the official date on the confession is December 20. There might even have been a long series of confrontations. Perhaps at the start Douglas had shown Johnson and the editors at the *Gentleman's Magazine* conclusive evidence of a few forgeries, and then Johnson and Douglas had gone to see Lauder, who immediately and casually admitted what he had done. He had himself forged some of the lines. Then later, when Payne and Bouquet exerted their pressure, demanding that he show all his evidence, Lauder had gone even further in his confession. But not until later in December was Johnson able to convince the Scot that a formal admission of guilt, in print, was necessary. Only after weeks of argument, we may guess, was Lauder convinced and ready to accept what Johnson wrote or dictated. Yet even then he had reservations.

Clearly Lauder was grateful to Johnson for all he had done to help him with his various projects, and he respected him as a scholar and writer. But looking back years later, he was not sure Johnson had been right in making him agree to a general confession. In Lauder's last blast at Milton, a pamphlet entitled *King Charles I Vindicated from the Charge of Plagiarism Brought Against Him by Milton and Milton Himself Convicted of Forgery, and a Gross Imposition on the Public,* which appeared in 1754, he described in detail his version of what happened in 1750:

> An ingenious gentleman [Johnson] (for whose amazing abilities I had conceived the highest veneration, and in whose candour and friendship I reposed the most implicit and unlimited confidence) advised me to make an unreserved disclosure of all the lines I had interpolated against *Milton,* with this view, chiefly, that no future critics might ever have an opportunity of valuing themselves upon small discoveries of a few lines, which would serve to revive my error, and keep the controversy eternally alive.
>
> With this expedient I then cheerfully complied, when that gentleman wrote for me the letter that was published in my name to Mr. *Douglas,* in which he committed one error that proved fatal to me, and at the same time injurious to the public. For, in place of acknowledging that such and such particular passages only were interpolated, he gave up the whole Essay against *Milton* as delusion and misrepresentation, and thereby imposed more grievously on the public than I had done, and that too in terms much more submissive and abject than the nature of the offence required.
>
> Though this letter, in many respects, contained not my sentiments, as plainly appears from the contradictory postscript

subjoined to it, yet such was my infatuation at that time, and implicit confidence in my friend, that I suffered it to be printed in my name, though I was previously informed by one of the greatest men of the age of its hurtful tendency, which I have since fully experienced to my cost.

That the gentleman meant to serve me, and was really of opinion that the method he proposed might probably prove effectual for rescuing me from the odium of the public, and in some measure restoring my character to the honour it had lost, I was then disposed to believe. His repeated acts of friendship to me on former occasions, in conjunction with a reputation universally established for candour and integrity, left me little room to doubt it: though it is certainly a most preposterous method for a criminal, in order to obtain pardon for one act of felony, to confess himself guilty of a thousand. However, I cannot but condemn myself for placing so implicit a confidence in the judgment of any man, how great or good soever, as to suffer his mistakes to be given to the public, as my opinion.[55]

Although this was hindsight, there can be no doubt of the fact that Lauder had almost immediately regretted his acceptance of Johnson's forced confession. Such an interpretation is clear from the last-minute Postscript, mentioned in this account, which Lauder added to his *Letter to Douglas*. Indeed, this Postscript is crucial for any understanding of his eventual break with Johnson.[56] Presumably Johnson had not seen this late addition, or may not even have heard about it, until it was published in January. When he read it he must have been tremendously shocked. Yes, Lauder admitted, he had interpolated a few lines into various authors he was quoting. But why was everybody so shocked? It had all been part of an elaborate joke. In this Postscript, Lauder insisted, he would at last "pull off the mask" and tell his true motives. What he had really meant to do was to find out how clever the admirers of Milton were. He had merely used a stratagem designed to discover how deeply the partisanship in favor of Milton was rooted in the minds of his admirers. If he really had meant to impose on the general public, he could easily have worked out another way of doing so, one which Douglas and the others would never have been able to expose. He could have ascribed lines to some imaginary author, whose works could never have been found. Instead he had merely been playing a game with his critics.

One can easily imagine Johnson's reactions to such an explanation. After all he had done to see that the crazy Scot had formally confessed his crimes, now to find him trying to wriggle out with such an unbelievable story. This was the last straw. The man must be completely out of his head.

And so after the first week in January 1751 Johnson probably washed his hands completely of Lauder and never talked to him again.

At the same time it is possible also to understand Lauder's motives. During December his reputation had obviously suffered irreparable damage, and he was being ostracized by many of his former friends. When Johnson and the others had told him that a complete admission would be best for his future career, they may have meant well, but he now believed they were wrong. When he had done what they asked he had made a major mistake, for he should have qualified his confession, or at least made it only partial. As a result, he decided to shift his ground, back to an earlier position. He would stay away from Johnson and try other ways to re-establish his reputation.

Consequently during the early months of 1751 Lauder strove valiantly to change his whole approach. There must be a better way to procure some forgiveness in powerful circles. In March he published *An Apology for Mr. Lauder, in a Letter Most Humbly Addressed to His Grace the Archbishop of Canterbury,* which tried to explain just what he had done, and why, and ended with a denial of any attempt to "depreciate the just reputation of Milton." The whole affair which had brought him "almost to the brink of ruin" could now be saved only if he was restored to favor by the Archbishop.[57] Also he wrote long letters to other prominent figures, pleading with them for forgiveness. In none of these did he ever mention Johnson by name or clearly refer to his involvement.

Lauder kept stressing that his desire had been to punish Milton for what he believed to have been a villainous crime against Charles I—the poet's stealing a prayer out of Sir Philip Sidney's *Arcadia* and forcing the printer of *Eikon Basilike* to assign it to his late Majesty. It was the Milton–Charles I confrontation that he now emphasized, and he shrugged off the whole matter of *Paradise Lost* and Milton's plagiarism. Writing to Birch, who would not see him, he summed up the matter this way:

> Thus have I told you sincerely the true motive that induced me to interpolate a few lines into some authors quoted by me in my late Essay on Milton, which has made as great a noise almost as if I had denied the divinity of our Saviour, ridiculed his miracles, or declared open war against heaven and earth; And yet not above twenty or thirty lines at most of Milton were affected by them, which I hope I have in my power amply to replace.[58]

Hardly anyone, it might be added, accepted such an explanation. Failing to convince anyone of his honesty, Lauder left England around

1756 and settled in Barbados, where he died in extreme poverty in 1771.[59] For him the whole affair had become the last bitter climax of a fruitless life inevitably leading to disaster.

For Johnson, on the other hand, the episode probably seemed a waste of time and energy. How could his kind heart have led him into such an unbelievable mess? And how could he have been so fooled? Why had he not understood from the start what Lauder was doing? Of course, there were a few other haunting questions. Why had he been so stern in insisting that the mad Jacobite make an overall confession? Why had he not kept in mind the difference between Lauder's obvious fabrications and his basic scholarly goals? In 1780 when Johnson was shown a recent book attacking him for his aid to a forger, all he could do was write in the margin: "In the business of Lauder I was deceived, partly by thinking the man too frantic to be fraudulent."[60]

CHAPTER V

The Rambler

WITH THE COMING OF the new year, 1750, there was little improvement in Johnson's situation. Tetty was ill much of the time, progress on the *Dictionary* slower than expected, and there were many other difficult problems. We do not know where at age forty he spent New Year's Eve to celebrate the end of 1749, but after three the next morning he was home writing down a characteristic prayer.

> Almighty GOD, by whose will I was created, and by whose Providence I have been sustained, by whose mercy I have been called to the knowledge of my Redeemer, and by whose Grace whatever I have thought or acted acceptable to thee has been inspired and directed, grant, O LORD, that in reviewing my past life, I may recollect thy mercies to my preservation in whatever state thou preparest for me, that in affliction I may remember how often I have been succoured, and in prosperity may know and confess from whose hand the blessing is received. Let me O LORD so remember my sins, that I may abolish them by true repentance, and so improve the year to which thou hast graciously extended my life and all the years which thou shalt yet allow me, that I may hourly become purer in thy sight so that I may live in thy fear, and die in thy favour, and find mercy at the last day for the sake of JESUS CHRIST. Amen.[1]

Unfortunately for a biographer, the winter months of 1750 which followed are a blank period. There are no surviving letters, no journal entries, or publications. Yet we do know that he lived through unusual events which appear to have had no effect upon him whatsoever. Shortly after noon on February 8 London experienced one of its worst earthquakes in modern times. For days the weather had been rainy, but on the morning of the eighth the rain and fog disappeared and everything was calm. Then suddenly about 12:15 the central parts of the capital were shocked by earth tremors, beginning near London Bridge and Southwark, then under the river through Cheapside and other parts of London. According to various reports, in places there were gaping holes, some chimneys fell, and stones came crashing down from new buildings. A few ships were overturned in the Thames. Inside houses, dishes fell off shelves and furniture rattled about.[2]

Apparently there were three distinct quakes, and some thought they heard a loud explosion up in the air. By one o'clock the streets were full of people, gaping at each other and wondering what had happened. Of course, many thought this was the voice of God, predicting doom for all mankind. And when, almost exactly a month later, early in the morning of March 8, there was a second tremor, similarly beginning in the east and moving west, there was further terror. The violence was even greater than before, with a great rustling noise of wind. More houses were damaged, bells rang without any human involvement, and there were more cracks in the ground. Some people reported that they saw a great ball of fire in the sky just before the quake. In the cellar of one house in Dean Street, Soho, a spring of water gushed forth and then disappeared the next day. According to the *London Magazine*: "The shock was so great in some parts, that the people ran from their houses and beds almost naked."[3] Again the shock seemed to come in three bursts.

What happened at 17 Gough Square? Up in the attic were desks overturned and books tossed all over the room? Downstairs were dishes smashed and windows cracked? Johnson seems never to have referred to these events at all. To look ahead—almost a month later, when Easter was approaching, there were various predictions of a third, and more disastrous quake. On Tuesday, April 3, Miss Talbot, writing to Miss Carter, referred to "the gloom that hangs over this town," when "young and old, happy and wretched, are all hurrying out of town, on the dreadful, though I trust idle expectation of some fate impending over it tomorrow and Thursday." Panic raged in the streets for three days and nights, as many waited for the judgment of God and possibly the end of mankind. But nothing happened. Nor have there been any tremors since then of comparable magnitude. Thus the so-called "earthquakes of 1750" have become a forgotten legend, remembered by a few historians. At the time, periodicals and newspapers recorded the events, but not Samuel Johnson. Apparently he soberly refused to be upset by mere aberrations of the physical world and was not to be mistakenly lured into blaming God for such temporary disturbances. Instead he went on with his work and his preparations for starting a new periodical.

As it became increasingly obvious that the original estimates of the time needed to complete a dictionary of the English language had been unrealistic, and since most of the money coming from the printers had to be used to pay the amanuenses, Johnson saw the need for some other source of regular income. Consequently he decided, after talks with the publisher Payne and others at gatherings of the Ivy Lane Club, to start a new biweekly series in the tradition of Addison's *Spectator*. But what should it be called? One suspects there may have been numerous suggestions, none of which seemed attractive. Even in our day many readers must keep wondering why Johnson finally chose *The Rambler*, a title which hardly describes the serious moral content of many of the essays. Arthur Murphy thought that it had been "probably suggested by the *Wanderer*," a poem which Johnson mentions with high praise in his life of Savage.[4] And Johnson did once admit that he thought of himself as a "straggler."

Johnson later told Sir Joshua Reynolds:

> When I was to begin publishing that paper, I was at a loss how to name it. I sat down at night upon my bedside, and resolved that I would not go to sleep till I had fixed its title. The Rambler seemed the best that occurred, and I took it.[5]

Certainly the choice was a memorable one for his career, even though foreigners might misinterpret the term. One visiting prince from the Continent, when dining in company with Johnson, and wishing to give some proof that he had read his work, proposed a toast to "Mr. Vagabond."[6] British readers soon sensed that the term meant only shifting subject matter and not lack of serious commitment. Indeed, the title became firmly attached to Johnson, and many people later referred to him as "The Rambler," or as "Rambling Sam."[7]

Following its notable predecessor, the new periodical was planned to appear twice a week, each Tuesday and Saturday, to be six pages in length (three leaves), and sell for 2d. But unlike the *Spectator* it was to contain no advertisements. The length of each essay ranged from 1,200 to 1,700 words, and gradually as the periodical continued, tended toward the lower number. The differences in length were accommodated by shifting blank spaces on the first and sixth pages. Nevertheless, from the start Johnson knew that he had to produce something within this range, and must gradually have developed a sense of just what could be included in such a space.

When did Johnson write the essays? Most of them probably at the last moment, on Monday and Friday nights. Cave once told Birch that copy for each *Rambler* "was seldom sent to the press till late in the night before the day of publication."[8] And when Mrs. Jane Aston Gastrell visited the Thomas Herveys in London during the time that Johnson was writing the *Rambler*, "the printer's boy would often come after him to their house, and wait while he wrote off a paper for the press in a room full of company."[9] How could he do it? One explanation comes in a later letter from Miss Hill Boothby, who pointed out to Johnson: "You can write amidst the tattle of women, because your attention is so strong to sense, that you are deaf to sound."[10]

Still, though he was dilatory, this did not mean that he casually dashed off whatever happened to be in his mind at the time. As Boswell shows, he kept a commonplace book full of notes and suggestions for possible essays.[11] And through the years he had developed a remarkable ability to plan pieces in his mind without wasting time in jotting down fragments. One might point out that in the autumn of 1748 he composed in one morning the first seventy lines of his greatest poem, *The Vanity of Human Wishes*, before putting any of it on paper.[12] It is likely that he had each essay well worked out in his mind and only needed an hour or so to jot it down, or dictate a version to send to the printer. Hawkins, who saw some of the original versions, insisted that Johnson "never blotted out a line."[13] Nor was there ever time for him to see proofs. The printers had to decipher what was given them as best they could, and although they made some errors, they were skillful and proficient.

Shortly before beginning the *Rambler,* Johnson soberly composed the following prayer:

> Almighty God, the giver of all good things, without whose help all labour is ineffectual, and without whose grace all wisdom is folly, grant, I beseech Thee, that in this my undertaking thy Holy Spirit may not be witheld from me, but that I may promote thy glory, and the salvation both of myself and others, —Grant this O Lord for the sake of Jesus Christ. Amen. Lord Bless me. So be it.[14]

From the start he obviously intended the series to have serious moral overtones. That much is certain. As it happened, his problem was not keeping this serious tone, but just the reverse. His difficulty was in providing enough light entertainment to satisfy ordinary readers.

Responsibility for the *Rambler* was solely Johnson's. For two years he produced all the essays except four—two by Elizabeth Carter, one by

Catherine Talbot and one by Samuel Richardson, the printer and novelist, the last understandably outselling all the others. Hester Mulso, later Mrs. Chapone, supplied four billets used in one of the numbers, and David Garrick and an old Lichfield friend, Joseph Simpson, parts of two others. But these were isolated contributions. For all intents and purposes, Johnson was the Rambler.

His original plan was to keep his authorship secret. When two gentlemen from the court of the Prince of Wales came to Edward Cave, to bring a list of seven new subscribers and also to inquire about the author's name, the publisher refused to give him away.[15] When Bubb Dodington, one of the Prince's political hangers-on, sent a letter "to the Rambler" inviting him to his house where he could "enlarge his acquaintance," Johnson declined, preferring to keep his anonymity as long as possible. But David Garrick and other friends who knew so well Johnson's characteristics soon made their suspicions widely known, and the scheme of secrecy collapsed. Nevertheless many readers were puzzled for some time. As late as August 9, Samuel Richardson was not certain who it was, and when writing to Cave was forced to guess. "There is but one man, I think, that could write them."[16] To this Cave replied, "Mr. Johnson is the *Great Rambler,* being, as you observe, the only man who can furnish two such papers in a week, besides his other great business."[17]

Johnson rarely, if ever, used unsolicited contributions from people he did not know well. Although there were constant reminders in the newspapers that communications to the editor might be left at St. John's Gate, or at the printer's in Paternoster Row, Johnson adamantly refused to fill his pages with ephemera of that sort, and later told Samuel Richardson that he had from the start made it a rule to write his own papers.[18] He had no intention of becoming a Georgian columnist, giving advice to troubled correspondents. Naturally such a decision irritated those who took the trouble to send in letters. When Richardson's prolific correspondent, Lady Bradshaigh, sent in a contribution, Johnson casually ignored it. One can scarcely blame her for complaining. Richardson agreed and insisted that Johnson "should not have advertised where letters for him should be taken in if he designed to be so little obliged to correspondents."[19]

Evidence seems to be conclusive that the immediate sale of the *Rambler* in London was not extensive, with fewer than five hundred copies of each number being sold.[20] It was no best seller. But Roy Wiles, in a study of early provincial newspapers, has shown that many *Rambler* essays, within a few weeks of the first printing, were being read by thousands of people who did not live in London.[21] The country papers pirated whatever they wanted, and evidently the *Ramblers* caught their eye. Well over half of them, at one time or another, were reprinted in the various country papers such as the *Bath Journal, Bristol Weekly Intelligencer, Western Flying Post, Salisbury Journal, Newcastle General Mercury, Nottingham Weekly Courant, Leed's Mercury,* to name only a few. Thus large numbers of readers outside London were able to keep up with the *Rambler.* Also many of the essays were reprinted in monthly magazines. Apparently the notion that Johnson's audience in 1750 was severely limited must be modified, for he was actually more popular at the time than he himself suspected.

Certainly the small sale in London was not due to any lack of effort on the part of the publisher, John Payne, or Cave, who was Johnson's sponsor. They pushed the new venture in every possible way. Indeed, the newspaper advertising must have been quite expensive.

After a few sporadic announcements in the daily papers, the first *Rambler* appeared on Tuesday, March 20, 1750. All the larger papers carried notices "this day is published," with the large advertisement including two Latin quotations: first, the three lines from Juvenal used as a motto for the first number, and second, two lines from Horace later used on the title page of the collected editions. Then on succeeding Tuesdays and Saturdays the publisher experimented with differing notices in a variety of papers, each time using a different Latin quotation, always the particular motto chosen by Johnson for the latest essay. These range in length from a single line of Horace to six lines from Boethius in No. 7. For the early numbers these notices chiefly appeared in such papers as the *London Evening Post* and the *Whitehall Evening Post.* Then the publisher decided to shift papers, perhaps hoping to reach another audience. This time he used the *General Advertiser.* On April 28, for example, there was a full advertisement for No. 12, containing six lines from Lucan's "Carmen ad Pisonem." From then on, through May, June, and early July, the advertisements continued to appear, again including the special Latin motto used on that particular *Rambler.* These range from one line of Persius to seven lines of Horace. Finally, for No. 32 no quotation was used, perhaps because Johnson had for this number selected as his motto three lines of Greek from Pythagoras. It may well be that the printers balked at the use of Greek in a casual newspaper advertisement, or lacked proper type. Whatever the reason, this marked the end of an amazing, if not unique, attempt to sell a periodical appearing twice a week through the use of Latin quotations.

It is well to remember that in the eighteenth century it was standard practice to allow newspaper advertisements to stand without change for long periods of time. Thus a "this day is published" notice might keep appearing for months after the actual publication date. Yet for the *Ram-*

bler the publisher insisted upon resetting part of each notice—not merely a word or a number, but quotations sometimes extending to seven lines. Why? It is difficult to say, but he may have hoped in this way to attract a wide cultured audience. If so, the attempt was unsuccessful. Not many readers in London apparently were ready to buy a copy of a twopenny paper just to see how the author exemplified some favorite passage in ancient literature.

Perhaps this unusual sales effort casts some doubt on the accuracy of what has been said about Johnson's method of composition. If it was his practice to dash off the essays in haste and send them to the printers without even rereading what he had produced, at least the motto must have been decided upon earlier, in time to be inserted in the next morning's newspaper advertisement.[22] If the motto had been chosen well in advance, then the general theme must also have been known to the printers. The early reports of haste may have been exaggerated. At times he may have sent in copy promptly, in time to make a few stop-press corrections.

Yet it happens that the Latin mottoes in the papers do not always exactly correspond to those printed at the top of the individual essays. In one instance there were four lines of Juvenal in the paper instead of two and a half actually used in the essay, which might suggest that Johnson had merely sent word of what he intended, and later decided to use only part of it. He might even have given the printers a tentative schedule of papers and mottoes, which he meant to follow.

At the start Johnson was not exactly sure what he meant to do. Indeed, describing in the first number the difficulty connected with any initial performance, he seems overly modest and almost apologetic. "I hope not much to tire those whom I shall not happen to please; and if I am not commended for the beauty of my works, to be at least pardoned for their brevity."[23] And he also commented: "If a man could glide imperceptibly into the favour of the public, and only proclaim his pretensions to literary honours when he is sure of not being rejected, he might commence author with better hopes, as his failings might escape contempt, though he shall never attain much regard." And even in the second number, on the necessity and danger of looking into the future, he stresses the uncertainties an author faces in trying to please all kinds of readers. As is shown in all his works, Johnson is never a compressed, firm starter.

But by the third number he could make a straightforward statement: "The task of an author is either to teach what is not known, or to recommend known truths, by his manner of adorning them." From then on he rarely lets his reader forget that the chief purpose of his project is moral instruction. The range of his topics was perhaps wider than some modern critics suggest, but his purpose was constant. His principal design, so he described it at the very end, was "to inculcate wisdom or piety."

The immediate reception was what might have been expected. Johnson's wife, Tetty, after a few numbers had appeared, said to her husband: "I thought very well of you before; but I did not imagine you could have written any thing equal to this."[24] And his friend Samuel Richardson insisted to Cave that though he did not read the *Ramblers* regularly as they came out, despite paying for them, he always "spoke of them with honour." He added: "I have the vanity to think that I have procured them admirers; that is to say, *readers*."[25]

James Elphinston, whose sister was married to the printer Strahan, was in Edinburgh when the first *Rambler* came out. It was sent to him without a name attached, but he immediately guessed who was the author.

> He consequently conceived the benevolent design of diffusing the work among his countrymen, as promising much instruction to them, and some profit to the author. It was immediately reprinted in Scotland in a minute and elegant manner. Mr. Elphinston not only superintended the press, and took every possible care of the edition, but likewise enriched it by a new and apposite translation of the mottoes.[26]

When the *Ramblers* were later collected in book form, Johnson followed the example of his Scottish friend and also included English translations of the classical mottoes.

Other people whom Johnson knew, such as Christopher Smart, reportedly praised the essays highly,[27] and James Ralph in the *Remembrancer* for April 21 began his "Rambling Letter" (reprinted in the April *Gentleman's Magazine*): "If a new writer, blessed with a vigorous imagination, under the restraint of a classical judgment, and master of all the charms and graces of expression, had not made his appearance to the public under the style and title of *The Rambler,* I would myself have assumed that character, as the most suitable to my own."

The newspapers and monthly periodicals not only reprinted some of the papers but also included a number of complimentary verses. Whoever wrote "To the Rambler" in the July *Gentleman's Magazine* started out with praise of Addison for his triumph over Vice and Folly, which, alas, had been followed by a return of gloom and chaos. But now,

> Happy for us! another Champion shines,
> Equal in genius and in great designs,
> To combat Vice, howe'er she changes place,
> To flash his light'ning in each guilty face,

To paint fair Virtue's awful-striking mien,
Who, to be lov'd, needs only to be seen,
. . . .
Proceed, Great *Rambler,* and with manly fire
War against crimes, and still make Guilt retire,
Till the detested Fiends shall shun the light,
Sunk in the shades of their primeval night.[28]

And in the *Daily Advertiser* for August 24 in "To the Author of the Rambler. On Reading his Allegories," the writer begins:

For thee, by whom their hostile hands were join'd,
Learning and *Wit* have all their pow'rs combin'd:
Wit wins for thee the *Graces* from the skies,
The *Virtues, Learning* for thy aid supplies.
Each *filial science* follows in the train,
And *Truth's fear'd daughter* visits earth again:
. . . .
         O! born without a patron to be great,
And not design'd to *copy* but *create,*
Still call new worlds, new beings into birth,
And bid *Saturnian* times return on earth.[29]

The October *Gentleman's Magazine,* while confessing that the *Ramblers* were "sent into the world from St. John's Gate" and thus there might be thought to be some selfish interest in praising them, passes on a quotation from "an ingenious and disinterested writer," the author of *The Student: Or Oxford and Cambridge Miscellany* (perhaps by Christopher Smart), which had appeared in a recent issue:

We beg leave to return our acknowledgments, for the noble and rational entertainments he has given us, to the admirable author of the *Rambler,* a work that exceeds any thing of the kind ever published in this kingdom, some of the *Spectators* excepted—if indeed they may be excepted. We own ourselves unequal to the task of commending such a work up to its merits —where the diction is the most high-wrought imaginable, and yet, like the brilliancy of a diamond, exceeding perspicuous in its richness—where the sentiments ennoble the style, and the style familiarizes the sentiments—where every thing is easy and natural, yet every thing is masterly and strong.[30]

With such encomiums, no author could complain!
Certainly, in cultivated circles the early essays were well received,

though sometimes with reservations. Thus Birch wrote to Charles Lyttelton on May 22:

> We have a periodical paper published here on Tuesdays and Saturdays in a sheet and a half, under the title of the Rambler. Nineteen numbers are already printed. The serious ones are in general excellent; but the author, who is Mr. Sam Johnson who gave us two winters ago the tragedy of "Irene" has not sufficient knowledge of the world to furnish out a paper of entertainment.[31]

In August, Cave wrote to Richardson:

> I have had letters of approbation from Dr. Young, Dr. Hartley, Dr. Sharpe, Miss C[arter], &c, &c, most of them, like you, setting them in a rank equal, and some superior, to the Spectators. . . . but notwithstanding such recommendation, whether the price of *two pence,* or the unfavourable season of their first publication, hinders the demand, no boast can be made of it.[32]

William Duncombe, when writing to Elizabeth Carter, added: "The Rambler gains ground every day, *viresque acquirit eundo.* It is a very rational performance, but I doubt wants more sprinklings of humour to make it popular."

On the other hand, many upper-class readers were not so pleased by the new essay series. Witness the comments made by the Marchioness Grey, when writing to Catherine Talbot on June 21:

> I see nothing new or clever in his essays, and the stories and characters he attempts are seldom well hit off or resembling common life; besides that every paper is full of so many hard words as really break my teeth to speak them. I can't say I shall have a much higher opinion of it even though it should be grown fashionable; but I can't readily imagine neither what should make it so, except its being now and then a little unintelligible.[33]

An example of the continued admiration for the Rambler's powers combined with fear as to his ultimate success may be found in the correspondence of Elizabeth Carter and Catherine Talbot. On May 28, at a time when both ladies were considering becoming involved in the project, Miss Talbot commented on her correspondent's "Vision," which she thought would "make an excellent *Rambler,*" although there might be a more serious moral.[34] It was finally used as No. 44. Miss Talbot's own allegory on the observance of Sunday appeared on June 30 as No. 30. She further commented:

> You see the author of the Rambler need not be put upon writing papers of amusement, as he takes to it of himself; but he ought to be cautioned to admit the letters of his correspondents with much care and choice, and if one might say so, not to use over many hard words. This must be said with great care. In yesterday's paper [No. 20] (a very pretty one indeed) we had *equiponderant*, and another so hard I cannot remember it [*adscititious*], both in one sentence. Your Vision and your verses will do more good than advice. However, when he writes papers of humour, there are many odd clubs, advertisements, societies, meetings, and devices of various kinds, which this age produces; and London swarms with what would afford as amusing subjects as any in the Spectator. The Marrying Register, the Threepenny Club in Essex-street, a most universal nursery of low, infidel orators; the Threepenny Masquerades, numberless follies and enormities. But these places should not be writ about without most particular enquiries, easily made in London.

Johnson was probably bombarded with suggestions of this sort, though he had little desire to do the kind of research Miss Talbot thought might be necessary. He found it easier to pull things out of his own mind. Still, his friends kept on making suggestions. As Miss Talbot continued,

> I am much pleased with Mr. Cave's account of the approbation this excellent paper has met with amongst some of the fine world [in the May *Gentleman's Magazine*]. Any hint that is known to come from you will have great weight with the Rambler, if I guess him right, particularly given in that delicate manner you so well understand.

Obviously the ladies were not certain just how their advice would be received. Knowing Johnson as well as they did, they understood his independent spirit and determination.

During the autumn the ladies kept up their comments, which so well represent the kind of split which developed in all of Johnson's ardent supporters—immense admiration for most of the essays, combined with a realization of certain of his weaknesses, which rendered *The Rambler* unappealing to many readers. This qualified praise became characteristic of almost all contemporary criticism. The new periodical was much more intelligent and discerning than most others being published at the time, but why did the author have to include so many difficult words and allow his style at times to become so verbose and turgid? And why couldn't he somehow include more variety? On September 28 Miss Talbot wrote:

> Pray how do you like the life of Lady Bustle's family? [No. 51] I think that is a paper of much humour, and there might be many more of the same sort in different ways. But what Mr. Johnson most excels in is the serious papers, that seem to flow from his heart, and from a heart amiable and delicate to a great degree.

Nevertheless, she could not refrain from adding, "The second of Euphelia [No. 46] is far-fetched and unnatural."

And on October 20, she continued:

> The Rambler is to me very entertaining. The letter from Mr. Frolick [No. 61] has a strain of humour, and the last from Rhodoclia [No. 62] will, if he makes use of it, give him an excellent opportunity to introduce humorous descriptions of, and reflections on, the London follies and diversions. . . . Mr. Johnson would, I fear, be mortified to hear that people know a paper of his own by the sure mark of somewhat a little excessive, a little exaggerated in the expression. In his Screech Owl [No. 59] were *so many* merchants discouraged, *so many* ladies killed, matches broke, poets dismayed! The numbers are too large. Two or three—five or six, is enough in all conscience in most cases.

The character of Suspirius, called the "screech-owl," which Goldsmith years later turned into his Croaker in *The Good-Natured Man,* became one of the best-known creations.

Nearly two months later, on December 17, Miss Talbot wrote again:

> I wish most violently you was in town, for I have set my whole heart upon the success of the Rambler (what a noble paper his last upon death [No. 78]) and you could talk more persuasively to the author than any body. Mr. Cave complains of him for not admitting correspondents; this does mischief. In the main I think he is to be applauded for it. But why then does he not write now and then on the living manners of the times?—the stage—the follies and fashions. I had a long battle about him t'other night.

Unfortunately, the "people of the world" were too perverse to accept Johnson's style of writing.

If he could get Lord Chesterfield to write one small paper for him—But I say all this with fear and trembling, for after all he is the best judge of his own schemes. Humour and the manners of the world are not his forte. . . . I do really now wish you would write a cheerful paper to the Rambler. Whether on Christmas merriment as laudable; and the town madness, and that of the age of continual joyless dissipation as illaudable—or on the hoops of these days, compared with those of the Tatlers, &c. and so on all sorts of caps, bonnets, aigrettes, col-oured capuchins, &c. &c. &c. on drums—on the improvement, and misuse of the stage and the French *comedies larmoyantes.* —or on anything or nothing.

To which Miss Carter replied on December 28:

I extremely honour your defence of the Rambler, and heartily wish it was in my power to give him any assistance, but you have much too high an opinion of my capacity, as you will be con-vinced by the nonsensical thing I enclose, merely to show you that I had rather make an imperfect attempt than seem to de-cline making any at all.

When Miss Talbot replied a few weeks later she called the piece sent her by Miss Carter "very pretty" but added that it had gone into her "con-sidering drawer, from whence nothing ever comes out again under half a year." It did finally come out of the drawer and eventually became No. 100 on "modish pleasures." The whole exchange shows how emotionally involved with the venture the two women were, and how anxious to do what they could to further its success.

Johnson's use of difficult words was one of the perpetual criticisms leveled at him by critics in his own day. But what could be expected from a lexicographer who spent much of his time defining the English lan-guage? Still, such words as "obtunded," "intumescence," "frigorifick" could scarcely appeal even to the most scholarly reader.

There is no denying that some of Johnson's sentences are wordy and ponderous. He was criticized for his "perpetual triplets" and for too much "antithesis and alliteration." He repeated himself too often. On the other hand, everyone recognized the "great strength and dignity" of his style, and in places it moves along with real velocity. Moreover, one should always remember that the first versions, which were the ones perused by readers in 1750, were hasty compositions, usually tossed off without careful revision. When the essays were later reprinted, Johnson, in addition to correcting misreadings of his handwriting which the printers had made, carefully changed the style in many places. He knew that some pieces were verbose. When working on revisions he did a good deal of shortening. As a sample, in No. 5, a meditation on Spring, at the ending of the fourth paragraph there is the passage: "If his affairs were disordered, he could regulate them in the spring; if a regimen was prescribed him, the spring was the proper time of pursuing it; if what he wanted was at a high price, it would fall its value in the spring." But in the version most modern readers see the passage reads: "If his health were impaired, the spring would restore it; if what he wanted was at a high price, it would fall its value in the spring." And in paragraph fourteen the ending of the last sentence was changed from "as to be able to accommodate itself to emergent occasions, and remark every thing that offers itself to present examination" to read "as easily to accommodate itself to occasional entertainment." Furthermore, in a still later revision he cut out many unnecessary words and phrases. Actually it is remarkable that the style throughout was as good as it was, when pieces were dashed off at such speed. What Mrs. Thrale later called his "facility of writing"[35] is nowhere more evident than in the *Rambler* papers.

The *Rambler* is often thought of as predominantly a sober, sonorous, moral work, with only flashes of humor.[36] There are a fair number of light, amusing essays, and Johnson's style sometimes is the source of the humor. He was quite willing to laugh at himself. There are scores of amusing commentaries on the use of philosophic words, disappointments of marriage, faulty education, disappointed fortune hunters, and other topics. If Johnson cannot ever quite catch the light touch of Addison and Steele, he does at times come close.

In form the *Rambler* essays tend to follow Addison's *Spectator*, though within that tradition there is more variety than one might suppose. Over sixty of the whole *Rambler* series are ostensibly letters to the editor, though really Johnson's own creation.[37] There are eight Eastern tales and eight other short allegories. There are a number of satirical portraits modeled on real people, such as Prospero (No. 200), which infuriated Garrick, or Gelidus (No. 24), who may have represented John Colson, whom Johnson had known when he first came to London. The man who purred like a cat and the one who barked like a dog in No. 188 were based on actual individuals. As Walter Jackson Bate points out, while we often think of the *Rambler* as being chiefly serious moral essays, fewer than half can strictly be labeled as such. It must be confessed that the ones many modern readers cherish are either general discussions such as those on the vanity of stoicism (No. 32), old age (Nos. 50 and 69), life in a garret (No. 117), the uncertainty of fame (No. 146), the impotence of wealth (No. 165), the fallacious hopes of youth (No. 196); or those which bear on modern problems like the unhappiness of women (No. 39) or the misery of prostitutes (No. 107). Two of the most moving tell of the tragic life of Misella, a prostitute (Nos. 170–171), possibly relating a real story picked up on one of Johnson's nocturnal rambles. Well over thirty of the essays could be regarded as literary criticism, including those on fiction (No. 4), biography (No. 60)—the first really important discussion of this genre to be published —and a number on Milton's works.

Although there is not enough space here for a thorough critical discussion of this major work of Johnson's middle years, a few points made by modern scholars should be mentioned. According to Edward Bloom, Johnson was one of the most skillful users of symbolic names, which are much more complex than many readers assume.[38] These name-devices are very adeptly integrated into the themes of the essays. To be sure, one must have a thorough grounding in Latin, Greek, and Oriental literature to understand what he is doing. The names were clearly meant to enrich the various levels of meaning. There are Dicaculus, a professional wit (No. 174); Gelasimus, a misguided scholar (No. 179); Papilius, the idler (No. 141); Quisquilius, the strange collector (Nos. 82, 177); and Misocapelus, the young trader (Nos. 116, 123). To appreciate the full significance of the basic satire, one must know Cicero, Quintilian, Plautus, and many other Roman authors. The use of these fictional names is a very important part of Johnson's satire of the petty social foibles of his day.

In our day emphasis is being placed more on Johnson's psychological skills. As Bate puts it,

> In Johnson, the pressing sense of the caged and bewildered struggle of the human heart for freedom prevents him from turning to any quick answer or cheap panacea. His practical humanism grows step by step from a clear-eyed exploration of the nature of this cage and this bewilderment.[39]

Johnson understands well the results of repressed sex drives, the frustrations of trying to channel desires into other areas, and the difficulty of satisfying man's "hunger for imagination." Indeed, Bate insists that "Johnson's own sense of the working of the human imagination probably provides us with the closest anticipation of Freud to be found in psychology or moral writings before the twentieth century." It is Johnson's astute understanding of the sources of man's foibles and weaknesses that stands out for twentieth-century readers of the *Rambler*.

D URING THE FIRST YEAR of his new periodical Johnson was also involved in a number of other matters unconnected with the *Rambler* or with his work on the *Dictionary*. Someone may have pointed out to him in Thomas Newton's recent edition of *Paradise Lost* a notice of the sad plight of Milton's only surviving granddaughter, who had been reduced, with her husband, to keeping "a little chandler's or grocer's shop" in Cock Lane.[40] His sympathy was at once aroused and he proposed various means of helping the impecunious Elizabeth Foster. At last Johnson persuaded Garrick to give a benefit performance of *Comus* at Drury Lane, and to speak a special prologue to be written by Johnson. It should be recalled that the year before he had helped the one-legged Scot, William Lauder, in his attempt to unravel Milton's use of modern Latin poets. Although Johnson was never a genuine Milton enthusiast, poverty always aroused his compassion, no matter who was involved.

In order to stir up interest in the benefit, Johnson wrote a letter which appeared in the *General Advertiser* on April 4, the day before the performance, in which he insisted that "to assist industrious indigence, struggling with distress and debilitated by age, is a display of virtue and an acquisition of happiness and honour."[41] How could anyone refuse "to lay out a trifle" for the benefit of the only surviving member of the family of "our incomparable Milton"? Perhaps it was because Johnson remembered the criticism that had been leveled at him for his help with Lauder's *Essay* that he thought it best to add: "There will be a new prologue on the occasion, written by the author of *Irene,* and spoken by Mr. Garrick." Happily, the benefit was a great success, and Elizabeth Foster received over £130.[42]

Not that his help for Milton's destitute granddaughter had changed Johnson's critical opinion of *Comus,* or of others of Milton's lesser works. In his prologue he says nothing about the merits of this particular work. Though he calls Milton "our mighty bard" and refers to the "universal praise" accorded his works, this is not the purpose of his plea. It is the lady's plight on which he concentrates.

> Unknown, unheeded, long his offspring lay,
> And want hung threat'ning o'er her slow decay.
> What tho she shine with no *Miltonian* fire,
> No fav'ring muse her morning dreams inspire;
> Yet softer claims the melting heart engage,
> Her youth laborious, and her blameless age:
> Hers the mild merits of domestic life,
> The patient suff'rer, and the faithful wife.
> Thus grac'd with humble virtue's native charms
> Her grandsire leaves her in Britannia's arms.[43]

And in various essays to come in the *Rambler* he anticipates the estimate of Milton's poems he would make many years later in the *Lives of the*

Poets. He was quite willing to call Milton "incomparable" but not to praise unduly works which he did not think first-rate.

During the summer and early autumn Johnson was involved in helping his friend Thomas Birch find a manuscript for which he was searching, and spent some time advising Charlotte Lennox about some of her enterprises.[44] Copy for the *Dictionary* kept slowly going to the printer, and by October Birch could write to Yorke:

> Johnson has printed off the three first letters of his English Dictionary, and designs to continue his *Rambler* till he has finished one year's course. He will then probably stop, for his bookseller complains of the want of encouragement, as himself does of the want of assistance.[45]

Everyone was curious as to how long he would continue. As the end of the first year of the *Rambler* approached, there were various rumors that Johnson meant in March 1751 to cease meeting last-minute deadlines every Monday and Friday nights. But somehow the publishers decided to carry on, despite continuing poor sales, and Johnson badly needed the four guineas a week. After all, for the first year he would have received over £200.[46]

On New Year's Day, 1751, he composed one of the shortest and simplest of his prayers.

> O Eternal God, who regardest all thy works with mercy, look upon my wants, my miseries, and my sins, grant that I may amend my life, and may find mercy both in this world and in the world to come by the help of thy Holy Spirit, for the sake of Jesus Christ. Amen.

Unfortunately, his miseries were not about to end.

CHAPTER VI

The Last of Tetty

DURING 1751 AND EARLY 1752 Johnson's life continued much the same, with work in the attic on the *Dictionary*, regular deadlines for *Ramblers* on Monday and Friday nights, convivial gatherings of the Ivy Lane Club on Tuesday evenings, and late rambles about the city when he could not sleep. Presumably Tetty was away some of the time, or confined to her room at Gough Square. So long as Johnson continued to earn his four guineas a week from the *Rambler* he had no desperate financial emergencies, but there were occasional sudden needs, as when he was forced to borrow two pounds from the publisher John Newbery on April 18, 1751: "I have just now a demand upon me for more money than I have by me: if you could conveniently help me with two pounds it will be a favour."[1] This was to pay a man named Thomas Lucy, and in July and August Johnson had to borrow a pound each time, again to pay Lucy. Were these purchases Tetty may have made?

On July 3 he received a note addressed to "Mr. Johnsten" at "Goof Squ., Flet Street," from a tradesman named William Mitchell in Chandos Street, Covent Garden, asking for £2, which, he said, Johnson's wife had owed him since August 12, 1749. Mitchell insisted that he had repeatedly called for and sent after the money until he was ashamed. Though the sum was small, he threatened to bring Johnson into court if the debt was not paid within a week.[2] Perhaps Newbery also took care of this. These small borrowings from Newbery may merely have been advances for Johnson's "Life of Cheynel" which appeared in the May, June, and July numbers of the *Student*, published by Newbery.[3]

It is not certain why Johnson decided to write this account of Francis

Cheynel, the active Presbyterian who represented Parliament in the late 1640s and attempted to reform Oxford University. Of course, it provided an opportunity to show his contempt for the man and his distaste for the Puritan position in the mid-seventeenth century. No one could ever call Johnson's description of Cheynel unbiased or objective. Throughout, Johnson uses phrases such as "turbulent, obstinate, and petulant," "his captious and petulant disposition," and "his natural vehemence," and describes him as indulging himself "in the utmost excesses of raging zeal." Moreover, Johnson's version of Cheynel's attempt to take over crucial university positions as "archivisitor," driving out many older officials and replacing them with radicals of his own breed, clearly shows where Johnson stands.

As an Oxford man himself, Johnson's sympathies, when evaluating the attempts of reformers to change his university, were all with the establishment. As he sums it up:

> A temper of this kind is generally inconvenient and offensive in any society, but in a place of education is least to be tolerated; for, as authority is necessary to instruction, whoever endeavours to destroy subordination, by weakening that reverence which is claimed by those to whom the guardianship of youth is committed by their country, defeats at once the institution; and may be justly driven from a society, by which he thinks himself too wise to be governed, and in which he is too young to teach, and too opinionative to learn.

For Johnson university education had to be a graded society.

In addition to this venture in partisan biographical writing, there were other matters to occupy some of Johnson's time. Always ready to advise and help his many friends, he ventured to propose to Samuel Richardson that he provide a subject index for the next revised edition of *Clarissa*.

> Though Clarissa wants no help from external splendour I was glad to see her improved in her appearance but more glad to find that she was now got above all fears of prolixity, and confident enough of success, to supply whatever had been hitherto suppressed. I never indeed found a hint of any such defalcation, but I fretted: for though the story is long, every letter is short.
>
> I wish you would add an *Index Rerum,* that when the reader recollects any incident he may easily find it, which at present he cannot do, unless he knows in which volume it is told; For Clarissa is not a performance to be read with eager-

ness and laid aside for ever, but will be occasionally consulted
by the busy, the aged, and the studious, and therefore I beg that
this edition by which I suppose posterity is to abide, may want
nothing that can facilitate its use.[4]

And he was involved with Richardson in a number of other matters.

For example, during the spring he was helping his favorite female
writer—at least his favorite of the moment—Charlotte Lennox, perhaps
with her translation of some excerpts from Sully's *Memoirs*, which appeared in March, and after that with her second novel *The Female
Quixote*. Just how much Johnson had to do with planning and writing
this piece of fiction we do not know, but from recent discoveries of Lennox
papers we can be sure that during the autumn of 1751 and early 1752 he
was acting as intermediary and helping her in other ways.[5]

Fanny Burney, in her later diary, recorded that Charlotte Lennox,
"upon her commencing writer," waited upon Johnson, and "at her request,
he carried her to Richardson." Then, according to Fanny, Johnson recalled that "when we came to the house, she desired me to leave her, 'for,'
says she, 'I am under great restraint in your presence, but if you leave me
alone with Richardson I'll give you a very good account of him.' "[6] Alas,
"poor Charlotte" never gave any report to Johnson. Nevertheless, when
her second novel was well along either she or Johnson somehow persuaded
Richardson to look at the manuscript and give his advice. It was then
submitted to him in installments. By November 2 Richardson could write
to Johnson that he had not yet had time to go through the whole manuscript, but that he liked what he had read. After asking if she needed it
back at once, he added:

> I am concerned that I was absent when you and she did me the
> favour of a call in Salisbury Court. I have been much indis-
> posed, and likewise much busied, or I would have craved leave
> to thank you for it in person. May I hope for a visit from you
> and that lady? Or shall I attend you?[7]

Pressure was being exerted on the well-known publisher Andrew
Millar to accept the novel, but there were some "unmerciful critics" who
were attempting to keep him from doing so, or at least that is what Charlotte Lennox thought. On November 21 she sent Richardson more of the
manuscript, and the next day he replied, with a number of suggestions, at
the same time insisting that he had spoken well of the work to Millar and
also to others. When she received this letter, late the same afternoon she
dashed off a reply, expressing her happiness in now having Richardson on
her side and agreeing to make some of the changes he had proposed.

Evidently the joint power of Johnson and Richardson proved irresist-
ible and the reluctant Millar did agree to publish *The Female Quixote*. But
there were still difficulties. As late as the middle of January, 1752, there
remained the question whether the work should be extended from two to
three volumes. Richardson, despite his own tendency to prolixity, wrote
to Mrs. Lennox on January 13 opposing any major reorganization and
suggesting that she consult Johnson before making any changes at the end
of volume two. It would be much better, Richardson thought, to get the
work out largely as it was.

> You are a young lady, have therefore much time before you,
> and I am sure, will think that a good fame will be your interest.
> Make, therefore, your present work as complete as you can, in
> two volumes; and it will give consequence to your future writ-
> ings, and of course to your name as a writer.

Johnson evidently supported Richardson, and the work went to
Millar. Yet still there were delays, this time in the typesetting. On February 3, 1752, Mrs. Lennox begged Johnson "to hurry the printing," if he
could do so without any inconvenience to himself. She said she would
"look upon it as a particular favour," and that with "a mind so generous
and compassionate" as his it was not too much to ask. In the same letter
she begged Johnson to use his interest with the booksellers "to procure me
some employment in the translating way, as this would be a great deal
easier than composition." Translating was something in which she was
already expert. She even asked his pardon for mentioning another favor
she hoped he would extend—help in finding work for her husband. "If
you would be pleased to recommend him to any little employment, your
interest as I am informed with several great people might easily procure
it." She promised that in another letter she would provide Johnson with
more details about her husband's "birth, misfortunes, and disappointed
expectations." She was obviously well aware of the way to arouse Johnson's
sympathy.

After all the troubles and delays, *The Female Quixote: or, The
Adventures of Arabella* finally appeared on Friday, March 13, 1752, printed
for "A. Millar, over-against Catherine Street in the Strand."[8] The dedication to the Earl of Middlesex was written by Johnson. He may also have
written the eleventh chapter of the concluding book, as some have suspected, and other sections.[9] We know that he provided vigorous help all
during the time the work was being written, and reputedly thought very
highly of the novel, despite certain weaknesses. Johnson even broke his
usual rule of not including quotations from the works of living writers in

the *Dictionary* and used one from *The Female Quixote* as an illustration of the proper use of the word "talent." Perhaps it would not be unfair to suspect that Johnson was somewhat prejudiced by the fact that in the novel the author called him "the greatest genius in the present age." Charlotte Lennox was very adept at flattery.

John Boyle, the 5th Earl of Orrery, was also involved in negotiations involving *The Female Quixote*. When writing to Richardson on December 10, Johnson referred to Orrery's favorable opinion of "our Charlotte's Book."[10] Johnson had been in touch with Orrery involving other matters. On November 7, 1751, the Earl had published his controversial *Remarks on the Life and Writings of Jonathan Swift*. Included in a list of those who were sent complimentary copies is "Mr. Johnson." At the same time Orrery asked Johnson's reaction to a guess he had made as to the possibility that Virgil may have alluded to Horace in a line in the *Aeneid*. To this Johnson speedily replied late in November in a long letter which has only recently been properly placed chronologically.[11] His largely negative evaluation was clearly the source of an annotation made in an interleaved copy of the *Remarks* kept by Orrery when preparing the second edition, which appeared about December 10. The fact that Johnson was willing to give up hours of valuable time to writing such a complex and learned reply shows his friendly attitude toward Orrery. The letter also must have greatly impressed Orrery, for over two months later, on February 15, he wrote to Johnson suggesting that they "correspond with that friendship which is above ceremony" and "write to each other not when we ought, but when we please." In other words, informally and not always with such scholarly erudition. Orrery also included a hope that he might be able to lure the author of the *Rambler* to visit him at Marston House in Frome, where he was recovering from an attack of gout. And he alluded to Charlotte Lennox and her work. "How is the fair enchantress, whose appearance I dare say will draw many to her castle? I shall be glad to be thought a knight errant in her train, or to be of any real service to those whom you number among your friends."[12]

At the same time that he was helping the Lennoxes, Johnson was also giving much time to the concerns of another pair who had aroused his deep sympathy. This was an elderly Welshman named Zachariah Williams and his daughter, Anna. As a young man Williams took orders but then became a "surgeon, physician, and projector," with wide scientific interests.[13] While in Wales he had proposed new methods for mining coal, but for a large part of his life his chief aim was to convince others that he had discovered a sure method for those at sea to determine the longitude. Since Parliament had offered a prize of £20,000 to anyone who could solve this difficult problem, here was a way for him to become rich. He had come to London in the 1720s, vainly trying to convince Sir Isaac Newton and other scientists that his solution, through variations of the magnetic needle, was correct. In 1729 he was admitted to the Charterhouse as "a poor brother pensioner," where he remained for some twenty years while he continued to experiment. Throughout he was largely supported and helped by his daughter, Anna, who made a meager living "particularly by her needle." She devoted most of her life to her father, "attending on him, begging for him, and fighting for him."

Unfortunately in the 1740s, with cataracts in both eyes, Anna's eyesight began to fail, though she was able to continue her sewing.

> During the lowness of her fortune, she worked for herself with nearly as much dexterity and readiness as if she had not suffered a loss so irreparable. Her powers of conversation retained their former vigour. Her mind did not sink under these calamities; and the natural activity of her disposition animated her to uncommon exertions.

From late 1745 her father became for most of the time bedridden, and he gradually alienated the officers of the Charterhouse with his demands for special services. When these failed, Anna moved in to nurse her father, though this was an obvious violation of the rules. After long haggling, an order for his expulsion was made in May 1748, and sometime later, according to his own account, at the age of 78 he was dragged from his bed, his room dismantled, and some of his scientific instruments smashed. Left alone and helpless on the floor all night, he was rescued by friends and carried to a temporary home.[14]

Somehow he had heard of Johnson's sympathy for anyone in deep distress and wrote him a letter in which he described the tragic situation which he and his daughter faced. Johnson came at once to see them and soon threw himself into their cause. *Rambler* No. 19 (May 22, 1750), which describes the danger of ranging from one study to another and the importance of an early choice of a profession, seems almost to have been written after hearing about Williams. And *Rambler* No. 67 (November 6), a dream which concentrates on the delusions of hope, describes meeting someone "on the point of discovering the longitude." This must have been at least partly inspired by Williams's moving story. Anna also made an immediate impression by her intelligence and delight in conversation and her refusal to be daunted by failing eyesight. Thus he invited both father and daughter to come to Gough Square to meet his wife. Apparently the two ladies at once were attracted to each other, and Anna Williams became a regular visitor. In time Tetty and Anna became intimate friends.

Anna Williams. (detail)

"Tetty," Johnson's wife, before her marriage to Johnson.

But it was not until the autumn of 1751 that Johnson threw himself into promoting the indigent old man's cause, revising and helping him write a long series of letters to prominent officials. Several years after Johnson's death some of these were printed in the *Gentleman's Magazine,* with the heading "Original Letters of Zachary [sic] Williams; some of them corrected, and others written, by Dr. Samuel Johnson."[15] These begin with an undated letter to the Earl of Halifax, then one of October 9, 1751, to the Lords of the Admiralty, and then others through October, November, December, and early January to Dr. James Bradley, an eminent astronomer, to Lord Anson and the Lords of the Admiralty. Alas, nothing was accomplished. Williams's proposal to base everything on variations of the compass seemed too uncertain for the experts. Apparently Johnson found the whole thing fascinating and may have been at least partly convinced of Williams's method, since some years later, just before the death of Williams, Johnson put together a pamphlet for his old friend explaining the whole theory.

What is important at this point in Johnson's life is the evidence the episode provides concerning his perpetual interest in scientific problems, and his continuing compassion for the poor and needy, particularly for intelligent failures who under different circumstances might have had useful careers.

All this while Johnson had other problems connected with his own work. As was pointed out in the last chapter, many of the *Ramblers,* hastily written at the last minute, were at times wordy and needed editing. He planned to do this revision when a collected reprint was to be published. There were thousands of minor verbal changes to make, sentences to be shortened, and ideas rephrased. He even intended to make some minor changes in the few pieces written by others. During the autumn of 1751 the first four volumes of the duodecimo collected edition were being printed, and from various ornaments used Duncan Eaves believes that Richardson was the printer, at least of the last volume.[16]

In his letter to Johnson of November 2 Richardson had added a postscript, indicating that Johnson had asked permission to make a few changes in his friend's essay (No. 97), shifting a few paragraphs and omitting a passage concerning ladies who frequent public places where "young fellows buzz about them as flies about a carcass, and they hear with greediness foolish things which they think pretty." Richardson was quite willing to give his permission—"You will do with it, what you please." He also added, "I am glad you are re-printing the *Ramblers.*"[17] Did this mean he had just heard about the plan? Or had just begun to receive copy?

Over five weeks later Johnson wrote to Richardson, but unfortunately the original letter has disappeared. All we know of it comes from a few quotations given in Sotheby's sale catalogue in 1875. One sentence which is quoted is obscure in its meaning. "I thought it necessary to inform you how it happened that I seemed to give myself so little trouble about my book when I gave you so much."[18] The only "book" that Johnson was having printed at this time was the collected version of the *Rambler,* and this must be what Johnson was referring to. Could Johnson have been making so many changes in proof that he was causing trouble for Richardson's compositors? Had he sent as copy the original issues, with manuscript changes which were hard to read? Or could he have sent copy made up partly of original issues and the rest in his own handwriting? Or was he merely making Richardson's subordinates do the proofreading? Until the complete letter is found we cannot be sure.

There continued to be delays, caused either by Johnson's numerous changes or by Richardson's printers. Though the four-volume duodecimo reprint was advertised on December 17 as one which "speedily will be published," it was not actually ready until early February 1752. Then readers were able to secure over half the numbers, in corrected form, and available bound either in calf at 12s. or in boards, or "sewed in blue paper," for a few shillings less.[19]

While helping Mrs. Lennox and Zachariah Williams and struggling with the revision of over half the *Ramblers,* Johnson had trouble keeping up with his commitment to the printers of the *Dictionary,* and this may have been when the proprietors became so angry that they even thought of cutting off his financial support.[20]

As the winter wore on, the condition of Tetty gradually worsened. She was probably bedridden, usually under the influence of alcohol and drugs, more and more fretful and full of complaints. It was a difficult time for her husband, who was trying desperately to move ahead with copy for the *Dictionary,* attempting to raise money to pay off the mortgage of the family house in Lichfield, and thinking of various ways of surviving. Possibly he was getting tired of the *Rambler.* Under such pressures, to be forced to toss off two serious essays a week was simply too much. A somber note had been creeping into some of the essays and in No. 202, in late February, he concentrated on poverty, sickness, and death. It was, he decided, time to quit.

By early March, he estimated, he would have produced enough to fill two more volumes of reprints. So in No. 207, on Tuesday, March 10, he aptly described his own condition:

So certainly is weariness the concomitant of our undertakings, that every man, in whatever he is engaged, consoles himself with the hope of change; if he has made his way by assiduity to public employment, he talks among his friends of the delight of retreat; if by the necessity of solitary application he is secluded from the world, he listens with a beating heart to distant noises, longs to mingle with living beings, and resolves to take hereafter his fill of diversions, or display his abilities on the universal theatre, and enjoy the pleasure of distinction and applause.

With fancy tired, and perseverance broken, Johnson could no longer refuse to rest. Thus the next to the last number ends with this admonition to himself:

He that is himself weary will soon weary the public. Let him therefore lay down his employment, whatever it be, who can no longer exert his former activity or attention; let him not endeavour to struggle with censure, or obstinately infest the stage till a general hiss commands him to depart.

Two days later on March 12, when thanking Charlotte Lennox for a copy of *The Female Quixote,* Johnson added: "Poor Tetty Johnson's illness will not suffer me to think of going any whither, out of her call. She is very ill, and I am very much dejected."[21] The next day he had the pleasure of giving Tetty some volumes of the first reprint of the earlier *Rambler* essays which she had so admired. In the set of volumes which still survives her name is written in Volumes II, III, and IV, and in III the date is given as March 13, 1752. (There is no signature in I, or in V and VI, which did not appear until summer 1752).[22] As her condition steadily weakened, her eyes may have often wandered to the bound volumes by her bedside.

On Saturday, March 14, the last number of the *Rambler* appeared (No. 208), with the author's explanation: "Time, which puts an end to all human pleasures and sorrows, has likewise concluded the labours of the Rambler. Having supported, for two years, the anxious employment of a periodical writer, and multiplied my essays to six volumes, I have now determined to desist." Because he had steadfastly attempted to "inculcate wisdom or piety" and had allotted only a few papers to "idle sports of imagination," he concluded by insisting that he looked back "on this part of my work with pleasure, which no blame or praise of man shall diminish or augment." All he wished was to be numbered among the writers who have "given ardour to virtue, and confidence to truth." With this the Rambler bade his serious readers adieu.

Over the weekend Tetty's condition continued to worsen. But Johnson still had various important business affairs to complete, and, by Tuesday, March 17, he could write to John Levett in Lichfield, who held the mortgage on the house, that he had "sold a property principally to satisfy you" (probably his republication rights to the *Rambler*) and would soon be able to give Levett "a draught of one hundred pounds upon a bookseller of credit payable on the first of May and negotiable in the mean time."[23] After trying to settle how much had been paid for him by Henry Hervey Aston, and some problem concerning Joseph Simpson, he ends the letter: "For any money above the hundred pounds I must beg you to accept my note for six months."[24]

In this business letter there is no sign of his emotional state, but the end for Tetty was near. Late that night, or early the next morning, she died—as a result, so Robert Levet later insisted, of her addiction to opium.[25] Johnson at once dispatched a note to his old friend Taylor, who was in London, telling him the news, and expressing his grief "in the strongest manner he had ever read." So Taylor told Boswell many years later. The letter was brought to him, Taylor added, "about three in the morning," and as it "signified an earnest desire to see him," he went as soon as he could get decently ready.[26] He found Johnson crying and in extreme distress. After talking for a short while, Johnson said, "Come, my friend, let us go to prayers," and they each prayed extempore, which temporarily calmed him. Later the same day Johnson dashed off another note to Taylor: "Let me have your company and your instruction. Do not live away from me. My distress is great." In daylight he could at least think of such mundane necessities as mourning clothes and asked Taylor to ask his wife what should be purchased and sent up to Lichfield for his mother and Tetty's daughter. Johnson ends: "Remember me in your prayers— for vain is the help of man."

The most immediate matter he had to face was Tetty's funeral. According to Hawkins, Johnson had intended to have her buried in the chapel in Tothill Fields, Westminster, but later changed his mind.[27] Why? The whole matter of Tetty's burial is one of the most difficult problems of Johnson's middle years. We know that on Thursday, March 26, her body was interred at the parish church in Bromley, Kent. But why Bromley? It is not to be forgotten that Johnson's good friend John Hawkesworth lived in Bromley, where his wife, a native of the place, had a thriving school. In late February Hawkesworth's father had died and thus he had just been through similar burial problems. The local undertaker, John Dunn, his surviving records show, was responsible for both the funerals of the elder Hawkesworth and Elizabeth Johnson.[28]

It may be possible, then, to put together a fairly reasonable account of what happened. We know that Hawkesworth, along with John Ryland, his brother-in-law, and Cave, were among those who came to console Johnson as soon as his wife's death became known. Tyers, indeed, claimed that Johnson, just as he had to Taylor, "sent for Hawkesworth, in the most earnest manner, to come and give him consolation and his company."[29] Possibly it was then that Johnson asked advice about funeral procedures and Hawkesworth offered to take charge and see that Tetty's body was transported to Bromley, some dozen or so miles from London. The decision may even have been made before Tetty's death. Perhaps Ryland's son, who also lived in Bromley, was involved. Here was an opportunity to lay Tetty to rest in the placid countryside which she had loved, rather than in the congested city which she hated.

Johnson, we know, watched Tetty being placed in the coffin, in a wool shroud as required by law, removed her wedding ring, and at the same time made certain vows relating to later actions.[30] A legal affidavit proving her burial in woolen would then have been carried with the coffin by the undertaker on a cart to Bromley. The "Register of Burials in the Parish of Bromley in the County of Kent" has for March 26 the entry: "Elizabeth Johnson of the Parish of St. Brides London." Because the name "Deneuen" as the signer of the affidavit is here written in the handwriting of the curate, Thomas Bagshawe, it appears certain that Bagshawe conducted the funeral service. Johnson was not there. From all surviving evidence he did not even visit her grave close to the Charity Children's Pew in Bromley Church until over a year later. It was thirty-two years after her death that he finally arranged for her gravestone to be erected.[31]

It is not clear when Johnson wrote a sermon which was later described as having been composed "for the funeral of his wife." In the summer of 1787 when Mrs. Piozzi visited Ashbourne, vainly trying to convince John Taylor that he should allow her to include Johnson's letters to him in her edition of Johnson's correspondence which she published the next year, Taylor showed her a copy of the sermon. After Tetty's death, so Taylor reported, Johnson had attempted to get him to compose a funeral sermon for a special service in London, but he had refused because he "would not commend a character he little esteemed."[32] When Johnson then sat down and wrote his version, Taylor still refused to preach it, and by his objections even "provoked the writer to tear the manuscript," which fortunately was later "carefully put together again and copied fair." When Samuel Hayes finally printed it in 1789, along with other sermons he had found in Taylor's possession, all he said was that Taylor had refused to do anything with it because he thought "the praise of the deceased was too much amplified."[33] Undoubtedly there never was any special service for Tetty, except that in Bromley.

The larger part of the sermon, it must be admitted, is merely made up of traditional comments about death, funerals, immortality, God's forgiveness of human frailty, hope, the necessity of resignation, and other generalities. Only late in the sermon did Johnson finally come to the reason for the whole composition. There are those, he explained,

> who have lived without any open or enormous crimes; who have endeavoured to propitiate God by repentance, and have died, at last, with hope and resignation. Among these she surely may be remembered whom we have followed hither to the tomb, to pay her the last honours, and to resign her to the grave; she, whom many who now hear me have known, and whom none who were capable of distinguishing either moral or intellectual excellence could know, without esteem, or tenderness. To praise the extent of her knowledge, the acuteness of her wit, the accuracy of her judgment, the force of her sentiments, or the elegance of her expression, would ill suit the occasion.

"Such praise," Johnson continued, would "little profit the living, and as little gratify the dead." Nevertheless, he went on,

> let it be remembered that her wit was never employed to scoff at goodness, nor her reason to dispute against truth. In this age of wild opinions she was as free from skepticism as the cloistered virgin. She never wished to signalize herself by the singularity of paradox. She had a just diffidence of her own reason, and desired to practise rather than dispute. Her practise was such as her opinions naturally produced. She was exact and regular in her devotions, full of confidence in the divine mercy, submissive to the dispensations of Providence. . . . She passed through many months of languor, weakness, and decay, without a single murmur of impatience, and often expressed her adoration of that mercy which granted her so long time for recollection and penitence. That she had no failing cannot be supposed; but she has now appeared before the Almighty Judge; and it would ill become beings like us, weak and sinful as herself, to remember those faults which, we trust, Eternal Purity has pardoned.

Hardly the view of Tetty we get from other more impartial observers! But in a funeral sermon, perhaps, as in lapidary inscriptions, the writer is not upon oath.

Still there is the nagging question of what it was that appears to have completely incapacitated Johnson for some time after Tetty's death —that kept him from attending her funeral, or from arranging any proper service in London. One explanation is that the strains and stresses of the last few days were too much for him and he was too ill to travel. A suggestion of this possibility comes in a recollection of Sir Joshua's nephew, young Samuel Johnson—how dependable it is impossible to tell—who later wrote to his sister, "I have been told that his [Johnson's] grief for the loss of his wife went near to cost him his life, that is, his despair drove him to drink which brought on a fever."[34] It is, of course, possible that Johnson's uncharacteristic overdrinking, if this actually occurred, was merely an attempt to ward off an attack of influenza or a bad cold, with a resulting high fever, which made it out of the question for him to go to Bromley.

Doubtless he never forgave himself for not doing so, and he could never forget. But in the turmoil of his uncontrollable grief, suspicions of his own personal guilt as the possible reason for his wife's unhappy final years, and the gnawing fear of being left alone, he could not easily pull himself together. One series of events which must have served partially to take his mind off himself was the entrance into the household at 17 Gough Square of two persons who were to influence greatly his later life.[35]

The first new member of the household was the almost blind Anna Williams, who during the winter had been a constant visitor. Some of her friends hoped that it might be possible to restore her sight through an operation. According to Hawkins, at Johnson's insistence he took Miss Williams to see the well-known surgeon, Samuel Sharp, of Guy's hospital, who agreed to do the operation without charge, provided the cataracts were sufficiently developed.[36] Because "her own habitation was not judged convenient for the occasion," Johnson and Tetty had kindly offered her the use of a room in their house, where she could be taken care of by the servants during and after the operation. Presumably all this was definitely arranged before Tetty's sudden death, and there was no change of plans. Apparently Miss Williams moved in almost immediately after Tetty's death, probably on the day originally agreed upon. Unfortunately, the operation was not a success. The trouble was that the cataracts were not far enough along, so that, to use Hawkins's wording, "the crystalline humour was not sufficiently inspissated for the needle to take effect," with the result that Miss Williams became totally blind.

For most of the rest of her life she remained a part of Johnson's household. Never a financial burden, she had meager support from a number of sources—from Lady Philipps, who made her a small allowance, from the Miss Wilkinsons and other Welsh friends. She brought her own furniture and her expenses were small, according to a later commentator, "tea and bread and butter being at least half of her nourishment."

A few weeks later a black boy, about ten years old, also became a part of the household. His name was Francis, or Frank, Barber.[37] Born a slave in Jamaica, he had been brought to England two years earlier by his master, Col. Richard Bathurst. After attending school in Yorkshire, he was for a short time in London with Dr. Richard Bathurst, the colonel's son and Johnson's close friend. Then in April 1752 he was put under the supervision of Johnson in Gough Square, where, as he later remembered, he found his new master "in great affliction." From one account he was sent to board at a "Mrs. Coxeter's" in order "that he might go to Black-friars school," a plan that did not work; as it turned out, he "went one day only for he caught the small pox." Whether he was treated for the disease at Mrs. Coxeter's or in Gough Square by Johnson's poor but trusted friend Robert Levet, we cannot tell. Indeed, Frank's illness might well have been another complicating factor in Johnson's life during this difficult period. Happily the boy survived and was later sent to "Mr. Desmoulins' writing school."

All this time Frank was still a slave of Colonel Bathurst, who is reputed to have officially freed him in his will, which was dated April 24, 1754, two years later. Obviously he had aroused Johnson's sympathy and compassion, and, as readers of Boswell will remember, except for several periods of separation Frank remained with Johnson until his death, and he became the chief heir and beneficiary of Johnson's will. During the early years of their association the boy's duties must have largely consisted of carrying messages and doing odd jobs about the house. He became indeed almost a symbol of Johnson's lifelong hatred of race prejudice and unfairness to other races.

As we have seen, immediately following Tetty's death Johnson was in a state of almost complete collapse. Only slowly did he begin to recover, and even then, according to Hawkins, his melancholy "was not, in degree, such as usually follows the deprivation of near relations and friends: it was of the blackest and deepest kind."[38] His memories of his departed wife were "of the terrific kind." And William Shaw, whose information came chiefly from Mrs. Desmoulins, who had lived with Tetty out in Hamp-stead, later insisted that Tetty's death so affected Johnson

that he grew almost insensible to the common concerns of life. He then stayed little within, where her image was always re-called by whatever he heard or saw. Study disgusted him, and books of all kinds were equally insipid. He carefully avoided his friends, and associated most with such company as he never saw before. And when he thought himself a burden, and felt the pressure of time becoming insupportable, the only expedient he had was to walk the streets of London. This for many a lonesome night was his constant substitute for sleep.[39]

Occasionally he tried to divert his somber thoughts by some mechanical labors, as when on April 14 he worked on an index to a commonplace book.[40] But for the most part he could not settle back into ordinary living.

It was not until five weeks after Tetty's death that Johnson was able to set down what he called "Prayers composed by me on the death of my wife." On April 24 he wrote:

> Almighty and most merciful Father, who lovest those whom
> Thou punishest, and turnest away thy anger from the penitent,
> look down with pity upon my sorrows, and grant that the afflic-
> tion which it has pleased Thee to bring upon me, may awaken
> my conscience, enforce my resolutions of a better life, and im-
> press upon me such conviction of thy power and goodness, that
> I may place in Thee my only felicity, and endeavour to please
> Thee in all my thoughts, words and actions. Grant, O Lord,
> that I may not languish in fruitless and unavailing sorrow, but
> that I may consider from whose hand all good and evil is re-
> ceived, and may remember that I am punished for my sins, and
> hope for comfort only by repentance. . . .[41]

The whole prayer, as George Irwin points out, is really a supplication for his own welfare. Tetty is never specifically named.

Even in the next prayer written on April 25, where his wife is men-
tioned, his chief concern is himself. What he needs is forgiveness and peace for his troubled soul.

> Grant me the assistance and comfort of thy Holy Spirit, that
> I may remember with thankfulness the blessings so long enjoyed
> by me in the society of my departed wife; make me so to think
> on her precepts and example, that I may imitate whatever was
> in her life acceptable in thy sight, and avoid all by which she
> offended Thee.

He pleads that he may be able to "perfect that reformation which I prom-
ised her," and to persevere in that resolution, "which I recorded in thy sight, when she lay dead before me."

Again on April 26, in the early hours after midnight, he concentrates on how he will himself be affected. There can be little doubt that John-
son's emotional reaction to Tetty's death was based in his own fears of loss of security and his own admissions of guilt and fear for the future. He is praying for himself, not for Tetty.

> O Lord, Governor of Heaven and Earth, in whose hands are
> embodied and departed spirits, if thou hast ordained the souls
> of the dead to minister to the living, and appointed my departed
> wife to have care of me, grant that I may enjoy the good effects

of her attention and ministration, whether exercised by appearance, impulses, dreams, or in any other manner agreeable to thy government.

Does this show Johnson's tentative belief in spirits? Or merely an uncertain hope that he might receive some permanent good from his present sad loss?

There was another prayer on May 6, and then a notation: "I used this service, written April 24, 25, May 6, as preparatory to my return to life tomorrow." He was ready to end his severe mourning, and on May 8 deposited these prayers among other memorials to Tetty, with the exclamation "Deus exaudi.—Heu!" which was written on a slip of paper pasted on the inside of a round wooden box in which he placed Tetty's wedding ring.[42] Although this terrible experience was over, it was never forgotten. He may have thought he was ready for a "return to life," but adjustment to a new kind of existence came slowly.

CHAPTER VII

The Widower and the Adventurer

IN THE SUMMER OF 1752 Johnson was still in a distraught condition as a result of Tetty's death in March. We know little about his daily life after this traumatic event, since none of his surviving letters are very informative, nor is there much about him in the correspondence of his friends. In late April Elizabeth Carter wrote to Miss Highmore, honoring "the just indignation you express at the cold reception which has been given by a stupid trifling ungrateful world to the Rambler," but there is no indication in the letter that Miss Carter knew anything about Johnson's present condition.[1] In Samuel Richardson's and the Earl of Orrery's letters to Charlotte Lennox there is no mention of Johnson.[2] In early July Johnson wrote a letter of condolence to Orrery, referring to his lordship's own recent illness, and consoling him upon the malevolent attacks of some scribblers directed at his recent book on Swift.[3]

We also know that Johnson was still trying to borrow money in order to pay off the loan from John Levett in Lichfield.[4] His letter in March, just before Tetty's death, had assumed too much. So, on July 26, he wrote again to Levett:

> I am extremely ashamed after what I wrote last to you with so much confidence, to have disappointed you, but I am really no otherwise than unfortunate in the affair. I then told you that I had sold a property, which was exactly true, but I have not yet received a third part of the money which I expected from it; a circumstance that, after what I had written shocked me so much that I could not bear to see you, as I expected to receive the rest every day, and was willing to spare us both so disagreeable an

interview. The thing has however given me more credit, so I am about to borrow the money, which I will immediately send you as soon as it comes to my hands, which cannot, unless every thing fail me, be but a few weeks.

Again, however, he was too optimistic, and it would not be until nearly five years later that Levett received his £100 and the mortgage was finally paid off.

During this period Johnson's distant friends and acquaintances must have wondered what he was doing. Could he be planning another periodical? When any new publication seemed to have some connection with Johnson's earlier works, it naturally stirred up speculation. For example, on August 22, 1752, Thomas Birch wrote to his patron Philip Yorke:

We had last week the first number of a paper intended to be continued every Thursday under the title of *The Impertinent,* printed in the same form and for the same bookseller [Bouquet] with the Rambler, which it greatly resembled in the style. But it so fully answered its title in the general opinion that its existence, like that of the insects called the ephemera, was determined within one day, and on Thursday last we were told by the publishers that we should have no more of them. I have too good an opinion of Johnson to assign to him a piece of so much malignity as well as petulance, but the suspicion will not easily be removed till he gives the public that satisfaction which he likewise owes to himself.[5]

In the August *Gentleman's Magazine,* which came out early in September, the author of the *Impertinent* was identified as the quack doctor John Hill, who, hoping to avoid detection, had slyly attacked the piece in his own periodical, the *Inspector.* It is unlikely that Johnson had anything to do with the exposure of Hill, for Hawkesworth probably wrote the devastating disclosure with help from other members of the club.[6]

Early in September a strange thing happened to Johnson, as it did to all inhabitants of Great Britain. He had gone to sleep on the night of Wednesday, September 2, but woke up on Thursday the fourteenth. This long sleep of eleven days was the result of an act finally passed by Parliament allowing the British to catch up with the Gregorian calendar which was in use on the Continent. There was no change in the days of the week, but the "new style" calendar forced a reorientation. Johnson quickly adapted to the new dating, and from this time on thought of his own birthday as occurring on September 18, rather than the seventh, and

Tetty's death, which had occurred on March 17, he now firmly fixed in his mind as having been on March 28.

By early autumn Johnson had returned to some kind of regular life. Doubtless he still walked around late at night, talking to wandering prostitutes and beggars. After an evening with the club, which was supposed to conclude about eleven o'clock, he found it difficult to head straight home.[7] Even though blind Anna Williams was gradually learning to wait up for him, ready to provide a cup of tea and more conversation, the prospect was not too exciting. He found it more diverting to listen to the pathetic tales of failures and to help with a gift of a small coin whenever he could. For Johnson the plight of the poor and needy became one of his most overpowering interests. His own sex life remained unchanged, for he had no physical relations with women.

During the day he spent much time with his amanuenses in the garret at Gough Square making slow progress on the *Dictionary.* Usually on Tuesdays he attended the regular meetings of the Ivy Lane Club. Here he was able to keep in touch with what was going on in the publishing world through his fellow-members John Payne and John Hawkesworth; indeed, *The Adventurer,* the next important periodical in his career, originated in discussions at the club. According to a much later account,

> the counsels of the club in Ivy Lane encouraged Hawkesworth to propose the plan of the Adventurer. Mr. J. Payne agreed to become the publisher, at the price of two guineas a number, copy-money. Hawkesworth was to be the editor and principal author of the work. Dr. Bathurst agreed to become an auxiliary.[8]

From various remarks made later by Payne and others it seems clear that Johnson, while he did not intend to write essays for the new periodical, was from the start involved in the planning, and even at times dictated general policies. The *Adventurer* was to be the same size as the *Rambler,* would sell at the same price (2d. a copy), and appear on the same days of the week (Tuesday and Saturday). Unlike the *Rambler,* the total number to be produced was determined at the start—one hundred and forty—just enough to fill four duodecimo volumes when reprinted. Like its predecessor, each essay was to have a Latin or Greek motto at the beginning, no English translation to be provided until the essays were reprinted as a collection. Readers not conversant with the classics were promised this later help. Appended to the first number was a note which stated that folio numbers would be "formed into regular volumes, to each of which will be printed a title, a table of contents, and a translation, of the mottoes and quotations."[9]

Since Hawkesworth was not himself a classical scholar, he depended on his friends for suggestions of suitable mottoes. According to Thomas Percy, Hawkesworth usually sent Johnson "each paper to prefix a motto before it was printed."[10] If this occurred, Johnson must have been in close touch with the project all the time. One thing he had learned from his earlier experience was that it was a mistake for any author to attempt to produce alone a semiweekly series of essays. There should be more variety than he had been able to supply in the *Rambler*. A much better plan would be to have from the start a commitment from other writers to provide a regular series of essays, always with some identification of authorship. To be sure, Johnson still believed that the basic goals were much the same as in the earlier periodical. Later in a letter he summed up what had been the opinion of the "fraternity" who had planned the *Adventurer*.[11] Basically it should consist of "pieces of imagination, pictures of life, and disquisitions of literature." And Payne, the publisher, when sending some of the first numbers to Thomas Birch, hoping that he would help publicize the venture, described the "ultimate design" as being "to promote the practice of piety and virtue upon the principles of Christianity; yet in such a manner that they, for whose benefit it is chiefly intended, may not be tempted to throw it aside."[12]

Perhaps Payne, writing to a clergyman, exaggerated the moral aspects of the plan. He and others were well aware that their chief problem was to attract a wider audience than the *Rambler* had ever enjoyed. There must be more light pieces, more amusing satirical essays. Thus Hawkesworth at first secured as his collaborator Bonnell Thornton, a young man under thirty, who had already shown his capacity for light satire. Thornton was also something of an eccentric.

The son of a London apothecary, he had been intimate with George Colman, William Cowper, and Robert Lloyd at Westminster School, all later members of the Nonsense Club and contributors to the *Connoisseur*. Although he took a degree in physic at Oxford, Thornton refused to accede to his father's wish that he become a practicing apothecary. Instead, he much preferred being a wit and a hack writer. There are various amusing stories which have come down to us describing Thornton's character, one telling what happened once when he slipped away from his studies in Oxford to go with a gay party to the theater in London where he was embarrassed to find his father occupying the very next box. Rushing back to Oxford, he surrounded himself with medical books and convinced his father, who had followed him there, that he must have mistaken another young man in the theater for his son.[13] Thornton's first published work appeared in Christopher Smart's *The Student,* and early in 1752 he began the *Drury Lane Journal,* as a rival to Fielding's *Covent Garden Journal.*

Some years later, Thomas Percy, in a letter to William Shenstone, described Thornton as

> a middle-sized man, with his face moderately full of pock-holes, with rather a fair complexion; but what will sufficiently distinguish him is a remarkable impediment in his speech, owing (I believe) to his having no roof of his mouth, by which he cannot pronounce several letters, particularly the theta, so that he never could articulate his own name.[14]

Nevertheless, despite his well-known eccentricities, and the fact that in the *Drury Lane Journal* Thornton had written an amusing burlesque of Johnson's style entitled "A Rambler Number 999999," the "fraternity" planning the *Adventurer* decided to seek his help. Presumably he had the light touch they needed.

And so Bonnell Thornton, while he was at the same time preparing to write a single weekly number of another new periodical, *The Spring Garden Journal*,[15] agreed to contribute every third number of the *Adventurer*. He was to be responsible for a third of the essays, and Hawkesworth two-thirds.

The choice of the title is perhaps further evidence of the desire of Payne and his advisors to attract more readers. If the Rambler had not strayed too far from his sober hearth, the Adventurer was intended to move about more widely and take a few more risks. Obviously there was no intention of providing a series of exciting adventures, all purely fiction, but it was hoped that readers would expect something different from the new periodical's earlier model.

On Tuesday, November 7, 1752, the first number appeared, with a motto from Horace referring to Hercules, and the essay dealing with the dangers and delights of a modern adventurer who considered himself a kind of literary knight errant, comparable to the classical heroes and medieval knights. Implied throughout were an adventurer's possible achievements. In the second number on Saturday, November 11, appeared an essay comparing intellectual and corporeal labor. Then, on the next Tuesday, November 14, came Bonnell Thornton's first piece, a light, ironic satire announcing a plan for a "most sublime pantomime in the modern taste." The pantomime is to be called "Harlequin Hercules." Signed "Lun *Tertius*," it was identified as being written by "A," as were all Thornton's contributions. For a while Thornton did what he was supposed to do, handing in essays 3, 6, and 9, which substantially lightened the tone of the series.

At the beginning the *Adventurer* was not, as the *Rambler* had been, widely advertised in the newspapers. Payne had evidently learned his lesson. It might be more useful, he suspected, to rely on other means of securing readers—perhaps by passing out large quantities of the first numbers, and by word-of-mouth gossip. He could certainly count on valuable coverage in the monthly magazines. The *Gentleman's Magazine,* for which Hawkesworth worked, was naturally a great help. In the November number, which appeared early in December, there were five pages devoted to an "Account of the new paper that has appeared this month, called the Adventurer," followed by summaries of the first four numbers and the whole of No. 5.[16] Then in each succeeding issue, as long as the new paper continued, the *Gentleman's Magazine* included at least one *Adventurer,* usually written by Hawkesworth himself; only two were by Johnson.

The *Scots Magazine* was even more generous with space. In its November and December numbers, including the annual Appendix, it repeated the *Gentleman's Magazine's* account and summary of the first four numbers, and then reprinted numbers 5, 7, 8, 12, 13, 14. In provincial papers there was also some publicity, for the *Salisbury Journal* of December 4 included the first *Adventurer,* and later a few other odd numbers.

From the start many of Johnson's friends suspected that he was responsible for some of the papers. Although Hawkesworth's writing was never quite as ponderous as that in some of the *Ramblers,* he did achieve a style much like that of his predecessor. Thus some readers were puzzled. Here was a new series which had much more variety than the *Rambler,* and yet sometimes sounded very much like it. Johnson must be involved, yet hardly anyone was sure. On November 11 Birch wrote to Yorke, "The Adventurer, of which the second number appeared today, is evidently from the same hand with the Rambler."[17] On December 17 Catherine Talbot, who had herself written a *Rambler,* wrote to Elizabeth Carter:

> Pray can you tell me any history of a new paper called the Adventurer? We hope much from it, though we have seen but one. It seems, with a style not unlike the Rambler, to go upon that amusing scheme which people expected from the title of The Rambler.[18]

Over a month later, on January 29, 1753, Miss Talbot, who had been ill with a cold, wrote again:

> I like the Adventurers; we all like them exceedingly, and I fancy they will soon become very generally fashionable. There was not a fault that the most captious found in the Rambler that is not obviated in these papers. They do not abound in harsh words, they are varied with a thousand amusing stories, they

touch with humour on the daily follies and peculiarities of the times.

. . . Don't think by commending the Adventurer I give up the cause of the Rambler; I discern Mr. Johnson through all the papers that are not marked A, as evidently as if I saw him through the keyhole with the pen in his hand.

Even if she had peered continually through all Johnson's keyholes, she would not have seen him writing any essays for the *Adventurer*. So far as we can tell, through November, December, and January he contributed nothing, though he may have revised some of Hawkesworth's pieces and may have talked to him about others.

Though not actually writing any of the essays, Johnson kept closely in touch with what was going on. At the same time he was cementing a new friendship with Joseph Warton, which in a few months proved to be useful to the *Adventurer*. An Oxford man and an excellent classical scholar, then rector of Winslade, Joseph Warton was completing a translation of the *Eclogues* and *Georgics* of Virgil. By early November this work was completed, except for the dedication. Now back in the country at Winslade, after some time in London, Joseph wrote to his brother Thomas at Trinity College, Oxford, on November 17, reporting on the state of his project.[19]

I have seen Johnson so very often that we have contracted close friendship and are quite intimate—Dodsley behaved throughout with the utmost civility and kindness. The last night he made a grand supper and invited all my acquaintance, Vansittart among the rest who was glad to see Johnson.

Warton then added another piece of news:

Thornton called and seemed piqued I should say to Johnson that he wrote the *Adventurer*. I told him I heard it at a coffee-house openly from 20 people which is true.

Apparently Thornton's authorship of the first "A" paper (No. 3) in the *Adventurer* was widely known, and one may suspect that Johnson did not need to be told.

According to the original plan, Thornton was to supply every third number and, as we have seen, he did so for a short time. But then something happened, and there was no piece identified as by "A" for No. 12, on December 16. Instead, the editor had to use a letter about infidelity, unsigned, but presumably by Hawkesworth himself. As a matter of fact,

Thornton did not contribute again until No. 19 on January 9. He may have left London early in December (his last essay for the short-lived *Spring Garden Journal* was on December 7), perhaps for a holiday. Once back in the city in early January, Thornton did for a short time fit back into the schedule, and contributed numbers 23 and 25. Then he did nothing until No. 35 (March 6), and his final number was No. 43 on April 3.

There is no convincing evidence to explain why—whether he was angling for another connection, or merely found the pressure to supply light variety in a serious periodical a bit too demanding. Or was this another sign of his habitual laziness and lack of energy? By February 1753 it must have become evident to Payne and Hawkesworth that some other plan was needed. With Dodsley's new periodical *The World* a rival for popular support among the literati, they had to move quickly. At once they began more advertising in the newspapers.[20] A suggestion which Johnson may have made was to enlist two of his own former female supporters, Catherine Talbot and Elizabeth Carter. In her letter to her friend on January 29 Miss Talbot, while indicating her suspicion that Johnson was responsible for some of the *Adventurers,* suggested:

> They want nothing but now and then a little of your assistance, for such writers should be assisted, that they may by the help of their correspondents now and then get a holiday. Look over your *considering drawer,* and if you have any old sketches that were intended for the Rambler, bring them up, I beseech you.[21]

Indeed, Miss Talbot may already have been approached, for it now appears probable that she wrote *Adventurer* No. 27, which appeared on February 6.[22] Moreover, David Fairer suggests that when Elizabeth Carter arrived in London on February 15 for a stay of some three months, she agreed to some kind of an arrangement to help the *Adventurer.*[23]

If the ladies could be counted on to enliven the periodical in their own way, what was still needed was a reliable scholar-critic to do literary essays. And so on March 8 Johnson wrote to Joseph Warton:

> I ought to have written to you before now, but I ought to do many things which I do not, nor can I indeed claim any merit from this letter, for being desired by the authors and proprietor of the Adventurer to look out for another hand, my thoughts necessarily fixed upon you, whose fund of literature will enable you to assist them with very little interruption of your studies.
>
> They desire you to engage to furnish one paper a month, at two guineas a paper, which you may very easily perform. We

have considered that a paper should consist of pieces of imagination, pictures of life, and disquisitions of literature. The part
which depends on the imagination is very well supplied, as you
will find when you read the papers; for descriptions of life there
is now a treaty almost made with an author and an authoress,
and the province of criticism and literature they are very
desirous to assign to the commentator on Virgil.

I hope this proposal will not be rejected, and that the
next post will bring us your compliance. I speak as one of the
fraternity though I have no part in the paper beyond now and
then a motto; but two of the writers are my particular friends,
and I hope the pleasure of seeing a third united to them will
not be denied to, dear Sir.[24]

Two allusions in this letter are puzzling. Who were the "author and
authoress" with whom a treaty was almost settled? Samuel Richardson
and Hester Mulso? And who were two of the writers for the *Adventurer*
who were Johnson's "particular friends"? Bonnell Thornton was certainly
not one of Johnson's close friends. Was one of them Richard Bathurst?
Hawkesworth and Elizabeth Carter certainly were, and it is tempting to
think that these are the two referred to. If the other "author" suggested
was Richardson, the expectation was wrong, for he never wrote anything
for the *Adventurer*.[25]

Warton may have been reluctant to take on this added responsibility,
and when replying to Johnson may have used as an excuse his prior agreement to write occasionally for the *World*. Or he may have written to
Dodsley for his advice. In any event, there survives a strange, torn fragment which appears to be Dodsley's reply, (written, it seems clear, about
the middle of March) which begins:

There are certainly very good papers in the Adventurer; it will
therefore be no discredit to be concerned in it: and if you can
make it profitable to your self, I beg you will not let any consideration for the *World* prevent your engaging in it.[26]

But he still asked for a piece for his own publication, which Warton had
earlier promised. As it turned out, Joseph Warton later contributed to
each periodical, sometimes writing essays for both at the same time.

Apparently pressure was exerted on Johnson as well to become a
regular contributor. After *Adventurer* No. 48, which came out on April
21, 1753, the remaining ninety-two papers were to be divided between
Hawkesworth, who was responsible for half, and Johnson and Joseph
Warton, each for a quarter.[27] Occasional contributions from the women,

such as hints for the story of Eugenio (Nos. 64, 65, 66) from Elizabeth Carter, and the story of Fidelia by Hester Mulso (Nos. 77–79), came by a roundabout route and were Hawkesworth's responsibility. What should be stressed here is that Johnson did twenty-nine papers in all for the *Adventurer,* four before the arrangement, and twenty-five afterward. Since he was supposed to write only two essays a month, it was not a particularly difficult assignment, even while he pushed ahead with copy for the *Dictionary.*

From all accounts he did not take the assignment very seriously. He may even have been willing to allow his good friend, the impecunious Dr. Bathurst, to pick up the fee of two guineas for some of the contributions. Years later Anna Williams, who was living in the Gough Square house at the time, told Boswell that because Johnson had given the essays to Bathurst, "he used to say he did not *write* them." The fact was that "he *dictated* them, while Bathurst wrote."[28] Johnson certainly composed them. Indeed, he confessed as much to Hill Boothby.[29]

The twenty-four papers hitherto ascribed to Joseph Warton were actually a family effort. Joseph's brother Tom and his sister Jane also had something to do with them.[30] This is apparent from a letter written by the brothers and Joseph's wife Molly to their sister Jane on April 26. Tom begins by saying:

> Jo and I have been both busying ourselves in writing for the Adventurer: so that if we call you a duenna, you may call us Don Quixotes. This is a profound secret! You know the *Adventurer* is a paper that succeeds the Rambler, under the inspection of Johnson; we beg your assistance in giving us some pictures drawn from real life, events you have actually met with in this fluctuating state of things. This won't be the first time you have appeared in print; you need not therefore be afraid of any maiden-blushes upon that trying occasion. Miss Carter is engaged with us, and would be proud to find another of her own sex employing her time in this manner. Authoresses, you know, are scarce and curious in this age. We know you can write if you please. Make yourself the heroine of one of your papers.[31]

Later in the same letter Molly commented: "My dear sister would laugh with me, if she was here to see them both engaged in the Adventurer, the poor little study crammed so full of books scattered about that there is scarce room for a mouse to creep in." The evidence seems conclusive that some of the "Z" papers were collaborations, others by one of the brothers, and one (No. 87) perhaps by their sister Jane.

If, as has often been pointed out, Johnson's essays for the *Adventurer* tended to be less serious in tone than many in the *Rambler,* they include also some of his most moving and revealing pieces, such as No. 108, "The Uncertainty of Human Things" and No. 120, "The Miseries of Life." Johnson was not merely dashing off light pieces for the general reader. His serious moral purpose was never deeply hidden.

Johnson's connection with the *Adventurer* lasted until its conclusion in March 1754. In Nos. 137 and 138, a week before the end, he considered the whole problem of the usefulness of writers and their alternating happiness and infelicity. He was, as he had told Payne earlier, trying to do what he thought each of the chief writers should do and "wind up" the papers "by some general subject."[32]

For Johnson the conclusion of the project must have brought mixed emotions—relief at the removal of one regular commitment and regret that such a worthwhile work should end. Even though he knew from the start that it had been planned to stop with No. 140, he may have had regrets. The women who had been involved were definitely dismayed. Catherine Talbot wrote to Elizabeth Carter on March 16:

> In vain have I, in every company, done honour to the Adventurer, by naming numbers of the most acknowledged taste, even in the fine world, who constantly read and admire them. Mr. Dodsley prevails [with his rival publication, the *World*] and the Adventurer will soon cease his delightful instructions.[33]

To which Miss Carter replied two days later from Deal:

> I am vexed and mortified to hear that the Adventurer is at an end. What an idea must it give one of the public taste, to find such a paper sunk for want of encouragement. To be sure, the fine folks of this world are as sagacious in finding out the formidable genius of instruction, however beautifully disguised, and run away from it with as much horror as good people do from a cloven foot. I have been equally unsuccessful in my preachings.

General disappointment did not quickly disappear. On June 10 Miss Talbot wrote again to Miss Carter about the *Adventurer:*

> Never was paper more lamented. Every body is impatient to have him begin on some new scheme. . . . Of all the admired papers of the Adventurer, I have heard no one more highly spoken of than that marked Y, which he says he received from an unknown hand, and of which I am sure you could tell me

more if you would. Now could not you procure another story
from the same hand?

Hawkesworth in his concluding *Adventurer,* while identifying Joseph
Warton as the author of the "Z" papers, and admitting his own general
editorship, had not given the name of the writer of the "Y" papers. Miss
Talbot, apparently, was not sure that it was Johnson, though she suspected
that Miss Carter must know. In any event, even in the fashionable clerical
circles which Miss Talbot frequented, Johnson's pieces were among the
ones most widely admired.

When the whole series was available in bound volumes, the *Adven-*
turer did reach many more readers. In early April 1754 newspapers carried
advertisements for a four-volume duodecimo, and also a two-volume folio
edition, as well as odd numbers of the original essays which would allow
collectors to complete their sets.[34] In the collected volumes the mottoes
were translated for the general reader. One new reader was Richardson's
friend Lady Bradshaigh. On May 21, 1754, after thanking him for recommending the *Adventurer* to her, she added:

> I have gone through the 4 volumes and am charmed. Most of
> them I greatly admire. Excellent things indeed! In a few of them
> I thought the style a little uneasy, and rather difficult to under-
> stand, but I shall read them again, with greater attention, and
> have sent for the folio edition, the small one being too pale a
> print for my eyes. I never before heard of Mr. Hawkesworth,
> but suppose this is not his first work. I am sorry they are so
> soon given up.[35]

To which Richardson replied:

> I am glad that the Adventurers please your ladyship. You think
> the style of some of them uneasy and difficult. The principal
> author has been thought an imitation of Mr. Johnson, the
> author of the Rambler. They have a high opinion of each other.
> Mr. Hawkesworth has written some very good things in Cave's
> magazine, as Mr. Johnson used to do.

And so the *Adventurer* became another set of volumes, easy to come
by and useful for dipping into. Neither a major event in Johnson's life,
nor financially very rewarding, the periodical did bring him definite com-
pensation, chiefly the close friendship with the Wartons.

But now back to Johnson's everyday life in Gough Square during
the winter and early spring of 1753. Continually plagued by memories of

Tetty, he could not get her off his mind. Could he have himself been partly responsible for his wife's unhappy condition during her last years? If so, how could he make up for it now? On New Year's Day in 1753 he pleaded with God:

> Make me to remember to thy glory thy judgements and thy mercies. Make [me] so to consider the loss of my wife whom thou hast taken from me that it may dispose me by thy grace to lead the residue of my life in thy fear.

And to this he added:

> I hope from this day to keep the resolutions made at my wife's death
>   To rise early
>   To lose no time
>   To keep a journal[36]

So far as we can discover, he was never able to keep any of these resolutions for long. His own incapacity for reform, indeed, was a recurrent theme in his prayers for the rest of his life.

On March 28 he wrote: "I kept this day as the anniversary of my Tetty's death with prayer and tears in the morning. In the evening I prayed for her conditionally if it were lawful."

It was not until Easter, on April 22, that Johnson could force himself to go to Bromley in Kent to see Tetty's grave. Constantly wrestling with a desire to see where she had been laid to rest, he was nevertheless for other reasons reluctant to make the short drive to Bromley. At last on Easter Sunday he composed this prayer:

> Ap.22.1753. O Lord, who givest the grace of repentance, and hearest the prayers of the penitent, grant that by true contrition I may obtain forgiveness of all the sins committed and of all duties neglected in my union with the wife whom thou hast taken from me, for the neglect of joint devotion, patient exhortation, and mild instruction. And O Lord, who canst change evil to good, grant that the loss of my wife may so mortify all inordinate affections in me that I may henceforth please thee by holiness of life.
>
> And, O Lord, so far as it may be lawful for me I commend to thy fatherly goodness the soul of my departed wife, beseeching thee to grant her whatever is best in her present state, and finally to receive her to eternal happiness.
>
> All this I beg for Jesus Christ's sake, whose death I am now about to commemorate, to whom &c. Amen.

In writing down the prayer he made an addition which Boswell later suppressed, obviously thinking it did not fit his own understanding of Johnson's marriage.[37]

> April 22 1753. As I purpose to try on Monday to seek a new wife without any derogation from dear Tetty's memory I purpose at sacrament in the morning to take my leave of Tetty in a solemn commendation of her soul to God.

Then on the following Monday Johnson wrote a fuller account of just what he had done.

> Ap. 23. Easter Monday. Yesterday as I purposed I went to Bromley where dear Tetty lies buried and received the sacrament, first praying before I went to the altar according to the prayer precomposed for Tetty and a prayer which I made against unchastity, idleness and neglect of public worship. I made it during sermon which I could not perfectly hear. I repeated mentally the commendation of her with the utmost fervour larme à l'oeil before the reception of each element at the altar. I repeated it again in the pew, in the garden before dinner, in the garden before departure, at home at night. I hope I did not sin. Fluunt lacrymae. I likewise ardently applied to her the prayer for the Church militant where the dead are mentioned and commended her again to Eternal Mercy, as in coming out I approached her grave. During the whole service I was never once distracted by any thoughts of any other woman or with my design of a new wife which freedom of mind I remembered with gladness in the Garden. God guide me.

Next Sunday, back in London, after further contemplation he wrote:

> Ap. 29 1753. I know not whether I do not too much indulge the vain longings of affection; but I hope they intenerate my heart and that when I die like my Tetty this affection will be acknowledged in a happy interview and that in the meantime I am incited by it to piety. I will however not deviate too much from common and received methods of devotion.

He continued to be tortured by conflicting pressures—his own sentimental memory of Tetty on one side, and his continuing strong sexual desires on the other. Other unmarried men might find sexual gratification with prostitutes, or affairs with other women, but not Johnson. His moral compunctions were too great. While he longed for love and affection, he was convinced that the only way to secure them must be in marriage. So he was cruelly deprived of what he thought was the supreme happiness man could ever attain. Indeed, Garrick was responsible for the story that when Johnson was once asked what was the greatest pleasure, he answered frankly "f—g and the second was drinking. And therefore he wondered why there were not more drunkards, for all could drink though all could not f—k."[38] For long periods of his life Johnson himself refrained from both these top pleasures of human existence.

But when he seriously considered remarrying there must always have been the disturbing thought that he might drive a second wife to drink and drugs, as he may have done to his first wife. Would it be fair to ask anyone to take such risks? And if he chose to remarry, despite all these possible reservations, which of his women friends should he ask? For the moment his was a general purpose, with no specific woman in mind.

He certainly never did remarry. If he ever decided on someone to ask, the chances are he never spoke to her about it. But he probably kept thinking about the possibility, and for years to come continued to consider different choices.

He kept busy in various ways. Copy for the first volume of the *Dictionary* was almost all in print, and he began work on the second volume early in April.[39] But lexicography did not occupy all his time. He sent Thomas Edwards, through Richardson, comments on a recent pamphlet on linguistic matters.[40] He spent some time unsuccessfully trying to find a publisher for a scheme of Richard Bathurst, and he was helping Charlotte Lennox in a number of ways.[41] Early in March she had solicited a favor for a young gentleman who was not yet married. When she berated Johnson for doing nothing, he tried to wriggle out by using as an excuse: "The reason for which I said nothing to Mr. Lennox was no less than that I had nothing to say."

Johnson all along had been helping Mrs. Lennox with her *Shakespear Illustrated*, a study of the playwright's sources, which was published in mid-May. In addition to writing the Dedication to the Earl of Orrery, he may well have given her other assistance, as Percy later suggested.[42] Johnson certainly thought highly of her and saw her frequently. About this time he wrote her a playful letter:

> I hope you take great care to observe the doctor's prescriptions, and take your physic regularly, for I shall soon come to enquire. I should be sorry to lose criticism in her bloom. Your remarks are I think all very judicious, clearly expressed, and incontrovertibly certain. When Shakespeare is demolished your wings will be *full summed* and I will fly you at Milton; for you are a bird of prey, but the bird of Jupiter.[43]

Among his literary contacts about this time Samuel Richardson was one of the closest. Johnson frequently was at his house in North End,

Fulham, and they advised each other about various projects. It was at Richardson's that Johnson met William Hogarth. When the painter first saw Johnson, so Boswell later describes the incident, "standing at a window in the room, shaking his head, and rolling himself about in a strange ridiculous manner," he thought the man must be crazy. But once Johnson began to talk, Hogarth rapidly changed his opinion. He was astonished, though at first he imagined that "this idiot had been at the moment inspired."[44]

At least once Johnson took Miss Williams with him to see Richardson. Hester Mulso, later Mrs. Chapone, in a letter to Miss Carter of July 10, 1753, described meeting them there. Richardson had been in better health than usual and had been very amiable in reading and talking to his guests. She added:

> We had a visit whilst there from your friend Mr. Johnson and poor Miss Williams. I was charmed with his behaviour to her, which was like that of a fond father to his daughter. She seemed much pleased with her visit; showed very good sense, with a great deal of modesty and humility; and so much patience and cheerfulness under his misfortune, that it doubled my concern for her. Mr. Johnson was very communicative and entertaining, and did me the honour to address most of his discourse to me. I had the assurance to dispute with him on the subject of human malignity, and wondered to hear a man who by his actions shows so much benevolence, maintain that the human heart is naturally malevolent, and that all the benevolence we see in the few who are good, is acquired by reason and religion. You may believe I entirely disagreed with him, being, as you know, fully persuaded that benevolence, or the love of our fellow-creatures, is as much a part of our nature as self love, and that it cannot be suppressed or extinguished without great violence from the force of other passions. I told him I suspected him of these bad notions from some of his Ramblers, and had accused him to you; but that you persuaded me I had mistaken his sense. To which he answered, that if he had betrayed such sentiments in the Ramblers, it was not with design, for that he believed the doctrine of human malevolence, though a true one, is not a useful one, and ought not to be published to the world. Is there any truth that would not be useful, or that should not be known?[45]

Johnson could never accept without argument the doctrines based on the belief that all was right with the world. But he also refused to believe that all was wrong with the world. Through God, goodness could be attained.

Another visit is described in Richardson's letter to Elizabeth Carter on October 2, 1753. Hester Mulso was visiting him at North End, Fulham, and he hoped she would stay on with the weather "soft and balmy." He added:

> Mr. Johnson *rambled* thither, principally on her account, last Sunday. He is in love with her. And extremely fond of her verses to Stella. Most magnificently does he express himself of them.[46]

Could Miss Mulso have been on Johnson's list of prospective spouses?

Johnson gave Richardson copies of some of his works, and Richardson showed Johnson some of the early volumes of *Sir Charles Grandison*. Not that Johnson completely approved of seeing only portions of a work, and not the whole. This was "a kind of tyrannical kindness to give only so much at a time as makes more longed for."[47]

Johnson kept giving Richardson all kinds of advice. Later he asked to be added to the subscription list for the octavo edition of *Grandison*, at the same time promising to push the volumes among other friends. Johnson followed the last portions of *Grandison* closely, and in March 1754, when acknowledging receipt of Volume VII, commented:

> You have a trick of laying yourself open to objections, in the first part of your work, and crushing them in subsequent parts. A great deal that I had to say before I read the conversation in the latter part, is now taken from me. I wish however Sir Charles had not compromised in matters of religion.[48]

But despite his many social and professional connections, this was not one of the happiest periods in Johnson's life. Bereft of a wife, unable speedily to complete a major project, plagued by other worries, he later described his existence to Thomas Warton as "broken off from mankind a kind of solitary wanderer in the wild of life, without any certain direction, or fixed point of view. A gloomy gazer on a world to which I have little relation."[49]

CHAPTER VIII

The Harmless Drudge

O N TUESDAY, April 3, 1753, Johnson wrote in his book of prayers:

> I began the 2d. vol of my Dictionary, room being left in the first
> for preface, grammar and history none of them yet begun.
>   O God who hast hitherto supported me enable me to pro-
> ceed in this labour and in the whole task of my present state
> that when I shall render up at the last day an account of the
> talent committed to me I may receive pardon for the sake of
> Jesus Christ. Amen.[1]

Pages including letters "A" to "K" were now in final form. He had
still to complete "L" to "Z" and then write the preliminary material.
Although it had taken him over seven years to complete the first volume,
he still had hopes of moving much faster with the second. After all, he did
have most of the quotations copied out by his amanuenses, and probably
had done some of the work on the etymologies and definitions for the
latter part of the alphabet. He and his helpers had finally worked out
efficient procedures. What he now had chiefly to do was to paste up this
material as copy for the printer.

It is likely that he still had two helpers—perhaps Peyton and William Macbean[2]—and they were determined to complete the work as
quickly as possible. As a result of this speeding up of the process, the second volume contained more mistakes than the first. With assistants perhaps less dependable, and because of his own increasing boredom, Johnson
apparently did not spend as much time choosing and shortening quotations. Nor was he as effective in catching errors in the proofs. All this
seems evident from the fact that some years later when preparing the

revised fourth edition for the printers he made many more changes and corrections in the latter part of the alphabet than in the earlier.[3]

But even with this determination to hasten the process it was not until over a year later that Johnson could begin to see light ahead. How much the delay was caused by mechanical problems and slowness of type-setting and how much by his own tendency to be dilatory, it is hard to tell. He never was capable of extended periods of hard work. As he once said to Boswell, he "always felt an inclination to do nothing."[4]

Moreover, he could hardly cut himself off completely from his close friends and their problems. And in order to keep alive, he had to do some other writing. So during 1753, as we have seen, he wrote twenty-four *Adventurers*, which brought him £50 8s., and five more in early 1754, bringing £10 10s.[5]

By April, 1754, the bulk of the text for the *Dictionary* was in print.[6] All Johnson needed to do was to make some corrections and to work on the critical portions to be inserted at the beginning of volume I. By July he was sufficiently advanced to think of taking a few weeks off to visit Oxford. There were various things he wanted to see in libraries there for last-minute checking. His chief contact in Oxford was now Thomas Warton, a fellow of Trinity College, with whom he had been involved in matters connected with the *Adventurer*. Warton had sent him a copy of his *Observations on Spenser's Faery Queen*, and after some delay Johnson wrote to him on July 16 to send his thanks. After various compliments to Warton for his "advancement of the literature of our native country," Johnson referred to his own lexicographical work "which now draws towards its end." But he could not complete the job adequately "without visiting the libraries of Oxford."[7] Looking ahead to writing a history of the language, and an English grammar, as part of the introductory ma-terial, Johnson needed contact with serious scholars who knew something about Anglo-Saxon and Germanic philology. Thus talk with linguistic experts probably was more on his mind than checking material in large libraries. He ended his letter somewhat vaguely: "I know not how long I shall stay or where I shall lodge, but shall be sure to look for you at my arrival, and we shall easily settle the rest."

As soon as he received Johnson's letter, Warton arranged for him to stay at Kettell Hall, a building next to Trinity which had originally been intended for use of commoners of the college. Within a fortnight Johnson arrived, and remained for about a month, with Warton acting as his host and guide.[8] For the most part, it proved to be a very pleasant and produc-tive vacation. Many years later Warton provided Boswell with a full account of this visit, the first time Johnson had been back since leaving the university in late 1729.

The first thing Johnson wanted to do was to visit his old college, Pembroke. The morning after his arrival he and Warton walked over, where he was pleased that all the old servants, "particularly a very old butler," recognized him, but annoyed by the cold reception of the Master, Dr. John Ratcliff, who would not even invite him to dinner or order a copy of the *Dictionary*. Once outside the Master's rooms, Johnson exploded: "There lives a man who lives by the revenues of literature, and will not move a finger to support it. If I come to live at Oxford, I will take up my abode at Trinity."

Since it was the vacation, few students or fellows were in residence. Johnson called on John Meeke, who had been in college at the same time and was now a fellow, and also on another, not identified. After what Johnson thought had been an insulting reception by the Master, he was gratified to have the two fellows press him to stay at Pembroke on his next visit. A return to old surroundings naturally brought mixed reactions.

If he still had some sentimental feeling for his old college, the sight of the easy, unproductive life of others of his own age there aroused resentment. As he left Meeke's rooms, Johnson remarked to Warton: "About the same time of life, Meeke was left behind at Oxford to feed on a fellowship, and I went to London to get my living: now, Sir, see the difference of our literary characters."

On other days they walked out to Ellsfield, a village about three miles from Oxford, to see Francis Wise, Radcliffe Librarian and Keeper of the Archives of the University. He and Johnson were immediately attracted to each other.

> At this place Mr. Wise had fitted up a house and gardens in a singular manner, but with great taste. Here was an excellent library, particularly a valuable collection of books in Northern literature, with which Johnson was often very busy.

As they returned to Oxford that evening, Warton "out-walked" Johnson, and

> he cried out *sufflamina*, a Latin word which came from his mouth with peculiar grace, and was as much as to say, *Put on your drag chain*. Before we got home I again walked too fast for him, and he now cried out, "Why you walk as if you were pursued by all the *Cabiri* in a body."[9]

Warton and Johnson took walks around Oxford, viewing the ruins of old abbeys and other sights. And Johnson gradually met a number of

Oxford scholars who became good friends. One topic of conversation with Warton must have been their common friend, the poet William Collins. Johnson had known Collins back in the forties in London, and thought highly of him, and he may have seen something of him in London in 1750 when Collins was working on a history of the Revival of Learning, or at least talking about it. But "Poor Collins" had had a complete breakdown, which was very distressing to his friends. Early in 1754 he had come to Oxford for a while and had had to be dragged away from his lodgings opposite Christ Church to be taken to a madhouse.[10] Undoubtedly Warton passed on all the terrifying details, particularly upsetting to Johnson with his own fears of insanity.

It may have been on this visit that Johnson made the mistake of ridiculing "Bishop Berkeley's American scheme" in the presence of his son, George Monck Berkeley, then a student at Christ Church, with the result that the young man was so upset that he "walked out of the room, and subsequently refused Johnson's repeated requests for permission to write a Life of the Bishop."[11]

While in Oxford Johnson could not completely shake off his responsibilities in London, and sent a brief note to Strahan:

> I shall not be long here, but in the mean time if Miss Williams wants any money pray speak to Mr. Millar and supply her; they write to me about some taxes which I wish you would pay.
> My journey will come to very little beyond the satisfaction of knowing that there is nothing to be done, and that I leave few advantages here to those that shall come after me.[12]

It was a pleasant time for Johnson, though he did not collect anything important from the Oxford libraries for his *Dictionary*. From scholars and their conversation and collections, yes, but not from institutional libraries.

The trip also had another welcome result connected with the completion of his great project. Sometime in casual conversation Johnson may have expressed his regret that he did not have an Oxford degree to show on the title page of his work; or it may have been Warton or Wise who brought up the subject. In any event, someone remembered that it was possible to secure an M.A. not in the ordinary sequence, but *honoris causa*, awarded for literary work outside the university. Once the possibility had been raised, Johnson's Oxford friends and admirers began the long process of backstage pressures and manipulation. Nothing could be done quickly, but some pushing in the proper places might be successful.

There can be no doubt that Johnson was pleased by the possibility and during the long autumn eagerly awaited news of progress.

The great project was definitely nearing completion. On September 21 Thomas Birch wrote to Yorke:

> Johnson's Dictionary, though entirely finished except the History of the English Language till the time of Queen Elizabeth, when his authorities commence, and a grammar of it, will not appear till March next. It will be 100 sheets larger than Chambers's Cyclopaedia.[13]

Although there was still much to do, Johnson did not give all his time to this one pressing need. It was in the summer and autumn of 1754 that he either first met, or became intimately involved in the affairs of, four men who would be important in his later life—Arthur Murphy, Robert Chambers, Bennet Langton, and Giuseppe Baretti.

Johnson's meeting with Arthur Murphy came about in a strange way. At this time, Murphy, a practicing dramatist, was also writing essays for a periodical called the *Gray's Inn Journal*. In June 1754 he and Samuel Foote, wit and dramatist, were on holiday for a few days in the country. When Murphy happened to mention that he had to return to the city to write a piece for the periodical, Foote suggested that instead he translate into English an Oriental tale from the April number of the French *Journal Étranger*, which they happened to have with them. This he did, and his version appeared in the June 15 number of the *Gray's Inn Journal*. At once readers recognized that the French piece was an unacknowledged translation of Johnson's *Rambler*, No. 190. When Murphy found out about his mistake he included an apology in the next number, and as soon as he could went to call on Johnson to explain what had happened. He found Johnson in the midst of a chemical experiment, "covered with soot, like a chimney-sweeper, in a little room, as if he had been acting Lungs in the Alchemist, making aether."[14] Johnson was not upset by what Murphy had done, and they got along famously. Apparently Johnson admired what he had already seen of Murphy's published work, and was pleased by his visitor's manners and his ability to quote Latin. Thus a friendship was formed which was never broken.

Robert Chambers was an ambitious young lawyer whom Johnson had met in London before Chambers accepted a fellowship at Lincoln College, Oxford. Years later Johnson would dictate large portions of a series of law lectures which Chambers was to give at Oxford, where he succeeded Blackstone as Vinerian Professor.[15] In November 1754 Johnson wrote to him in Oxford, sending various requests to check manuscripts and make transcriptions, some to be passed on to Thomas Warton at Trinity. The letter ends: "I hope, dear Sir, that you do not regret the change of London for Oxford. Mr. Baretti is well, and Miss Williams, and we shall all be glad to hear from you."[16] Evidently an agreeable young man eager to be of service in any way he could, Chambers was a welcome addition to the Johnson circle.

Johnson's first meeting with Bennet Langton was the result of the young man's admiration for *The Rambler* and his determination somehow to meet the author. In the autumn of 1754, when he and his father, with his uncle Peregrine and a friend, came to London for three months, he saw his opportunity.[17] By chance they stayed in lodgings in a house often visited by Johnson's friend Robert Levet. Once young Bennet had mentioned his wish to his landlady, she introduced him to Levet, who easily obtained Johnson's permission to bring him to Gough Square. It may well be that the name Langton was not wholly unfamiliar to Johnson, for the elder Langton, who was an active country squire, was well known to Pope's friend, Joseph Spence, and possibly to Garrick, Dodsley, and Edward Young. In any event, sometime in October or November, 1754, the meeting took place. According to Boswell, the young man

> was exceedingly surprised when the sage first appeared. He had not received the smallest intimation of his figure, dress, or manner. From perusing his writings, he fancied he should see a decent, well-dressed, in short, a remarkably decorous philosopher. Instead of which, down from his bedchamber about noon came, as newly risen, a huge uncouth figure, with a little dark wig which scarcely covered his head and his clothes hanging loose about him. But his conversation was so rich, so animated, and so forcible, and his religious and political notions so congenial with those in which Mr. Langton had been educated, that he conceived for him that veneration and attachment which he ever preserved.[18]

As a matter of fact, young Langton was himself far from ordinary. As one writer later described him, "He was a very tall, meagre, long-visaged man, much resembling . . . a stork standing on one leg near the shore. . . . His manners were in the highest degree polished; his conversation mild, equable, and always pleasing."[19] Of course, when he was seventeen Bennet's conversation may not have been so polished, or his height quite six feet six inches, as it was in later years. Laetitia Matilda Hawkins provides other details of Langton's appearance. He had a "mild countenance," with "elegant features," and a "sweet smile." When seated, he often twisted one leg around the other, "as if fearing to occupy more space than was equitable" and with his body "inclining forward as if wanting strength to support his height." His usual practice was to have his snuff box in his hand while conversing.[20]

From their first meeting Johnson recognized Langton as an intelligent, serious-minded young man. He even took him to see Richardson, making clear to his young companion that the novelist had little to talk about except his own works. Though Johnson tried vainly to bring him out into more general themes, all Richardson would talk about on that occasion was a translation of *Clarissa* into German.[21]

This first meeting of Johnson and Langton occurred almost three years before the latter entered Trinity College, Oxford, where Thomas Warton was to be his tutor. He was to see Johnson a number of times before then.

During the autumn of 1754 Johnson was also deeply involved in a bizarre affair which needs to be described in detail. It all had to do with an acquaintance who was gradually becoming a close friend, an Italian named Giuseppe Baretti.[22] Although Johnson was basically insular in his prejudices, he did accept visiting foreigners who settled in London and who impressed him with their intelligence and serious approach to literature and life. Baretti was one of these. According to Baretti's own later account, Mrs. Lennox, while preparing to publish a translation of various works used by Shakespeare in writing his plays, wished to acquire some proficiency in the Italian language, and sent her husband to the Orange Coffee House to see if he could find some Italian there who would be willing to exchange tuition in his language for lessons in English. Baretti happened to be there and at once accepted the offer. Sometime late in 1752 or early the next year, Mrs. Lennox introduced him to Johnson.[23] Evidently the two men took to each other at once, for by 1754 they were on excellent terms. Baretti consulted Johnson on various matters. Although he did not always accept the older man's advice, and at times the ties were strained to the limit, the relationship was one of mutual respect.

In the spring of 1754 Baretti was approached by William Huggins, who had been working for some twenty years on a translation of Ariosto's *Orlando Furioso* into English *ottava rima*. Eager to secure expert help, Huggins sent a young clergyman, the Reverend Temple Henry Croker, to see Baretti, with instructions to fetch the Italian visitor by any means he could. Some arrangement was agreed upon. On May 24 Baretti wrote to Croker, who was perhaps acting as chaplain to Huggins, that he was quite ready to come down to look at the manuscript. Unfortunately, Baretti had been suffering from a stubborn fever, and a week later wrote again apologizing for his failure to show up. He hoped to see him shortly.[24]

Early in June, then, Baretti traveled out to Huggins's estate, Headley

Park near Farnham in Surrey, for a delightful stay of about two months in the English countryside. The temperate climate and the cider and beer cooled his fiery blood, and he evidently enjoyed his visit very much, while he struggled valiantly with the English verse rendering of Ariosto's lines. On August 8, just after returning to London, Baretti wrote a long, enthusiastic letter to a friend in Milan.[25] As part of his reward, so Baretti described the whole matter, Huggins had paid all his expenses, generously giving him a handsome gold watch worth at least forty guineas, as well as a note for a similar amount. In addition, Huggins had offered him the use of a little neighborhood house and garden with the right to as many deer from the park as he needed for his table. He even tried to saddle him with a relation as a wife. When the translation was published it was to have a preface in English by Baretti, and he was to receive the chief share of the payments. At least that was Baretti's understanding of the arrangement. When he left the Huggins ménage, so Baretti insisted, the whole family had been in tears and made him promise to return for Christmas.

But Baretti must have misunderstood some of Huggins's remarks. Indeed, most of his assumptions appear to have been unfounded. It all started over the matter of the watch. Huggins claimed he had merely lent it to Baretti to take with him when he went for a walk before dinner. Baretti thought it had been given him as a present. He certainly failed to give it back, and he took it with him when he finally left Headley Park. Despite all Huggins's later efforts, Baretti steadfastly refused to return the watch and later pawned it. Then the web became even more tangled.

Again it appears to have been Temple Henry Croker who acted as one of Huggins's emissaries in the matter of the watch. Inevitably Croker was viewed by Baretti as one of his mortal enemies. Once threats were used, Baretti secured protection from the Sardinian ambassador and thought he was safe. There may even have been attempts to force Baretti's landlord to allow a search of his premises. In any event, both sides were soon furious.

Johnson was apparently involved in the whole matter from the start, and late in July had heard of what Baretti was doing for Huggins. When Johnson reached Oxford he passed on all the details to Thomas Warton, and once he was back in London he heard Baretti's side of the subsequent argument. A clergyman named Charles Holloway visited Joseph Warton at Winslade in Hampshire, where he also found Thomas Warton, who had come down from Oxford. From fragments of Holloway's diary, which still remain at Trinity College, Oxford, it is clear that they talked over the "Ariosto scheme," and that Thomas Warton said that Johnson had told him about Huggins's gift to Baretti of forty guineas and a gold watch, as payment for his assistance.[26] Huggins had also mentioned to Baretti something he had received from the Wartons, but exactly what that was is not clear. Anyway, Johnson "looked upon it as a trifle," though he did think certain papers should have been returned.

A week later Holloway repeated in his diary most of the same details, but insisted that Baretti had secured the watch "by an artifice." He further added that Huggins's translation "was also to be revised by Johnson."

While there is no conclusive evidence that Johnson had ever promised to revise the translation, some people at least thought so. And it is quite possible that when he looked forward to the completion of the *Dictionary* he began to speculate how he would be able to keep alive. Helping the well-to-do Huggins was a reasonable possibility.

During the autumn most of the participants consulted Johnson, and he tried as long as he could not to take sides. He wrote to Huggins and advised Croker, and at the same time read Baretti's communications. But nothing seemed to resolve the argument. Consequently, he wrote again to Huggins on November 9, trying as best he could to make clear his position:

> I find that I am likely to suffer the common fate of inter-meddlers, and receive no thanks on either side. I can however solace myself with my good intentions without any disturbance from the event of a transaction in which nothing but my benevolence gave me any interest. I supposed you desirous to recover a favourite watch, and proposed a way which is certainly the most speedy, and I believe the cheapest; if you are more affected by the provocation than the loss, and more intent on resentment than the disputed property, I have no means of pacification to offer. But your letter makes it necessary for me to tell you that neither the loss nor the provocation is my fault. The loss I endeavoured to repair, and should have procured restitution, or willingness in restitution, had not this new expedient been found out, by which the only conviction, which I pretend to have raised, conviction of inability to defend himself, was for a time suspended, without the least knowledge or cooperation of mine. The provocation I endeavoured to prevent, by making up the quarrel in which I was wholly on the side of Mr. Croker. In this attempt I failed and the feud proceeded. Mr. Baretti showed me his letter before he sent it, but he did not show it for advice, and I observed neutrality so scrupulously as not even to mend his English lest he should have it to say that I concurred with him. The second letter he did not bring until he had sent it, and when he gave it to me told me "You will not like it." He told the truth.
>
> Your warm assertion of yourself to me is therefore unnec-

essary for I never pretended to think you in the wrong. The particular question about which I remember myself quoted, you have justly distinguished in your letter to Mr. Croker, and I have nothing to object further. Your vindication of Mr. Croker is yet less proper, for I have always maintained him to be in the right, and endeavoured to convince him how easily he might prosecute the work without the help which he regretted to have lost. Mr. Croker was indeed the man for whom I was chiefly solicitous, as he was the only man that could be much hurt. I have opposed Mr. Baretti in the whole process of this difference and in the proposal meant him no favour, nor as any favour did he acknowledge it; what I said of his condition he would resent more than he would thank me for my interposition.

One angry paragraph seems to be the consequence of an oversight in you or me. You have read, or I have written *hospitality* for *hostility*; if you look on my letter you will find that *hospitality* could not or should not be the word. The laws of *hospitality* no man ever within my knowledge charged you with breaking; the *rules of generous hostility* Mr. Croker has certainly broken if not by his application to the Sardinian Envoy, which I mentioned with no great vehemence because at worst I thought it only circumstantially blamable, yet surely by his attempt on the landlord, of which I might speak more harshly, and speak truth. He is however a good man who in such a quarrel does but one thing wrong.

I will repeat it again that I have endeavoured honestly and, what is more, kindly, to moderate the violence of this dispute; if I had succeeded I should at least have spared you the impropriety of such a letter as you have been pleased to send to . . .[27]

When his correspondent replied with further allegations, Johnson bowed out of the controversy. On November 14 he wrote again to Huggins:

I was led by your letter to suspect that you had received some misinformation, but I could not conceive what might be charged upon me. I see that fiction has no limits, to show you on what allegations some will venture, I assure you that I never in my life saw either the Venetian Resident, or the landlord, nor ever sent a message to either, nor have any reason to be certain that either knows my name, or knows of my existence. I think, Sir, I may fairly claim that whatever shall be said to my disadvantage in this affair may be judged by this specimen. I hinted before that Mr. Croker has, I sincerely think without

his fault, whisperers or clamourers about him, who want only
to do mischief, or make themselves sport. If I had not happened
to have written, what must I not have been thought?

I hope, Sir, to have now made an end of this subject, which
shall no longer disturb me, and I sincerely wish that it may
cease likewise to disturb you. I should be glad that every good
mind were left to the enjoyment of itself.

If you shall please to continue this correspondence upon
more pleasing topics, it will be considered as a favour. . . .

Although Johnson refused to do any more negotiating, this was not
the end of the dispute. When it became evident to Huggins and his
backers that Baretti thought himself safe under the protection of the
Sardinian ambassador, they applied to Sir Thomas Robinson, one of the
Secretaries of State, to force the ambassador to withdraw his protection.
This he did, and finally the watch was secured from the pawnbroker and
returned to Huggins.

Joseph Warton, when summarizing the sequence of events for his
brother Thomas at Oxford, commented: "What a strange story! and how
difficult to be believed!" Then he added further gossip which he thought
rendered the whole story even more incredible.

Huggins wanted to get an approbation of his translation from
Johnson but Johnson would not though Huggins says it was
only to get money from him. To crown all he says that Baretti
wanted to poison Croker. . . . By some means or other Johnson
must know this story of Huggins. How infamous is it if it should
be false![28]

When the translation of Ariosto appeared in a privately printed
version the next spring, no translator's name was given, but the dedication
to the King was signed by Croker. Many readers thus assumed that he was
responsible for the whole work. A year or so later, when an official version
was published, Huggins's name was given as translator, and Croker's dedication was omitted. So the quarrels continued to proliferate. Certainly the
whole affair must have been very annoying to Johnson.

He did, nevertheless, remain on friendly terms with Baretti, even
after the excitable Italian was accused of murder some years later. They
often walked the streets of London together late at night and talked of
many things. Perhaps their rapport might not have been quite so close
had Johnson known of the existence of some verses which Baretti had
written to Charlotte Lennox, urging her to be a poet rather than a prose
writer, and which included suggestions that she ignore Johnson's bad

advice. In this ode Johnson quite obviously is portrayed as a villain—an inflexible Englishman who thinks a graceful poetic nothing a sin and a vice, whose heart is full of austerities, whose voice speaks terrible words.[29] It would be far better, Baretti implied, for her to choose himself as her adviser. When all the evidence is assessed, then, Baretti could hardly be called a dependable, devoted friend. Still, for many years Johnson retained a deep feeling for him.

Despite such digressions as this with Baretti and Huggins, Johnson throughout the autumn of 1754 was struggling to move through the last stages with the *Dictionary*. Just when final copy was dispatched to the printers is uncertain, though when it arrived there must have been a sigh of relief from all concerned. Boswell recounts how Andrew Millar, the bookseller who had chiefly been in charge, and whose patience during the long years had been sorely tried, exclaimed when the last sheet was received, "Thank God I have done with him." When the messenger who had taken the copy told Johnson what had occurred, he remarked with a smile, "I am glad that he thanks God for any thing."[30] But tempers quickly cooled, and Johnson could later call Millar "the Maecenas of the age," and say, "I respect Millar, Sir; he has raised the price of literature."

As he struggled on, in the back of his mind was the possibility that somehow he could secure an Oxford degree before the two volumes were published. When writing to Thomas Warton on November 28 his first thought was to send thanks to his friend and Mr. Wise "for the uncommon care" they had taken in his interest, and to ask whether he could "do anything to promoting the diploma."[31] Then some weeks later, on December 21 he wrote again:

> I am extremely sensible of the favour done me both by Mr. Wise and yourself. The book cannot, I think, be printed in less than six weeks, nor probably so soon, and I will keep back the title page for such an insertion as you seem to promise me. Be pleased to let me know what money I should send you for bearing the expense of the affair and I will take care that you may have it ready in your hand. . . . I shall be extremely glad to hear from you soon again to know if the affair proceeds. I have mentioned it to none of my friends for fear of being laughed at for my disappointment.

In his letters there were also questions about "Poor dear Collins," books he had promised to send Wise, Warton's own "Spenserian design," and the death of Dodsley's wife and his suffering. His own condition was not much better.

Even by February 1, 1755, he had heard nothing definite, and was beginning to be a little anxious.

> I now begin to see land, after having wandered, according to Mr. Warburton's phrase, in this vast sea of words. What reception I shall meet with upon the shore I know not, whether the sound of bells and acclamations of the people which Ariosto talks of in his last canto or a general murmur of dislike. . . . I hope however the critics will let me be at peace, for though I do not much fear their skill or strength I am a little afraid of myself, and would not willingly feel so much ill-will in my bosom as literary quarrels are apt to excite.

Then three days later he did receive news that there was progress, though when he wrote to Warton again on February 13 he urgently wanted to know "in what state my little affair stands." It must have been a tantalizing experience. It was not until February 25 that relief came and he could dash off a note to Warton that Dr. King, Principal of St. Mary Hall, Oxford, had brought him the diploma, and he now had "the full effect" of his friends' care and benevolence. He enclosed a letter written in Latin to George Huddesford, the Vice-Chancellor, expressing his deep appreciation, which he hoped Warton would read, and if approved would seal and present to Huddesford.

At last the long, worrisome wait was over, and the title page could be printed with "Samuel Johnson A.M." officially in place. On March 20 he wrote again with the news that he expected to see the *Dictionary* "bound and lettered" the next week. With that off his mind, he thought he might come up to Oxford for Easter. Five days later, however, when expressing his pleasure at hearing that the Vice-Chancellor liked his letter, he indicated that he hoped to see Warton soon in London. From the long exchange of letters one thing is obvious: for the time being, at least, Tom Warton had become one of Johnson's best friends.

While all this was going on, something else which was to be of later importance had occurred. On Thursday, November 28, the hundredth number of the periodical *The World* contained an anonymous essay praising the dictionary "soon to be published," with kind words for Johnson's other works. Then, a week later, in No. 101, on December 5, there was further praise. Although the essays were unsigned, word soon got around that the author was the Earl of Chesterfield, the well-known statesman, wit, and letter writer, who was noted as one of the most eminent patrons of the day.[32] There can be little doubt that Dodsley, the publisher of the *World,* passed on the information to Johnson, who was suddenly faced with a difficult decision. He had somewhat unwillingly addressed the *Plan of a Dictionary* to Chesterfield in 1747. Most people then assumed that the Earl would be the patron for the whole project. But nothing much had happened. What should Johnson do now?

Clearly there were a number of options. If he felt so inclined, he could call upon the Earl bearing fervent thanks and then with his permission dedicate the *Dictionary* to him. This would show that he got the message, and as a result he would receive a normal, acceptable gift from his lordship. Or he could ignore the whole business, giving the impression that he had no idea who had written the essays. Or he could write a formal letter of thanks to Chesterfield, and then see what happened. Or he could compose an angry letter, in which he would make clear that the Earl, after the initial phase, had done nothing important to aid the project, that Johnson himself was solely responsible and owed nothing to any patron.

Apparently, however, Johnson could not decide immediately what to do. Very soon the authorship of the essays became widely known, and by the middle of January one periodical, when reprinting the first one, attributed it to Chesterfield. But still Johnson did nothing. To be sure, there is a story which cannot be substantiated but which Joseph Fowke later told, that Johnson wrote his letter only after he knew that Chesterfield was ready to give him £100 on the assumption that the *Dictionary* would be dedicated to him.[33] It might be that something like this was the final nudge. All we know is that early in February he decided to adopt the last option. Why?

Many attempts have been made to explain Johnson's true reason.[34] There had never been any outright quarrel or definite break. Certainly after a gift of £10 in the early stages Chesterfield had been no help to the indigent lexicographer. For seven long years Johnson had had to struggle on with no financial assistance from his supposed patron, so that his growing resentment is easily understandable. Moreover, his attitude toward Chesterfield's political position was definitely not more favorable. Yet there had not been any quarrel. Johnson later told Boswell that there never was any specific reason why they could not remain on easy terms, and that the well-known story (later the source of a famous nineteenth-century painting) telling of Johnson's fury after a long wait in Chesterfield's waiting room when he saw Colley Cibber walk out the door, had no foundation whatever.[35] Johnson had visited the Earl a few times and been forced to wait, but it was "his Lordship's continued neglect" that caused the final break.

When Chesterfield once was asked why he had not kept in touch with Johnson, he lamely gave as his excuse that Johnson had changed addresses and he did not know where he was living.

The message that Johnson sent in February 1755 has long been recognized as one of the great letters of all time. Packed into six fairly short paragraphs are all the exasperations and pain of years of frustration and disdain. The satirical touches are keen and to the point. No one could ever be uncertain just what he meant. He could not accept the condescending praise which his lordship had expressed in his essays in the *World*. Johnson insisted on standing firmly on his own feet.

The letter begins with two paragraphs filling in the background. Then he comes to the heart of the matter.

> Seven years, my Lord, have now passed since I waited in your outward rooms or was repulsed from your door, during which time I have been pushing on my work through difficulties of which it is useless to complain, and have brought it at last to the verge of publication without one act of assistance, one word of encouragement, or one smile of favour. Such treatment I did not expect, for I never had a patron before.[36]

Then after a reference to Virgil,

> Is not a patron, my Lord, one who looks with unconcern on a man struggling for life in the water and when he has reached ground encumbers him with help? The notice which you have been pleased to take of my labours, had it been early, had been kind; but it has been delayed till I am indifferent and cannot enjoy it, till I am solitary and cannot impart it, till I am known and do not want it.
>
> I hope it is no very cynical asperity not to confess obligations where no benefit has been received, or to be unwilling that the public should consider me as owing that to a patron, which Providence has enabled me to do for myself.

How did Chesterfield react? With his usual urbanity. He showed the letter to various acquaintances, pointing out especially well-written passages, and left it out on his table for all to read. If he was annoyed in any way, he never showed it.

The reactions of Johnson's close friends, when they heard about the affair, were mixed, with admiration for Johnson's independence and integrity, but regret that he had been unwilling to accept the obvious financial rewards which Chesterfield's patronage would have brought him. Dodsley felt that Johnson "had a property" in the *Dictionary* which he should have used, and William Adams, his old college friend, was sorry he had written such a letter. But Johnson never wavered, and posterity has supported him. Not that this famous letter marked the end of patronage in England, as critics such as Thomas Carlyle have maintained, but it was an important milestone in the movement for independence of the modern author. Johnson speaks out firmly on the side of the writer, rather than supporting the wealthy class.

Word of the approaching publication spread outside London, and some people who had never met Johnson were excited by the prospect. Charles Burney, then organist in a church at King's Lynn in Norfolk, enthusiastically gathered the names of six inhabitants of the region, including himself, who wished to secure copies. In February he wrote a fulsome letter of compliment to Johnson, stressing how much he had admired his periodical works, which he thought "models of true genius, useful learning, and elegant diction, employed in the service of the purest precepts of religion, and the most inviting morality," and apologizing for keeping Johnson from his "useful labours."[37] But, he added, "it is the fate of men of eminence to be persecuted by insignificant friends as well as enemies; and the simple cur who barks through fondness and affection, is no less troublesome than if stimulated by anger and aversion." It was seven weeks before Johnson found time to acknowledge Burney's letter by telling him that copies of the *Dictionary* might be secured easily through Dodsley.[38] Johnson invited his correspondent to favor him with another letter, which he did, but they did not meet for some years.

As soon as word of Johnson's Oxford degree had been received, the booksellers began to advertise the coming work.[39] On February 27 and through March there were notices in the newspapers that the *Dictionary* would "speedily be published." Strahan had also run off reprints of the 1747 *Plan,* and these were offered free to prospective subscribers. The price set for the two huge folio volumes containing over 2,500 double-columned pages and weighing close to twenty-five pounds was £4 10s., a clear indication that they did not expect to attract purchasers with modest means. The price was almost twice that of any other dictionary then available. At a time when one could get drunk for a penny and under the table for tuppence, and when some weekly wages were only a few shillings, the appeal was to the well-to-do. Two thousand copies of the first edition were printed.[40]

By April 1 advertisements were more specific, announcing definite publication on April 15, a promise which, happily, was to be kept. As the great day approached, Johnson may well have lost some of the "frigid tranquillity" to which he had referred in his Preface. Finally the long labor was over, and he could sit back and await the public response.

CHAPTER IX

The Dictionary

I N THE LONDON NEWSPAPERS of April 15, 1755, and on succeeding days came the announcement: "This day is published—"

> A Dictionary of the English Language: in which the words are deduced from their originals and illustrated in their different significations by examples from the best writers. To which are prefixed A History of the Language, and a Grammar. By Samuel Johnson, A.M.[1]

Reviews in the periodicals began to appear in a few weeks' time. They were full and for the most part complimentary. Thus in the opening pages of the April *Gentleman's Magazine*, Johnson's good friend John Hawkesworth described the work in detail and insisted that honor should be given Johnson "who alone has effected in seven years what the joint labour of forty academicians could not produce to a neighbouring nation in less than half a century."[2] Alluding to the Preface, Hawkesworth added: "It is written with the utmost purity and elegance; and though it is only an avenue to the dusty deserts of barren philology, it abounds with flowers that can shoot only on poetic ground; it delights the passenger without detaining him by the way." As a sample of what readers may expect to find, Hawkesworth at the end of the review gives the entry for the word "aim," to prove "that a Dictionary may be an entertaining as well as an useful book."

Other reviews tended to mix praise with reservations. As a sample, the April *Monthly Review* provided such a long account (over thirty pages) that they had to apologize to their readers for having to omit some of their usual monthly sections.[3] Included were many pages from Johnson's Preface, in which he explained just what he was doing. Then the anonymous reviewer (Sir Tanfield Leman) added:

> Such is Mr. Johnson's account of what he has endeavoured, and barely to say that he has *well* performed his task would be too frigid a commendation of a performance that will be received with gratitude by those who are sincerely zealous for the reputation of English literature: nevertheless, lavish as we might justly be in its *praise,* we are not blind to its *imperfections*; for *some* we have observed, even in the short time allowed us in the inspection of this large work, nor are all of them equally unimportant. Some may, perhaps, expect that we should point out what appear to us as defects, but this we decline, because most of them will be obvious to the judicious and inquisitive reader; nor are we inclinable to feed the malevolence of little or lazy critics: besides which our assiduous and ingenious compiler has, in a great measure, anticipated all censure by his apological acknowledgments. Upon the whole, if the prodigious extent of this undertaking, and the numerous difficulties necessarily attending it, be duly considered; also that it is the labour of one single person . . . instead of affording matter for envy or malignancy to prey upon, it must excite wonder and admiration to see how greatly he has succeeded.

Portions of this long review were reprinted in the April number of the *Scots Magazine.*

There were other accounts in the April *London Magazine,* the July-August *Journal Britannique* (by Matthew Maty), and in the June *Edinburgh Review.* This last was a thirteen-page balanced review by Adam Smith.[4] Beginning with the customary general compliments, "When we compare this book with other dictionaries, the merit of its author appears very extraordinary," Smith added that the excellence was so great "that it cannot detract from it to take notice of some defects." His chief objection was that the work was not "sufficiently grammatical." What the user needed were more discussions of different classes and meaning. To show what he meant, Smith quoted two of Johnson's sections—for "but" and "humour"—and then added samples of how he would have included more critical comments explaining normal usage. It might be pointed out that if Johnson had provided such full explanations, and still kept all his quotations, it would have necessitated adding a third volume. Smith's suggested approach would have been useful, but hardly practical.

The immediate reaction of contemporary readers was what might have been expected, with high praise from his friends, vigorous attacks by rivals or those who disagreed with his method, and divided opinions, praising some parts and condemning others. In the *Public Advertiser* for April 22 there were some complimentary verses by David Garrick, stressing English superiority over the French, and ending with the lines

> First Milton and Shakespeare, like Gods in the Fight,
> Have put their whole Drama and Epic to flight:
> In Satires, Epistles, and Odes would they cope,
> Their Numbers retreat before Dryden and Pope;
> And Johnson well-arm'd, like a Heroe of Yore,
> Has beat Forty French, and will beat Forty more.[5]

This was repeated in the *Gentleman's Magazine* for April and elsewhere.

Thomas Birch, who had been shown proofs of parts of the work just before publication, wrote to Johnson on April 3, congratulating the public on the appearance of a work which would be of such "service to the present age and to posterity," admiring the "industry, accuracy, and judgment" which Johnson had shown, and promising him the "approbation and thanks of every well-wisher to the honour of the English language."[6] Of course, this was largely formal praise. To his own friends Birch was less enthusiastic.

Even Johnson's close friends, when writing to each other, had reservations. For example, Tom Warton, writing to his brother Joe on April 19, commented:

> The Dictionary is arrived; the preface is noble: he tells the world that he performed the work "in sickness and in sorrow, in distress and inconvenience; not lulled in the soft obscurities of retirement, or sheltered in academic bowers; without the assistance or the *patronage* of any: as I shall gain or lose nothing by censure or applause, I dismiss the work from my hands with *frigid tranquillity,* careless of either." There is a grammar prefixed, and the history of the language is pretty full; but you may plainly perceive strokes of laxity and indolence. They are two most unwieldy volumes.[7]

Evidently Warton had been trying to think of some Oxford post which Johnson might secure, for he explained to his brother that one which had been proposed would not be available for forty years. Near the end of the letter he added, "I expect tonight a solemn letter from Johnson."

He wrote again on May 9: "Johnson's Dictionary is mightily liked here, but men who don't know what it is to *write,* and yet think they have a right to *judge,* pretend to carp." To which his brother replied that he had seen the reviews in the periodicals, adding that "his preface is fine."[8]

Perhaps the most disapproving evaluation came from Thomas Edwards, friend of Richardson and ironical opponent of Warburton's edition of Shakespeare, who in two letters to Daniel Wray accused Johnson of many errors.[9] To be sure, Edwards was a stalwart Whig, and much of his attack was politically based. In his first letter on May 23 he accused Johnson of including too many quotations from earlier writers, many of them useless, so that the *Dictionary* has become "a vehicle for Jacobite and high-flying tracts." Johnson, he thought, had cited too much from "party pamphlets of Swift" and from South's sermons. Then he added:

> But what most offends me is his crowding his work with those monstrous words from the things called Dictionaries such as adespotick, amnicolist, androtomy &c. words, if they may be called words, merely coined to fill up their books and which never were used by any who pretended to talk or write English.

Edwards found fault also with the printing—too many words misspelled, some lines misplaced and an author's name put in a wrong line. Over three weeks later, in his second letter to Wray, Edwards sums up his objections:

> Every page of Johnson, as I go on, convinces me of the truth of your observation that his needless number of authorities is intolerable; were these properly reduced and the long articles from Miller and Chambers together with the monsters from the Dictionaries left out, the work for ought I know might be brought into half the compass it now takes. But in its present condition it is, as most books lately published seem to be, nothing but a bookseller's job.

As it happened, Johnson never was aware of these particular attacks; yet he must have heard something like them from others.

Johnson's own personal prejudices showed clearly in a few of the definitions, though some of those which have been most objected to were either meant to be humorous, or have not been properly understood. For example, the Whigs of Johnson's time naturally disliked having their party called "a faction," when "Tory" was defined as "one who adheres to the ancient constitution of the state, and the apostolical hierarchy of the church of England." But as has recently been pointed out by Donald Greene, it is a mistake to consider Johnson's definitions in isolation, merely as examples of his idiosyncratic way of thinking. They must always be judged together with the accompanying quotations. Johnson is never rigid in his definitions. Normally they develop from his huge collection of illustrative material. Johnson's notorious definition of "Whig," so Greene insists, "is merely to direct the reader to the 'illustration' which follows it—a long and detailed exposition by the historian Gilbert Burnet (himself a staunch 'Whig') of how the word came into use."[10]

There are many amusing anecdotes describing the reactions of ordinary readers, such as Johnson's response when a lady asked him how he could possibly have made the mistake of defining "pastern" as the "knee of a horse." "Ignorance, Madam, pure ignorance," was his candid reply. Or the time a gentleman complained that his friend had vainly looked for the word "ocean." After triumphantly pointing out the definition to him, Johnson added, "Never mind it, Sir; perhaps your friend spells *ocean* with an *s*." And there is the account of his reply to some ladies who had praised him for not including all "naughty" four-letter words—"What, my dears! then you have been looking for them?"[11]

A young Irishman named Samuel Whyte was staying in London with the older brother of the wife of Johnson's friend Thomas Sheridan. Long afterwards he set down his recollection of what happened one day when he "rather abruptly" walked into the drawing room and found his host and Sheridan, and two other men "with two large folios on the table between them; Johnson's Dictionary, then but lately published."[12] One of the volumes lay open and the first word that caught his eye was "helter-skelter," which Johnson had suggested came from an old English expression meaning "the darkness of hell." The young man was not convinced and called out, "That's a very far-fetched etymology." The other three gentlemen appeared thunderstruck, and "staring at him for a moment, cast a significant glance towards the window, where stood an odd looking figure, which he had not before noticed, observing the boats passing on the Thames." This was Johnson himself, whom Whyte had never met. His host, "again casting an eye towards the window," asked Whyte, "Well, young sir! I suppose you can give a better derivation." To which Whyte replied, "O yes, sir! from the Latin; hilariter celeriter, merrily and swiftly; won't that do?" The older men made no reply, "but they hustled him out of the room as fast as they could," after some "judicious animadversions on his temerity." Fortunately, they thought, Johnson had been completely "absorbed in his own contemplations," and the young man had avoided "what perhaps he deserved, a good rap over the knuckles." Or perhaps Johnson would even have praised his good sense.

Inevitably there were complaints from readers who tried to look up a word but could not find it, as when Catherine Talbot and some friends wished to see what Johnson had to say about "athlete," but could find only "athletic."[13] Johnson had made no attempt to include everything. He left out "port" as a wine, although including other wines. He was purposely selective and included only about 40,000 words, not as many as were in Nathan Bailey's earlier *Dictionary*, though the total content was greater. Many readers were certain to disagree with some of his choices.

One of Johnson's generalizations drew a witty satirical reply from John Wilkes in a newspaper.[14] In his prefatory Grammar Johnson pointed out that the letter "H"

> seldom, perhaps never, begins any but the first syllable in which it is always sounded with a full breath, except in heir, herb, hostler, honour, humble, honest, humour and their derivatives.

To this Wilkes commented:

> The author of this remark must be a man of a quick *appre-hension*, and *compre-hensive* genius; but I can never forgive his *un-handsome be-haviour* to the poor *knight-hood*, *priest-hood*, and *widow-hood*, nor his *in-humanity* to all *man-hood* and *woman-hood*.

Wilkes also mentioned other words like *cow-herd, shep-herd, be-hind, un-healthy,* etc.

Just the same, Johnson still thought he was right, although in the fourth edition some years later he added a further explanation: "It some-times begins middle or final syllables in words compounded, as *blockhead*, or derived from the Latin, as *comprehended*."

One definition almost brought Johnson into court for defamation. In the Library of the Custom and Excise in London there is a document which describes the horror of the Commissioners of Excise on the appear-ance of the first edition of the *Dictionary*, when they found "excise" de-fined as "a hateful tax levied upon commodities and adjudged not by the common judges of property, but wretches hired by those to whom excise is paid."[15] At once they consulted the Attorney General, asking his opinion whether such a statement "will not be considered as a libel," and if so "whether it is not proper to proceed against the author, printers and pub-lishers thereof, or any and which of them by information or how other-wise." Nothing happened immediately, but on November 29 William Murray (later 1st Earl of Mansfield), the Attorney General, answered: "I am of opinion that it is a libel—but under all the circumstances I should think it better to give him an opportunity of altering his definition; and in case he don't to threaten him with an information." Time was thus allowed Johnson to correct his error. Resolutely, he refused to be frightened, and the same definition appeared unaltered in later editions. But the Board members, though there is evidence that they did keep watching for some reaction, never thought it wise to bring legal action.

A rival lexicographer, John Maxwell in Ireland, who had begun work as early as Johnson, and who had announced his coming work in the papers, on September 6 wrote to his brother listing all of Johnson's weaknesses.[16] According to Maxwell, Johnson did not go back far enough in choosing his authorities, ignored Scottish words and local dialects and phrases, omitted obsolete terms, the names of many religious sects, of rare animals, and many other things. He was "poor in his etymologies," and "confused and unmethodical" in "ranging" his "senses of words." Moreover, he thought there were numerous other defects. But when Maxwell published a specimen of his own work, which modern critics find "fantastic," it was obvious that he could not be taken seriously.

The worst attack of all came much later in a collection of ancient Scottish verses published in 1786.[17] Johnson, so the writer insisted, did not know "what he ought to have studied before he wrote a Dictionary; much less how to write a Dictionary itself." And the writer continued:

> Next age will pronounce his work, what it really is, a disgrace to the language. His examples, though already allowed his sole merit, are as ill-chosen as his etymologies; and very many are misquoted, or given to wrong authors, so that, such as they are, they can scarcely be depended upon. Any schoolmaster might have done what Johnson did. His Dictionary is merely a glossary to his own barbarous works. Indeed, that a man of very small learning (see his works), but confessedly quite ignorant of the Northern tongues, should pretend to write a dictionary at all; that a man, confessedly without taste, should attempt to define the nicer powers of words, a chief province of taste; that a man, confessedly the very worst writer in the language, save Sir Thomas Browne, and whose works are true *pages of inanity,* wrapt in barbarism, should set up for a judge of our language; are all ideas to excite laughter.

An obvious economic basis for adverse criticism was the high price put on the two volumes by the publishers. Only the well-to-do could afford such expensive acquisitions. So in late May the publishers came up with what may have seemed a possible solution, but one which scarcely had much chance of succeeding. Proposals were issued for a second edition, substantially the same text as that of the first, but to be issued in weekly parts.[18] For sixpence a week a reader could look forward to receiving 165 numbers, extending for three years and nine weeks, while for a shilling a week he could get the whole of it in half the time. But a user who had received up to "G" must have been frustrated if he wanted to look up a word beginning with "S." Apparently the success of this serial second edition was not outstanding. During the first ten years only between three and four thousand copies of the huge folio edition were sold.

What did do well was an octavo abridgment which appeared early the next year, selling for ten shillings. Drastically condensed, with quotations omitted, explanations shortened, and a number of words left out, these two smaller volumes sold at least 40,000 copies between 1756 and 1786. This became the standard authority in many households and was the one which Becky Sharp, in Thackeray's *Vanity Fair,* flung contemptuously from the coach as she departed from Miss Pinkerton's Academy.[19]

It might be useful also to point out that a third edition of the folio appeared in 1765, with only a few changes. All the while, Johnson, who was well aware of many mistakes and imperfections, had been keeping lists of possible corrections. These were finally embodied in the fourth edition of 1773. Recent studies have shown how extensive they were. One estimate is that there were over 15,000 changes in the two folio volumes, with many quotations omitted, others substituted, definitions changed or abridged, errors corrected. It was a major revision. Thus the fourth edition is now accepted as the best, representing more fully what Johnson wanted the *Dictionary* to be.[20]

When modern scholars attempt to evaluate Johnson's overall achievement they make clear that there was little new or original in his approach except his choice of quotations for moral purposes.[21] His work was merely the culmination of a long tradition. Earlier lexicographers on the Continent and in England had experimented with every device he used. Yet if he made no discoveries, Johnson was the first in England to combine in one reliable work the various functions we now demand of a dictionary.

Any idea that he may have had at the start that he would be able to fix the English language by his work was shown to be unrealistic as he moved along. He ended by being largely empirical, merely attempting to describe how words had been used by serious writers of the past, and through this evidence trying to explain normal usage. Moreover, he saw clearly the complexity of his subject—the many significations taken on by ordinary words—and was the first to attempt to provide as accurately as he could all the various shades of meaning. For the word "take" there are 134 meanings, and for "set" almost ninety. Even if today we can see many things more he should have done, as well as some errors, the overall coverage is astonishing.

Johnson's etymologies are often faulty; he was ignorant of Germanic philology; his accounts of grammar and the history of the language are not acceptable by modern standards; his selection of words is bookish and deficient in terms of commerce and trade; his style is sometimes cumbersome. But considering the state of philological studies in his time, Johnson avoided many pitfalls, and most of his definitions deserve high praise.

As we have seen, from the start some people poked fun at particular definitions and used them as a sign of Johnson's prejudices and pedantry. But the perverse examples make up only a tiny fraction of the work, and some like "oats" were meant to be amusing adaptations of earlier definitions. In every way Johnson was far ahead of his rivals. Those who had preceded him in England had not tried to define accurately all common words. Bailey obviously assumed that his readers knew what many words meant, so that there was no need for any full definition. Thus in his *Dictionarium Britannicum* of 1736 he defines "mouse" as "an animal well known," "cat" as "a domestic creature that kills mice," and "net" as a "device for catching fish, birds, &c." A typical example of how Johnson moves well ahead of his predecessors is the word "wheel." Bailey describes it vaguely as "a round utensil for various uses" while Johnson is more explicit, "a circular body that turns round upon an axis." Although Bailey gave long lists of words, with synonyms and some explanations of difficult terms, he made no attempt to illustrate correct idiom with examples from the works of major authors. All these deficiencies Johnson set out to remedy when he began his great project in 1746.

It is customary to laugh at the ponderous way Johnson defined simple objects. But at least he did not avoid the task. "Network" is a celebrated example—"any thing reticulated, or decussated, at equal distances, with interstices between the intersections." "Cough" is another which has provided much merriment: "a convulsion of the lungs, vellicated by some sharp serosity. It is pronounced *coff*." But in Ephraim Chambers's *Cyclopaedia* (second edition, 1738) "cough" is described as "a disease affecting the lungs, occasioned by a sharp serous humour, vellicating the fibrous coat thereof, and urging it to a discharge by spitting." Johnson at least condensed Chambers's verbose definition.

It was easy for those who were looking for things to attack to find what they sought. If some definitions were too complicated, others were too simple. James T. Callender in his *Deformities of Dr. Samuel Johnson,* published in 1782, pointed out several examples: "boy" ("a male child; not a girl"), "a runner" ("one that runs"), "husband" ("the correlative to wife: a man married to a woman"), "butter" ("an unctuous substance"), "parsnip" ("a plant").[22] Boswell could not resist pointing out various other amusing instances.

Not all Johnson's definitions would meet twentieth-century standards. It was easy for his contemporaries to point out some that they thought useless or wrong, and the inexorable march of language has rendered many of his judgments obsolete. Today we would scarcely call "lesser" "a barbarous corruption of *less*," (though basically Johnson was right), or "tiny" "a burlesque word." Most readers today accept "prig," "ruse," and "shabby" without question. We do not think quite so badly as did Johnson of "tiff," "ignoramus," and "stingy." Yet we may smile to find "lingo" included, and agree that it is "a low cant word." But examples such as these represented only a very small percentage of the total coverage. Today, we recognize that the definitions are one of the chief strengths of Johnson's *Dictionary*. They have been the basis for the work of all modern lexicographers.[23]

Johnson's greatest contribution, however, did not come in the verbal part of the work. Although he may jokingly have referred to himself as "a harmless drudge," he had a more exalted ideal always before him. In addition to being a linguistic authority, his *Dictionary* was to be a great storehouse of philosophy, theology, history, and literature. By the judicious choice of quotations he meant to instruct and inspire his readers, so that the man who actually looked up the meaning of even the homeliest word would also be provided with some practical or moral guidance. Occasionally the application may make us smile. Thus Johnson illustrated the use of the noun "table" by a sentence from the philosopher John Locke: "Children at a *table* never asked for any thing, but contentedly took what was given them." And the entry for "razor" contained a quotation from Richard Hooker: "Zeal, except ordered aright, useth the *razor* with such eagerness, that the life of religion is thereby hazarded." Johnson's own strong opinions are reflected everywhere in the selections. As Carlyle put it, "Had Johnson left nothing but his *Dictionary*, one might have traced there a great intellect, a genuine man."[24]

In this way the *Dictionary* became an extensive anthology of English prose and verse. In the first volume alone, from A through K, there are about 24,000 quotations from the English poets, with more than 8,500 from Shakespeare, over 5,600 from Dryden, 2,700 from Milton; and there were some 10,000 from the philosophers, with over 1,600 from Locke, and some 5,000 from religious writers. The two volumes contained over 116,000 quotations, and Johnson had collected twice that many. No wonder people regarded the *Dictionary* as more than a reference work! Robertson, the Scottish historian, is said to have read it through twice. Robert Browning, so says one of his biographers (Mrs. Sutherland Orr), qualified himself for the profession of literature "by reading and digesting the whole of Johnson's Dictionary." Others used it for general education, as well as to enlarge their vocabularies.

In his own time, and for many years thereafter, Johnson's *Dictionary*, even with all its minor defects, was recognized as a major achievement in the development of modern culture. The accomplishment of one lone scholar, slaving away in an attic in Gough Square, dominated the field for the next hundred years. Increasingly, foreign visitors to London asked to meet this man who by himself in such a short time had produced such a remarkable work. The Reverend Dean Jacob Serenius, author of an Anglo-Danish dictionary, wrote from Sweden on March 5, 1757, to Edward Lye in England:

> Nothing will be perfect, much less a Dictionary. But if any thing comes near perfection it is that of your Johnson's work. I am astonished at that gentleman's labour which is enough for two men's life. Pray let me know the character of him and his employment.[25]

So Johnson came to be called "Dictionary Johnson."

CHAPTER X

Still the Hack

IF PUBLICATION OF the *Dictionary* established Johnson's international reputation, it did nothing to improve his desperate financial condition, at least not for some time. When the booksellers arranged a tavern meeting to settle all accounts, they produced large numbers of receipts for money advanced him, some for very small sums. The records, instead of becoming a basis for an additional payment, showed that he had been overpaid. The original agreement signed back in 1746 had stipulated that he be given the overall sum of £1575. Actually he had received more than £100 over that amount. As one later account put it, Johnson "was confounded on finding the balance against himself, for he kept no account, and that he had been working for some time for nothing. The creditor instantly became the debtor. The booksellers generously made him a present of the difference, and paid his reckoning for him."[1] Johnson was deeply grateful, and always thought of booksellers as generous men. Nevertheless, he still had to live, and he could see no substantial source of income.

For the moment, he thought of doing some traveling, for relief from all the strains of the winter and spring. But where should he go? He knew he ought to go up to Lichfield to see his mother; he wanted to talk to his friends in Oxford; and he even considered a trip into Lincolnshire to visit his young friend Bennett Langton. Langton had written to him twice, and on May 6, 1755, Johnson dispatched an answer:

> I have indeed published my book, of which I beg to know your
> father's judgment and yours, and I have now stayed long

enough to watch its progress into the world. It has, you see, no patrons, and I think has yet had no opponents except the critics of the coffeehouse, whose outcries are soon dispersed into the air, and are thought on no more: from this therefore I am at liberty, and think of taking the opportunity of this interval to make an excursion, and why not then into Lincolnshire, or to mention a stronger attraction why not to dear Mr. Langton? I will give the true reason which I know you will approve. I have a mother more than eighty years old, who has counted the days to the publication of my book in hopes of seeing me, and to her, if I can disengage myself here, I resolve to go. . . .

I shall rejoice to hear from you till I can see you, and will see you as soon as I can, for when the duty that calls me to Lichfield is discharged, my inclination will hurry me to Langton.[2]

But nothing happened. Less than a week later, on May 13, he wrote to Thomas Warton in Oxford:

I am grieved that you should think me capable of neglecting your letters, and beg that you never will admit any such suspicion again. I purpose to come down next week, if you shall be there, or any other week that shall be more agreeable to you; therefore let me know. I can stay this visit but a week but intend to make preparations for a longer stay next time, being resolved not to lose sight of the University. . . . I think to come to Kettle Hall.

The same day he wrote to his old schoolmate, Edmund Hector, in Birmingham: "I shall come into the country if I can this summer, and will certainly visit him whom I have so often visited in former days. Are you too come to the age in which *former days* begins to have an awful sound, and to impart an idea mixed of pain and pleasure?" But still he made no move.

Almost a month later he wrote to Warton:

It is strange how many things will happen to intercept every pleasure, though it [be] only that of two friends meeting together. I have promised myself every day to inform you when you might expect me at Oxford, and have not been able to fix a time. The time however is, I think, at last come and I promise myself to repose in Kettle Hall one of the first nights of the next week. I am afraid my stay with you cannot be long, but what is the inference? We must endeavour to make it cheerful. I wish your brother could meet us, that we might go and drink tea with Mr. Wise in a body.

Then two weeks later he wrote again:

To talk of coming to you and not yet to come has an air of trifling, which I would not willingly have among you, and which, I believe, you will not impute to me when I have told you that since my promise, two of our partners are dead, and that I was solicited to suspend my excursion till we could recover from our confusion. . . . I hope now to see you next week, but next week is but another name for tomorrow which has been noted for promising and deceiving.

It was Paul Knapton and Thomas Longman, both of whom had shares in the *Dictionary,* who died so unexpectedly. Somehow Johnson could not tear himself away.

It was more than temporary matters of this sort that kept Johnson from deciding what to do. He was in a difficult state of indecision. Why could he not bring himself to go to see his mother? If he went to Oxford, could that be thought of as a sign of lack of affection for his parent? Which should come first?

Earlier I have described the divided, almost contradictory feelings Johnson had in regard to his mother. In one way he thought he loved her, but somehow he could not admire her. And now he could not bring himself to face her. During the eighteen years since leaving Lichfield he had not been back. As George Irwin has suggested, "The very thought of coming face to face with his mother again, of hearing her voice again, aroused unaccountable, devastating emotions."[3] Actually he did not travel to Staffordshire at all in the summer of 1755; nor did he ever do so until after his mother had died.

His feelings about the midlands were probably further complicated by his emotional involvement with a pious lady named Hill Boothby, who was living at Tissington in Derbyshire. Johnson had first met Miss Boothby in 1739, when he was visiting his old friend John Taylor in Ashbourne.[4] For years afterward he did not see her, but when, a year after Tetty's death, he had resolved to seek a second wife, Hill Boothby was one of those he must have considered. A year older than himself, she was learned, religious, and physically attractive. Even though years later Johnson admitted to Mrs. Thrale that Miss Boothby "pushed her piety to bigotry, her devotion to enthusiasm" and that she had "somewhat disqualified herself for the duties of *this* life, by her perpetual aspirations after the *next*,"[5] she nevertheless had all the qualities he most admired in a woman. On the other hand, he knew that she was not available, for at the time of the death in March 1753 of her close friend, the wife of her cousin William Fitzherbert, she had promised to devote her life to bringing up their children. And Johnson knew that nothing would make her break this solemn commitment. Thus he was caught in an impossible situation and could never bring himself to go up to see her.

But while he was trying to make up his mind where to go outside of London for a rest, and vacillating as to other matters, he kept up some social life. Indeed, two other ladies who may have been on Johnson's hypothetical list of possible candidates for his second wife were the intelligent and attractive Cotterell sisters, daughters of an admiral who lived in London. Boswell says that Johnson met the Cotterells as early as 1738, when he was living in Castle Street, and frequently used to visit the two ladies "who lived opposite him,"[6] but Charlotte Cotterell, who became Mrs. Lewis, later wrote to Mrs. Piozzi that "we never saw Johnson till some years after his wife died," and it was about a year after that "when Mr. Reynolds met him at Fanny's."[7] Thus it would appear that Johnson did not meet the Cotterells until 1754 or 1755.

From one of Johnson's surviving letters, dated July 19, 1755 (whether to Frances or to Charlotte is not clear), it is evident that his feelings for the sisters had a sentimental tinge. Miss Cotterell had been out of town, perhaps up in the midlands; when Johnson accidentally heard that she was back he quickly rushed over to see her. It turned out that she was not at home, but she lost no time in writing to apologize, and evidently to invite him, and some others, to return. In his immediate answer he explained what had happened:

> When I had missed you I went away disappointed, and did not know that my vexation would be so amply repaid by so kind a letter. A letter indeed can but imperfectly supply the place of its writer, at least of such a writer as Miss Cotterel, and a letter which makes me still more desire your presence is but a weak consolation under the necessity of living longer without you; with this however I must be for a time content, as much content at least as discontent will suffer me, for Mr. Baretti being a single being in this part of the world, and entirely clear from all engagements, takes the advantage of his independence and will come before me, for which if I could blame him I should punish him, but my own heart tells me that he only does to me what, if I could, I should do to him.[8]

Then came a reference to his stepdaughter, Lucy Porter, in Lichfield, who had evidently also been doing some traveling.

I hope Mrs. Porter when she came to her favourite place, found her house dry, and her woods growing, and the breeze whistling, and the birds singing, and her own heart dancing. And for you, Madam, whose heart cannot yet dance to such music, I know not what to hope; indeed I could hope everything that would please you, except that perhaps the absence of higher pleasures is necessary to keep some little place vacant in your remembrance for Madam, your most obliged most obedient and most humble servant   Sam: Johnson

Just why Miss Cotterell at the time was incapable of enjoying "higher pleasures" is not clear—perhaps because she did not have a house in the country. Certainly there is an emotional quality in Johnson's letter which is surprising. He admired both Cotterell sisters, and may even have hoped that one of them might sentimentally reciprocate.

Although Johnson was pleased to visit people in the upper class, he did not think it necessary to make any effort to dress up for the occasion. With his lack of money he could not buy any new clothes. Once when he visited Miss Cotterell there occurred an episode which Frances Reynolds recounts, having heard the story from her brother:

> His best dress was at that time so very mean that one after-noon as he was following some ladies up stairs, on a visit to a lady of fashion, the housemaid, not knowing him, suddenly seized him by the shoulder and exclaimed, "Where are you going?" striving at the same time to drag him back; but a gentle-man who was a few steps behind prevented her from doing or saying more, and Mr. Johnson growled all the way up stairs, as well he might. He seemed much chagrined and apparently dis-posed to revenge the insult of the maid upon the mistress. Unluckily, whilst in this humour, a lady of high rank happen-ing to call on Miss Cotterell, he was much offended with her for not introducing him to her Ladyship, at least not in the manner he liked, and still more for her seeming to show more attention to this Lady than to him. After sitting some time silent, medi-tating how to *down* Miss C., he addressed himself to Mr. Rey-nolds who sat next him, and, after a few introductory words, with a loud voice said, "I wonder which of us two could get most money by his trade in one week, were we to work hard at it from morning till night." I don't remember the answer, but I know that the lady, rising soon after, went away without knowing what trade they were of. She might probably suspect Mr. Johnson to be a poor author by his dress, and because neither a porter, a chairman, or a blacksmith, trades much more suitable to his apparent abilities, were not quite so suitable to

the place she saw him in. This incident Dr. Johnson used to mention with great glee—how he had *downed* Miss C., though at the same time he professed a great friendship and esteem for that lady.[9]

It must be admitted that Charlotte Cotterell, many years later, in a letter to Mrs. Piozzi, denied that the story was completely accurate. It was true that the Duchess of Hamilton and Lady Donegal had come for a visit while Johnson and Reynolds "were sitting with Fanny," but Charlotte insisted that Fanny

> cannot recollect that there was any offense, nor that any party seemed offended; the conversation she does not recollect, except that when the Ladies were gone Johnson said to her, thank you Madam, *I was never in company with a Duchess before.*[10]

The summer of 1755 was a difficult time for Johnson. As Arthur Murphy later commented,

> His mind, at this time strained and over-laboured by constant exertion, called for an interval of repose and indolence. But indolence was the time of danger; it was then that his spirits, not employed abroad, turned with inward hostility against himself.[11]

With all his uncertainty came the customary qualms of conscience and a determination somehow to change his habits. Thus on July 13 he wrote in his journal:

> Having lived hitherto in perpetual neglect of public worship and though for some years past not without an habitual reverence for the sabbath yet without that attention to its religious duties which Christianity requires, I will once more form a scheme of life for that day such as alas I have often vainly formed which, when my mind is capable of settled practice, I hope to follow.
>   1 To rise early and in order to it to go to sleep early on Saturday.
>   2 To use some extraordinary devotion in the morning.
>   3 To examine the tenor of my life and particularly the last week and to mark my advances in religion or recession from it.
>   4 To read the Scripture methodically with such helps as are at hand.

5 To go to church twice.
6 To read books of divinity either speculative or practical.
7 To instruct my family.
8 To wear off by meditation any worldly soil contracted in the week.[12]

Perhaps suggested by the sixth part of this entry, Johnson also wrote down a prayer about this time with the title "On the Study of Philosophy, as an Instrument of Living":

> July. O Lord, who hast ordained labour to be the lot of man, and seest the necessities of all thy creatures, bless my studies and endeavours; feed me with food convenient for me; and if it shall be thy good pleasure to intrust me with plenty, give me a compassionate heart, that I may be ready to relieve the wants of others; let neither poverty nor riches estrange my heart from Thee, but assist me with thy grace so to live as that I may die in thy favour.

Almost thirteen years later Johnson found among his papers a copy of this undated prayer, and added the note: "This study was not pursued." At the same time, finding another prayer labeled "Study of Tongues," he added the note: "Of this prayer there is no date, nor can I tell when it was written; but I think it was in Gough-Square, after the Dictionary was ended. I did not study what I then intended. Transcribed June 26, 1768."

As a matter of fact, none of his emotional resolves made any change in his habits. Although he knew he should lead a more regular life, he lacked the firm determination to force himself to change.

After all his vacillation, Johnson did finally reach Oxford by early August.[13] All we know about this visit to his university is that he was kept up so late talking to Wise, the librarian, that he could not say goodby to Robert Chambers and thank him for his "company and kindness." Consequently he dispatched a note to Chambers, who was going to London: "As you are soon to come to town I shall be glad if you will pay my barber whom I forgot for a week's shaving etc. and call at Mrs. Simpson's for a box of pills which I left behind me, and am loath to lose." It was always useful to have younger friends ready to do errands, when one was in an absent-minded mood. We know also that while in Oxford Johnson spent some time looking at manuscripts of Sir Thomas More's writings.

There is no evidence as to how long this visit to Oxford lasted, but once back in London, he returned to his footloose existence. Arthur Murphy describes Johnson's life about this time:

He resigned himself to indolence, took no exercise, rose about two, and then received the visits of his friends. Authors, long since forgotten, waited on him as their oracle, and he gave responses in the chair of criticism. He listened to the complaints, the schemes, and the hopes and fears of a crowd of inferior writers, "who," he said, in the words of Roger Ascham, "lived, *men knew not how, and died obscure, men marked not when.*" He believed that he could give a better history of Grubstreet than any man living. His house was filled with a succession of visitors till four or five in the evening. During the whole time he presided at his tea-table. Tea was his favourite beverage.[14]

Who were all these unimportant people who drank tea with Johnson and occupied his time? Once during this period Johnson wrote down a list of people he knew, for what purpose no one can tell. Were they visits he had to repay, or merely the most active of his present acquaintances? It is a fairly long list of forty-one names (only last names, with no identifying first names), not alphabetically arranged. Most of the people can easily be identified, though there are mysteries.

The list was shown to John Wilson Croker by Thomas Harwood, the historian of Staffordshire, and Croker included it in his notes.[15] Since then the manuscript has disappeared from sight.

There were five Ivy Lane Club members who were still active: Richard Bathurst, John Hawkesworth, John Hawkins, John Payne, and John Ryland. There were seven publishers: Robert Dodsley, David Henry of the *Gentleman's Magazine,* Andrew Millar, John Newbery, Thomas Osborne, William Strahan, and Jacob Tonson; four friends with Lichfield connections: Capt. David Brodie (Molly Aston's husband), David Garrick, Joseph Simpson and John Taylor of Ashbourne; three women: Mrs. Desmoulins (Tetty's former companion and not yet a member of Johnson's household), Ann Gardiner (wife of a tallow chandler), and Charlotte Lennox. Those with literary connections of some sort were James Elphinston (Strahan's brother-in-law), Richard Gifford (a poet), James Grainger (poet, or James Granger, biographer), John Boyle, Earl of Orrery, Samuel Richardson, William Rose (schoolmaster and translator), and Thomas Tyers (author, who later wrote a short life of Johnson).

Others were Joseph Fowke (East India Company official), Johnson's physician, Dr. Thomas Lawrence, Joshua Reynolds (painter), Sir Thomas Robinson (colonial governor), and Thomas Wilson (rector of St. Margaret's, Westminster). All these we can identify with some certainty. But there are a few whom we cannot. Was "Baker" supposed to be David (dramatic writer) or George (physician)? Did "Lloyd" refer to Robert (writer), or Sampson (banker), or someone else? Was "Gregory" Dr. John (who came to London in 1754)? Was "Weston" Edward (editor of the *London Gazette*)?

There are six names which are not easily identified: Craster, Drew, Garden, Gully, Sherrard, and a second Millar. (The name appears twice in the list, and one must have been the publisher. Could the other have been someone with the name Miller?) Of course, some of these may have been misreadings of Johnson's difficult handwriting. For example, "Sherrard" could have been meant to be "Sheward" for "Seward." And might "Gully" have been meant to be "Collet," Johnson's barber? We will never know until the original manuscript turns up. But at least the list does give an idea of the range of Johnson's connections.

The fact that the *Dictionary* publishers Paul Knapton and Thomas Longman, who died in June 1755, are not included would suggest that the list was set down after that date, and since Reynolds is included along with Bathurst, who left England late in 1756, it must have been made in late 1755 or 1756.

Full of uncertainty and lacking energy, Johnson could not decide what to do next professionally. He badly needed money, but how should he get it? For a time he picked up odd writing jobs which would not take much time, almost anything that was remunerative. Indeed, for the next year he was involved in more miscellaneous activity than ever before. He did some editing, wrote prefaces and dedications for his friends, perhaps some periodical reviews, may have composed some sermons, and possibly composed a famous parliamentary speech. Anything that was not immoral and brought him some cash was acceptable. And he considered plans for several larger projects.

He had in 1754 helped Zachariah Williams (the father of blind Anna, who lived in his house at Gough Square) prepare *An Account of an Attempt to Ascertain the Longitude at Sea,* and had touched up a preface and perhaps some footnotes for Baretti's *Introduction to the Italian Language.*[16] He helped Mary Masters with her *Familiar Letters and Poems on Several Occasions,* and, as Boswell put it, "illuminated" her work "here and there with a ray of his own genius."[17] Late in the autumn he provided a dedication for Charlotte Lennox's translation of *Sully's Memoirs,* did the dedication and possibly portions of a preface for William Payne's *Introduction to the Game of Draughts,* and composed a new preface for the octavo edition of his own *Dictionary.*[18]

He may well have done shorter pieces for periodicals such as the *Gentleman's Magazine,* and when Zachariah Williams died on July 12, 1755, he wrote an obituary for one of the newspapers.[19]

The ascription to Johnson of some of these miscellaneous pieces must remain conjectural. For instance, Hawkins later claimed that before 1760 Johnson composed "pulpit discourses" at the request of "sundry beneficed clergymen" for a regular fee of two guineas. Hawkins added:

> and such was his notion of justice, that having been paid he considered them so absolutely the property of the purchaser as to renounce all claim to them. He reckoned he had written about forty sermons; but, except as to some, knew not in what hands they were.[20]

He evidently found writing sermons not too difficult, and once said, "I have begun a sermon after dinner, and sent it off by post that night." Alas, it is impossible to be sure just when many were written, or when or where they were delivered.

Nearly ten years later, in 1765, Thomas Birch wrote to his patron Philip Yorke, who had succeeded to the Earldom of Hardwicke, that he had been told that the first parliamentary address of William Gerard Hamilton which he delivered in November 1755, the one which gave him the nickname "Single-Speech," had really been drafted by Samuel Johnson.[21] Unfortunately, there is no other corroborating evidence. To be sure, we know that in the early sixties Johnson did some work for Hamilton. But did he in November 1755? Unfortunately no copies of the speech have ever come to light. Still, we know something of the contents from a random comment by Horace Walpole, who had heard it delivered. On November 15, 1755, he wrote to Henry Seymour Conway that the speech "was set, and full of antithesis, but those antitheses were full of argument."[22] How better could one describe the style of Samuel Johnson?

As for larger projects, there is some evidence that Johnson even began work on a commercial dictionary. William Cooke, in his short life of Johnson which appeared shortly after Johnson's death, included the story that

> he soon after the publication of his Dictionary, made a proposal to a number of booksellers convened for that purpose, of writing a *Dictionary of Trade and Commerce*. This proposal went round the room without his receiving any immediate answer; at length a well known *son of the trade,* since dead, remarkable *for the abruptness of his manners,* replied, "Why Doctor, what the D---l do you know of trade and commerce?" The Doctor very modestly answered, "Not much, Sir, I confess in the *practical* line—but I believe I could glean, from different authors of authority on the subject, such materials as would answer the purpose very well."[23]

Murphy even claims that Johnson was paid for some work on this project.[24] But when it turned out that another author, Richard Rolt, was working on a similar scheme and was probably more advanced, Johnson gave up the idea and may have turned over to him what materials he had collected. In any case, when Rolt's *Dictionary of Trade and Commerce* was published in February 1756, it contained a preface written by Johnson.

In mid-December Johnson had a bad attack of a bronchial ailment, and on the twenty-ninth wrote to an old friend, Lewis Paul, in Hammersmith:

> I would not have you think that I forgot or neglect you. I have never been out of doors since you saw me. On the day after I had been with you I was seized with a hoarseness which still continues; I had then a cough so violent that I once fainted under its convulsions. I was afraid of my lungs. My physician bled me yesterday and the day before, first almost against his will, but the next day without any contest. I had been bled once before, so that I have lost in all 54 ounces. I live on broths, and my cough, I thank God, is much abated so that I can sleep.[25]

He promised to come to visit him as soon as his doctor gave him permission to travel. "Change of air is often of use." The next day he wrote a long letter to Hill Boothby, who was also very ill:

> It is again midnight, and I am again alone. With what meditation shall I amuse this waste hour of darkness and vacuity. If I turn my thoughts upon myself what do I perceive but a poor helpless being reduced by a blast of wind to weakness and misery.

Although he could not explain the reason for his sudden illness, he imputed it "to some sudden succession of cold to heat, such as in the common road of life cannot be avoided, and against which no precaution can be taken." His present illness, he continued, had depressed his confidence and made him reconsider all his vain "resolutions of a better life." He pleaded with her:

> Continue, my dearest, your prayers for me, that no good reso[lu]-tion may be vain. You think, I believe, better of me than I deserve. I hope to be in time what I wish to be, and what I have hitherto satisfied myself too readily with only wishing.

Near the end of the letter, paraphrasing Descartes, Johnson added, "It is as good a consequence 'I write therefore I am alive.' I might give another

'I am alive therefore I love Miss Boothby,' but that I hope our friendship may be of far longer duration than life."

The same day he also wrote to his stepdaughter, Lucy Porter, in Lichfield:

> I have been ill for about a fortnight with a cold which was extremely troublesome, and produced a cough that I one night fainted away. This has pretty much hindered me, and put my affairs a little behindhand, and my physician tells me I must go out of London to recover. All this, however, I should not have troubled you with sending an hundred miles, but for a particular reason. A report was yesterday running in the town that I was dead; the report was occasioned by my illness and the death of my next neighbour; I am afraid the story should get into the papers, and distress my dear Mother. I therefore write to tell you that though not quite well, I am almost well, that I am coming down soon, that I wish you all many very many happy years.[26]

Then on December 31 he wrote another long letter to Hill Boothby, with affectionate phrases like "Dear Angel," and ending with "I love you and honour you, and am very unwilling to lose you." Most of the letter, however, was filled with fascinating medical advice.

> Give me leave, who have thought much on medicine, to propose to you an easy and I think a very probable remedy for indigestion and lubricity of the bowels. Dr. Laurence has told me your case. Take an ounce of dried orange peel finely powdered, divide it into scruples, and take one scruple at a time in any manner; the best way is perhaps to drink it in a glass of hot red port, or to eat it first and drink the wine after it. If you mix cinnamon or nutmeg with the powder it were not worse, but it will be more bulky and so more troublesome. This is a medicine not disgusting, not costly, easily tried, and if not found useful easily left off.
>
> I would not have you offer it to the doctor as mine. Physicians do not love intruders, yet do not take it without his leave. But do not be easily put off, for it is in my opinion very likely to help you, and not likely to do you harm. Do not take too much in haste; a scruple one in three hours or about five scruples a day will be sufficient to begin, or less if you find any aversion. I think using sugar with it might be bad, if syrup, use old syrup of quinces, but even that I do not like. I should think better of conserve of sloes. Has the doctor mentioned the bark?

In powder you could hardly take it; perhaps you might bear the infusion?[27]

Perhaps it was Johnson's conscience that made him take "five scruples a day."

Despite the fact that on New Year's Day Johnson thanked God for his "recovery from sickness," his troubles were far from over. And there continues to be one haunting question. Might this serious illness have been not merely physical but in some way related to his guilty feelings about his mother? As George Irwin has suggested, could it have been one way of justifying his refusal to go up to the midlands to see his mother and the ailing Hill Boothby?[28] There can be no doubt that his desperate feelings of guilt were still there.

Johnson wrote to Hill Boothby every few days, once twice in a single day. It is the most emotional series of letters in his entire lifetime, filled with such terms as "My Sweet Angel," and "my Dearest." On January 3 he wrote again, with news of his health:

I am extremely obliged to you for the kindness of your enquiry. After I had written to you Dr Lawrence came, and would have given some oil and sugar, but I took Rhenish and water, and recovered my voice. I yet cough much and sleep ill. I have been visited by another doctor today, but I laughed at his Balsam of Peru. I fasted on Tuesday, Wednesday and Thursday, and felt neither hunger nor faintness.

But his chief concern was for her own progress, for the news of her ill health was ominous. On January 8 he dashed off a short note beginning, "I beg of you to endeavour to live," and then added: "I am in great trouble; if you can write three words to me, be pleased to do it. I am afraid to say much, and cannot say nothing when my dearest is in danger." Waiting for news of her condition was almost unbearable.

When news of Hill Boothby's death on January 16 reached Johnson he was overwhelmed. As Baretti once told Mrs. Thrale, Johnson "was almost distracted with his grief, and that the friends about him had much ado to calm the violence of his emotion."[29]

In his customary manner he at once wrote a prayer:

O Lord God, almighty disposer of all things, in whose hands are life and death, who givest comforts and takest them away, I return thee thanks for the good example of Hill Boothby, whom thou hast now taken away, and implore thy grace, that

I may improve the opportunity of instruction which thou hast afforded me, by the knowledge of her life, and by the sense of her death; that I may consider the uncertainty of my present state, and apply myself earnestly to the duties which thou hast set before me; that living in thy fear, I may die in thy favour. . . .[30]

Despite all his physical and emotional problems, however, Johnson was able during January 1756 to rouse himself to help sell tickets for a benefit performance which he had persuaded Garrick to arrange for the support of Miss Williams, who was still living in the Gough Square house. He wrote numerous notes, begged leave "to trouble" Thomas Birch and John Ryland with blocks of tickets, urged Elizabeth Carter to stir up interest, and asked help of Catherine Talbot. He interceded with one of the Cave family at St. John's Gate to print the tickets. And on January 22 he undoubtedly was among the audience who watched Aaron Hill's *Merope* and *The Englishman in Paris* at Drury Lane. The friendly publicity evidently worked, and Anna Williams was the richer by some £200.[31]

Even by February his physical problems were not over. One eye became inflamed, and it did not quickly return to normal. In a letter to Richardson he remarked: "The inflammation is come again into my eye, so that I can read very little."[32] Apparently the trouble continued for some time.

With one crippling illness after another, Johnson had not been able to do much writing. Finally, the inevitable happened, and on Tuesday, March 16, he was arrested for debt and carried to a sponging house. He was not worried, for he was sure that one of his friends would act quickly to rescue him. Thus he wrote to Samuel Richardson:

I am obliged to entreat your assistance; I am now under an arrest for five pounds eighteen shillings. Mr. Strahan from whom I should have received the necessary help in this case is not at home, and I am afraid of not finding Mr. Millar. If you will be so good as to send me this sum, I will very gratefully repay you, and add it to all former obligations.[33]

According to one apocryphal anecdote, Johnson later told someone that while in the sponging house he was so sure of his deliverance that before Richardson's reply arrived he joked with "the rascal" who had him in custody, and "did so over a pint of adulterated wine, for which, at that instant, I had no money to pay."[34] As expected, Richardson at once sent six guineas, eight shillings more than was needed, and Johnson was free to go home, and able to pay for the adulterated wine. Three days later he wrote again to Richardson, to send thanks for his generous help, and included as a present a copy of his recently published edition of Browne's *Christian Morals*.

Something else that aggravated Johnson's dismal condition was the gradual dissolution of the Ivy Lane Club. Of the ten original members only a few were still active. Salter and McGhie were either dead or dying; Barker had moved away from London; Dyer no longer attended; Hawkesworth was "forming new connections"; and Hawkins had married a well-to-do lady and preferred to stay home in the evening. As Hawkins described what had happened, "The consequence was that our symposium at the King's Head broke up, and he who had first formed us into a society was left with fewer around him than were able to support it."[35] For some years Johnson found himself without a regular club to stimulate talk and convivial entertainment.

The mental breakdown of one of Johnson's young friends, Kit Smart, was the cause of some miscellaneous writing early in 1756. As pointed out earlier, Smart had highly praised the *Rambler* essays in *The Student,* and in 1751 Johnson had written his "Life of Cheynel" for this periodical. In the late autumn of 1755 a contract was signed by Smart and Richard Rolt as writers, Edmund Allen as printer, and Thomas Gardner, bookseller, to produce a new periodical to be called *The Universal Visiter and Monthly Memorialist*.[36] The writers were supposed to supply two-thirds of the copy and each would then receive a quarter of the profits. There were other stipulations which later caused much controversy. The chief trouble was that by the time the first number appeared on February 2, 1756, Smart was suffering from a mental disorder, or at least was showing signs of the madness to come, though he still seemed able to do some writing or could use pieces he had written earlier. Nevertheless, it was soon apparent that if he were to meet his responsibilities for half of the literary sections he would have to obtain help. Fortunately this was readily available, and Johnson, Garrick, Thomas Percy, Charles Burney, and others stepped in to fill the gap.

Hawkins insists that all essays signed "**" were by Johnson, but Boswell accepted only three.[37] Modern scholars continue to dispute the matter. It may well be that the asterisks were not meant to identify a single person, but only to refer to Smart or one of his replacements. The first contribution that we can be certain came from Johnson's pen appeared in the March issue, "Further Thoughts on Agriculture," which followed a piece by Rolt which had appeared the month before. Johnson also wrote the leading article in the April issue, a bitter and caustic attack on the present state of literature in England. He stressed the hardships of modern authors, "like wolves in long winters," who

> are forced to prey on one another. The *Reviewer,* and *Critical Reviewers,* the *Remarkers,* and *Examiners,* can satisfy their hunger only by devouring their brethren . . . they are hungry, and hunger must be satisfied; and these savages, when their bellies are full, will fawn on those whom they now bite.[38]

The tone and theme mirror Johnson's own distressed condition in March and early April 1756.

In the May issue Johnson supplied a "Dissertation on the Epitaphs Written by Pope." His possible contributions to the January, February, and June numbers remain controversial. What appears most likely is that they were provided in late February and March, before his commitment to the new *Literary Magazine.*

Whether Johnson was paid for his contributions, or gave them as a present to help the situation of the rapidly disintegrating Christopher Smart, is not known. Johnson's later comments show that he was never quite clear just what he was doing or why. Apparently he was not certain what Smart's contract involved. But at least by May he was dubious as to how much good he was achieving. Years later he remarked to Boswell:

> I wrote for some months in "The Universal Visitor" for poor Smart, while he was mad, not then knowing the terms on which he was engaged to write, and thinking I was doing him good. I hoped his wits would soon return to him. Mine returned to me, and I wrote in "The Universal Visitor" no longer.[39]

There can be little doubt that his work for this periodical was merely a casual interlude, stemming from a concern for one of his fellow writers.

All in all, this was one of the unhappiest periods of Johnson's life. His constant troubles—emotional, physical, financial, social—kept him in a black mood of despondency. Somehow he must find regular employment to occupy his time and bring in sufficient money to keep him going. Fortunately this would soon be possible with the start of a new periodical, the *Literary Magazine,* and of a large new project, an edition of the works of Shakespeare.

CHAPTER XI

Speaking His Mind—
The Literary Magazine

By mid-April 1756 Johnson was still eagerly trying to find some journalistic work which would help him stay alive. On the fifteenth he wrote to Joseph Warton, who had become second master of Winchester School, commenting on Warton's *Essay on Pope* and asking for news of "poor dear Collins." As for himself, Johnson added that he had not lately done much. "I have been ill in the winter, and my eye has been inflamed, but I please myself with the hopes of doing many things with which I have long pleased and deceived myself."[1]

One of the "things" he had long been thinking about was the possibility of starting an international periodical. Many years later William Adams described to Boswell a visit he had made to Gough Square near the end of 1755 or early 1756:

> He found the parlour floor covered with parcels of foreign journals and English reviews and he told Dr. Adams he meant to undertake a Review. "How Sir," said Dr. Adams, "can you think of doing it alone. All branches of knowledge must be considered in it. Do you know mathematics? Do you know natural history?" Dr. Johnson answered, "I must do as well as I can. My chief purpose is to give my countrymen a view of what is doing in literature upon the continent, and I shall have in a good measure the choice of my subjects." Dr. Adams suggested it would be better for him to do the reverse and having a high esteem for Dr. Maty he then mentioned that he had just laid aside his *Bibliothèque Britannique* and Dr. Johnson might do

well to take his assistance. Dr. grew angry—and said "Damn Maty—little dirty-faced dog—I'll throw him into the Thames."[2]

His detestation of Maty possibly stemmed from the latter's criticism in the *Journal Britannique* of his *Dictionary* and of his relations with Lord Chesterfield.

In one of Johnson's "memorandum-books" seen by Boswell there is the entry:

> *The Annals of Literature, foreign as well as domestic.* Imitate Le Clerk—Bayle—Barbeyrac. Infelicity of journals in England. Works of the learned. We cannot take in all. Sometimes copy from foreign journalists. Always tell.[3]

The older journals he was thinking of imitating would have been Jean Le Clerc's *Bibliothèque Universelle et Historique* (1686–1693) and his later continuations; Pierre Bayle's *Nouvelles de la République des Lettres* (1684–1687); and Jean Barbeyrac's *Bibliothèque raisonnée des Ouvrages des Savans* (1728–1753).

Johnson doubtless was also considering various associates he might ask for help. One puzzling surviving scrap of paper with Johnson's handwriting may have been somehow connected with these plans. Certainly all the names listed there are those of close friends of the mid-1750s. On the scrap is written:

> Mr Levet / White I think
> ~~Mr Southwell—Gent~~
> Mr Hawkins English
> Mr Southwell Baron
> Mr Derrick Magazine
> Mr Murphy—Clarissa[4]

Could he have thought of depending on Levet, who lived with him in Gough Square, for advice on medical matters? And Hawkins on music or the law? Perhaps Samuel Derrick might review other magazines, and Arthur Murphy do a piece on *Clarissa*? Could Johnson have been uncertain about Thomas Lord Southwell's title, and unsure of his chief interests? Alas, the little scrap remains a mystery.

Nothing specific came from his plans, at least for the moment, but Johnson was soon to be acting editor for a new periodical not so international in scope. This was the *Literary Magazine, or, Universal Review.* William Faden, who had been the printer of the *Rambler,* and the publisher Joseph Richardson were in charge. Faden, indeed, may have been the nominal overall editor.[5] It is possible that Faden and Richardson, who handled all financial details and the routine collection of material, had from the start planned to hire Johnson as a kind of general literary editor who would be responsible for articles and reviews.

The format was to be large and handsome, including maps and illustrations in each issue. And as a new idea, the magazine was to come out in the middle of each month instead of at the beginning, as did rival periodicals. Although it was called the *Literary Magazine,* it was meant to concentrate mainly on politics and historical concerns.

No one seems to know what Johnson's official position was, or how much he was paid. He himself never mentioned these details and, in fact, at the beginning did not wish it to be generally known that he was involved with the new periodical. On July 31, some months after the start, he wrote to his young friend Robert Chambers in Oxford that a contribution Chambers had sent in had come too late to be included in the last issue, but that they had had "more materials than room" and so had not been inconvenienced. Then he added, "I have sent it already to the press, unread, for the next month, and am much obliged to you for doing it. I will contrive to find you more work. . . . But you must not tell that I have any thing in it. For though it is known conjecturally I would not have it made certain."[6]

The first number appeared in the middle of May, 1756, the same month that England formally declared war on France, the beginning of the Seven Years' War. From later evidence we know that Johnson was responsible for almost half of this inaugural issue. He wrote the two-page general introduction called "To the Public," in which the purpose of the periodical was clearly stated and its contents outlined. Then came a long "Introduction to the Political State of Great Britain." In addition, he provided at least five book reviews, and probably revised and made additions to at least three other pieces—a short "History of Minorca," extracted from John Armstrong's earlier history; "A Description of the Anatomy of a Manatee, or Sea-Cow, Found near an Island to the East of Kamtschatka"; and six pages of "Historical Memoirs," summing up events since the beginning of 1756. In places there are typical Johnsonian passages, and though we cannot be certain Johnson was involved, there is enough evidence to suggest that he did at least some of the editing and may have supervised portions of the rest. Some routine sections, on the other hand, such as those containing chronological series of recent events, lists of deaths and promotions, stock market prices, two pages of music and poetry, and an article "On the Inconveniences and Disorders Arising from Strait Lacing in Stays" were undoubtedly put together by others on the staff. Even so, most of the important sections were his.

In his general introduction Johnson clearly states the intention of the proprietors "to give the history political and literary of every month." Despite the prominence of "literary" in the title, the emphasis was on other concerns. The arts came second. And anyone reading Johnson's long survey of the political situation in Great Britain, beginning in the sixteenth century and ending with the reasons for the present conflict with France, must have sensed that the stance would be anti-administration and anti-Newcastle. It must be admitted that his historical summaries, on the surface, were simple and unprejudiced, but the emphasis was on the American colonies, and Britain's failure to keep up with the French. "It is unpleasing," he wrote, "to represent our affairs to our own disadvantage; yet it is necessary to show the evils which we desire to be removed." Among the evils which Johnson lists is the fact that France has sent out better governors: "A French governor is seldom chosen for any other reason than his qualifications for his trust. To be a bankrupt at home, or to be so infamously vicious that he cannot be decently protected in his own country, seldom recommends any man to the government of a French colony." The implications as to how the British make their selections are obvious. French officers "are commonly skillful either in war or commerce, and are taught to have no expectation of honour or preferment but from the justice and vigour of their administration." Furthermore, the French have developed more friendly relations with the natives; they have admitted Indians "by intermarriage to an equality with themselves," and have been honest in their dealings with them. "Our factors and traders, having no other purpose in view than immediate profit, use all the arts of an European counting-house to defraud the simple hunter of his furs." Not the kind of introduction which would arouse great enthusiasm in the business community! How accurate Johnson was as to French practice is of little importance; what he was obviously doing was using all the devices of a brilliant writer to attack the English colonial counterparts.

At the same time that he was giving most of his time to this new periodical, Johnson also reactivated another scheme which had been in the back of his mind for a long time. Eleven years earlier, in 1745, he had issued proposals for a new edition of Shakespeare, but Jacob Tonson, who with his associates controlled the copyrights, blocked the scheme.[7] Reluctantly Johnson accepted the verdict. But in 1756, with Johnson's increased reputation and the passage of time, Tonson changed his mind. A new edition might be a worthwhile enterprise.

So on June 2 Tonson and Johnson signed an agreement for the publication of Shakespeare's dramatic works, "to be printed on a good paper and letter in eight volumes octavo."[8] In consideration of Johnson's "care and trouble" in preparing the edition, he was to receive 250 sets free, to sell to subscribers. And if there were more subscribers Johnson could secure other volumes by paying one guinea a set. Subscribers would be expected to pay one guinea to Johnson at the start and another when receiving the completed set. Thus Johnson presumably would receive well over 500 guineas in all for his labors.

There never was any doubt in his mind as to his reasons for doing the edition. When Hawkins congratulated him on being finally engaged "in a work that suited his genius," Johnson insisted that his motives were purely practical, not literary.

> I look upon this as I did upon the dictionary: it is all work, and my inducement to it is not love or desire of fame but the want of money, which is the only motive to writing that I know of.[9]

In his *Proposals,* which were dated June 1, 1756, Johnson made clear just what he intended to do.[10] The business of an editor should be to "correct what is corrupt, and to explain what is obscure." These were the two things he planned to do, by showing how obscurities had resulted from the changes in colloquial language since Shakespeare's time, and the differences in reading habits. Corruptions of the text, for which Shakespeare had provided no reliable authority, would be corrected by a careful collation of the oldest surviving copies, and all important variations would be noted so that a reader would not have to rely solely on someone else's judgment, but would have "the means of choosing better for himself." Moreover, Johnson promised to read the books which Shakespeare had used and in this way compare passages with their sources. But he would not continue a practice of some earlier editors who insisted on pointing out which were beautiful passages and which they thought bad. Johnson believed his chief duty was to provide as authoritative a text as possible, and in cases of controversial matters to include in his notes examples of both sides. While not wishing to appear too egotistical, he did suggest that someone who had just considered "the whole extent" of the English language was better fitted than others to ascertain Shakespeare's "ambiguities, disentangle his intricacies, and recover the meaning of words now lost in the darkness of antiquity." It was a forthright statement, strong and confident in tone, and the goals were admirable.

As with the *Dictionary,* Johnson at the start was unrealistic about the time necessary to do the job. He estimated a year and a half—that is, completion before Christmas 1757. And with proper concentration it might have been done. Actually it took him nine years, slightly longer than for his lexicographical project. But, as before, the work did help him to live during difficult times.

Once *Proposals* were passed out to Johnson's immediate friends, money began flowing in. On June 22 he wrote to Thomas Birch: "Being, as you will find by the proposal, engaged in a work which requires the concurrence of my friends to make it of much benefit to me, I have taken the liberty of recommending six receipts to your care, and do not doubt of your endeavour to dispose of them."[11] Others apparently were also saddled with subscriptions to pass around. Samuel Richardson in July wrote to Thomas Edwards: "Have you seen Johnson's Proposals for a new edition of Shakespeare? I will inclose you one of them."[12] Thomas Warton, at Trinity College in Oxford, actually secured twelve subscriptions, we know from his own records, and sent twelve pounds to Johnson.[13] For a while Johnson may even have had more money than he needed.

Most of Johnson's time in the spring and summer of 1756 would have been spent in preparing copy for the *Literary Magazine*. In the second number, which appeared in the middle of June, he provided vigorous remarks on the new Militia Bill, in which his own antiwar sentiments and country Tory bias are clearly shown; he also furnished some comments on a letter from a French refugee in America, three or four reviews, and possibly some other pieces. In the third number his contributions were not quite so extensive, though he did a number of reviews and provided pertinent observations on recent treaties with Russia and Hesse, which arranged for the hiring of large numbers of mercenaries, and he apparently acted as editor for the monthly historical memoirs. Then in No. 4, which appeared about the middle of August, he may well have been responsible for at least eight reviews and for what many think was his most astute political essay: "Observations on the Present State of Affairs."

One cannot be absolutely certain what reviews Johnson wrote, or what editing he did to various miscellaneous pieces. Scholars have argued about such matters in the past, and will continue to do so in the future.[14] What is obvious is that during the first four numbers Johnson was largely in control, providing the most important literary, political, and historical contributions, and seeing to it that books which interested him were reviewed.

Unfortunately his labors were not very successful. The *Literary Magazine* did not at once attract a wide audience. In a fairly long letter to Charlotte Lennox on July 30 Johnson shows clearly how involved he was with the new periodical, and he also includes some information proving its lack of success.[15] Mrs. Lennox had been irked by reviews of her translation *Memoirs of the Countess of Berci,* which had appeared in April in the *Monthly Review* and *Critical Review,* and had complained to Johnson. After agreeing that the reviewers had, "according to their plan, showed their superiority of knowledge with some ostentation," he insisted that they had not said anything bad enough to justify her resentment. They had commended her style and mentioned her with "great respect." Neither of the evaluations intended her "any hurt." Thus she had better forget all about the matter.

He added that when her husband had brought him a copy of the *Berci,* and had said that his wife wanted him "to say something about it," he had assumed that she wished him to talk to Andrew Millar, the publisher. If she was hoping for a review in the *Literary Magazine* that was another matter. As he pointed out, "There is so little room in the monthly book, that I believe no mention will ever be made in it but of originals, or books of science or learning. This rule, however, I would gladly break to do you either service or pleasure." Certainly the *Literary Magazine* did not normally have much to say about translations of other works. Still, he added:

> If there be any episode, or little story, more your favourite than the rest, that can be separated and will fill about four or five columns, I will press its insertion, and let it have its natural weight with the public. But I do not think it worth your while, our readers are few, and I know not when they will be more. . . . If you can point me out a passage that can be referred to the present times, I will press for a place in the Gentleman's Magazine, and write an Introduction to it; if I can not get it in there I will put it in the new book [the *Literary Magazine*], but their readers are, I think, seven to one.[16]

With only one-seventh as many subscribers as the *Gentleman's Magazine,* the publishers of the *Literary Magazine* must have been greatly disappointed. Perhaps one reason may have been the unpopular political position taken by the new periodical.

Although at the start Johnson may not have taken too partisan a stand, any reader would have sensed that the *Literary Magazine* was not supporting the war with France, nor was it enthusiastic about the situation in the American colonies. And this opposition was clearly based on moral grounds. The settlers, Johnson kept repeating, had not treated the natives fairly, traders were unethical, governors of provinces tended to be dishonest and inefficient, and the war itself was wasteful and unnecessary.

As an example, there are the opening paragraphs of the "Historical Memoirs" in the third number, which most experts now attribute to Johnson.[17] In the second number, the month before, reasons had been adduced to explain why the Indians in North America had come to support the French and "to take up the hatchet against us." Now Johnson explains why.

While the French have been endeavouring by every artifice that human policy could suggest to establish an interest among them, our governors there, trusting to the increasing strength of the rising colonies, or perhaps having an eye only to their present gain, have for a series of years taken no care to cultivate new friendships with the ancient inhabitants, nor has the government been at much expense to cement the old.

A people, therefore, thus neglected by one foreign nation and courted by another could not remain forever in doubt to which side to join their force. War was both their pride and their profession; and they saw this additional motive to determine their choice, that the French were in general poor, active, and enterprising; the English wealthy, laborious, and peaceable; hence they could not but conclude that as the spoils would be greater by warring against the latter, the hazard in obtaining those spoils would also be less.

The natives could not be blamed for siding with the French, for they saw clearly where their best interests lay. Moreover, those violent attacks by Indians upon the British settlers could be explained by their own bad treatment in the past, as well as by the lures of the French.

It was in the fourth number of the magazine, which appeared in mid-August, that Johnson allowed his moral indignation to have full rein. His own government was corrupt, its policies all wrong, and management inept. It was time that the supine English public awoke to what was going on. His stinging opening paragraph of the "Observations" has so much relevance for twentieth-century readers that it has been widely quoted:[18]

The time is now come in which every Englishman expects to be informed of the national affairs, and in which he has a right to have that expectation gratified. For whatever may be urged by ministers, or those whom vanity or interest make the followers of ministers, concerning the necessity of confidence in our governors, and the presumption of prying with profane eyes into the recesses of policy, it is evident that this reverence can be claimed only by counsels yet unexecuted, and projects suspended in deliberation. But when a design has ended in miscarriage or success, when every eye and every ear is witness to general discontent or general satisfaction, it is then a proper time to disentangle confusion and illustrate obscurity, to show by what causes every event was produced, and in what effects it is likely to terminate; to lay down with distinct particularity what rumour always huddles in general exclamations, or perplexes by undigested narratives; to show whence happiness or calamity is derived, and whence it may be expected, and honestly to lay before the people what inquiry can gather of the past, and conjecture can estimate of the future.

After this strong blast at "executive privilege" and his argument for making public all the evidence, Johnson moves speedily into the reasons for his moral indignation.

> The general subject of the present war is sufficiently known. It is allowed on both sides that hostilities began in America, and that the French and English quarrelled about the boundaries of their settlements, about grounds and rivers to which, I am afraid, neither can show any other right than that of power, and which neither can occupy but by usurpation and the dispossession of the natural lords and original inhabitants. Such is the contest that no honest man can heartily wish success to either party.
>
> It may indeed be alleged that the Indians have granted large tracts of land both to one and to the other; but these grants can add little to the validity of our titles till it be experienced how they were obtained: for if they were extorted by violence, or induced by fraud, by threats, which the miseries of other nations had shown not to be vain, or by promises of which no performance was ever intended, what are they but new modes of usurpation, but new instances of cruelty and treachery?

Other excuses, too, Johnson implied, are fallacious. "It cannot be said that the Indians originally invited us to their coasts; we went uncalled and unexpected." The war, then, is only "the quarrel of two robbers for the spoils of a passenger." And with continued sneers at both nations for clamoring with vehemence "about infractions of limits, violation of treaties, open usurpation, insidious artifices, and breach of faith," Johnson keeps stressing that the fundamental urges, at least on the English side, were commercial, a desire for more wealth through expanded trading.

If anyone in the administration read this blast one can easily imagine the reaction. Most merchants certainly would have found Johnson's emphasis on moral, rather than practical, considerations disturbing. They thought of themselves as moral people, but never considered foreign trade, even when it might involve cheating natives at the other end, as immoral. And extending the empire seemed a patriotic duty. Thus from the start many readers were probably upset by the position taken by the new magazine.

For example, in "The History of Minorca" which appeared in the first number, presumably edited, if not partly written, by Johnson, it is computed that holding this Mediterranean island, captured by the English in 1708, cost England at least £50,000 a year. Moreover, some three hundred of the garrison of three thousand soldiers died annually from bad climate, local conditions, diet, etc. For all this expenditure, the writer asks, what advantages are there for Britain except to provide harbors for naval vessels? Indeed, the writer ends by saying that he would willingly give up both Minorca and Gibraltar, always sources of tension with Spain.[19] Their usefulness in expanding the empire eastward the writer ignored. Again, this was not a suggestion which could have been heartily welcomed by patriotic Britons eager to increase colonial possessions and foreign trade.

Yet not many violent objections by contemporary readers have turned up.[20] If there were many protests, few were put into print. All that we know definitely is that Johnson's "Observations" was the last political piece that he contributed to the *Literary Magazine*. After the fourth number he continued to write reviews of books—at least for a time—but never any more general opening essays or commentaries on contemporary history. The proprietors somehow eased him out of the post as general editor. Were Faden and Richardson under pressure from the government? Or from their colleagues? Or was the change merely a sign of their own unhappiness over Johnson's point of view and their fears for the future of the new magazine if it should continue to take such a strong anticommercial and anticolonial position? There is no way to tell. But any reader who moves from No. 4 to No. 5 of the magazine will at once sense a change. Issue No. 5 begins with notes on the naval engagement off Minorca and minutes of General Fowkes's court-martial, but draws no overall conclusions. The only general discussion in the fifth number is "A View of the Importance of Our Plantations in America to Their Mother Country," which was clearly a reply to Johnson's earlier essay. The "Historical Memoirs" this time have a completely different tone from those supervised by Johnson, being much more patriotic and favorable to the war. The only two contributions which can definitely be ascribed to Johnson are continuations of reviews which began in earlier numbers. It might thus be argued that Johnson had nothing at all to do with the preparation of No. 5, which appeared in the middle of September.

One must always remember that while the *Literary Magazine* had been from the start anti-Newcastle, it supported Pitt, who actually would conduct the war more effectively. The proprietors were basically not antiwar. They could tolerate Johnson's blasts at Newcastle, so long as they concentrated on the administration's graft and inefficiency, but when Johnson went farther and condemned Britain's making war at all, then the proprietors really became alarmed. By the end of the summer it was becoming more and more clear that Newcastle was beaten.[21] To be sure, the actual shift, with Pitt taking over, did not occur until late November and early December, but this delay was largely caused by the King's dislike of Pitt.

The supplanting of Johnson as general editor of the magazine in late August or early September thus must have come partly from a conviction that Pitt had won, and also from a fear that Johnson's strong antiwar blasts were dangerous for all concerned. His searing attacks on British overall policy, and his anticolonial and anticommercial stance, were too shocking. The proprietors simply could not take any more.

Possibly they all talked it over in a friendly manner and agreed upon the shift. Or perhaps Faden and Richardson merely took charge and made the decisions as to what should go into subsequent issues. It may be significant that the piece written by Robert Chambers of Oxford, referred to in Johnson's letter at the end of July and sent "unread" to the printers, has never been identified and may not have been used.

It must be admitted that this is largely speculation. There is another possible explanation for the shift. Johnson's ill health in the autumn of 1756 could have forced him to give up editorial supervision for the periodical. Arthur Murphy suggested as much, when he claimed to have been brought in to do reviews and essays for the *Literary Magazine* about this time.[22] Nevertheless, when all the evidence is considered it does appear likely that after the fourth number of the magazine there was some major change in policy.

After a month, however, Johnson did provide some reviews. In No. 6, which appeared in mid-October, he probably contributed at least four, and in No. 7 perhaps the same number. Some of these, such as his discussions of Charlotte Lennox's *Sully's Memoirs* and the memoirs of Elizabeth Harrison, were largely uncontroversial. If some of the others did provide opportunities for political jibes, the proprietors perhaps decided that a few could be tolerated so long as the general policy of the magazine was clearly patriotic and acceptable to the present government.

In his account of Lewis Evans's *Map of the Middle British Colonies in America,* which appeared in the sixth number, Johnson was able to include some skeptical remarks about the value of colonial expansion, though the review was not hostile. Evans's arguments as to the potential value of the Ohio Valley, Johnson insisted, would not "prove that this system is right, or in other words, that it is more productive than any other of universal happiness."

Moreover, his analysis of various pamphlets connected with the celebrated case of Admiral Byng, later executed for cowardice and negligence in the Minorca expedition (in Nos. 6 and 7), shows Johnson's hatred of the government in power. Since Donald Greene has summarized all the important evidence in this shocking case, there is no need to repeat it all here. One of Johnson's comments shows exactly where he stood. Both pamphlets endeavor to prove that "Mr. Byng is stigmatized with infamy, and pursued with clamours artfully excited to divert the public attention from the crimes and blunders of other men, and that while he is thus vehemently pursued for imaginary guilt, the real criminals are hoping to escape."[23]

Once he was released from editorial supervision of the *Literary Magazine,* Johnson fell back on securing Shakespeare subscriptions as his chief means of financial support. On September 28 he wrote to an unidentified correspondent: "My good friend Mr. Vaillant has communicated to me your kind intention of contributing to the success of my Edition of Shakespeare. I have sent you a dozen of receipts signed."[24] Requests kept coming in from all over the country. For example, Benjamin Victor, a theatrical manager in Ireland, in a letter to the publisher George Faulkner in Dublin, acknowledged a present of bound volumes of the *Rambler,* adding that he had long esteemed the author as "a foremost genius" in the kingdom, and asking to be listed as a subscriber to Johnson's edition of Shakespeare.[25]

One may suspect that during the autumn of 1756 Johnson might have been ill and was not very busy. Still clinging to the notion that he would get up to the midlands to see his mother and renew old memories of his birthplace, he had earlier written to an old friend Richard Congreve at Leacroft near Lichfield: "I fully persuade myself that I shall pass some of the winter months with my mother; I would have come sooner but could not break my shackles."[26] Yet even his release from some of his responsibilities made no difference. He did not leave London soon.

Meanwhile he had been actively involved with the affairs of Lewis Paul, inventor of the "roller-spinning" machine.[27] Indeed, almost a third of Johnson's surviving letters for 1756 are to Paul. That Johnson had been actively concerned with the early development of this spinning machine, back in the 1730s, is very unlikely, but he later served as an intermediary between Paul and a number of Johnson's close associates—Cave, Dr. James, and Thomas Warren of Birmingham—who invested in the projects. And he undoubtedly kept closely in touch with Paul's frenzied schemes. Paul had been able to meet some of his expenses through loans from supporters, but there were always problems—trying to decide who owed whom, how to keep the factories going, how to settle various claims and involved finances. By 1756 Cave was dead, but Paul, who had been operating a factory in Northampton, was in deep trouble, partly because of Warren's bankruptcy and James's failure to pay what he owed. Acting as go-between, Johnson tried to collect from James, to secure agreements from the others, and to interest further investors. Apparently from his letters in 1755 and 1756 he was not attempting to help Paul sell more spindles, but to use them as security to borrow money. Somewhere along the way, Paul was arrested for debt and spent some time in a debtor's prison. It must be admitted that the whole business is obscure, but there can be no doubt as to Johnson's active involvement.[28]

It may even have been through Paul that Johnson in November 1756 paid a visit to the Foundling Hospital, during the first year of unlimited admissions. It was on this visit that he asked the children various questions and was horrified that they were not well instructed in their catechism. He "found not a child that seemed to have heard of his creed, or the commandments."[29] Johnson complained so strenuously that a teacher of religion was hired the next February.

Accompanying him that day were "some ladies with another gentleman."[30] Could this have been Paul? We know that Johnson wrote a letter signed by Paul to the Duke of Bedford, asking him to see that a spinning wheel be installed in the Foundling Hospital, "its structure and operation being such that a mixed number of children from five to fourteen years may be enabled by it to earn their food and clothing."[31] Paul offered to exhibit a model of his machine to his Grace, in order to show how it worked. Though undated, the letter could have been written about this time, for in it the writer referred to himself as "an old Man oppressed with many infirmities."

With his increasing reputation, Johnson naturally became the object of pleas for advice and help from other ambitious writers. Some time in November 1756 a poet (we do not know his name) submitted a blank verse piece for his opinion, and upon receiving no response, called several times at Gough Square without finding Johnson home. To further complicate matters, Johnson lost, or mislaid, the letter which had accompanied the manuscript, and thus did not know the poet's name or address. Finally Johnson did write a paragraph of criticisms—succinct and to the point, but scarcely very palatable to the author.

> To give opinions of manuscripts is to me never pleasing, nor do I think an author just to himself who rests in any opinion but that of the public. Something however I will say. I think too much of the work past in digression. The paragraphs are too long, and the sense too much deduced from line to line so as to require more attention than readers are willing to bestow. The author may improve his work perhaps with no great difficulty

The 1756 portrait of Johnson by Reynolds as it appeared in an engraving on the frontispiece to Boswell's Life of Johnson.

The 1756 Reynolds portrait of Johnson as it now appears in the National Portrait Gallery.

by breaking it into shorter paragraphs. He seems too much to have studied Thomson, a man of genius, but not very skillful in the art of composition.[32]

Among his best friends at this time was Joshua Reynolds. After their meeting, probably in the summer of 1755, they saw a great deal of each other, though, according to James Northcote, Reynolds was not at first much pleased by Johnson's visits.

> He frequently called in the evening and remained to a late hour, when Mr. Reynolds was desirous of going into new company, after having been harassed by his professional occupations the whole day. This sometimes overcame his patience to such a degree that, one evening in particular, on entering the room where Johnson was waiting to see him, he immediately took up his hat and went out of the house. Reynolds hoped by this means he would have been effectually cured, but Johnson still persisted and at last gained his friendship.[33]

By late 1756 they were such good friends that Reynolds painted Johnson for the first time. This three-quarter-length portrait of Johnson was undoubtedly Reynolds's idea and was not commissioned by the penniless writer. The portrait remained in the painter's house for some thirty-five years. Reynolds gave it to Boswell, who had an engraving made for the frontispiece to his *Life of Johnson*.[34]

One incident at the painter's house provided a sidelight on Johnson's interest in young people. A fourteen-year-old girl with her father were among the guests one day when a dispute arose concerning a passage in Milton's *Paradise Lost*. The father, John Joshua Kirby, teacher of perspective to George III, turned to his daughter and

> enquired if she had not the book in her pocket, it being a great favourite of hers, and he probably knowing that it then made a part of her daily studies. The book was accordingly produced and opened at the disputed part.

Johnson was so struck

> with a girl of that age making this work her pocket companion, and likewise with the modesty of her behaviour upon the occasion, that he invited her the next day to his house, presented her with a copy of his Rambler, and afterwards treated her with great consideration.[35]

Sarah, who later was Mrs. Trimmer, became a famous writer of books for the moral instruction of children.

Another incident which probably occurred about this time concerned a boy from Lichfield who was a student at Charterhouse in London. His name was Charles Howard, and Johnson in his earlier years had been kindly received in the house of the boy's father. Later Howard told Boswell that while at the Charterhouse his father had written to him suggesting that he

> pay a visit to Mr. Samuel Johnson, which he accordingly did, and found him in an upper room, of poor appearance. Johnson received him with much courteousness, and talked a great deal to him, as to a school-boy, of the course of his education, and other particulars. . . . He added that when he was going away Mr. Johnson presented him with half-a-guinea; and this, said Mr. Howard, was at a time when he probably had not another.[36]

Although Johnson was always sympathetic and friendly with young people, he did at times have some troubles. It was in late 1756 or early 1757 that he suffered a major inconvenience when his young black servant, Frank, ran away to serve an apothecary named Farren in Cheapside. What caused the rupture no one can tell. Boswell refers to it merely as "some difference with his master."[37] In a letter to Paul about this time Johnson explained his difficulty in communicating with the remark that "my boy is run away, and I knew not whom to send."[38] A few months later, on March 10, 1757, Johnson wrote to Charlotte Lennox that "I have no servant, and write therefore by the post."[39] Fortunately Frank was not gone very long. Perhaps he found working for an apothecary more tiring than working for a dilatory hack writer.

In addition to receiving random subscriptions to his Shakespeare project, Johnson earned something from special jobs for his publisher friends. For the opening number on January 1, 1757, of a new paper called the *London Chronicle*, later one of the most distinguished newspapers of the century, Johnson wrote the preliminary discourse, for which Dodsley paid him one guinea. He was an expert at the sort of balanced explanatory writing which inspired confidence in readers. As a sample, there was this sentence:

> Of remote transactions the first accounts are always confused and commonly exaggerated; and in domestic affairs, if the power to conceal is less, the interest to misrepresent is often greater, and what is sufficiently vexatious truth seems to fly from curiosity; and as many enquiries produce many narratives, whatever

engages the public attention is immediately disguised by the
embellishments of fiction.[40]

The winter of 1757 could not have been a busy time for Johnson, though
he did provide an opening paragraph for Baretti's *Italian Library*, which
came out in February, and, at Newbery's suggestion, a dedication to
members of parliament for John Lindsay's *Evangelical History*, published
in April.[41]

It is likely that it was in early March 1757 that Johnson was invited
to Samuel Richardson's to meet Edward Young, author of the immensely
popular poem in blank verse, *Night Thoughts*, and to hear him read a
revised version of his critical "Conjectures on Original Composition."
Since Johnson was never a great admirer of blank verse, his account of the
evening, later passed on to Boswell when they were on Skye in the
Hebrides, could hardly be called unprejudiced. After Young had read his
piece, Johnson "made his remarks," stressing chiefly that "he was surprised to find the Doctor receive as novelties" what Johnson "thought very
common thoughts."[42] He then went on to say that he believed Young "was
not a great scholar, nor had studied regularly the art of writing. He said
there were very fine things in his *Night Thoughts*, though you could not
find twenty lines together without some extravagance." Although after
this first meeting Young "pressed" Johnson to visit him at his home in
Welwyn, so Boswell reported, Johnson always "intended it, but never
went."

During the spring he continued to advise Charlotte Lennox, and in
March wrote her about a French volume he had seen at Dodsley's which
she might turn into English.[43]

If he ever seriously thought of leaving London, he did nothing about
it. According to Boswell, about this time Bennet Langton's father in
Lincolnshire offered Johnson a living with a rectory at his disposal, if he
were willing "to enter into holy orders."[44] But Johnson refused, doubting
that his temper and habits were suited to the life of a clergyman. There
are stories also that Johnson once considered going to India, or to the East
Indies, though it is doubtful that these have any firm basis. The two letters
he received from his dear friend Richard Bathurst, who had emigrated to
Barbados, which he called an "execrable region," could hardly have moved
him to consider going there.[45]

For the most part his time was spent either jotting down some short
piece of journalism or considering how to proceed with his Shakespeare
project. As Hawkins put it, "when he was not writing he was thinking."
And at least some of his expenses were being taken care of by stray Shakespeare subscriptions, as when Edmund Hector in Birmingham sent money

through Johnson's mother in Lichfield.[46] In his usual prayer, he thanked God for forgiveness for his "vain imaginations," and pleaded for help to "shake off sloth, and to redeem the time misspent in idleness."[47]

For No. 13 of the *Literary Magazine,* which appeared in mid-May, he provided some valuable reviews, his first contributions for four months. Perhaps the most important was a three-part evaluation, which continued through the July number, of Soame Jenyns's *A Free Enquiry into the Nature and Origin of Evil.* Much has been written about this, and there is no need to examine it thoroughly here.[48] For those who may still cling to the old notion that Johnson was at heart a rigid reactionary, a Tory of the old school, the review of Jenyns is crucial.

The basic paradox in Johnson is that despite an innate love of freedom and a hatred of oppression and slavery, he was at the same time convinced that some kind of subordination was necessary. In order to achieve peace and stability central government must be absolute. On the other hand, he refused to accept the philosophic theory of the Great Chain of Being, normally used by conservatives to excuse poverty and inequality. Although he would agree that society should consist of many gradations, Johnson felt that an individual, through his own efforts, ought to be able to move up in the scale. He was appalled by Jenyns's apparent willingness to allow the poor to remain so because that was their obvious position in the Great Chain. He could never agree that universal education was wrong because it might render a person unhappy in his social position. As he put it,

> The privileges of education may sometimes be improperly bestowed, but I shall always fear to withhold them lest I should be yielding to the suggestions of pride, while I persuade myself that I am following the maxims of policy; and under the appearance of salutary restraints, should be indulging the lust of dominion, and that malevolence which delights in seeing others depressed.

It was a stinging review, one which Jenyns never forgave. But only after Johnson's death did he dare to retaliate with a petulant satirical epitaph in which he described his reviewer as "a sleeping bear."

> Religious, moral, generous, and humane
> He was—but self-sufficient, rude, and vain;
> Ill-bred and overbearing in dispute,
> A scholar and a Christian—yet a brute.[49]

Book reviewing could involve Johnson in other kinds of difficulties. Indeed, his final complete break with the *Literary Magazine* came as a result of a review. One of his best-known and wittiest contributions to the magazine is his discussion of Jonas Hanway's *Journal of Eight Days Journey and an Essay on Tea,* which also appeared in No. 13, in mid-May. In his book Hanway had thought it necessary to attack the use of tea as a beverage, insisting that it was almost as dangerous as gin, and should be rooted out.

For such a compulsive tea-drinker as Johnson, this demanded vigorous rebuttal. But along with his defense of his favorite beverage Johnson could not resist also mentioning the visit he had made the previous November to the Foundling Hospital, of which Hanway was a governor. The failure there to indoctrinate the children in religious principles and their catechism was, Johnson insisted, "equally pernicious with gin and tea."[50] These remarks were reprinted in the *London Chronicle* for May 17, and in the *Gazetteer* the next day, described merely as having been written by "a truly good man and a very able writer." Hanway and the other governors of the hospital were horrified. How they reacted is disclosed in the surviving minutes of their weekly meetings.

On May 25, at a meeting which Hanway did not attend, the governors directed the hospital's solicitor to visit the printers and find out who had written the anonymous review. If the printers refused to tell, the solicitor was authorized to threaten prosecution for libel. The next day, May 26, Hanway published a letter of rebuttal, which appeared in the *Gazetteer.* Unfortunately no copy of the issue of May 26 appears to have survived. But its contents are pretty clearly indicated in Johnson's reply in No. 14 of the *Literary Magazine.* As Boswell pointed out, this was the only known instance of Johnson's condescending to reply to any journalistic attack. But what Boswell did not know is that the governors of the hospital seriously considered bringing him into court for libel.

In a full account of the whole episode, Ruth McClure points out that the governors had some reason to be apprehensive. If their new policy of unlimited admissions to the hospital should lead to more public criticism of this kind, they might be in trouble, since the survival of the hospital depended entirely on financial gifts from well-to-do benefactors. They had worked hard to keep it going and viewed with great alarm such offensive comments.

On June 1, John Wilkie, publisher of the *London Chronicle,* for whom Johnson had written the "Preliminary Discourse," and who probably knew Johnson well, appeared at the General Committee's weekly meeting. He "acknowledged his offense and undertook to publish such acknowledgement in the next *London Chronicle.*" This he did not do, though he did publicly apologize some weeks later.[51] Similarly Charles Say, printer of the *Gazetteer,* apologized for reprinting the item, but would do no more. J. Richardson, publisher of the *Literary Magazine,* when he attended a meeting on June 15, "denied that it was in his power to discover the author" but added that he was convinced that "the author would avow the truth of the said libel." Knowing Johnson as well as he did, the publisher was certain that his book reviewer would not back down. Indeed, in the next issue of the magazine (just about to appear, if not already out), Johnson, still anonymous, reiterated the truth of his statements.

Since none of the printers, even after further threats of prosecution, would divulge the name of the writer, who himself remained recalcitrant, the governors sent their solicitor to consult with the Attorney General, Charles Pratt, later Lord Camden, about the possibility of bringing at least Richardson into court. For various legal reasons nothing was done, and there, so far as the Foundling Hospital was concerned, the matter ended. Hanway always remained furious at Johnson, but there was nothing he could do about it.

For Johnson, who was not obliged to testify in court, the affair had another result. For the proprietors of the *Literary Magazine* this must have been the last straw. Johnson was never asked to do another review, or, at least, nothing of his ever appeared in later numbers. Only continuations of his earlier reviews, which must have been written before the Hanway affair, were included. For all intents and purposes, with his reply to Hanway Johnson's connection with the magazine was terminated.

By this time it should have become obvious to all concerned that the prospects were not bright for a forthright, brilliant journalist who attacked the war policy of his own government and frankly said what he thought about sensitive philanthropical institutions. In the twentieth century someone taking Johnson's position might have an immense following, with the prospect of selling large numbers of copies of his writings. But not in the mid-eighteenth century! At that time acceptance depended upon what the writer was opposing. If he was representing some political group which was out of power but wished to regain control, then he would be applauded by that side and sneered at by the other. His future depended on how many wealthy supporters he had. But an attack on the whole commercial colonial system on which the wealth of England depended could expect no support from any of the regular political parties. Should anyone suggest, as did Johnson, in effect, that it would be better for his own country to remain a second-rate power, rather than to steal lands from natives or to conquer far-off countries with great trading potential, he would never be tolerated by wealthy patrons or commercial interests. The proprietors of the *Literary Magazine* obviously had a problem on their hands.

Something had to be done. But how? With a famous moralist and conservative writer like Johnson, whose personal reputation was above reproach, the proprietors could scarcely risk a scandal. They had to find some way of easing him out of his position with the magazine. As we have seen, they persuaded him to concentrate on book reviewing, and not writing political comments. Then when even his reviewing got them into trouble, they attempted to convince him that he would be better off concentrating on other projects. If only they could push him gently into work for other publishers, they could do what they wanted with the *Literary Magazine* (eventually it proved a failure and ended after another year). So in No. 13, in the same number of the *Literary Magazine* which carried Johnson's controversial attack on Hanway, Faden and Richardson included an enthusiastic four-page announcement of Johnson's proposed edition of Shakespeare, possibly hoping in this way to entice more subscribers to send in money on which Johnson could live. After many compliments which stressed Johnson's perfect capacity for the job, there came this paragraph:

> But all these matters are so well set forth by Mr. Johnson himself that we recommend to all our readers an attentive perusal of the following proposals, which we are inclined to think they will find to be an instructive piece of criticism, condensed into a narrow compass, and written in a masterly style. Whoever chooses to see the points there insisted on, enlarged, enforced, and illustrated with taste and erudition, will have an opportunity of doing it on or before next Christmas, when we are assured the work will be published. Our editor speaks for himself as follows [then comes a quotation from Johnson's 1756 *Proposals*].[52]

By repeating Johnson's own original unrealistic estimate of the time he would need to complete the edition, the proprietors may have seen another way to give him a push. Knowing Johnson as well as they did, and realizing how much still had to be done on the project, they could hardly have thought his projected seven months sufficient. Although it is possible that Johnson ceased writing for the magazine on his own initiative, and even that the proprietors urged him to remain, the factual evidence to the contrary is suggestive. The *Literary Magazine* never included advertisements in its pages, nor was it their policy to discuss books or projects which were not yet completed. Thus the praise of Johnson's Shakespeare was a distinct break with former practice. By putting in some 3½ pages touting this work, the proprietors were clearly hoping for some resulting action. And it appears to have been successful. Johnson at least at this point did end his connection with the magazine, and sporadically gave his time to other projects.

Apparently Johnson never held any grudges against Faden and Richardson,[53] and probably was sorry the next year to see the magazine cease publication, even though he could not have been happy with its changed political stance. Johnson had other ways to exist—Shakespeare subscriptions kept drifting in, and later he wrote uncontroversial short essays known as *The Idler*. To be sure, he had not changed his mind about political matters. In the autumn of 1757 he could actually "without premeditation or hesitation" dictate a short speech to a friend who possibly planned to speak at a meeting of the Common Council of the City of London supporting a request to the King for an investigation of the unsuccessful Rochefort expedition. As Johnson put it,

> We have raised a fleet, and an army; we have equipped them; we have paid them; they set out with the favour and the good wishes of the whole nation. Great advantage was expected from the secrecy of our counsellors, and the bravery of our commanders. They went out, and they are come back again, not only without doing, but without attempting to do anything.[54]

It was time the public knew what really happened.

> But no nation has yet suffered themselves to be exhausted, in sending out fleets and armies, without enquiring what they have done, and why they have done nothing. Caligula once marched to the sea-coasts and gathered cockle-shells: our army went to the coast of France, and filled their bellies with grapes. Caligula's expedition has been, to this day, the subject of merriment, and we can only avert from ourselves the like contempt by enquiring rigorously by whose fault our troops and ships have been equally ridiculous.

Even William Pitt's later victorious leadership did not change Johnson's fundamental attitude toward war and colonial expansion. Despite his failure to arouse any strong support, or to gain for himself a prominent place as a political and historical commentator, he continued to hold resolutely to his moral view of international affairs.

CHAPTER XII

The Idler

D URING THE LATE SPRING of 1757 Johnson was worried by financial pressures from Lichtfield. The mortgage on his mother's house, where he had been born, was still not paid (the original agreement in 1739 had been for £80, plus interest of 4½ percent). For years he had been saying he would find the money somehow, but had been able only to send small portions. Finally John Levett, who held the mortgage, decided to use stronger measures, even threatening foreclosure, which would have meant forcing Sarah Johnson out of the house. At least that appears clear from what evidence has survived, though some of the reconstruction of the sequence of events has to be guesswork. There is a note, dated June 7, written by Lucy Porter, Johnson's stepdaughter, who lived with his mother, apparently to Levett.

> I shall take it as a particular favour if you will not mention the ejectment, or cause it to be delivered to Mrs. Johnson till I have spoke to you again, which I shall be glad to do the first opportunity. She has been very poorly for some time and is too weak at present to bear the shock of such a thing and I believe the very naming of it would almost destroy her. I hope you need not be under any apprehensions concerning the money as I will do my utmost endeavour to procure it as soon as I can. Your complying with the above request will infinitely oblige.[1]

Perhaps a copy of this note was sent to Johnson, along with other details. In any event, the very next day, June 8, Johnson arranged to borrow £100 from Jacob Tonson, the publisher, probably as an advance on the Shakespeare edition. Then on June 21 Johnson wrote to Levett. After apologizing for being so slow in making the final payment, Johnson estimated the total for principal and interest as being £146. Of this he believed he had in the past paid £46, through Henry Hervey Aston, John Asbridge, and Lucy Porter, though his recollection of the earlier payments was not altogether clear.

> The money paid by Mr. Aston was I am very confident three years interest, but if I was to declare upon oath, I would not go to the utmost. Ten pounds I could swear to. I suppose you do not think I would cheat you of ten or twelve pounds, nor do I believe you would require them unjustly of me.[2]

He had that day sent his mother a bank note of £100, which he hoped would settle what he owed, an affair he was sorry had been "so long and so uneasily protracted." He continued: "Be so kind as to spare my mother all the trouble you can." If his estimate of the total amount was wrong, he promised to do whatever Levett thought correct.

Once the bank note reached Sarah Johnson, all was cleared, and fortunately Levett was willing to accept Johnson's vague explanations. On the original indenture, which still survives, Levett on June 27, 1757, acknowledged receiving from Samuel Johnson "(by the hands of Mrs. Lucy Porter) the sum of £98 in full of all principal money and interest due upon the therein within written mortgage, he having allowed to the said Mr. Johnson the sum of £44 (which was alleged to have been paid in part)."[3]

During June Johnson was busy with his edition of Shakespeare, subsisting on subscriptions which continued to be sent in from all over, and retaining his optimism about an early publication date. The terms of the original contract had stipulated that all eight volumes were to be published in eighteen months—that is, allowing about two months for each volume and two more for corrections, writing a Preface, and inserting late notes.[4] Apparently, he had not planned very extensive research or thorough explanations. Over ten years earlier he had edited *Macbeth* and may well have been collecting similar annotations for the other plays during the intervening years. But even with such loose plans, his optimistic predictions were scarcely realistic.

After more than a year he could write to Thomas Warton on June 21, 1757, "I am printing my new Edition of Shakespeare," but that did not mean all of it.[5] Probably various plays were set in type separately, once he had enough annotation ready, and only later was the order of the whole edition established. In June he had enough for one volume set in type, and when Thomas Percy wrote to William Shenstone on November 24, after describing how he had been seeing Johnson often in London, he added: "He is not yet got through the second volume yet seems to think he shall publish Shakespeare before Easter."[6] On December 24 Johnson could still write to Charles Burney that he expected to publish in March.

When March 1758 arrived and still no complete printed edition, he pushed the prediction forward to "before summer."[7] And it may be that by April many plays had been set in type, which would lead one to suspect that at the start Johnson never thought of the process as so time-consuming, or as full, as it later became.

Of course, as the months flew by he did not give all his time to this project. When writing to Thomas Warton in June 1757, introducing an Italian scholar who "has a mind to see Oxford," Johnson had intimated that he hoped to receive full news from Warton, who was now Professor of Poetry at Oxford. So he added: "I long to see you all, but cannot conveniently come yet. You might write to me now and then, if you were good for anything, but honores mutant mores. Professors forget their friends."

With such slow progress, Johnson's conscience continued to prod him, and when celebrating his birthday on September 18 he wrote a prayer asking for "another year of probation," with repentance for "vain thoughts," "sloth," and "folly," so that he could "by diligence redeem the time lost." Specifically he asked pardon for "idleness, intemperate sleep, dilatoriness, immethodical life," "lust," "neglect of worship," and "vain scruples."[8] Despite all his regrets for idling and weakness of purpose, he could not change his unproductive life.

Because he tended to think of the Shakespeare edition as a short-term project, he continued to weigh other possibilities. For example, if he should chance to move to Oxford (and he did evidently at times consider the remote possibility), what kind of "literary business" might he be involved in there? In October he confided some of his ideas to one of his friends, though in strict confidence. "The schemes of a writer are his property and his revenue, and therefore they must not be made common."[9] Still, he confessed that he had seriously been considering four schemes which might be possible: "An Ecclesiastical History of England," "A History of the Reformation (not of England only, but of Europe)," a life of Richard the First, and one of Edward the Confessor.

When talking to Thomas Percy, Johnson also mentioned another project which always lay at the back of his mind, particularly after what he must have taken as the partial failure of his work for the *Literary Magazine*. As Percy commented to Shenstone, Johnson "talks of undertaking a kind of Monthly Review upon a new plan: which shall only extend to the choicest and most valuable books that are published not in England only but throughout Europe: something like the Acta Eruditorum Leipsiensia:

&c."[10] It was at this time that Percy showed Johnson the manuscript of his collection of old ballads, and Johnson expressed a desire to see it printed.

Johnson had, as usual, been helping other friends with various works. He composed a dedication for Charlotte Lennox's *Philander: A Dramatic Pastoral,* which was published in December 1757, and for her *Maintenon;* he provided a preface for John Payne's *New Tables of Interest,* published in late February 1758; and he helped Saunders Welch, Fielding's former friend, with his *Proposal to Render Effectual a Plan to Remove the Nuisance of Common Prostitutes from the Streets,* which came out in May. E. L. McAdam believes Johnson wrote some paragraphs and may have corrected others.[11] Moreover, it was rumored that Johnson did some writing for Lord Charles Hay, a major general, who was later court-martialed for some reflections he had made on the conduct of Lord Loudoun in Nova Scotia. When Langton took Johnson to see Hay, the latter approved what Hay was composing for his defense, though how much he helped him is still uncertain.[12]

None of this, however, brought much financial support, and subscriptions for the Shakespeare were drying up, though Johnson kept sending out copies of the *Proposals* and forms for receipts. As might have been expected, in February 1758 Johnson was again arrested for debt and on the tenth dispatched a note to Jacob Tonson:

> An accident has happened to me which Mr. Strahan will tell you, and from which I must try to be extricated by your assistance. The affair is about forty pounds. I think it necessary to assure you that no other such vexation can happen to me for I have no other of any consequence but to my friends.[13]

Tonson at once provided the £40 and Johnson signed a promise to pay the amount "on demand."

Another regular weekly stipend for his writing was clearly needed to keep Johnson out of the hands of his creditors. The *Rambler, Adventurer,* and, for a short time, the *Literary Magazine,* had served that purpose. Why not another such periodical? Somebody seems to have caught the message. Whether it was John Newbery who had the idea of starting another newspaper to be called *The Universal Chronicle or Weekly Gazette,* and persuaded Johnson to agree to provide each Saturday a short front-page essay, has never been determined. Everyone assumes that Newbery was the power behind the project, although first John Payne's and then Robert Stevens's and William Faden's names were on the colophon. And the title of the paper kept changing.[14]

Once the overall plans were fixed, Johnson was easily involved. He wrote a two-part introductory essay, occupying all the front page and part of the second, of the first number of the paper which appeared on April 8, 1758. Here he explained clearly just what the paper was supposed to do, and generalized on the duty of a journalist, both as historian and moralist. He also attempted to make clear what kind of an audience the planners hoped to reached. The *Universal Chronicle* was not designed merely for people of eminence, for students or statesmen, but also was addressed "to women, shopkeepers, and artisans, who have little time to bestow upon mental attainments, but desire, upon easy terms, to know how the world goes; who rises and who falls; who triumphs and who is defeated."[15] This information the paper resolutely promised to provide.

Johnson was quite committed to providing material which would be light in tone and attractive to the ordinary reader. In the second number of the *Universal Chronicle* on April 15, 1758, the first of the *Idler* essays appeared. They kept coming regularly for the next two years—104 in all— of which Johnson wrote all but twelve (three by Thomas Warton, three by Joshua Reynolds, one each by Bennet Langton, Bonnell Thornton, and William Emerson, and three whose authorship is unknown). For these he was paid at the rate of three guineas a paper. It was rather more than he received for the *Ramblers* or *Adventurers*, but in this instance he was supposed somehow to share in the profits of the new paper. For the rest of 1758, he received £113 8s. merely for *Idler* papers, and for 1759 the series brought him £144 18s. In early 1760 it amounted to £34 13s.[16] When the *Idler* was published by Newbery in two volumes, Johnson received an additional £84 2s. 4d. All in all, it was a welcome financial help during difficult times.

From various well-known stories one might assume that Johnson did not take the assignment very seriously and tossed off *Idlers* at the last minute. Bennet Langton told Boswell that about this time when Johnson was in Oxford he asked one evening how long it was before the post left for London. On being told "about half an hour," he exclaimed, "then we shall do very well," and dashed off an *Idler* which had to be in the capital the next day. When Langton expressed a desire to read what he had written, Johnson replied, "Sir, you shall not do more than I have done myself." He quickly folded up the sheets and sent them off.[17]

But this did not mean that he had not thought long and seriously about the piece before hurriedly writing it down. One has to understand how Johnson worked. Thomas Percy explained it best.

> Johnson's manner of composing has not been rightly understood. He was so extremely short-sighted, from the defect in his eyes, that writing was inconvenient to him; for whenever

Johnson's letter to Jacob Tonson, written from debtor's prison, February 10, 1758.

he wrote he was obliged to hold the paper close to his face. He, therefore, never composed what we call a foul draft on paper of anything he published, but used to revolve the subject in his mind, and turn and form every period, till he had brought the whole to the highest correctness, and the most perfect arrangement. Then his uncommonly retentive memory enabled him to deliver a whole essay, properly finished, whenever it was called for. The writer of this note has often heard him humming and forming periods, in low whispers to himself, when shallow observers thought he was muttering prayers, etc.[18]

This was Johnson's method with all his compositions. There is no evidence that he was more casual about the *Idlers* than anything else.

From the start, however, the *Idler* essays were intended to be lighter in tone than the *Ramblers* and *Adventurers*. Because they appeared in a newspaper, and not separately, they were supposed to reach a wider audience. At first the essays occupied about two-and-a-half of the three columns on the first page, though gradually they tended to grow shorter. The remaining seven pages of the paper contained news of the week, stock market reports, lists of new books and advertisements, all the customary newspaper fillers. But since most of the material was secondhand, derived from other papers, the *Universal Chronicle* never became as popular as the editors had hoped. Nevertheless, the *Idler* essays were often reprinted in contemporary periodicals and reached a wide audience. Indeed, they were so widely pirated in such periodicals as the *London Chronicle* and the *Grand Magazine,* among others, that Johnson felt forced to write a protest, which appeared in the *Universal Chronicle* early the next year, threatening ironically that if this continued they would feel obliged to do likewise with pieces from other sources.[19]

That the *Idlers* were meant to appeal to all kinds of readers is clear from an amusing letter which the editors included in the *Universal Chronicle* of May 6, 1758, soon after the new project began. "Tim. Tape," the writer of the letter, claimed to be a haberdasher, with six men in his shop and so busy on Saturdays that he could use six more. He subscribes to the *Universal Chronicle* because it has so much news. Then he added:

But, Mr. Publisher I don't like the man who writes the first page of it; (Mr. Idler, I think his name is) for though I myself never read such sort of stuff, and should be much better pleased if that part of the paper too was filled with news, yet my servants, for no other reason than that they like the man's name, are always reading his nonsense, when they should be minding their business. No longer ago than last Saturday I lost thirty papers of middling pins, forty yards of coxcomb, and I don't know how many pieces of ribbon.

This, Mr. Publisher, is a very sad affair; and, I hope, out of consideration to me, who, as I said before, like the paper, that you will either publish it on some other day in the week, or discharge Mr. Idler. If neither of these requests can be complied with, and you should want more *Idlers,* I desire you will take my servants into your pay, as they will be of no further use to, Sir, your humble servant.[20]

One may suspect that, despite the efforts of Newbery and his henchmen, few servants or laborers wasted their time reading *Idlers.* Still, there can be no doubt as to Johnson's determination to make his essays more palatable. They are shorter than the earlier *Ramblers,* with fewer hard words and more short sentences, and in a style tending toward that of the later *Lives of the Poets.* Critical essays are less analytic. Fewer literary quotations are included, and gradually classical mottoes were eliminated. There is increased focus on contemporary events, with more casual allusions.

At the start, choice of a name must have been the basic problem. The first number cleverly handles that. "It will be easily believed of the Idler, that if his title had required any search, he never would have found it." But he who is satisfied with what is easiest to find escapes fruitless labor. "Every man is, or hopes to be, an Idler." Thus no appellation could be better to "denote his kindred to the human species." Scarcely any name could be imagined which would arouse less envy or competition. And so, with further comments on the Idler's character and what might be expected from his essays, there came a promise of continued variety. The Idler might sometimes "descend into profoundness, or tower into sublimity," but such "violent exertions of intellect" will not be frequent. And to save himself work, he would welcome letters from readers—short, with no words wasted in "declarations of esteem." "Conscious dullness has little right to be prolix, and praise is not so welcome to the Idler as quiet."

Such jocular invitation to correspondents in the second and then in the third number further explained some of the Idler's problems. His predecessors had had a wide range of vices and follies to attack, with "the whole field of life before them," while those like himself who follow "are forced to peep into neglected corners, to note the casual varieties of the same species, and to recommend themselves by minute industry, and distinctions too subtle for common eyes." After such warnings to readers, Johnson finally in No. 4 tackles a serious subject—the growing support of hospitals and the increasing schemes of charity in his time.

From there, Johnson moved to a satirical proposal for a female army.

No modern soldiers, he insisted, have any duties which a lady could not perform. Anyone can pull a trigger. Consider the disastrous surrender of General Braddock at Fort Duquesne in the colonies in July 1755:

> The troops of Braddock never saw their enemies, and perhaps were defeated by women. If our American general had headed an army of girls, he might still have built a fort, and taken it. Had Minorca been defended by a female garrison, it might have been surrendered, as it was, without a breach; and I cannot but think that seven thousand women might have ventured to look at Rochefort, sack a village, rob a vineyard, and return in safety.[21]

Number 6 tells of the exploits of Miss Pond, who a few weeks before had concluded a thousand-mile ride on a single horse. And so on. There were many amusing discussions of such topics as punch and conversation, bargain hunting, a lady's journey to London, an author's frustrations in trying to get his book published. Following the example of Steele and Addison, Johnson created characters whose names echoed their traits—Ned Drugget, Dick Shifter, Sam Softly, Sim Scruple, Bob Sturdy, Tom Tempest, Phil Gentle, Dick Wormwood, Tim Wainscot, and many others. In the *Idler* the satiric portraits tended to be more agreeable and favorable than in the earlier series. More have been drawn from real people such as Jack Whirler (No. 19, Newbery himself), Tom Restless (No. 48, Thomas Tyers), Sophron (No. 57, whose name Johnson could not later remember), and Sober and Gelaleddin (Nos. 31, 75, Johnson himself). Perhaps the most popular has been Dick Minim (Nos. 60, 61), a hilarious burlesque of the traditional literary critic, passing judgment at coffeehouses, attending theatrical rehearsals, and discovering hidden beauties in ordinary poems. This is certainly Johnson at his best in light satire.

His light style and amusing satire did not mean that Johnson completely suppressed all his serious ideas. In the *Idlers* one can find some of his most perceptive attacks on social conditions of his time. Witness two papers on arrest for debt (Nos. 22 and 38), undoubtedly stirred up by his own unhappy experiences. As he saw clearly, "The prosperity of a people is proportionate to the number of hands and minds usefully employed." Idleness, he insisted, was an economic waste.

> The confinement, therefore, of any man in the sloth and darkness of a prison is a loss to the nation, and no gain to the creditor. For of the multitudes who are pining in those cells of misery, a very small part is suspected of any fraudulent act by which they retain what belongs to others. The rest are imprisoned by the

wantonness of pride, the malignity of revenge, or the acrimony of disappointed expectation.

For an individual creditor "to be the judge of his own cause" and decide who should go to jail, seemed to Johnson unfair.

> Since poverty is punished among us as a crime, it ought at least to be treated with the same lenity as other crimes; the offender ought not to languish, at the will of him whom he has offended, but to be allowed some appeal to the justice of his country. There can be no reason why any debtor should be imprisoned, but that he may be compelled to payment; and a term should therefore be fixed in which the creditor should exhibit his accusation of concealed property.

Although Johnson himself had never languished long in a jail, and when arrested was quickly bailed out by friends, he saw clearly the terrors of the system.

> The misery of gaols is not half their evil; they are filled with every corruption which poverty and wickedness can generate between them; with all the shameless and profligate enormities that can be produced by the impudence of ignominy, the rage of want, and the malignity of despair. In a prison the awe of the public eye is lost, and the power of the law is spent; there are few fears; there are no blushes. . . . Thus some sink amidst their misery, and others survive only to propagate villainy.

There were essays attacking slavery (Nos. 11 and 87), adverse comments on British military expeditions overseas (No. 5 and 39), discussion of political credulity and inconsistencies occurring in historical descriptions of events (No. 20), and corruptions of newswriters (No. 30).

> Scarce anything awakens attention like a tale of cruelty. The writer of news never fails in the intermission of action to tell how the enemies murdered children and ravished virgins; and if the scene of action be somewhat distant, scalps half the inhabitants of a province.
>
> Among the calamities of war may be justly numbered the diminution of the love of truth by the falsehoods which interest dictates and credulity encourages. A peace will equally leave the warrior and relator of wars destitute of employment; and I know not whether more is to be dreaded from streets filled with soldiers accustomed to plunder, or from garrets filled with scribblers accustomed to lie.

Among the other serious papers in the *Idler* there was an important critical discussion of the art of biography (No. 84), and two discussions of the art of translation (Nos. 68, 69). One might point out that Joshua Reynolds's three essays (Nos. 76, 79, 82) on style and criticism of painting served as the stimulus for the painter's later famous *Discourses*. Yet even so, the *Idler* must be thought of as one of Johnson's lighter productions.

Although the *Idlers* were largely nonpolitical, this did not mean that Johnson had given up his opposition to the war with France. His sense of moral outrage continued to be just as strong, and in August and September 1758 he contributed five short, anonymous comments on the war to the *Universal Chronicle,* then called *Payne's Universal Chronicle.*[22] The first four were labeled "Observations" and may have been intended as the start of a series of short remarks to which he could add whenever he so desired. But Johnson seemed doomed to failure as a political commentator. What followed was almost a repetition of events two years before with the *Literary Magazine.*

As Johnson's severity increased, his fourth "Observation," in the paper of September 9, turned into a devastating attack on military celebrations and public glory. On September 6 the few "French colours" captured by the British at Louisbourg had been paraded before the King and then carried to St. Paul's for a great thanksgiving service. Johnson thought all this asinine and said so. The capture of a minor French island could hardly be thought of as a triumph.

> But how were these colours got, whence did they come, and what did they cost? They were not gained by a decisive victory; there is no army defeated, France is not much weaker than she was before, and the war, however successful, is not much nearer to an end. They were not torn down from the walls of Paris or Toulon; they were not brought from Minorca, in return for those which we lately lost. They came from a place so obscure and inconsiderable that its name is known only to the French and English; and are purchased at an expense, which would be barely countervailed by the conquest of a province on the Continent, or the defeat of a royal army.

This aroused at least one patriotic reader who wrote an angry letter of protest that the paper printed on September 16. The anonymous correspondent angrily objected to what he called the falsehoods and ignorance which he found in the last "Observations." To this the "Observator" replied in the paper on September 30 with what Donald Greene calls "an utterly devastating counterattack." Newbery and Payne evidently suspected that such vigorous thrusts at patriotic fervor would hardly bring in new readers for their paper. With sales not very encouraging, it might be more sensible to avoid controversies like this. And so there were no more "Observations" by Johnson on political topics in the *Universal Chronicle*. Of course, the later *Idler* 81 (November 3, 1759) could be considered a scathing attack on the war with France, but this was part of a well-established series of light essays.

In the late spring and summer of 1758 Johnson was nearing the end of his long residence in the house at 17 Gough Square. It had never been a sumptuous home, and since Tetty's time the condition of the place had steadily declined. We can sense something of its state from an account of a visit by Charles Burney sometime in the late spring of 1758. The organist from King's Lynn in Norfolk dined and had tea with Johnson and was introduced to the blind Miss Williams. After dinner Johnson proposed that they go up to the garret, where they found "about five or six Greek folios, a deal writing-desk, and a chair and a half." As Burney later described the episode to Boswell, "Johnson giving to his guest the entire seat, tottered himself on one with only three legs and one arm."[23] The desks used by his amanuenses when the *Dictionary* was in progress were evidently gone.

To assuage Burney's curiosity, Johnson told him the tragic story of Anna Williams and her unsuccessful cataract operation, and then, as definite proof of his claim to be actually moving ahead with the edition, showed him some printed volumes of Shakespeare's plays. The two men talked about earlier Shakespearean critics, Theobald and Warburton, and some of the difficult problems Johnson would have to face when handling their work.

Another description of the Gough Square garret about the same time may be found in Northcote's later account of how Joshua Reynolds first introduced the sculptor Louis-François Roubiliac to Johnson:

> Johnson received him with much civility, and took them up into a garret, which he considered as his library; where, besides his books, all covered with dust, there was an old crazy deal table, and a still worse and older elbow chair, having only three legs. In this chair Johnson seated himself, after having, with considerable dexterity and evident practice, first drawn it up against the wall, which served to support it on that side on which the leg was deficient.[24]

We cannot be certain how many persons were living in the house at this time. Anna Williams would have been in one of the bedrooms above the ground floor, probably having one maid with her in the dressing room.

Johnson and Dr. Levet were on the next floor, and there might have been a cook, or a maid, in the basement. From all accounts the physical condition of the house was abominable, but neither blind Miss Williams nor Johnson, whose eyesight was not much better, saw enough of the dirt or disrepair to cause them discomfort. For years the house had been larger than he needed, but, although Johnson must have been conscious of rattling around in the big dingy place, he never summoned the necessary energy to do anything about it.

What finally, then, caused him to change addresses? Was it continued financial pressure? Or was it someone else's idea? Were his immediate neighbors unhappy about Johnson's noisy nightly habits and eager to have him move? Was Johnson really to blame? There are two surviving stories, how reliable it is impossible to tell, both suggesting that Johnson left by request.

A later popular journalist, drawing a parallel between Johnson and Diogenes the Cynic, pointed out that Diogenes never carried his laziness to such lengths as Samuel Johnson. The former kept his tub "sweet and clean" and "when he was under certain pressing necessities," "retired to a place at a convenient distance." But as for Johnson, "when he lived in one of Sir Harry Gough's houses, that gentleman give him warning that he might get his premises properly aired and cleansed."[25]

Hector later told Boswell that "Sir Harry Gough told Hector he was obliged to put him [Johnson] out of one of his houses in Gough Square for the neighbours complained they could not get rest for a man who walked all night and talked to himself."[26] Probably this occurred at some time in the late summer or early autumn of 1758. All we know certainly is that before Michaelmas (September 29) Johnson's name was removed in various local records of rent and tythes, and the name of Thomas Bodward was substituted. At the same time the amount of the rent was lowered from £26 to £24. The condition of the house may have been so bad that Bodward refused to pay what Johnson had been paying for the past few years.

The surviving Guildhall records show that Johnson had paid his "impropriate tythes" and "augmentation dues" at midsummer 1758, and he had paid his land tax on July 28, but he was listed as failing to pay the "Poors Rate" for the first two quarters.[27] For other taxes such as those for "lamp ledger" the records are missing. We do know that generally through the mid-fifties he had paid what was assessed. Two years before, in September 1756, he had paid 17s. 4d. "for and towards the cleaning repairing and beautifying" of St. Bride's Church.

When Thomas Bodward took Johnson's place as tenant of 17 Gough Square, no payments of charges were immediately listed. Moreover, he does not appear to have actually held the house for more than six months.

The entries for Lady Day (March 25, 1759) show William Addenbrooke taking over. For the next few years it was Addenbrooke who held the lease.

But did Johnson, when he gave up his lease of the house in September 1758, actually move out completely? There is no surviving evidence to suggest his having any other address for the next six months. It is tempting to guess that Johnson may have worked out some kind of an agreement with Bodward which would allow him to stay on for a while in one room, keeping his belongings there. He may thus still have been there early in 1759. Not until Addenbrooke came in, in March 1759, was Johnson perhaps forced to move. We know that his next lodging was Staple Inn.

Anna Williams, however, probably did have to move out and possibly Dr. Levet as well. In July Johnson's black servant, Frank, ran away again and joined the Navy. Miss Williams, we know, took over from John King the neighboring house, which she kept for some years, and where Johnson regularly visited her.[28]

From the surviving Guildhall records we can also tell who were Johnson's immediate neighbors, the ones whose complaints may have stirred Sir Harry Gough to ask him to leave. Because tenants shifted rapidly, Johnson remained in Gough Square for much longer than any of his neighbors. In early 1758 those who lived close by were John King, John Rayner, John Hilditch, and Richard Landrake, and on the other side of the Square were Elizabeth Scarlet, John Regley, William Revil, Charles Morgan, and John Chamberlaine. Curiously, not one of these names ever appears in Johnson's letters or journal entries, or in any surviving anecdotes.

Wherever he was living, Johnson kept working, perhaps half-heartedly, on his Shakespeare. By Langton, now Warton's pupil, he sent up to Oxford copies of some of the plays which were in print, pleading with Warton not to show them to others. He agreed to let his two friends see them, "on condition that you both hide them from everybody else."[29] In the same letter he asked Warton to send on any more notes on Shakespeare, which he was very glad to have. And he still kept sending out copies of his *Proposals* and forms for receipts. Some of his friends who lived outside London such as Percy, Warton, Thomas Edwards, Alexander Drummond, and James Grainger, sent in subscriptions, but they were beginning to see that there was little likelihood of speedy publication. Grainger, writing to Percy on June 27, 1758, commented, "I have several times called on Johnson to pay him part of your subscriptions: I say part, because he never thinks of working if he has a couple of guineas in his pocket."[30] Almost a month later he added that Johnson's Shakespeare "movet sed non promovet"—"I shall feed him occasionally with guineas—and in the

meantime I have inclosed you four more subscriptions as you desired."
During the autumn Johnson continued to advise young Langton, helped
Chambers with his attempt to secure a fellowship at Oxford, and wrote to
William Drummond in Scotland about the education of his son.[31]

But the most exciting event of this autumn was the production of his
friend Robert Dodsley's tragedy *Cleone* at Covent Garden on December
2, 1758.[32] It had been the center of heated controversy, and Johnson had
been involved for some time. The origin of the play went way back to the
early forties, when Dodsley had shown the first plan to Alexander Pope.
Following Pope's suggestion, Dodsley had expanded the play from three
acts to five and made other changes. By the summer of 1756 he was passing
the manuscript around among his friends, among them Shenstone, Graves,
Hawkesworth, and Johnson. At first Johnson thought it had "more blood
than brains" but later changed his mind and became a loyal supporter.
Almost all the readers were moved by the tragic plot which Dodsley had
adapted from a seventeenth-century story of St. Genevieve, who had suffered every kind of attack, torture and privation, and finally died a saint.
Dodsley changed the names, reorganized the story, and intensified the
horrors. Cleone, the heroine, is driven mad, and there is a concluding
scene which horrified many observers. Indeed, when Dodsley submitted
the play to Garrick, hoping for a production at Drury Lane, the latter
called it "a cruel, bloody, and unnatural play," and would not put it on.
John Rich at Covent Garden, after some pressure, agreed to produce the
tragedy.

Late in November, at Dodsley's request, numerous well-known people
came to rehearsals, among them Lord Lyttelton, Lord Chesterfield, and
Johnson. Everyone was full of advice.

George Anne Bellamy, who played the leading part, was determined
not to be pushed into doing anything she thought unsuitable. She saw
clearly that it would be a mistake to overdo the tragedy, and decided
instead to underplay some of the sensational scenes. *Cleone* she read as a
domestic, not an imperial, tragedy; thus she insisted on dressing simply
and would not wear the traditional hoopskirt. In her own later recollections she said that Dodsley told her he and all his friends thought she was
not being "forcible enough in the mad scene," but she petulantly refused
to take suggestions, with the result that the author began to regret his
choice of her for the part. Johnson, too, she remembered, was irked at the
rehearsal, and when she came to repeat the words "Thou shalt not murder," he "caught me by the arm, and that somewhat too briskly, saying at
the same time, 'It is a commandment, and must be spoken, "Thou shalt *not*
murder." ' "[33] Not knowing Johnson then as well as she did later, the
actress very much resented his pinch and his domineering attitude and

resolutely refused to change her style. All these arguments apparently made her ill, and the opening had to be postponed for a few days.

When the great day finally arrived (Saturday, December 2) and the theater filled with Dodsley's partisans, many of them dubious about what might happen, there was tension in the air. But Mrs. Bellamy was proved right. Her interpretation was a great success and the audience alternately cheered and wept. As she later described what occurred,

> The applause was repeated so often when I seemingly died, that I scarcely knew, or even could believe, that it was the effect of approbation. But upon hearing the same voice which had instructed me in the commandment exclaim aloud from the pit, *"I will write a copy of verses upon her myself,"* I knew my success was insured, and that *Cleone* bid fair to run a race with any of the modern productions.

Johnson, when reporting the event to Langton, commented:

> *Cleone* was well acted by all the characters, but Bellamy left nothing to be desired. I went the first night and supported it as publicly as I might; for Doddy, you know, is my patron, and I would not desert him. The play was very well received. Doddy after the danger was over went every night to the stage side, and cried at the distress of poor Cleone.[34]

Thus the play, despite David Garrick's open opposition, was an unqualified success. The night before the opening, so we are told, at the Bedford coffeehouse Garrick had declared that *Cleone* was "the very *worst* piece ever exhibited," and as a rival for theatergoers he had scheduled for the same night as the opening Susanna Centlivre's *The Busie Body*.[35] To be sure, the morning after *Cleone's* success Garrick wrote to Dodsley with warm felicitations, which occasioned a sharp rebuff. To this Garrick made a stinging retort, referring to Dodsley's "peevish answer." And so the quarrel continued. But happily for Dodsley the public came to see his tragedy; there were thirteen consecutive performances, and four more later in the season—an excellent record for those days.

Johnson, while well aware of the serious quarrel, evidently tried not to take sides openly. On Christmas Day he had dinner at Garrick's. Arthur Murphy remembered the occasion chiefly because it was the first time that he had ever seen Johnson willingly allow himself to be contradicted in conversation.[36] The subject had to do with the affairs of Bengal in India, something Johnson knew little about. The man who contradicted him successfully was a young Irishman whose name was Edmund Burke.

CHAPTER XIII

Rasselas

OFTEN ON NEW YEAR'S DAY Johnson would write down a prayer, full of regrets and pleas for forgiveness for countless minor errors and omissions, things he should have done and those he meant to do in the future. But with the coming of 1759 there was no prayer, or at least none that has survived. Perhaps this says something about his indecisive condition at the time. He was certainly living a disjointed life. When young Langton sent him some meat from Lincolnshire, Johnson commented in a long letter on January 9: "I have left off housekeeping and therefore made presents of the game which you were pleased to s[end me]."[1] The pheasant he gave to Samuel Richardson, the bustard to Dr. Lawrence, and "the pot" he deposited with Anna Williams, "to be eaten by myself." Presumably he dined wherever he could—at some nearby coffeehouse, or at Miss Williams's rooms nearby, or with some other friend.

Hanging over him was an ominous threat from his birthplace. He knew that his mother, who was almost ninety, was very ill. But how seriously? After warnings he had received from Lucy Porter, he became very worried and on Saturday, January 13, wrote to his mother:

Honoured Madam,
    The account which Miss gives me of your health pierces my heart. God comfort and preserve you and save you, for the sake of Jesus Christ.
    I would have Miss read to you from time to time the Passion of our Saviour, and sometimes the sentences in the Communion Service, beginning *"Come unto me, all ye that travel* [sic] *and are heavy laden, and I will give you rest."*
    I have just now read a physical book which inclines me to

think that a strong infusion of the bark would do you good. Do, dear mother, try it.

Pray send me your blessing, and forgive all that I have done amiss to you. And whatever you would have done, and what debts you would have paid first, or anything else that you would direct, let Miss put it down; I shall endeavour to obey you.

I have got twelve guineas to send you, but unhappily am at a loss how to send it to-night. If I cannot send it to-night, it will come by the next post.

Pray, do not omit anything mentioned in this letter: God bless you for ever and ever.

From other surviving letters it is possible to put together a fairly complete account of what happened during the next excruciating week. As George Irwin suggests, he kept writing with the "jumbled feelings of a troubled child," still somehow afraid of the tyrant of his child-hood.[2] Forever craving maternal acceptance, he nevertheless could not bring himself to visit Lichfield to face his dying mother. It was too terrible a prospect to think of. Thus there is a sense of pious urgency throughout his letters, filled as they are with a kind of affection, sympathy, tenderness, yet also with "feelings of unworthiness, guilt, and self-concern."

After hearing more bad news, Johnson three days later wrote again to his mother and to Lucy.

Dear honoured Mother
Your weakness afflicts me beyond what I am willing to communicate to you. I do not think you unfit to face death, but I know not how to bear the thought of losing you. En-deavour to do all you [can] for yourself. Eat as much as you can.

I pray often for you; do you pray for me. I have nothing to add to my last letter.
I am, dear, dear mother, your dutiful son

A letter to Lucy contained more practical considerations—the fact that he had the night before dispatched twelve guineas to them, his desire to thank "Kitty" (Catherine Chambers), his mother's maid, for "her tenderness for her mistress," and most of all his deep gratitude to Lucy herself for all she was doing. But there was no suggestion at all that he himself was consider-ing coming to Lichfield.

On Thursday, January 18, he scrawled another short note to his mother.

I fear you are too ill for long letters; therefore I will only tell you, you have from me all the regard that can possibly subsist

in the heart. I pray God to bless you for evermore, for Jesus
Christ's sake. Amen.
    Let Miss write to me every post, however short.

On Saturday there came another:

> Neither your condition nor your character make it fit for me
> to say much. You have been the best mother, and I believe the
> best woman in the world. I thank you for your indulgence to
> me, and beg forgiveness of all that I have done ill, and all that
> I have omitted to do well. God grant you his Holy Spirit, and
> receive you to everlasting happiness, for Jesus Christ's sake.
> Amen. Lord Jesus receive your spirit. Amen.

In these letters there is little personal love or deep affection. It is filial
duty, honor, and guilt for his own unworthiness which dominate his
thoughts.
    In his letter to Lucy on the twentieth Johnson for the first time
mentioned the possibility of his coming to see his dying mother.

> I will, if it be possible, come down to you. God grant I may yet
> [find] my dear mother breathing and sensible. Do not tell her
> lest I disappoint her. If I miss to write next post, I am on the
> road.

But he did not go, if, indeed, he ever even seriously considered doing so.
    Meanwhile, Johnson was facing interrelated financial problems.
Once the inevitability of his mother's death was accepted, he could see
clearly the need for money—to pay doctor's bills, and eventually for her
funeral and other debts. How could he raise enough? He could hardly ask
any more advances from Tonson. There must be another way. For a time
he had been thinking about a longish Eastern tale he had intended to write
some day. It was all there in the back of his mind. Now was the time to
write it down. Characteristically, what he needed was some stringent
emergency to get him moving. So, as his mother lay dying, he found a kind
of diversion in putting together the whole story largely in the evenings of
one week. At least that is what he later told Joshua Reynolds.[3]
    His topic did not represent some new interest. While at Oxford, over
twenty-five years earlier, he had been fascinated by reading the travels in
Abyssinia of Father Lobo, and his first large published volume was a translation of that work. During the following years he had continued to read
widely about that remote part of the world, and in the early fifties he had
composed a number of Eastern tales for his *Rambler* series.[4] In late Feb-

ruary 1752 Johnson published as *Rambler* Nos. 204 and 205 the story of Seged, Lord of Ethiopia, the chief theme being his search for happiness. Indeed, it was a strange coincidence that while his wife Tetty was dying he composed a story based in Abyssinia, with themes very similar to those in the story he was writing while his mother was in her last days. Seged and Rasselas come to similar conclusions about the impossibility of finding happiness in this world. When faced with the loss of his last close relative, Johnson apparently sought release for pent-up emotions in the same way he had when Tetty was approaching the end. The two inevitable losses were strangely intertwined.

On Saturday, January 20, he wrote to the printer, William Strahan, referring to a conversation they had had the night before. What they had been talking about was a work to be called "The Choice of Life, or The History of —— Prince of Abissinia." It would make two small volumes. Although the work was to be published anonymously, he expected the authorship to be immediately known.

The price which he originally asked the publisher, William Johnston, was seventy-five pounds (or guineas) a volume, with twenty-five additional for the second edition.[5] But he indicated that he would agree to go down to sixty pounds if he could retain all the rights, or forty if he were to share the profits and retain half the rights. What was vital was that he must have thirty pounds in advance on Monday night. At the end of his letter to Strahan, Johnson added, "Get me the money if you can."

Over the weekend Johnson did not go to visit his dying mother. Was it because he could not raise the necessary cash? A publisher who had perhaps seen parts of *Rasselas,* knowing the author's tendency to postpone and delay, would not give him an advance—not even the small sum of twenty pounds—until the whole manuscript was in his hands. This is the explanation given in four short biographical accounts published soon after Johnson's death.[6]

A more likely explanation is psychological. At times we know he had enough money available, and in an emergency such as this he could have easily borrowed enough from a friend for such a short trip. Could Johnson have been merely using the negotiations with his publisher as another way to justify not going?

By Monday Sarah Johnson was dead. She was buried in Lichfield on Tuesday, January 23; on that day her son in London set down a long prayer:

> Almighty God, merciful Father, in whose hands are life and death, sanctify unto me the sorrow which I now feel. Forgive me whatever I have done unkindly to my mother, and whatever

I have omitted to do kindly. Make me to remember her good precepts and good example, and to reform my life according to thy holy word, that I may lose no more opportunities of good; I am sorrowful, O Lord; let not my sorrow be without fruit. Let it be followed by holy resolutions and lasting amendment, that when I shall die like my mother I may be received to everlasting life.

      I commend, O Lord, so far as it may be lawful, into thy hands the soul of my departed mother, beseeching thee to grant her whatever is most beneficial to her in her present state.[7]

For one like himself, "about to return to the common comforts and business of the world," he pleaded for "such diligence in honest labour, and such purity of mind" that he might improve every day in grace. And he ends with these comments:

I returned thanks for my mother's good example, and implored pardon for neglecting it.
I returned thanks for the alleviation of my sorrow.
The dream of my brother I shall remember.

What he dreamed about his brother Nathaniel, who is suspected of having committed suicide over twenty years before, we will never know.

      On the same day he wrote to Lucy Porter:

You will conceive my sorrow for the loss of my mother, of the best mother. If she were to live again, surely I should behave better to her. But she is happy, and what is past is nothing to her; and for me, since I cannot repair my faults to her, I hope repentance will efface them. I return you and all those that have been good to her my sincerest thanks, and pray God to repay you all with infinite advantage. Write to me, and comfort me, dear child. I shall be glad likewise if Kitty will write to me. I shall send a bill of twenty pounds in a few days, which I thought to have brought to my mother; but God suffered it not. I have not power or composure to say much more. God bless you and bless us all.

Then on Thursday he wrote again to Lucy:

You will forgive me if I am not yet so composed as to give any directions about anything. But you are wiser and better than I, and I shall be pleased with all that you shall do. It is not of any use for me now to come down, nor can I bear the place; if you want any directions Mr. Howard will advise you. The twenty pounds I could not get a bill for tonight but will send it on Saturday.

He was able to send the note for twenty pounds on Saturday, the twenty-seventh, and promised ten more when she needed it.

> I am not able to determine any thing. My grief makes me afraid to be alone. Write to me dear child.
> I should think it best that you stayed in the house, and that Kitty carried on the trade. She has been very good, and is my old friend. Tell me what you would have done. God bless you.

Despite his emotional ups and downs, he was composed enough that week to write a calm dissertation on death as No. 41 of the *Idler*.[8] Purporting to be a letter commenting on the death of a friend, it really represents Johnson's own anguished loss. Some evils of life, he wrote, are accidental, against which no advance planning can be effective. But other miseries which time brings silently on us we tend to ignore.

> That it is vain to shrink from what cannot be avoided, and to hide that from ourselves which must some time be found, is a truth which we all know, but which all neglect, and perhaps none more than the speculative reasoner, whose thoughts are always from home, whose eye wanders over life, whose fancy dances after meteors of happiness kindled by itself, and who examines every thing rather than his own state.
> Nothing is more evident than that the decays of age must terminate in death; yet there is no man, says Tully, who does not believe that he may yet live another year; and there is none who does not, upon the same principle, hope another year for his parent or his friend; but the fallacy will be in time detected; the last year, the last day must come. It has come and is past. The life which made my own life pleasant is at an end, and the gates of death are shut upon my prospects. . . .
> These are the great occasions which force the mind to take refuge in religion: when we have no help in ourselves, what can remain but that we look up to a higher and a greater power; and to what hope may we not raise our eyes and hearts, when we consider that the greatest power is the best.

For ten days Johnson could not bring himself to write to Lucy in Lichfield, explaining, when he finally did: "I had no reason to forbear writing, but that it makes my heart heavy, and I had nothing particular to say which might not be delayed to the next post." Lucy, after all, was "the only person now left in the world with whom I think myself connected." As to practical matters, he hoped she and Kitty Chambers would continue to run the bookstore, at least for a while. "My mother's debts, dear mother! I suppose I may pay with little difficulty, and the little trade may go silently forward." It should be a good way for Kitty to pass the rest of her life. Lucy could have any part of the house she wished. In his present situation he sadly could not invite her to join him in London: "I am very solitary and comfortless, but will not invite you to come hither till I can have hope of making you live here so as not to dislike your situation."

On February 15 Johnson wrote again, pleased that the two women agreed with his proposals:

> Kitty shall be paid first, and I will send her down money to pay the London debts afterwards, for as I have had no connection with the trade, it is not worth while to appear in it now. Kitty may close her mistress's account and begin her own. The stock she shall have as you mention.

Two weeks later there was another letter, with not too much to say, but urging Lucy to keep acting for him "without the least scruple," and hoping that she would make it a rule to write to him at least once every week, "for I am now very desolate, and am loath to be universally forgotten." So far as we know, she did not.

Meanwhile, between bouts of despondency and self-incrimination and spurts of energy when he worked on chapters of his Eastern tale, Johnson did have some social life. The unpublished diary of Thomas Percy, a clergyman from Easton Maudit in Northamptonshire, who had been introduced to Johnson several years before by another clergyman, James Grainger, gives us some information.[9] On February 21, 1759, Percy noted that he had breakfasted at Grainger's, dined at a tavern with Johnson, and spent the evening at Grainger's, where another guest had been Oliver Goldsmith. He even noted down Goldsmith's address, "at Mrs. Martin's in Green Arbour Court, Little Old Bayley." This is the first time that Percy mentions Goldsmith in his diary, and he identified him as the author of *The Present State of Polite Learning*. On the same page Percy notes: "NB recommended by Mr. Johnson for any literary curiosity to apply to Mr. Jackson in Clare-Court, Drury Lane."

Unfortunately, some of the pages immediately following have been torn out, but on Thursday, March 1, Percy breakfasted at Grainger's and dined at Horseman's in Ivy Lane, where the Ivy Lane Club used to meet. Then he called on Johnson and had tea with Miss Williams, where he also met "Mr. Swinfield's sister." The latter part of the evening he spent at the Grecian coffeehouse writing letters. Among other things Percy was doing on this trip was attempting to sell some of his own writings. Thus he read portions of his so-called "novel" *Hau Kiou Choaan* to Dodsley, who published it two years later.

On Friday, March 2, he breakfasted at Mr. Orelbar, Jr.'s [?], then went to Dodsley's, then saw a live crocodile, and dined at Mr. Perrin's. He had tea at Mrs. Rolt's, called on Mr. Notts, visited a museum, supped at Grainger's, and called on Johnson. Quite a day! To have seen Dodsley, Johnson, and a live crocodile all in the same day must have been invigorating. The very next day he sat all morning with Goldsmith.

On Monday, March 5, he spent most of the day at Johnson's and Miss Williams's. With Baretti and Dodsley also present, Percy read aloud his Chinese tale. Later he supped on lobster at the Unicorn. Although Johnson still may have kept one room at Gough Square, where he could have talked to male friends, he nearly always was at Anna Williams's for tea. There were plenty of coffeehouses nearby if he was really hungry.

Johnson was now near the end of one of the crucial periods of his life. For over a decade he had lived in Gough Square, and it was there he did most of the work on the *Dictionary* and wrote the *Rambler* and *Adventurer* papers; it was there that Tetty died, and he was probably sleeping there when his mother passed away in Lichfield. The place was packed with memories. But at last he was going to have to sever connections completely with the house, since William Addenbrooke was taking over. So on Friday, March 23, 1759, he wrote to Lucy Porter: "I beg your pardon for having so long omitted to write. One thing or another has put me off. I have this day moved my things, and you are now to direct to me at Staple Inn, London."[10]

During the next few years Johnson would be moving about, renting temporary quarters. For a short while he would stay in Holborn, where, at Staple Inn, he had both rooms and meals at an inexpensive rate. The promissory note he had signed for John Newbery, for £42 19s. 10d., on March 19 may have provided money for an advance payment.[11] In any event, he stayed at Staple Inn until mid-June, but then went up to Oxford where he remained for over seven weeks, one of his longest visits. Was he even thinking of remaining there permanently? He came back to London in the autumn, and then rented rooms at Gray's Inn, north of High Holborn, where he stayed at least through the next winter. Uncertain just where he wanted to be or what to do, Johnson for a while aimlessly moved about.

But now back to the composition and publication of his Eastern tale. As we have pointed out, there are some difficult problems. What did he originally mean to call it? When was it all written down? What did he intend when he described the size of the work to Strahan in his letter of Saturday, January 20, "It will make about two volumes like little Pompadour"? What did he mean when he told Strahan that he would "deliver the book" on Monday? And if the writing was then almost done, why did it take so long to move through the press? Gwin Kolb has wrestled with these questions, and there is no need to fill in all the details here.[12]

That Johnson had begun to compose his tale before hearing of the death of his mother is clear. But his estimate of how long it would take to complete the writing, like most of his predictions, was unrealistic. No doubt it took longer than one week. His reference to "little Pompadour" was possibly to a translation which he had agreed to do for the publisher William Johnston and has little relevance here. The price Johnson was to receive was finally set at £100 for the first edition of the two small volumes and £25 for the second edition.

Even the publishers do not seem to have been sure of the title, or whether the work would be ready when promised. On Friday, March 30, they announced in the *Public Advertiser* that on Thursday next (April 5) would be published, "elegantly printed in two pocket volumes," *Rasselas, Prince of Abyssinia. A Tale,* to be published by R. and J. Dodsley in Pall Mall, and W. Johnston in Ludgate Street. This was repeated the next day, but when Thursday came there was no *Rasselas.* Then on Friday, April 13, there came a similar advertisement, with publication now promised for "next week." On the following Wednesday April 18, came "On Friday will be published," though on Thursday it was advertised as published. Still, April 20 appears to have been the date of publication.[13] The title of the work was finally *The Prince of Abissinia. A Tale.* The name "Rasselas" never appeared in the title of any editions published in Johnson's lifetime, nor is the author's name given on the title page. But at last the *Tale* was available for readers, and Johnson received his £100.

It was a simple story, with little plot—like all Eastern tales, episodic in form—the account of a prince named Rasselas, who was confined in a kind of earthly paradise in the highlands of Ethiopia where, in spite of having everything he could desire, he was bored. Eagerly he wished to see more of the world. Eventually, with his sister Nekayah and her maid and his philosopher companion, Imlac, he was able to escape through a tunnel. They made their way to the great city of Cairo, where they set about observing real life. What they were most eager to find was the true source of human happiness. So they examined, one after another, everything which was reputed to bring satisfaction, but nothing proved to be the perfect solution. Thus in the end Johnson did not provide the simple answer for which romantic optimists were searching. His last chapter, "in which nothing is concluded," merely leaves the travelers vaguely planning to return to Abyssinia. And that was it. Not a very compelling story to hold readers spellbound.

But for those who savor Johnson's dry wit and pithy generalizations, the tale has had a continuing fascination. It has been translated into foreign languages more often than any other of his works. David Nichol Smith used to say that *Rasselas* was the touchstone by which you could determine whether you could ever be a true Johnsonian or not. If you found it tiresome or hard to understand, then you might be a Boswellian but not a Johnsonian. Since this is the test, it seems important here to make clear just how it was originally produced, how it was received by contemporaries, and how it has been judged by modern critics.

Once published, Johnson's *Rasselas* (we call it that, though Johnson did not) had a mixed reception. Johnson's close friends and admirers praised it, and others immediately pointed out many defects. Reviews in the monthly journals, beginning in May, clearly showed this split, ranging from high compliments in the *Gentleman's Magazine,* probably by Hawkesworth, to qualified praise in the *London Magazine,* to adverse reaction in the May *Monthly Review*.[14] Most of the other periodicals merely included extracts, with no comment, or long quotations together with a brief quotation from the *Gentleman's Magazine.* Hawkesworth's coverage was not very thorough. All he did was to quote some portions of the early chapters and then at the end advise readers who would like to know what happened later to go to "subsequent chapters." Here would be found "the most elegant and striking pictures of life and nature, the most acute disquisitions, and the happiest illustrations of the most important truths."

The most glowing compliments came in a set of verses which appeared in *Lloyd's Evening Post,* for May 2–4, 1759. Undoubtedly written by one of Johnson's avid admirers, it had the title "On Reading *Rasselas,* an Eastern Tale." In twenty-six lines the author pulls out all the stops.

> Prior a hum'rous Tale politely tells,
> And in a vein of pleasantry excells:
> Johnson his oriental pearl displays,
> And shines a glory of unsully'd rays;
> He best, each avenue, which guards the heart,
> Takes by surprize, with ev'ry grace of art;
> Pictures of such rich colours he depaints
> We bend the knee, as Romans to their Saints;
> So pure his diction, and his thoughts so bright,
> His language shines an insula of light;
> A tide of vivid lustre pours along,
> That ev'n his prose is melody and song;

> What depth of sentiment, what height of thought,
> With what sublime, exalted morals fraught!
> So Amazon's vast river rolls his state,
> A limpid sea, magnificently great!
> A thousand rivers fill his ample stores
> A thousand nations his extended shores,
> Ten thousand fountains, like young Hebes, bring
> Translucent cups, from each perennial spring;
> Lost in his bosom, torrents rage in vain,
> And send, thro' him, their tribute to the main,
> Stupendous cataracts, from Andes toss'd,
> In his deep wave, are eminently lost,
> Like rolling centuries, they pass away,
> Sunk in the ocean of eternal day.[15]

A review in the April *Critical Review,* which attributes the work to "the learned and sensible author of the *Rambler,*" largely concentrates on difficulties of his style and approach. For an author dealing with moral subjects it is essential that great skill be used to convey knowledge and teach while one diverts. "Tedious reflections, long dissertations and laboured disquisitions" should be avoided. The thread of the narrative should not be broken. Unfortunately, the reviewer suggests, Johnson has failed to meet these standards.

> He has in a simple, but elegant tale, couched in the method of dialogue, the most important truths and profound speculations. No plot, incident, character, or contrivance, is here used to beguile the imagination. The narrative might have been comprised in ten lines; all, besides a flowery description of the *happy valley,* will please philosophers, but possibly be laid aside as unintelligible by the readers of novels.[16]

After citing one short chapter (XVIII) as a sample, the reviewer ends with this summation:

> Upon the whole, we imagine the talents of the author would appear to more advantage had he treated his different subjects in the method of essays, or form of dialogue. At present, the title page will, by many readers, be looked upon as a decoy, to deceive them into a kind of knowledge they had no inclination to be acquainted with.

An anonymous reviewer in the *London Magazine* pointed out that the work contained "the most important truths and instructions, told in an agreeable and enchanting manner," but written in Johnson's "usual nervous and sententious style."

Of all the early reviews by far the most critical was by Owen Ruffhead in the May *Monthly Review*.[17] Ruffhead was hardly an unbiased critic. A few years earlier he had been a loyal supporter of the Whigs who were backing the Seven Years' War, and he had started a paper to rival one edited by Arthur Murphy. The result had been much name-calling and vituperation, so much so that Johnson in the *Literary Magazine* had expressed the hope that neither paper would be long-lived. Although Johnson's comment was anonymous, Ruffhead no doubt knew who had written it and had been awaiting his chance to get even with the writer.

In his review of *Rasselas* Ruffhead shows clearly what he thinks of a "learned writer" attempting to produce a popular romance, where "sprightliness of imagination" is needed. Johnson was obviously out of his element.

> He wants that graceful ease, which is the ornament of romance; and he stalks in the solemn buskin, when he ought to tread in the light sock. His style is so tumid and pompous that he sometimes deals in *sesquipedalia,* such as *excogitation, exaggeratory,* &c. with other hard compounds, which it is difficult to pronounce with composed features—as *multifarious, transcendental, indiscerptible,* &c.

And there were further remarks about "this inflated style."

Throughout, Ruffhead confessed, he could not discover "much invention in the plan, or utility in the design." And after some lengthy quotations of remarks by the Prince and his sister, Nekayah, Ruffhead remarks that it would have been better for the author to have done nothing, rather than produce what he had. "Whoever he is, he is a man of genius and great abilities; but he has evidently misapplied his talents." If any ladies, misled by the title page, "expect to frolic along the flowery paths of romance," they will find themselves instead "hoisted on metaphysical stilts, and borne aloft into the regions of syllogistical subtlety and philosophical refinement."

Nevertheless, despite such comments, the sales were good enough to justify an immediate second edition. When preparing this, Johnson evidently read over his tale carefully and made a good many changes and corrections. Three of the chapter headings were changed, and there were omissions or introduction of whole clauses and numerous changes of words and phrases. For this second edition Johnson was paid in three installments, £10, £6 6s., and £8 14s., beginning on May 21.[18]

The usual practice of reviewers at the time was to include short sections of a new work, without any comments. This had the obvious advantage of avoiding taking a stand. Thus the *London Chronicle* ran a long series of extracts; the *Grand Magazine of Magazines, The Caledonian Mercury,* the *Edinburgh Magazine,* the *Universal Magazine,* among others, merely included extracts without comment.[19] The most complimentary evaluation came at the end of the year, in the *Annual Register,* then edited by the young Edmund Burke, who had met Johnson in late 1758. While admitting that the tale is not so full of incidents or so diverting as it might have been, Burke insisted that even with these defects

> perhaps no book ever inculcated a purer and sounder morality; no book ever made a more just estimate of human life, its pursuits, and its enjoyments. The descriptions are rich and luxuriant, and show a poetic imagination not inferior to our best writers in verse. The style, which is peculiar and characteristical of the author, is lively, correct, and harmonious.[20]

The reactions of ordinary readers, as might have been expected, were divided. Johnson's close friends, while admitting that the work could hardly be called a novel, or a major work of fiction, still thought of it as a superb moral tract. Others not in the inner Johnson circle, like Richardson's friend, Hester Mulso, were dismayed. On April 28, shortly after *Rasselas* appeared, she wrote to Elizabeth Carter:

> I take it for granted Mr. Johnson's Abissinian Tale has reached you; and pray tell me whether, with all your veneration for the author, you were not grievously disappointed in it? I know you have always thought me a profane wretch about him, as well as Doctor Young; but do for once give your judgment fair play against the man's name, and tell me whether you do not think he ought to be ashamed of publishing such an ill-contrived, unfinished, unnatural, and uninstructive tale? I know you will say there is a great deal of good sense, and many fine observations in it.[21]

What, she asks, is the real moral of the work? Was it

> that human life is a scene of unmixed wretchedness, and that all states and conditions of it are equally miserable; a maxim which, if adopted, would extinguish hope, and consequently industry, make prudence ridiculous, and, in short, dispose men to lie down in sloth and despondency?

After Miss Carter tried to defend Johnson, Miss Mulso wrote again on July 15:

> I allow the justice of every thing you have said relating to Mr. Johnson and his Rasselas. I own I was very angry with him for the conclusion, considering it as a conclusion, but I have since heard that he proposes going on with the story, in another volume, in which I hope he will give us antidotes for all the poisonous inferences deducible from the story as it stands at present. Alas! poor Mr. Johnson has, I fear, considered the worst side of the character of human nature, and seems to be little acquainted with the best and happiest of its affections and sensations. ...
>   I cannot but admire his truly philosophical manner of placing the advantages and disadvantages of each situation before us.

Others of Johnson's female friends thought his view of humanity too pessimistic, but they recognized that the work had been produced at a bleak time in his life, and besides that the tale was also filled with humor. Indeed, one modern scholar calls Rasselas Johnson's greatest comic work.[22] Many of the so-called weaknesses which contemporary critics found in the work now seem to be exaggerated. Viewed from a twentieth-century position, Rasselas seems to be more carefully constructed, less fragmentary and one-sided than was once assumed. As we today see it, Rasselas is one of the most characteristic works of Johnson, worth studying on many levels, and from various points of view.[23]

Today there is more emphasis on Johnson's shrewd psychological insights, and a number of twentieth-century scholars have concentrated on this approach.[24] Just as in the Rambler essays, Johnson in Rasselas clearly shows his keen understanding of the causes of frustration. He provides subtle insights into the caged, bewildered struggle of human beings for identity. Many passages, indeed, may seem startlingly like modern psychiatric analysis.

For us it is tempting to see Rasselas in conjunction with Voltaire's Candide, written about the same time. Neither could have influenced the other, nor did they approach the problems in the same way, but both intended to attack the principles of Leibniz and the complacent view of the deists and benevolists that "all's right with the world." Both were written hurriedly at white heat, Voltaire's in the summer of 1758, though it did not appear in print until January 1759 in Paris, and in England not until about a week after the publication of Rasselas.[25] An English translation was promised by the next month. Actually two were soon available.

Thus in the summer of 1759 English readers had an opportunity to compare the two remarkable works, so alike in many ways, and yet so dissimilar. Both have heroes brought up in a sheltered atmosphere who after a series of disillusioning adventures in which the evils and disappointments of life are exposed, decide to go back to retirement—Candide to cultivate his garden, and Rasselas to Abyssinia.

Though alike in form and general theme, the two works are utterly different in tone and style. It is not enough to say that one is thoroughly British and the other Gallic. Their whole approach is different, in no way more than in the matter of narrative technique. *Candide* moves rapidly. There is a constant succession of exciting episodes, as the characters travel about the world, even to South America, and the reader is scarcely ever able to catch his breath, so eager is he to see what happens next. Johnson's narrative, on the other hand, is almost static. His characters travel from Abyssinia to Cairo, make short expeditions in the neighborhood, but that is all. To Johnson the story was unimportant, merely a framework in which to set his musings on life. The result is that there is always a temptation for the reader to stop after each paragraph, sometimes after each sentence, to savor the ideas.

If one tends to read Johnson slowly, the reason is not basically because of his prose style. Its difficulty for modern readers has been vastly exaggerated. Despite the traditional impression, Johnson does not have a sesquipedalian style. He does not ordinarily use many long words or cumbersome expressions. One of his most characteristic sentences, which ends a superb chapter in *Rasselas,* is made up almost solely of monosyllables. "No man can taste the fruits of autumn while he is delighting his scent with the flowers of the spring; no man can, at the same time, fill his cup from the source and from the mouth of the Nile." Out of forty words, thirty-seven have only one syllable. And yet the sentence has all of Johnson's stately tone and formal rhythm. Obviously it is not vocabulary alone which produces his easily-recognized effects. Nor is it length of sentences. Some of the great Romantics, notably Lamb and De Quincey, often write much longer sentences than Johnson. To be sure, one can easily find places in *Rasselas* where the sentences are packed with polysyllables and may appear overly complex, with excessive parallelism and antithesis, but this is far from the most important point about his style. What gives it its unmistakable quality is the combination of formal rhythms and superbly compressed observation. His constant use of the general abstraction, and his careful choice of slow-moving musical effects, produce the impression of stately movement, even in monosyllabic prose.

It is the compact and pithy quality of so many of the sentences which causes readers to stop and muse over Johnson's summations.

> Human life is everywhere a state in which much is to be
>   endured, and little to be enjoyed.
> Marriage has many pains, but celibacy has no pleasures.
> Domestic discord . . . is not inevitably and fatally necessary; but
>   yet it is not easily avoided.
> It is difficult to negotiate where neither will trust.
> Many were in love with triflers like themselves; and many
>   fancied that they were in love when in truth they were
>   only idle.
> Such . . . are the effects of visionary schemes; when we first form
>   them we know them to be absurd, but familiarize them by
>   degrees, and in time lose sight of their folly.

Another important difference between *Candide* and *Rasselas* exists in the characters. Voltaire's philosopher, Pangloss, who keeps constantly insisting that this is the best of all possible worlds, is a fool. His counterpart, Imlac, is often the mouthpiece for Johnson's most serious ideas. The chief personages in *Candide* are much more individualized. They themselves experience the horrors of life. Candide is beaten, enslaved, has many narrow escapes from death; Cunegonde sees her parents butchered before her eyes, is raped, and suffers every kind of physical torture. The main characters in *Rasselas* are almost untouched, being merely observers. Nothing untoward happens to Rasselas and Nekayah, and even the kidnapping of unlucky Pekuah ultimately proves to have been no disaster.

Certainly Johnson was aware of the savagery in life. At times he sums up terrifying events unforgettably in a few words. When Rasselas examined the happiness of high station he found that "almost every man who stood high in employment hated all the rest, and was hated by them, and that their lives were a continual succession of plots and detections, stratagems and escapes, faction and treachery." And the episode closes with the terse remark: "In a short time the second Bassa was deposed. The Sultan that had advanced him was murdered by the Janisaries, and his successor had other views and different favourites."

But of much more importance to Johnson was the problem of happiness in private affairs. Voltaire shocks us into a realization of the precariousness of our physical well-being, and the selfishness and cruelty of most human actions. Johnson, instead, shows the basic defects of human character, even when unaffected by external events. Is happiness, he asks, to be found in youth and gay society, in simple pastoral life, in withdrawal, in absorption in science, or in marriage and domestic concerns? One after another is examined and found wanting. Some men are perhaps happier than others, but none is truly content. Nor may he ever be. The modern reader who is willing to move at Johnson's pace is held enthralled as each human desire is held up and shown to be basically forlorn. If at first each may seem to contain the answer to man's hopes, on careful study it is shown to have some flaw.

Surely, one might say, a simple hermit must be happy, withdrawn as he is from the cares and duties of everyday existence. No, says Johnson, nor will removal of temptation ensure goodness. Sadly the hermit confesses to Rasselas, "the life of a solitary man will be certainly miserable, but not certainly devout." In the end the hermit confides that he has decided to return to civilization. "They heard his resolution with surprise, but after a short pause offered to conduct him to Cairo. He dug up a considerable treasure which he had hid among the rocks, and accompanied them to the city, on which, as he approached it, he gazed with rapture."

Candide is witty in one way—with biting irony and mockery— *Rasselas* in another—with skeptical yet compassionate understanding. Voltaire is filled with bitter disgust, Johnson with melancholy resignation. Yet he, too, could satirize with keen irony. It is his skill in fashioning a devastating phrase, in embodying in a single compressed statement the ripeness of deep observation, that makes *Rasselas* worth reading over and over again.

Perhaps Joseph Wood Krutch was right in claiming that Johnson in one respect is more of a cynic than Voltaire, because he sees no possibility of reform.[26] Even in his own day many of Johnson's friends, among them Boswell, Hawkins, and Fanny Burney, felt that his outlook in this book was too gloomy and somber.[27] No wonder that Hazlitt called it "the most melancholy and debilitating moral speculation that ever was put forth."[28] But recent critics who have been stressing the religious convictions of Johnson refuse to agree. Johnson, they insist, is a realist, not a pessimist. As one recent writer puts it, "If happiness is possible on earth, in the sense which the travelers define it, then for Johnson there would be no need for heaven."[29]

Johnson's position is not that of a railer or misanthrope. He has no patience with vain regrets or attempts at withdrawal. Moreover, in his wise evaluation of human existence there is ample room for the comic. Thus it is quite possible to call *Rasselas* a comedy, though it must be in the sense that Dante's masterpiece is also a divine comedy. Although from one point of view Johnson's is a despairing commentary, from another it is also an inspiring recognition of man's heroic struggle and his hope for something better after death.

So *Candide* and *Rasselas* come down to us as twin assaults on man's pride and self-confidence—the one brilliant, shocking, and devastating in its revelation of man's villainy; the other somber and reflective, yet equally shrewd in its dissection of our failures and flagging hopes.

Johnson's *Rasselas* still has something vital to say to twentieth-century readers. Hilaire Belloc summed up what should be said when he wrote in the *New Statesman* in 1925: "Every man ought to read *Rasselas,* and every wise man will read it half-a-dozen times in his life . . . for never was wisdom better put, or more enduringly."[30]

CHAPTER XIV

Struggling to Keep Alive

D URING THE SUMMER OF 1759 Johnson spent most of his time out of London. In a letter to Lucy Porter on August 9 his comment that he had been in Oxford for seven weeks would suggest that he must have arrived in late June.[1] But we know very little about this visit, exactly where he stayed or how long, whom he saw or what he did. Almost all the evidence which has survived comes from a fragment of a letter which has never been traced. In it Johnson refers to having been in his Oxford gown ever since he had arrived. "It was at my first coming quite new and handsome." Presumably it did not remain so long.

What may have drawn Johnson to his old university this summer was the formal installation of the Jacobite Earl of Westmorland as Chancellor. The ceremonies began on July 3 with a

> grand procession of noblemen, doctors, &c, in their proper habits, which passed through St. Mary's, and was there joined by the masters of arts in their proper habits; and from thence proceeded to the great gate of the Sheldonian theatre, in which the most numerous and brilliant assembly of persons of quality and distinction were seated, that had ever been seen there on any occasion.[2]

If only we could have seen Johnson there in his proper Master's habiliments!

Then on the sixth there was a speech by Dr. William King, principal of St. Mary Hall, probably full of Jacobite allusions, at which Johnson clapped his hands until they were sore.

For lighter diversions Johnson went swimming three times, his first such exercise for years, and once vainly tried to persuade Robert Vansittart, an old friend, to climb over a wall. Was this after the frolic at University College when Johnson is reputed to have put away three bottles of port without being the worse for it?[3]

Johnson may this summer even have been seriously thinking of moving to Oxford, but he was not very excited about the prospect, for in his letter to Lucy Porter early in August, while praising his recent reception, he had to confess that "I have no great pleasure in any place." Practical considerations still had first priority, and he asked her how much might still be needed to pay his mother's debts. From some miscellaneous writing he expected to receive some money "in a short time." But his journalistic work was obviously based in London. Thus late in the summer he probably was back in rented rooms, this time at Gray's Inn, near High Holborn. Like Staple Inn, where he had stayed in the late spring, Gray's Inn was a temporary residence where he remained for a time while he was looking around. This was not in a part of the city where he wished to remain for the rest of his life. Somewhere nearer Fleet Street would be better.

Besides, he still was not certain whether he would ever get back his black servant, Frank, who was still in the Navy, where he first served on the ship *Golden Fleece*.[4] In March 1759, with the help of Tobias Smollett and John Wilkes, arrangements were begun for Frank's discharge, but when Johnson left the city for Oxford in the summer nothing was settled. Frank, by now serving on the *Stag*, was at sea when his former master, now living at Gray's Inn, decided to make another attempt. On November 9, 1759, Johnson apparently wrote to Sir George Hay, one of the Lords Commissioners of the Admiralty, asking his help.

> I had a negro boy named Francis Barber, given me by a friend whom I much respect, and treated by me for some years with great tenderness. Being disgusted in the house he ran away to sea, and was in the summer on board the ship stationed at Yarmouth to protect the fishery.
>
> It [would] be a great pleasure and some convenience to me, if the Lords of the Admiralty would be pleased to discharge him, which as he is no seaman may be done with little injury to the King's service.
>
> You were pleased, Sir, to order his discharge in the spring at the request of Mr. Wilkes, but I left London about that time and received no advantage from your favour. I therefore pre-

sume to entreat that you will repeat your order, and inform me
how to cooperate with it so that it may [be] made effectual.

I shall take the liberty of waiting at the Admiralty next
Tuesday for your answer.[5]

But still nothing happened quickly.

The *Stag* docked later in November, and a number of times in the
spring of 1760, but Frank stayed on, listed in the Muster Books as "L.M."
or "Land. Mn," that is, not a sailor by calling. It is clear that Frank had
no particular desire to get out, for years later he told Boswell that he
finally came back to civilian life "without any wish of his own."[6] It was
not until the summer of 1760 that he was officially discharged, and he did
not return to his old master until the autumn.[7]

There is very scanty information about Johnson's temporary stay
in Gray's Inn; there are only two known letters written from there in
November and December 1759. Boswell had nothing important to tell.
The one story which is definitely associated with this period appeared in
the *European Magazine* about twelve years after Johnson's death, but it
is not clear what other persons were involved. Here is the way the story
was told:

> Mrs. C— having subscribed for several copies of Johnson's first
> edition of Shakespeare, she told Mr. M— (a particular acquaint-
> ance of the Doctor) that she wished above all things to be intro-
> duced to the author, and that she would waive all ceremony
> and pay him the first visit. Johnson, being apprized of this, con-
> sented, and a morning was appointed for the rendezvous. The
> parties accordingly arrived at Johnson's chambers in Gray's
> Inn about one o'clock; when, after thundering at the outer
> door for near a quarter of an hour, Mr. M— at last peeped
> through the key-hole, and observed Johnson just issuing from
> his bed, in his shirt, without a night-cap (which by the by he
> never wore), the *pot de chambre* in one hand and the key in the
> other. In this situation he unlocked the door, when, spying a
> lady, he gravely turned round, "begged she would walk into an-
> other room, and he would have the pleasure of waiting on her
> immediately."
>
> As soon as ever Mrs. C— had recovered her surprise, she
> observed to Mr. M—, "what a fortunate thing it was for her
> that Johnson's milliner had not cheated him of his linen as
> much *before* as she had *behind*.[8]

Clearly Johnson was following his normal habit of late rising.

During the autumn Johnson secured some help in the *Idler* series
with three essays by Joshua Reynolds. He was helping Charlotte Lennox

in various ways with her translation from the French of Brumoy's *Greek Theatre*.[9] But his chief involvement probably was in a project, begun by Newbery, of a twenty-volume series to be called *The World Displayed*. First Johnson provided a paragraph for the advertisement (or proposals) which appeared in the newspapers at the end of October.

> Curiosity is seldom so powerfully excited, or so amply gratified, as by faithful relations of voyages and travels. The different appearances of nature, and the various customs of men, the gradual discovery of the world, and the accidents and hardships of a naval life, all concur to fill the mind with expectation and with wonder; and as science, when it can be connected with events, is always more easily learned and more certainly remembered, the history of a voyage may be considered as the most useful treatise on geography, since the student follows the traveller from country to country, and retains the situation of places by recounting his adventures.[10]

Then in his full Introduction, which appeared in the first volume published December 1, he discussed some of the works to be included. Naturally, he also added a number of general comments of his own. Even though, with the surrender of Quebec in September 1759, England and Pitt were apparently winning the great war with France, this did not materially change Johnson's attitude towards colonial expansion. This he clearly showed in some of his generalizations, such as: "The Europeans have scarcely visited any coast but to gratify avarice and extend corruption; to arrogate dominion without right and practice cruelty without incentive." And he lashed out with fury in an often-quoted passage:

> The first propagators of Christianity recommended their doctrines by their sufferings and virtues; they entered no defenseless territories with swords in their hands; they built no forts upon ground to which they had no right, nor polluted the purity of religion with the avarice of trade or insolence of power.
>
> What may still raise higher the indignation of a Christian mind, this purpose of propagating truth appears never to have been seriously pursued by any European nation; no means whether lawful or unlawful have been practised with diligence and perseverance for the conversion of savages. When a fort is built and a factory established, there remains no other care than to grow rich. It is soon found that ignorance is most easily kept in subjection, and that by enlightening the mind with truth, fraud and usurpation would be made less practicable and less secure.

When describing how one Portuguese admiral used gaudy presents to calm down native opposition to a settlement, Johnson remarked:

> The work was now peaceably continued, and such was the diligence with which the strangers hastened to secure the possession of the country, that in twenty days they had sufficiently fortified themselves against the hostility of negroes. . . . In this fort the Admiral remained with sixty soldiers, and sent back the rest in the ships, with gold, slaves, and other commodities. It may be observed that slaves were never forgotten, and that wherever they went they gratified their pride if not their avarice, and brought some of the natives, when it happened that they brought nothing else.

Of course, they always built a church for services of worship, but this modified not at all their commercial negotiations with the Negroes.

Johnson also became involved in another controversy, the construction of a new bridge over the Thames at Blackfriars. The issue was whether an elliptical or a semicircular arch was to be preferred. Eventually the design offered by the architect William Mylne, which was elliptical in form, was chosen. But Johnson came out for that proposed by Mylne's rival, John Gwynn, who later became one of his good friends, and who was for semicircular arches. After some investigation and thought, Johnson decided that practical considerations should prevail over aesthetic, and he wrote three letters to the *Gazetteer,* which appeared in the issues of December 1, 8, and 15, 1759. His solution to the problem was simple:

> The first excellence of a bridge built for commerce over a large river is strength; for a bridge which cannot stand, however beautiful, will boast its beauty but a little while; the stronger arch is, therefore, to be preferred, and much more to be preferred, if with greater strength it has greater beauty.[11]

In what followed, Johnson proved conclusively, at least from his practical point of view, that the semicircular arch was stronger. So he ended by recommending to any who might still doubt "which of the two arches is the stronger, to press an egg first on the ends, and then upon the sides."

Johnson's emphasis on practical considerations did not mean that he had no interest in the problems of artists. Indeed, as far back as December 1756 Johnson had been elected a member of the Society for the Encouragement of Arts, Manufactures, and Commerce, commonly called the Society of Arts, the only group which included painters, sculptors, and workers in the decorative arts, and in March 1757 paid his dues of two guineas. He had been proposed by James Stuart, later known as "Athenian Stuart" because of his advocacy of Greek architecture. From surviving minutes of meetings we can tell something of Johnson's active participation in various activities of the society.[12] In February 1758 he proposed his friend James Grainger for membership, and in May Johnson was appointed to a special committee which was discussing plans for establishing a charity house which could be used by repentant prostitutes. Remembering Johnson's *Rambler* essays on the sad plight of prostitutes and his habit of talking to them late at night on the streets, one can surmise that he became an active member of the committee. Unfortunately in the end nothing came of the project.

Occasionally Johnson may have taken part in open discussions at the general meetings of the society. Boswell passes on a number of vague stories which cannot be accurately placed, though they may have had some factual basis. For example, Sir William Scott mentioned that Johnson once confessed that he had several times tried to speak at meetings of the society, but "had found he could not get on."[13] And Johnson told William Gerard Hamilton that once when he rose to deliver a speech which he had prepared, "all my flowers of oratory forsook me."

On the other hand, Andrew Kippis, when describing how the great room of the society was for a time the place where many persons tried to display their oratorical skill, and how Goldsmith once was obliged to sit down in confusion, insisted that he had heard Johnson speak there "upon a subject relative to mechanics, with a propriety, perspicuity, and energy which excited general admiration."[14]

In the autumn of 1759 and early the next year Johnson was drawn into some other important activities of the society. In London up to this time there had been no easy way for creative artists to exhibit their works. In 1755, a number of leading artists formed themselves into a committee and published a statement of their aims, but because of various rivalries nothing came of the project. The one place where beautiful paintings had been displayed was at the new Foundling Hospital, which had been presented with a number of fine works of art. As these were much admired, it was natural that there should be talk about the desirability of more extensive exhibitions of the work of creative artists, of the famous and the little known alike.

Finally, early in November 1759, at the Foundling Hospital proposals were initiated for some definite action, and a week later at a gathering at the Turk's Head Tavern in Gerrard Street, Soho, a committee, including a number of Johnson's close friends, was formed to set in motion arrangements for the first extensive public exhibition ever to be held in London. The most pressing problem was that of finding a room large enough to hold all the paintings, sculptures, and other objects to be shown. One obvious solution was to request the use of the spacious room in the Strand belonging to the Society of Arts. But to do so would require a formal petition, and the practical artists, quite sure of their ability to handle a brush or chisel, may not have been quite so certain of their skill in letter writing. And so the matter lagged.

At the fourth meeting, on January 19, 1760, however, someone among the thirteen who attended made a proposal. Why not ask the help of a professional writer? And he obviously had someone in mind—a man who was friendly with members of the group, known to be in sympathy with their aspirations for greater public recognition, and noted for his skill in fashioning memorable phrases. Thus the secretary recorded: "Resolved— that Mr. Johnson may have the form of a letter drawn up by this society to correct, in order to be sent to the Society for the Encouragement of Arts &c to solicit the use of their room for the exhibition." Unfortunately, Reynolds, who may well have initiated the idea, was not actually present at this meeting, and again there was no speedy action. Two weeks later, on February 2, however, with Reynolds in attendance, another resolution was passed authorizing a special meeting of the committee on the next Saturday "to peruse the letter given to Mr. Johnson for his correction," and to arrange to have this dispatched to the Society of Arts. Still, it was not until February 26 that what had been prepared was ready to show to the group. On that day there was another meeting, when the secretary recorded a resolution that a letter and plan, to be signed by the chairman, Francis Hayman, be sent to the society.

That the "Mr. Johnson" referred to in the minutes was Samuel there is no doubt. The rhythms of the concluding sentence of the letter he had produced—"The public concurrence of the Society will give to a new practice that countenance which novelty must always need, and the arts will gain dignity from the protection of those whom the world has already learned to respect"—and the writer's insistence that "elegance and ingenuity are most valuable when they contribute to the purposes of virtue" are characteristic. Indeed, it is unlikely that much of the original draft remained intact after Johnson's rewriting. If Reynolds and others supplied the factual details, the general wording must be Johnson's.

Of course, Johnson was himself a member of the society being addressed, though slightly in arrears with his dues.[15] In the spring of 1760 he was two years behind, but on March 25 after paying four guineas he was once again in good standing. The reason sometimes given for Johnson's paying up what he owed has been his support for membership of Robert Dossie. More likely the chief factor was the continued negotiations over the proposed exhibition.

Johnson did not attend the meeting of the Society of Arts on March 3, 1760, when the matter was discussed, but Reynolds and Hayman were there and along with Garrick were appointed to a special committee to consider the proposal.[16] The Society was not ready to lend its rooms without retaining some definite control of what went on. They would not allow any charge for admission and also insisted upon postponing the date two weeks. Having no choice at this late date, the artists had to accept or give up the whole project.

Finally on April 21 the exhibition opened; it was a great success. Sixty-nine artists were represented with 131 works. There were large crowds, at times even unruly ones, and windows were broken. One estimate of the total attendance was over twenty thousand people. Partly to circumvent the society's ban on an admission fee, the artists charged sixpence for each catalogue, and since over six thousand were sold, when it was over the artists were in funds. They gladly voted various payments to people who had helped with arrangements—half a guinea for one man, ten for another and his son, one for another, four for someone else, and a handsome piece of plate for the secretary. Then at the end of the minutes for the meeting of May 12 comes the entry: "Ordered that thanks be returned to Mr. Johnson for his great assistance to the Committee of Artists and that Mr. Reynolds return the same." The action suggests that Johnson's help involved more than the mere rewriting of the letter of request. He may possibly also have drafted the formal letter of thanks sent to the Society of Arts in mid-May, although the style is not distinctively Johnsonian.

The first exhibition having been so successful, it was natural that the artists should think of arranging a second. The following November meetings began again. On the fourteenth a new committee was elected, and on the twenty-fifth Hayman was reelected Chairman. Following this the group passed a series of resolutions containing various suggestions for the next exhibition, ending with the statement: "Resolved—that the above minutes be the substance of the letter to be sent to the Society. Mr. Reynolds is desired to request Mr. Johnson to continue his good offices to the artists."[17] That Mr. Johnson was so inclined appears from the minutes of the next meeting of the committee, at which time the secretary reported having received the draft of a letter as requested.

Again, as in the earlier revision, the lame half-sentences, the awkward phrases and unexpressed assumptions of the minutes were reshaped into a dignified, forceful letter. A mixed-up explanation of the choice of June for the exhibition was turned into a moral issue—"lest any man should a second time suffer the disgrace of having lost that which he never sought"—and the reminder of last year's "inconvenience" caused by "inferior" people crowding the rooms was elaborated into a memorable short paragraph: "The exhibition of last year was crowded and incommoded by the intrusion of great numbers whose stations and education made them no proper judges of statuary or painting, and who were made idle and tumultuous by the opportunity of a show." Although the basic ideas are the same, a new element has been added. Here is the Rambler, seeing all human actions as moral choices or social dilemmas.

About the same time Johnson helped some of the artists in another project. Early in November 1760, following the accession of George III, there were drafted great numbers of formal addresses to the throne. Every town and county, organization and group, wished to carry up to St. James's some expression of enthusiastic welcome to the new sovereign. Consequently, during the last weeks of 1760 the *London Gazette* and other newspapers were packed with these addresses. In the minutes of the committee of artists there is no mention at all of any plan to join in this mass outburst of loyalty, yet evidently something must have been done by a representative section of the same individuals. On the first page of the *London Gazette* of January 6–10, 1761, there appeared an address to the King from the "painters, sculptors, and architects," probably written by Johnson. Boswell thought so, and the style is certainly Johnsonian. As a sample, here is the third paragraph:

> It is our happiness to live in the age when our arts may hope for new advances toward perfection, assisted by the favour of a British King, of a monarch no less judicious to distinguish than powerful to reward: who knows the usefulness and value of that skill which delights the eye with beauty, but not corrupts the manners by unlawful passions, and which has been hitherto learned in foreign countries, for want of sufficient encouragement in our own.[18]

Although the source of Boswell's information was not given, he undoubtedly had good authority for the ascription.[19] The piece is contained in a manuscript list of Johnson's publications and fugitive pieces, which still survives in the Yale collection.[20]

One might guess that the same procedure was followed as in the other cases of help given by Johnson to the artists. Reynolds came to Johnson with a rough sketch of the main points to be made. After some general discussion, the sheet was left with him for consideration. He then reworked the sentences and added the moral sentiments, emphasizing art which pleases but does not corrupt, and insisting on its subservience to virtue and religion. It is impossible to tell just when it was written, but on January 10, 1761, the text was released by the Court officials.[21]

When plans were being made by the committee of artists for the next exhibition, various differences arose, one of the most difficult being their proposal to charge a shilling for each catalogue and to make this serve as an entrance fee. For a while there was an impasse, with continued arguments, but there is no evidence that Johnson had anything to do with these later negotiations.[22]

Not that all this work for the practicing artists reflected any change in Johnson's own general attitude toward the visual arts. Nearsighted as he was, and unable to see anything clearly at a distance, he had never been noted for keen admiration of paintings. It is easy to document his later obvious lack of interest in them. There is the well-known story of his visit, with Boswell and Reynolds, to the house of Richard Owen Cambridge in Twickenham. As soon as they had been welcomed by their host, Johnson "ran eagerly on one side of the room, intent on poring over the backs of books. Sir Joshua observed (aside), 'He runs to the books, as I do to the pictures: but I have the advantage. I can see much more of the pictures than he can of the books.' "[23] And there are other accounts of Johnson's candid admission of how little painting meant to him. Although he was happy to help his friends in any possible way, he did not change his fundamental position. He could see few basic moral values in mere visual representation.

Thus after the first two exhibitions he could comment to his friend Baretti in Milan: "This exhibition has filled the heads of the artists and lovers of art. Surely life, if it be not long, is tedious, since we are forced to call in the assistance of so many trifles to rid us of our time, of that time which never can return."[24]

This did not mean any hypocrisy on Johnson's part. He was fully in support of the artists' project. From the beginning it had been advertised as a philanthropic venture, with the proceeds of the first exhibition designed to aid elderly, indigent artists, though gradually this side of the project was pushed aside. Stress was always given to recognition of serious-minded artisans who worked with their hands. Honest labor, which injured no one, should be encouraged. Besides, the necessity for man to fill up the vacuity of life by every means possible was one of Johnson's recurrent themes. As one critic recently put it, "Johnson's basic metaphor for human experience is the empty receptacle which cannot tolerate its own emptiness."[25] In man there is this ever-present dichotomy—the "inherent need of the mind to be filled with 'objects of attention' and the elusive nature of the objects offered it by temporal experience."

The aims of the group of artists may well have appeared to Johnson as one innocent means of filling up the vacuity of life. Whatever he thought of the objects to be exhibited, he was glad to help in any way he could.

To move back to early 1760, we should point out that shortly before the opening of the first exhibition, in April 1760, the final number of Johnson's *Idler* appeared in the last issue of the *Universal Chronicle*. If he was for the moment relieved to have the weekly pressure taken away, it had been the *Idler* which had for the last two years been his only regular source of income. Now that was gone. Instead he had to fall back on various small jobs which he did to help his friends, possibly a few essays for Charlotte Lennox's *Lady's Museum,* and one of the "Trifler" papers in that miscellany.[26]

Occasional glimpses of what he was doing appear in the records of societies to which he belonged. One, known as "The Associates of Dr. Bray," was a semireligious benevolent organization designed to supply reading matter to colonial clergy. The annual membership fee was a guinea, and there were monthly business meetings at Mr. Bird's bookshop in Ave Mary Lane, attended usually by eight or ten members. On April 6, 1760, Johnson's name was proposed, and he was unanimously elected a member. At the next meeting on May 1 he was one of eight listed as attending. Another who was there that day was Benjamin Franklin.[27] Thus we know that the two men at least once were in the same room, and presumably talked to each other. According to the surviving minutes of the meeting, the Associates heard a report about their lending library at Bampton, Westmorland, and voted to establish a library at Llandaff. The most interesting item of business was probably the reading of a letter from the supervisor of a Negro school in Philadelphia in the colonies, where eleven boys and twenty-four girls were enrolled. All received instruction in reading and religion, and the girls were also taught needlework.

Johnson undoubtedly approved. The nature of the discussion that day could not have proved particularly fascinating, for he never attended another meeting, though years later he did contribute to the funds of the Associates, and he may have gone to some of the annual dinners. No records were kept of those who attended these social functions. So all we have is one brief glimpse of Johnson and Benjamin Franklin, listening to dull reports about library facilities and projects of that sort. Perhaps they also had brief arguments on the side; they certainly would not have agreed on many topics.

From various other sources unavailable to Boswell we do know something about Johnson's activities during the summer of 1760. On June 29, when dining with Joshua Reynolds, he met an interesting Jesuit scholar, mathematician, and astronomer from the shores of the Adriatic, Roger Joseph Boscovich.[28] Later they dined together at the home of Mrs. Cholmondeley, the actress Peg Woffington's younger sister, whom Johnson once described as "a very airy lady," and at Dr. John Douglas's. Since Boscovich during his visit to England wrote full letters back to his brother and friends, we can date some of the meetings, though Boscovich had little specific to say about Johnson's actual conversation or appearance. All he did was identify him as "one of the leading men of letters in England, author of a celebrated dictionary" and "one of the great men of letters of the country." As always with visiting church dignitaries, Johnson spoke in Latin "with a dignity and eloquence" that astonished Boscovich.

At Joshua Reynolds's Johnson gave Boscovich a letter to young Robert Chambers at Oxford, who liked to show eminent visitors around. Boscovich found him delightful—"a young man of the highest parts, and a nature so sweet, modest at the same time, charming and gracious, that he is enchanting." Thus if he failed disappointingly to provide any frank comments on Johnson, Boscovich was not sparing in praise of others with more obvious graces.

Arthur Murphy gives a fuller account of the dinner later in the year at Dr. Douglas's. At first the conversation was mostly in French, and Johnson, uncertain as to his pronunciation, kept quiet. But later the topics changed, as did the language.

> For the rest of the evening the talk was in Latin. Boscovich had a ready current flow of that flimsy phraseology with which a priest may travel through Italy, Spain, and Germany. Johnson scorned what he called colloquial barbarisms. It was to his pride to speak his best. He went on, after a little practice, with as much facility as if it was his native tongue. One sentence this writer well remembers. Observing that Fontenelle at first opposed the Newtonian philosophy, and embraced it afterwards, his words were: *Fontenellus, ni fallor, in extrema senectute fuit transfuga ad castra Newtoniana.*

From the still unpublished diary of Thomas Hollis we can fill in more about another episode in the summer of 1760.[29] Hollis was a violent Whig, a great enthusiast for the Commonwealth, a benefactor of Harvard College in the colonies, and a supporter of all revolutionary causes. Not the type one would expect to find in any way associated with Johnson! But one of Hollis's benefactions did arouse support, an attempt to raise money in order to clothe French prisoners of war. Early in June 1760, Hollis dined repeatedly with the publisher John Payne, planning a publication for the committee. Apparently there had been some difference of opinion as to whom to ask to write an introduction, and the one finally chosen did not please all members. Perhaps as an afterthought, Johnson's name was suggested as an alternative, and with the backing of Hollis, Payne agreed to serve as intermediary. Johnson willingly agreed, and provided some forceful pages. Thus on June 19 Hollis noted in his diary:

> Mr. Payne with me in the evening relating to the intended publication of the charity respecting the French prisoners. Received of him, at the same time, a MS of Mr. Johnson's, composed at my request and for which I have presented him with five guineas, which MS I hope will be allowed to serve as an Introduction to the before mentioned publication, notwithstanding that another Introduction had been already agreed upon by the committee.

Once he saw Johnson's manuscript, Hollis was convinced of its superior merit, and he was determined to ensure its acceptance. But evidently this required some negotiation. For a group of radical Whigs to approve of something written by such a well-known Tory as Johnson was not easy. They had to see exactly what was said. Yet in this instance Johnson's kind heart and sympathy for war prisoners were involved, and he hated the war with France more than did most Whigs. Thus there was no real argument.

On June 23 Hollis commented in his diary that he had shown Johnson's suggested piece to Dr. Macaulay, "which paper was approved highly by the Dr. to my great satisfaction." Two days later he added:

> Called afterwards on Mr. Corbyn, the Quaker, Mr. Gwilt, and Mr. Smith, to show them Mr. Johnson's paper respecting the French prisoners; which paper was approved highly by the two first, and was assented to under various conditions, and uneasily by the latter, who is the author of the Introduction which was agreed to, for want of a better, by the Committee.

On the twenty-sixth he called upon King's Serjeant George Nares, who also highly approved; and on the twenty-eighth he added:

> At Sir Joseph Hankey's and Dr. Fothergil's to show them Mr. Johnson's paper respecting the French prisoners, which was approved highly by them both. . . . Wrote Mr. Brand and inclosed to him Johnson's paper before mentioned for his perusal.

By the thirtieth it was evident Hollis's tactics had been successful.

> In the evening Mr. Payne with me to inform me, that Mr. Smith on hearing that all the other gentlemen of the Committee for clothing French prisoners now in town approved Mr. Johnson's paper, had approved it likewise, and in a hand-

some manner. Received Mr. Brand's approbation to it likewise in a very pretty letter....

Finally, over three weeks later, on July 23, came the formal transaction.

> Dined with Mr. Johnson at a tavern. At a Committee for the Relief of French prisoners of war held at the Crown and Anchor in the Strand. Settled everything ultimately for the intended publication; and among other resolutions agreed that Mr. Johnson's manuscript should serve as an introduction to the publication in place of Mr. Smith's.

From the diary it is apparent that Hollis and "Mr. Johnson" continued to see each other, but the trouble is that among Hollis's associates there were at least three Johnsons, and he never supplies a first name. Thus we cannot always be certain which one he is referring to. We do know that early the next year he tried to talk Samuel Johnson into writing a dissertation for the Society of Arts on the polite arts, the state of the nation, and life in general. Despite the attractive offer of five guineas, Johnson declined "as not sufficiently informed of the several matters."[30]

Johnson's Introduction to the *Proceedings of the Committee on French Prisoners*, which appeared in August, is one of his most moving appeals. Only one argument, Johnson suggests, can be raised against helping in every way we can the prisoners of war—that by relieving Frenchmen we forget the miseries of our own poor. But even if this is admitted, all that it proves is that "to relieve the French is a good action, but that a better may be conceived." Still, "how little virtue could be practised, if beneficence were to wait always for the most proper objects, and the noblest occasions, occasions that may never happen, and objects that never may be found?" So he concluded:

> That charity is best of which the consequences are most extensive; the relief of enemies has a tendency to unite mankind in fraternal affection, to soften the acrimony of adverse nations, and dispose them to peace and amity; in the mean time, it alleviates captivity and takes away something from the miseries of war. The rage of war, however mitigated, will always fill the world with calamity and horror: let it not then be unnecessarily extended; let animosity and hostility cease together, and no man be longer deemed an enemy than while his sword is drawn against us.[31]

Some time during the summer of 1760 Johnson moved again, this time renting chambers just off Fleet Street up one flight of stairs at No. 1

Inner Temple Lane. He was probably subtenant of either Sir Thomas Bootle or Sir James Barrow, to whom he paid an annual rent of about fifteen or sixteen guineas.[32] Here he remained for about five years, and it was here that he was living when he first met Boswell.

He was settled into his new quarters when his servant Frank was released from the Navy on October 22, or at least that is what Frank later told Boswell.[33] After long delays he was finally back with his master, and presumably had a small space to sleep somewhere in the apartments, with Miss Williams, Levet, and other former companions living nearby. Frank served as messenger boy, brought in food, and did minor jobs around the place.

Although the original buildings are gone, we can describe from various sources something of what the place was like. A Cambridge student, Baptist Noel Turner, and a friend were thinking about making a new translation of Plutarch's *Lives,* and on a trip to London they decided to consult Johnson about the possibility. Turner met Dr. Levet, who willingly the next morning brought him at breakfast time to see Johnson. This is how Turner many years later described what happened:

> His residence was then in some old fashioned rooms called, I think, Inner Temple Lane, No. 1. At the top of a few steps the door opened into a dark and dingy looking old wainscotted ante-room, through which was the study, and into which, a little before noon, came rolling, as if just roused from his cabin, the truly uncouth figure of our literary Colossus, in a strange black wig, too little for him by half, but which, before our next interview, was exchanged for that very respectable brown one in which his friend Sir Joshua so faithfully depicted him. I am glad, however, I saw the queer black bob, as his biographers have noticed it, and as it proved that the lustre of native genius can break through the most disfiguring habiliments. He seemed pleased to see a young Cantab in his rooms, and on my acquainting him with the business on which I had taken the liberty of consulting him, he rather encouraged our undertaking than otherwise; though after working at it for a few months we found the work too tedious and incompatible with other pursuits, and were obliged to relinquish it. After this, the great man questioned me about Cambridge, and whatever regarded literature, and attended to my answers with great complacency.[34]

A few years later the painter Ozias Humphry, when telling his brother about a visit to Johnson, described passing through "three very dirty rooms" before coming to "a little one that looked like an old counting house, where this man was sat at his breakfast. The furniture of this room was a very large deal writing-desk, an old walnut-tree table, and five ragged chairs of four different sets."[35] Others stressed the decrepit, filthy condition of most of the rooms—"the abode of wretchedness." Arthur Murphy records that once when someone paid Johnson "a morning visit, intending from his chambers to send a letter into the City," he found to his surprise that his host was "without pen, ink, or paper."[36] Indeed, Murphy insisted that Johnson lived here "in poverty, total idleness, and the pride of literature."

From his annual birthday prayer jotted down on September 18, it is clear that Johnson was well aware of all the mistakes he was making. He knew he was lazy and unproductive. But he had for many years known that. This time, along with the usual resolves to rise earlier, to get more done, to keep a journal, to go to church, and to study religion, there was a new item which appears for the first time—"To drink less strong liquors."[37] As long as Tetty had been alive, Johnson had resolutely refrained from alcoholic beverages of all kinds. But after her death he apparently relaxed and by 1757 was beginning to drink again. By 1760 he evidently thought he was imbibing too much.

According to Boswell, when Johnson was living here and had no "regular system of life," he often inadvertently went without his customary large meals. He once had

> fasted for two days at a time, during which he had gone about visiting, though not at the hours of dinner or supper; that he had drunk tea, but eaten no bread; that this was no intentional fasting, but happened just in the course of a literary life.[38]

Once, indeed, he had "fasted" from Sunday's dinner to that on Tuesday, "without any inconvenience." Johnson's theory was that it is "best to eat just as one is hungry."

It was his custom not to go to bed before two o'clock in the morning, drinking cup after cup of tea after supper and finding it difficult to go to sleep. From many accounts, he did not usually get up the next day until almost noon, and sometimes even after that, and then loved to have people about him for relaxed talk. William Maxwell, at this time Reader (assistant preacher) of the Temple Church, described what Johnson's existence was like:

> His general mode of life . . . seemed to be pretty uniform. About twelve o'clock I commonly visited him, and frequently found

him in bed, or declaiming over his tea which he drank very
plentifully. He generally had a levee of morning visitors, chiefly
men of letters.[39]

It is likely he had other visitors as well. Any man with his kindness
of heart and interest in the poor and needy would be sure to draw constant
pleas. Hawkins reported that a neighboring shopkeeper at the corner told
him that during the time that Johnson lived on Inner Temple Lane
"more enquiries were made at his shop for Mr. Johnson, than for all the
inhabitants put together of both the Inner and Middle Temple."[40]

Not everyone who lived in the Temple area became Johnson's friend.
A young man named William Cowper, who at this time lived at No. 3
Inner Temple Lane, on the same side but across the passage leading into
Hare Court, apparently never met Johnson. As Charles Ryskamp phrases
it, "Johnson left no word indicating that he ever heard of Cowper, Cowper
no suggestion that he ever knew Johnson."[41] Although they must often
have passed each other in the Lane, nothing seems to have brought them
together.

There can be no doubt of the veneration accorded him by the many
writers and journalists who paid him visits. Charles Burney later told
Boswell that when he went to see Johnson in 1760 he happened to arrive
before his host was up, and being shown into the room where he was expected soon for breakfast, Burney looked around for some kind of a
memento he could take away to send to one of his good friends in Norfolk,
as a relic of the "admirable" great man. But finding nothing better to his
purpose, he cut some bristles off the hearthbroom and enclosed them in a
letter to his country enthusiast, "who received them with due reverence."[42]

Not that his visitors were unaware of their host's many eccentricities
and his slovenly appearance. Ozias Humphry described him to his brother
this way: "He is a very large man, and was dressed in a dirty brown coat
and waistcoat, with breeches that were brown also (though they had been
crimson), and an old black wig; his shirtcollar and sleeves were unbut-
toned; his stockings were down about his feet, which had on them, by way
of slippers, an old pair of shoes." But once talk began, the situation
changed. "Everything he says," Humphry commented, "is as *correct* as a
second edition; 'tis almost impossible to argue with him, he is so sententious and so knowing."[43]

One could never be sure just what to expect when going up the stairs
at No. 1 Inner Temple Lane. Baptist Noel Turner on his second visit
found Johnson absent, "and when Francis Barber, his black servant,
opened the door to tell me so, a group of his African countrymen were
sitting around a fire in the gloomy ante-room; and on their all turning

their sooty faces at once to stare at me, they presented a curious spectacle."[44]

Johnson himself was never certain who might turn up or when. It was about this time that a celebrated incident occurred which Boswell describes with gusto. Johnson's young Oxford friends, Langton and Beauclerk, had been at a tavern until about three in the morning, and then thought of going to see if Johnson would not join them in a ramble.

> They rapped violently at the door of his chambers in the Temple, till at last he appeared in his shirt, with his little black wig on the top of his head, instead of a nightcap, and a poker in his hand, imagining probably that some ruffians were coming to attack him. When he discovered who they were, and was told their errand, he smiled, and with great good humour agreed to their proposal: "What, is it you, you dogs! I'll have a frisk with you."[45]

He was soon dressed, and they wandered around Covent Garden talking to the greengrocers, imbibing a bowl of punch called "Bishop" (defined in Johnson's *Dictionary* as "a cant word for a mixture of wine, oranges, and sugar") at a tavern, before walking to the Thames and then rowing to Billingsgate. When Langton, tired after the night's dissipation, left at breakfast time, Johnson was still so pleased with the night's relaxation that he continued his rambles with Beauclerk.

With the move to Inner Temple Lane Johnson had entered a period of little productivity and increased socializing. With no regular weekly essays to compose in a hurry and little prospect of completing speedily any of his long-term projects, he lapsed into almost total inactivity, except on the social level. Not that he was unaware of his weaknesses. As we have seen, in his birthday prayer he clearly showed his concern. And he continued vaguely to talk about various other projects. Thomas Birch wrote to Yorke on October 25:

> Sam Johnson is in treaty with certain booksellers to supply three papers a week in the nature of essays like the *Rambler,* at the unusual rate (if my account be true) of three guineas a paper. But I question whether even the temptation of so liberal a reward will awaken him from his natural indolence enough to fulfill his engagement.[46]

Birch was right. Johnson did nothing about starting another periodical. During the late autumn and through the winter, life continued as before. By Easter Eve, 1761, he was so upset that he wrote down one of the longest and most explicit prayers of his career.

> Since the Communion of last Easter I have led a life so dissipated and useless, and my terrours and perplexities have so much encreased, that I am under great depression and discouragement, yet I purpose to present myself before God tomorrow with humble hope that he will not break the bruised reed.
>   Come unto me all ye that travail.
>   I have resolved, I hope not presumptuously, till I am afraid to resolve again. Yet hoping in God I steadfastly purpose to lead a new life. O God, enable me, for Jesus Christ's sake. My Purpose is
> 1 To repel vain and corrupt imaginations.
> 2 To avoid idleness.
>   To regulate my sleep as to length and choice of hours.
>   To set down every day what shall be done the day following.
>   To keep a journal.
> 3 To worship God more diligently.
>   To go to church every Sunday.
> 4 To study the Scriptures.
>   To read a certain portion every week.
>   Almighty and most merciful Father look down upon my misery with pity, strengthen me that I may overcome all sinful habits, grant that I may with effectual faith commemorate the death of thy son Jesus Christ, so that all corrupt desires may be extinguished, and all vain thoughts may be dispelled. Enlighten me with true knowledge, animate me with reasonable hope, comfort me with a just sense of thy love, and assist me to the performance of all holy purposes, that after the sins, errours and miseries of this world I may obtain everlasting happiness for Jesus Christ's sake. To whom &c. Amen.
>   I hope to attend on God in his ordinances to morrow. Trust in God O my soul. O God let me trust in Thee.[47]

Unfortunately, the next year was not much better.

CHAPTER XV

Friend and Talker

FROM THE AUTUMN OF 1760 to the spring of 1762 Johnson produced very little. It was a fallow period in his life as a writer. Instead, his social life widened, and he doubtless spent more time in talking. For the biographer, then, all that is possible is to present a potpourri of descriptions of his closest friends, some notion of how he lived, details of what little he did write, and some surviving anecdotes from these years.

It would appear that once he could drag himself out of bed by noon he would have all kinds of people about him; but he also spent much of his time with friends away from home. With no large kitchen or full-time cook of his own, Johnson did not have a fixed or regular schedule of meals. If he had dinner, it would most likely be either with some new acquaintance or business associate at a tavern, or as a guest at the home of an old friend. There were many of the latter, and he had numerous invitations. At times he may even have had commitments to dine with this person or that on regular days. At other times he fended for himself, on the spur of the moment. Supper would depend on where he was in the early evening.

Usually Johnson had tea with blind Anna Williams at her house, either in the afternoon or late at night on his way home. The diary entries of Thomas Percy and others show clearly how all of the Johnson circle expected to meet him and others at Miss Williams's. But there one would not expect to get much more than endless cups of tea. Apparently Anna Williams was very skillful in presiding over the tea table. Even though blind, she had worked out a way to gauge the height of liquid in a cup, so as to know just when to stop pouring. She moved her fingers up the outside of the cup feeling the warmth, and not inside as sometimes rumored. With remarkable patience and endurance, never certain just when Johnson would turn up, she nevertheless waited for him until the early hours of the morning if necessary.[1] His sense of time was unreliable, to say the least.

Since Johnson kept no day-to-day diary, we are forced to rely on others for details concerning his engagements. Much, indeed, has to be guesswork. There were some people whom Johnson saw regularly, among them his publishers, Dodsley, Newbery, and Payne. And there were David Henry and other connections at the *Gentleman's Magazine,* who may have come to talk about possible reviews or other minor jobs. At times Johnson used to dine with the Garricks, where he would hear talk about the theater and meet interesting new people, among them Edmund Burke. Sometimes he would go to dine with Samuel Richardson, when he had something he wished to discuss with his host, and was willing to listen to him talk interminably about himself.

Then there was a money scrivener and member of the Common Council of London named Jack Ellis. A bachelor who entertained well, Ellis was much more than a mere businessman. An amateur poet for over seventy years, he had also translated Ovid's *Epistles.* Somewhere, sometime, his path crossed Johnson's, and they became fast friends. As one later account described him, Ellis was "temperate, regular, and cheerful." He always was a pleasing companion and "joined in the conversation of his friends with ease, freedom, and politeness. He abounded in anecdote, and told a story with great success." Moreover, "he was charitable to the poor and unfortunate," and benevolent in many ways. No wonder Johnson enjoyed his society. Indeed, Johnson once told Boswell that the "most literary conversation" he had ever enjoyed was at the table of Jack Ellis.[3] For a time, Johnson used to dine regularly with him once a week.

Then there was the strange impostor, George Psalmanazar, one of the most successful liars who ever lived.[4] It was he who claimed to have been a native of Formosa and made up a language and history of that distant country which had Oxford scholars completely fooled. When later in life he happened to read William Law's *Serious Call* (also a crucial book in Johnson's life), Psalmanazar made a complete turnaround and confessed his deception. In the end he became one of the most pious and devout men that Johnson ever knew. But just when the two first met has never been established, whether back in the 1740s when Johnson wandered the streets of London with Richard Savage, or later, after the death of his wife, when he was again footloose.

In his late years Psalmanazar lived in Ironmonger Row and spent much of his time in a frowsy alehouse in Old Street, Clerkenwell. Here reputedly there met a group which Johnson later called a club, but the exact makeup of the group is vague. Only three persons have ever been suggested as active members—Johnson, Psalmanazar, and a "metaphysical tailor" named Hoole, whose nephew later became one of Johnson's good friends. Around cheap, soft wood tables, on benches or high-backed settles, the group would sit for long hours and talk. One topic we may be sure they never mentioned was Formosa. Johnson once admitted that he had been afraid even to mention China. Although Psalmanazar had publicly in print in 1747 acknowledged the fictitious nature of his earlier *Description of Formosa,* his complete confession did not appear until after his death. He left the manuscript with his kind landlady, Sarah Rewalling, whom he owed much for unpaid rent and other supplies. Johnson, while undoubtedly curious about the notorious earlier career of this now venerable figure, was apparently quite willing to accept without question his later devout stance.

From various surviving accounts, Psalmanazar was the ruling spirit of that club in Old Street. The fact that he was now an opium addict, keeping alive through his daily dosage of ten or twenty drops of Sydenham's mixture (laudanum, a tincture of opium), made no difference to Johnson. After all, Johnson himself at times used laudanum. There was no stigma involved. Everyone used it, more or less as we use aspirin today. Laudanum was the accepted remedy for pain, and no one cared whether or not a person became addicted. Psalmanazar, by his convincing religious faith, his regular life and humility and goodness, so impressed Johnson that he was willing to take him as he was. Like the neighboring children who reputedly deferred to this remarkable old man, Johnson greatly admired him. Indeed, he occupied for Johnson a higher sphere, and Johnson refused ever to argue with him. Once he even went so far as to say that he "would as soon have thought of contradicting a bishop." Undoubtedly the strange assortment of companions that Johnson found in this Old Street club provided pleasant relaxation when he had nothing more important to do.

Johnson also kept in close touch with Arthur Murphy, whom he had first met in 1754. Admittedly, Murphy had his prickly side, for he was constantly quarreling, or at least arguing, with Garrick and others. As far back as 1757, when he was writing for the *Literary Magazine,* Murphy had made some uncomplimentary remarks about the classical scholarship of the Reverend Thomas Francklin, vicar of Ware and lecturer at St. Paul's, formerly a professor of Greek at Cambridge and translator of Sophocles.[5] This stirred up a bitter quarrel, with sharp attacks on both sides connected with Murphy's play *The Orphan of China.* When the two men met in the Bedford Tavern early in March 1759 they were unsparing in abuse, so much so that Francklin brought Murphy into court on March 10. Nothing serious came of the court action. Both restrained themselves for a time.

But in 1760 Francklin, in his *Dissertation on Ancient Tragedy*, had scornful things to say about Murphy, calling him "formerly a wretched actor," and Murphy was again stirred into action. His published reply, dated from Lincoln's Inn October 10, 1760, *A Poetical Epistle to Samuel Johnson*, appeared on October 22. On the twenty-fifth Thomas Birch commented in a letter to Yorke,

> The poet in his *Advertisement* expresses his satisfaction in reflecting that as the great Dryden had his Parson Milbourne so the author of the *Orphan of China* is not so inconsiderable, but that he has also his Parson Francklin. The poem is formed upon the plan of Boileau's second satire: Mr. Murphy does not forget to record in a note the late Greek professor's blunder in his account of Mr. Gray's Ode in the *Critical Review,* in confounding the *Aeolian Lyre* with *Aeolus's Harp,* and giving to the modern Mr. Ossuald [?] what by classic authority belonged to the ancient Sappho.[6]

Most of Murphy's satire, of course, was directed at his opponent, Francklin, but what interests us here are some thirty lines in praise of Johnson. The poem begins:

> Transcendant Genius, whose prolific vein
> Ne'er knew the frigid poet's toil and pain;
> To whom Apollo opens all his store,
> And ev'ry Muse presents her sacred lore;
> Say, pow'rful Johnson, whence thy verse is fraught
> With so much grace, such energy of thought;
> Whether thy *Juvenal* instructs the age
> In chaster numbers, and new-points his rage;
> Or fair *Irene* sees, alas! too late
> Her innocence exchang'd for guilty state:
> Whate'er you write, in ev'ry golden line
> Sublimity and Elegance combine;
> Thy nervous phrase impresses ev'ry soul,
> While harmony gives warmth and rapture to the whole.[7]

Other lines which come later continue the high praise.

> Tell, for you can, by what unerring art
> You wake to finer feelings ev'ry heart?
> In each bright page some truth important give,
> And bid to future times thy Rambler live.

That Johnson was flattered by such high compliments, even when connected with a nasty quarrel in which he may have played some part, is likely. And he must have been happy to have the *British Magazine* give favorable mention to Murphy's satire. Moreover, the *Critical Review* also included further comment on Johnson's genius and candor.[8]

Possibly about this time, Johnson went with Murphy, Foote, and Wedderburne to Bedlam, where one could watch the antics of the insane by paying two pence. Foote later gave an entertaining account of Johnson's watching a madman beating his straw, supposing it was the Duke of Cumberland so hated by Scots for his cruelties during the "forty-five."[9]

One of Johnson's early friendships was slowly beginning to deteriorate. This was with John Hawkesworth. For many years he and Johnson had an intimate relationship, but by the early 1760s they were drawing apart. In a later summary of Hawkesworth's career the statement was made that sometime before 1762 Hawkesworth had "begun to estrange himself much from the society of Johnson and was even intoxicated to such a degree by the popularity of his writings that he no longer esteemed Johnson to be, in native talents, at all superior to himself."[10] But the break came slowly.

Sometime around 1760 Hawkesworth put together a three-act play using Eastern characters, hoping that Garrick would produce it at Drury Lane. He showed the play to Johnson, who made various suggestions, and to Garrick. Indeed, a manuscript of the play with their annotations survived for a time.[11] Unfortunately, Garrick was unwilling to spend all the money necessary to provide the elaborate scenery which Hawkesworth thought necessary, and so the project languished. But then another idea struck him. England now had a new King, youthful and impressionable. Why not restructure his story so that the sentiments might be useful to a novice monarch? Thus he turned it into a long Eastern tale, with the title *Almoran and Hamet*. It was published in the spring of 1761, in two small volumes like *Rasselas*, and at the same price. The work was dedicated to King George III, with his formal permission. Hawkesworth was obviously hoping to make an impression on the King, and possibly reap some rewards. The tale was at once widely reviewed, though for the most part all that was included in the reviews were long summaries of the plot. One reviewer in the *Library* for June, after pointing out that "ingenious Dr. Hawkesworth" had in the *Adventurer* shown his skill in producing Oriental stories, added that the new tale was

> lively, elegant, picturesque, interesting, and calculated to enforce, in the strongest manner, the most uniform and steady sentiments of piety and virtue. Were we disposed to suggest

anything amiss in it, we might observe that, like Rasselas, it is sometimes too abstract in its reasoning for a composition of such a kind; and that the conclusion would have been more satisfactory if it had been less abrupt.[12]

How did Johnson like the tale? There is a later story that after the publication of *Almoran and Hamet* someone asked Johnson if he had read the tale. To which Johnson replied, "No! I like the man too well to read his book."[13] If Hawkesworth ever heard that Johnson had not read his tale, this might have contributed to their break. But all this would have been before Hawkesworth's later reputed delight in finery and rich clothes and Johnson's reference to him as a coxcomb.[14] It was increasing pride on Hawkesworth's part which eventually led to strains in their close relationship.

By 1761 Johnson was on intimate terms with the hack writer Oliver Goldsmith. Probably Goldsmith was already a regular attendant at what Thomas Birch called Johnson's daily levee, where he would patiently bear all his host's superior thrusts.[15] On May 31 Johnson made his first visit to Goldsmith at his home in Wine Office Court, where there was a large dinner party. This was the occasion which Percy described long afterward when Johnson was unusually careful about his appearance. Goldsmith had asked Percy to bring Johnson to the party, and as they went along Percy was much struck by the neatness of his companion's dress. He had on a new suit of clothes, a new wig, well powdered, and everything else was dissimilar to his usual practice. When Percy asked the reason for this transformation, Johnson replied, "Why, Sir, I hear that Goldsmith, who is a very great sloven, justifies his disregard of cleanliness and decency by quoting my practice, and I am desirous this night to show him a better example."

It was not until the summer of 1762 that the best-known incident in the relationship of the two men occurred, when Goldsmith was arrested for debt by his landlady and not allowed to leave his rooms.[16] His first move was to dispatch an appeal for help to Johnson, who at once sent him back a guinea and then as soon as he was dressed went over to Wine Office Court for a talk. When he arrived, he found that Goldsmith had already used the guinea to buy a bottle of Madeira. Johnson at once put the cork in the bottle, desired Goldsmith to be calm, and began to talk about possible means of extricating him from his difficulties. What Johnson took away with him was a manuscript, how near completion is uncertain, of a novel, *The Vicar of Wakefield,* for which Newbery paid sixty pounds. He did not publish it, however, until four years later, after Goldsmith had made a name for himself with his poem *The Traveller.*

The incident shows clearly how much Goldsmith depended upon Johnson, and how Johnson felt inclined to help his sometimes foolish friend. Theirs was a close, if sometimes hilarious, relationship.

Christopher Smart was no longer around, for he was confined (though it is not clear just where) because he was at least partly mad. Before his last breakdown, Kit Smart had been one of Johnson's good friends. Smart used to relate that the first conversation he ever had with Johnson "was of such variety and length that it began with poetry and ended at fluxions [differential calculus]."[17] Tom Tyers, whom Johnson had taken off as "Tom Restless" in the *Idler,* and who later became joint manager of Vauxhall Gardens, also had numerous recollections of the richness of Johnson's conversation. In his short *Life* of Johnson, Tyers later insisted that Johnson "always talked as if he was talking upon oath. He was the wisest person, and had the most knowledge in ready cash this writer had the honour to be acquainted with." Tyers added that Johnson's advice was sought by all kinds of persons. "He was known to be a good casuist, and therefore had many cases for his judgment." Compliment after compliment Tyers heaped upon him:

> He said the most common things in the newest manner. He always commanded attention and regard. If he wrote for money, he talked for reputation. His person, though unadorned with dress, and even deformed by neglect, made you expect something, and you were hardly ever disappointed. His manner was interesting; the tone of his voice and the sincerity of his expressions, even when they did not captivate your affections, or carry conviction, prevented contempt.[18]

There can be no doubt as to the respect and high admiration with which Johnson's many friends and followers regarded him.

It was never difficult to draw Johnson into sharp altercations. If anyone said something he disagreed with, he saw no reason to keep quiet. For example, there was the Scot, Adam Smith, whom Johnson met at Strahan's sometime in September or October 1761.[19] It is difficult to tell just what triggered the explosion, but the two disagreed on many basic issues. One anecdote, told in various forms, has it that when Adam Smith "was expatiating on the beauty of Glasgow," Johnson was so irritated that he cut him short and exploded, "Pray Sir, have you ever seen Brentford?" Since Brentford was a symbol of urban unattractiveness, Smith must have been shocked. People soon learned that above all else Johnson loved to argue. Anyone wishing to savor the wisdom of his sallies had to be willing to put up with some strenuous verbal exchanges.

Johnson's few surviving letters give fleeting glimpses of how he spent his time. He went to the theater occasionally when some old friend was involved either as author or actor. As we have seen, he actively supported Dodsley on the appearance of his *Cleone,* and he probably went to see Murphy's *The Orphan of China* and others of his plays. When the elder Thomas Sheridan played in *Cato* and *Richard III,* Johnson was in attendance. Not that he thought Sheridan much of an actor. Writing to young Langton in October 1760, Johnson told of Sheridan's success, at the same time commenting on his faults, "some of natural deficience, and some of laborious affectation."[20] Specifically, Johnson added,

> He has, I think, no power of assuming either that dignity or elegance which some men who have little of either in common life can exhibit on the stage. His voice when strained is unpleasing, and when low is not always heard. He seems to think too much on the audience, and turns his face too often to the galleries.

Doubtless, Johnson thought of himself as a critic of acting. But despite Sheridan's faults, Johnson wished him well, chiefly because, as he admitted, he liked his wife.

On Christmas Day, 1760, Johnson dined at Garrick's, where there were also a number of his close friends, the two Wartons, Arthur Murphy, and Edmund Burke. Someone mentioned Samuel Foote, actor and dramatist, who was in Dublin at the time, and the story was told that he had been horsewhipped by an irate apothecary whom he had burlesqued on stage. Such takeoffs were Foote's stock in trade, and he was called "the modern Aristophanes." Garrick then commented, "But I wonder that any man would show so much resentment to Foote: he has a license or a patent for such liberties: nobody ever thought it *worth his while* to quarrel with him in London." To which Johnson added: "And I am glad to find that the man is *rising* in the world."[21] When Foote later heard about what had been said, he let it be known that he would in a short time burlesque Johnson as the Caliban of literature on the London stage. Upon hearing this bit of news, Johnson sent word to Foote that the theater was intended for the reformation of vice, and if Foote did what he planned Johnson promised to go from the boxes to the stage "and correct him before the audience."

Years later, when Boswell asked Johnson if Foote had really thought of exhibiting him, Johnson replied that he had, but fear had restrained him.[22] "He knew I would have broken his bones. I would have saved him the trouble of cutting off a leg; I would not have left him a leg to cut off." Another version of the story was told to Boswell later by Tom Davies. Once when dining with Davies, Johnson asked what was the common price of an oak stick.[23] When told that the price was sixpence, Johnson said: "Why then, Sir, give me leave to send your servant to purchase me a shilling one. I'll have a double quantity; for I am told Foote means to *take me off*, as he calls it, and I am determined the fellow shall not do it with impunity." Davies took care to inform Foote of Johnson's threat, which "effectually checked the wantonness of the mimic." Whichever version one chooses to believe, it is clear that Foote changed his mind. Happily no ill will resulted; Johnson used to say that for broad-faced mirth Foote had no equal. Although he was not a complete mimic, Foote was very entertaining, "with a kind of conversation between wit and buffoonery."[24] What Johnson may not have suspected was that although Foote had given up the scheme of public mimicry of Johnson, he still liked to take him off in private gatherings.

Not all Johnson's talking companions were male, but the ladies left fewer recollections. One surviving anecdote from Christopher Smart's wife, Anna Maria, Newbery's stepdaughter, describes a dinner she once had with Johnson and two Italians, while her husband was confined for madness. According to her daughter, Anna Maria often used to describe the occasion, but what she remembered was not what people said, but the menu—what they ate, or did not eat.[25]

> The dinner consisted of two very large fowls and nothing else; neither vegetables, pastry, nor any other eatable, and of liquor not one drop. What seems more remarkable was that none of the company asked for any beverage. However, soon after the removal of the cloth the tea was served up.

Johnson visited and admired a number of ladies in the neighborhood. There was Charlotte Lennox, whom he was constantly helping, and Mrs. Gardiner, wife of a tallow-chandler on Snow Hill, who was "not in the learned way, but a worthy good woman."[26] He would see Elizabeth Carter from Deal whenever she was in London, and there was Sarah Kirby, later Mrs. Trimmer, writer of children's books. And, of course, there were Mrs. Masters, the poet, whose work Johnson may have revised, and Mrs. Macaulay.

One young woman, Anne Penny, showed her admiration early in 1761 by publishing a rendering in verse of *Rambler* Nos. 186 and 187. The title was *Anningait and Ajutt: A Greenland Tale inscribed to Mr. Samuel Johnson A.M.*, and the poem began with eight lines of laudatory verses:

> O! Johnson, fam'd for Elegance and Sense,
> Whose Works, Instruction and Delight dispense;

Where nice Correction charms our wond'ring Eyes,
And in whose Lines embellish'd Beauties rise;
Say! will you deign this humble Verse to hear,
Spring from your Thoughts, and nurtur'd by your Care:
A Female Bard, unknown to Wit or Fame,
To you inscribes what from your Genius came.[27]

The poem was favorably reviewed both in the *Critical Review* and the *Gentleman's Magazine*.

In mid-May 1761, Thomas Percy arrived in London for a fortnight's visit, and his diary gives another glimpse of the everyday life of the Johnson circle.[28] During the previous autumn Johnson had been negotiating for Percy with two publishers, Dodsley and Andrew Millar, about his proposed collection of old ballads. Both publishers were interested and made offers, but Percy had not been able to decide which to take. He was now ready for some decisions. After arriving on the evening of Tuesday, May 19, Percy the next morning first called on Dodsley and then went to spend the day with Johnson for important advice. He and Johnson dined together and later had tea at Johnson's rooms; Miss Williams and the actor Charles Macklin were also present. Of the latter, Johnson told Percy that he had been "2 or 3 and 20 before he learnt to read," a bit of gossip which Percy at once jotted down in his diary.

On this trip Percy had come down from Easton Maudit with a bag full of material which might make books. The problems were to know which ones to do first, and how extensive to make them, and which of the publishers to choose. These were the chief topics of his long talk with Johnson. In a report he sent to William Shenstone a few days later he said he had "held a council of war with Mr. Johnson."[29]

The time was filled with negotiations. On Thursday, March 21, Percy "bargained with Dodsley for Solomon's Song and Runic Poetry." Of more importance was his collection of ballads, but he apparently was still not certain what to do, for he added in his diary, "Called on Mr. Millar." As Percy describes the negotiations to Shenstone, Dodsley had come to think better of the chief project than originally, and had agreed to Percy's financial terms. Millar also would have paid the same amount, but "he wanted to lay me under some difficulties about the execution, that prevented us from coming to an agreement." As a result, Percy noted on Friday: "Sold Dodsley my old ballads," and on Saturday he noted, "Went with Dodsley to Hughes the printer Sold Chin. Misc. and 3 Matrons [*Miscellaneous Pieces Relating to the Chinese* (1762) and *The Matrons* (1763)]." Thus in a few days of strenuous negotiating Percy had arranged for the publication of five works, which in all would amount to eleven volumes.

When writing to Shenstone on the twenty-second, telling him all the news and describing many of his major decisions, he added at the end:

> Mr. Johnson and I have had a good deal of talk about you: I explained to him the reason why you did not write to him, and I believe he is entirely satisfied on that head. He even talks of taking a journey down to the Leasows:—but this you must not much depend on; he is no more formed for long journeys than a tortoise. 'Tis two years that he has been resolving to come and see me, who consider myself as in the neighbourhood of London.

After all this busy professional talk, Percy was ready for some diversion and on Monday, May 25, he dined and had tea with Goldsmith, and the two then visited an exhibition in Spring Gardens. Apparently it was not until Tuesday, the twenty-sixth, that he saw Johnson again. That morning he had begun reading at the new British Museum, which had opened in January 1759. Later he dined with Johnson at Mrs. Williams's and remained there for the evening. At that time, Johnson received a full account of all the plans. The next day Percy breakfasted with Garrick, attended a rehearsal of *King Lear,* dined with his close friend Thomas Apperley, and spent the evening with Johnson. On the twenty-eighth he dined at Dodsley's, again had tea with Miss Williams, and then went to see Edmund Allen, the printer. On the twenty-ninth he saw various people at Garrick's, and somewhere along the way passed on a pound to Johnson —a subscription for the Shakespeare edition from John Orlebar of Hinwick in Bedfordshire. Evidently subscriptions were still appearing out of the hinterland. On Saturday he was again at Garrick's and Johnson's, and then on Sunday, the thirty-first, he went in the evening to a large party at Goldsmith's in Wine Office Court, the occasion of Johnson's first visit to Goldsmith's home.[30]

Through the next week Percy saw a performance of George Colman's *The Jealous Wife,* visited Johnson at least twice, and saw Goldsmith a number of times. An unfortunate injury to his eye kept him from reading as he had planned in the British Museum; still he attended a meeting of the Antiquarian Society, went to Vauxhall Gardens, and spent a whole day with Edward Capell, the Shakespeare scholar. It had been a valuable visit, as he reported to Thomas Warton in Oxford.[31] All he had to do now was to put together "a select collection of the best and most practical" of his old ballads, hoping to have them ready by the next winter. Actually, *The Reliques of Ancient Poetry* in three volumes would not be published until 1765. For Johnson, Percy's visit must have been a diverting interlude.

It was stimulating to advise someone who had so many ideas and such
varied interests.

Some insights into Johnson's own evaluation of his rather footloose
existence comes from a long letter he wrote on June 10, 1761, to Giuseppe
Baretti in Italy.[32] After apologizing for not answering Baretti's earlier
communications, Johnson claimed that the large piece of paper he was
using was proof that this time he really meant to give him a full account.

> Yet it must be remembered that he who continues the same
> course of life in the same place will have little to tell. One week
> and one year are very like another. The silent changes made by
> time are not always perceived, and if they are not perceived,
> cannot be recounted. I have risen and lain down, talked and
> mused, while you have roved over a considerable part of Europe.

Then, after comments on the changes in government which had occurred
since Baretti left England, he wrote: "We were so weary of our old King
that we are much pleased with his successor; of whom we are so inclined
to hope great things, that most of us begin already to believe them." And
after further comments on the exhibition of the Society of Artists, Johnson
comes to what was most important.

> I know my Baretti will not be satisfied with a letter in which I
> give him no account of myself; yet what account shall I give
> him? I have not since the day of our separation suffered or done
> anything considerable. The only change in my way of life is
> that I have frequented the theatre more than in former seasons.
> But I have gone thither only to escape from myself. We have
> had many new farces, and the comedy called *The Jealous Wife,*
> which, though not written with much genius, was yet so well
> adapted to the stage and so well exhibited by the actors that it
> was crowded for near twenty nights. I am digressing from myself
> to the playhouse; but a barren plan must be filled with epi-
> sodes. Of myself I have nothing to say, but that I have hitherto
> lived without the concurrence of my own judgment; yet I con-
> tinue to flatter myself that when you return you will find me
> mended. I do not wonder that where the monastic life is per-
> mitted every order finds votaries, and every monastery inhabi-
> tants. Men will submit to any rule by which they may be ex-
> empted from the tyranny of caprice and of chance. They are
> glad to supply by external authority their own want of con-
> stancy and resolution, and court the government of others when
> long experience has convinced them of their own inability to
> govern themselves.

At this time, Johnson was presumably working on his edition of Shakespeare. On June 1, 1761, five years had passed since he had issued his proposals, whereas he had thought he would complete the project in a year and a half. But in five years what had he done? What plays were now in print, or set in type? And what explanatory notes were at least in a first version? We know that the celebrated *Preface* was still only gestating in his head. But how many of his long notes arguing with Warburton had been completed? Were his explications of *King Lear, Hamlet, Macbeth,* the ones modern critics like to cite, in type? In 1758 those sections were in print, which Johnson sent up to Oxford for Thomas Warton to see. And in August 1761 Thomas Birch wrote to his patron, Philip Yorke, that two volumes of Johnson's edition had been sent to the press.[33] But which ones?

Subscriptions still kept dribbling in. In March 1762, John Ash, a physician, sent three to Warton.[34] And Johnson retained his remarkable optimism. In his letter to Baretti in July 1762 he commented, "I intend that you shall soon receive Shakespeare." But "soon" actually turned out to be three years.

During this period Samuel Johnson's creative writing, so far as we can tell, was almost nonexistent. Indeed, that he was able to exist on what he received from his writing seems impossible. In his survey of Johnson's known revenue as a writer all David Fleeman was able to find for this year and a half was one payment from the publisher Newbery of £84 2s. 4d. as Johnson's two-thirds share of the receipts from a small duodecimo edition of the *Idler,* which appeared late in 1761.[35] Of course, he received a few guineas now and then for minor editing and writing of dedications. Still, he must have been constantly borrowing from booksellers and friends, with destitution always staring him in the face.

Apart from the work for the Society of Artists which was described in the last chapter, the only writings that Johnson produced were a dedication for his good friend Charlotte Lennox for a second edition of her novel *Henrietta,* a piece on the approaching coronation of George III, a bit of editorial work for an edition of the works of Roger Ascham, and some further writing for his artist friends.[36] None of this could have taken much of his time.

The revised edition of *Henrietta* was published on March 19, 1761, but the new dedication to the Duchess of Newcastle was dated November 20, 1760. Although it was unusual for an author to supply a new dedication for a second edition of a book, Mrs. Lennox in this instance did have a special reason. As she made clear in a letter to the Duchess, Mrs. Lennox was desperately trying to find a position for her husband and was hoping the Duchess would help. She did in fact find him a job, and also acted as godmother to Charlotte's first child. With all this hanging fire, Mrs. Lennox was very eager to have the dedicatory address done as well as possible, and naturally turned to her ever-ready helper Johnson, who had already written at least five other addresses for her. There is no doubt that this one is Johnson's. "The style of the Dedication itself is decisive," as Allen T. Hazen points out; "Mrs. Lennox never wrote like this."[37] One sentence is conclusive: "To obtain the approbation of a judgment like yours, it is necessary to mean well; and to gain a kindness from such benevolence, to mean well is commonly sufficient."

During the summer of 1761 Johnson and his friend the architect John Gwynn put together a pamphlet having the full title *Thoughts on the Coronation of His Present Majesty King George the Third, Or, Reasons Offered against Confining the Procession to the Usual Track, and Pointing Out Others More Commodious and Proper. To Which Are Prefixed, a Plan of the Different Paths Recommended, with the Parts Adjacent, and a Sketch of the Procession*. It was published on August 8, and priced at 1s. 6d. Gwynn is supposed to have provided the "facts" and specific details, and Johnson, so Donald Greene believes, wrote the text.[38] Since the coronation took place on September 22, it is hard to see how Johnson and Gwynn thought their specific suggestions, such as tearing down the old Gate-House and raising the height of the seats for spectators, might be accomplished. But at least the accompanying map would have been useful for spectators.

What chiefly spurred Johnson on was a desire—singularly modern in its approach—to encourage a closer relationship between the ruler and his subjects. "All pomp is instituted for the sake of the public. A show without spectators can no longer be a show." The new King should be better known by the ordinary people.

> By the late method of conducting the coronation all these purposes have been defeated. Our kings, with their train, have crept to the temple through obscure passages; and the crown has been worn out of sight of the people. Of the multitudes, whom loyalty or curiosity brought together, the greater part has returned without a single glimpse of their prince's grandeur, and the day that opened with festivity ended in discontent.[39]

What was of greatest importance was to make it possible for large numbers of the population to have some clear idea what their monarch was like, and at the same time for the King to be better aware of who made up his nation. The closer the contact, the better.

Throughout the year Johnson may have done some work on an edition of the English works of Roger Ascham, which John Newbery had talked him into doing. The reason was ostensibly to help a poor schoolmaster named James Bennet, of Hoddesdon in Hertfordshire. Possibly it all started in 1754 when Francis Newbery, the publisher's son, went to Bennet's boarding school. By January 1758 proposals for a subscription for an edition were issued, at which time a two-paragraph advertisement written by Johnson was added. Thus by 1761 Johnson had been involved with the project for at least three years. According to Francis Newbery, it was "intended as an aid to Mr. Bennet, who was under some pecuniary embarrassments."[40] Just how much of the editing was done by Bennet, who had no pretensions to scholarship, though he was reputedly a good classicist, or by Johnson, who had been brought in to help, is difficult to decide. We can be certain that Johnson composed the dedication to the Earl of Shaftesbury, a life of Ascham, and some of the notes, though in general the editing was perfunctory. Progress had been slow, and by October 1761 Newbery thought it necessary to print an apology in the *London Chronicle*.[41] Not until January 1762 did the work finally appear. It was hardly received with acclamation, and probably did not bring Johnson much financial help.

In the spring of 1762 Johnson was again called on for help by his artist friends, who were planning a third exhibition.[42] There had been the usual discussions about a suitable place, which again turned out to be one of Cock's big rooms in Spring Gardens. And there were various problems concerning a catalogue. In Joshua Reynolds's engagement book for March 15, 1762, he noted that at 2 P.M. he was to see "Mr. Johnson." Then the next day, the sixteenth, at a meeting of the artists which Reynolds attended, the secretary recorded "a motion being made and seconded that Mr. Johnson be requested to give a motto for the catalogue and that Mr. Hayman make a design agreeable thereto." On the eighteenth Reynolds saw "Mr. Johnson" again. Twelve days later, at a meeting of the committee, there was some discussion of the design, but nothing concerning the motto. Indeed, in later meetings of the committee there never was any discussion of the classical quotation to be chosen by Johnson, though the catalogue, when it appeared, did carry a line from Martial—"*Aurea si Tuleris Dona, Minora Feres.*"

On April 12 Reynolds noted that he had an engagement at 1 P.M. with "Mr. Johnson," but at a meeting of the committee the next day nothing was reported. Finally, on the twentieth, at another meeting, the secretary's minutes record "Mr. Reynolds having presented a preface which was agreed to and ordered to be printed." Instead of merely bringing in a motto, Reynolds produced something of much greater importance.

Johnson's Preface appeared in the catalogue of the exhibition which opened on May 17, 1762. His authorship is generally accepted. The style, the tone, and the rhythms are Johnsonian. If Reynolds may have made the original suggestion and the two men worked together as they put the piece together, it was Johnson who did the actual writing.

In some circles there had been criticism of the earlier exhibitions, as motivated by avarice and false vanity on the part of the contesting artists. In answer to this, Johnson readily admits that "all who offer themselves to criticism are desirous of praise," but he goes on to insist that

> this desire is not only innocent but virtuous, while it is un-debased by artifice and unpolluted by envy; and of envy or artifice these men can never be accused, who, already enjoying all the honours and profits of their profession, are content to stand candidates for public notice, with genius yet unexperi-enced, and diligence yet unrewarded; who, without any hope of increasing their own reputation or interest, expose their names and their works only that they may furnish an oppor-tunity of appearance to the young, the diffident, and the ne-glected. The purpose of this exhibition is not to enrich the artists, but to advance the art; the eminent are not flattered with preference, nor the obscure insulted with contempt; whoever hopes to deserve public favour is here invited to display his merit.[43]

Johnson does not show in the Preface any envy of those painters who were doing very well financially while he was starving. When writing to Baretti a few months later, he merely mentioned that Reynolds was now making six thousand pounds a year.[44]

In this same letter Johnson passes on the latest news of his various friends. He and Miss Williams "live much as we did"; Dr. Levet has been married, though there is "much suspicion that he has been wretchedly cheated in his match"; Richardson has died of apoplexy. And then he tells of a trip he finally took during the winter to the midlands to visit his old home. He had not been back to Lichfield since 1740. The description in the letter to Baretti leaves little doubt as to his reaction.

> Last winter I went down to my native town, where I found the streets much narrower and shorter than I thought I had left them, inhabited by a new race of people, to whom I was very little known. My play-fellows were grown old, and forced me to suspect that I was no longer young. My only re-maining friend [unidentified] has changed his principles, and was become the tool of the predominant faction. My daughter-in-law [stepdaughter] from whom I expected most, and whom I met with sincere benevolence, has lost the beauty and gaiety of youth, without having gained much of the wisdom of age. I

wandered about for five days, and took the first convenient opportunity of returning to a place where, if there is not much happiness, there is at least such a diversity of good and evil that slight vexations do not fix upon the heart. . . .

Moral sentences appear ostentatious and tumid when they have no greater occasions than the journey of a wit to his own town: yet such pleasures and such pains make up the general mass of life; and as nothing is little to him that feels it with great sensibility, a mind able to see common incidents in their real state is disposed by very common incidents to very serious contemplations. Let us trust that a time will come when the present moment shall be no longer irksome; when we shall not borrow all our happiness from hope, which at last is to end in disappointment.

Not that everything was dull and dreary. He did have some unusual experiences in London. Early in 1762 Johnson was drawn into a strange controversy about which much has been written. This was the episode of the so-called Cock-Lane Ghost.[45] A child of twelve, by means of knocks and strange sounds, supposedly relayed a shocking accusation from a ghost named Frances Lynes, later known as "Scratching Fanny," that she had been poisoned by her lover while she lay sick with smallpox. The weird sounds were so cleverly produced that for a time no one was able to prove them contrived. Immense curiosity was aroused, and the newspapers were filled with accounts of the affair. As a result, the narrow lane near her house was jammed with coaches. Horace Walpole, the Duke of York, and many others attended a séance.

Finally it became obvious to some gentlemen that a serious attempt should be made to study the case. The credulous public should be provided with all the facts. Stephen Aldrich, Rector of Clerkenwell, conferred with John Douglas, who had been influential in the exposure of Lauder, and Douglas went to see Johnson, who agreed to serve on an examining committee. On the evening of February 1, 1762, Douglas escorted Johnson to Aldrich's house, where they were joined by a large group of others, sixteen in all, eager to find out exactly what was going on. What followed was written down by Johnson at the end of the evening and approved by others of the committee. Here is the way Johnson summed up what was done:

> *February 2.* Last night many gentlemen eminent for their rank and character were, by the invitation of the Rev. Mr. Aldrich of Clerkenwell, assembled at his house for the examination of the noises supposed to be made by a departed spirit, for the detection of some enormous crime.

About ten at night the gentlemen met in the chamber in which the girl, supposed to be disturbed by a spirit, had with proper caution been put to bed by several ladies. They sat rather more than an hour, and hearing nothing went down stairs, where they interrogated the father of the girl, who denied in the strongest terms any knowledge or belief of fraud.

The supposed spirit had before publicly promised, by an affirmative knock, that it would attend one of the gentlemen into the vault under the church of St. John, Clerkenwell, where the body is deposited, and give a token of her presence there by a knock upon her coffin; it was therefore determined to make this trial of the existence or veracity of the supposed spirit.

While they were enquiring and deliberating, they were summoned into the girl's chamber by some ladies who were near her bed, and who had heard knocks and scratches. When the gentlemen entered, the girl declared that she felt the spirit like a mouse upon her back, and was required to hold her hands out of bed; from that time, though the spirit was very solemnly required to manifest its existence by appearance, by impression on the hand or body of any present, by scratches, knocks, or any agency, no evidence of any preternatural power was exhibited.

The spirit was then very seriously advertised that the person to whom the promise was made of striking the coffin was then about to visit the vault and that the performance of the promise was then claimed. The company at once went into the church, and the gentleman to whom the promise was made went, with one more, into the vault: the spirit was solemnly required to perform its promise, but nothing more than silence ensued. The person supposed to be accused by the spirit, then went down, with several others, but no effect was perceived. Upon their return they examined the girl but could draw no confession from her. Between two and three she desired, and was permitted, to go home with her father.

It is therefore the opinion of the whole assembly that the child has some art of making, or counterfeiting, particular noises, and that there is no agency of any higher cause.[46]

This straightforward account was at once published in the newspapers, not as a communication, but as a piece of news, and it also appeared in the February number of the *Gentleman's Magazine*. But there were variations in the texts. Four uses of the word "supposed" which appeared in the *St. James's Chronicle* number of January 30–February 2, were changed to "pretended" in *Daily Advertiser* for February 3. Perhaps it all depended on how the editor felt.

The fraudulent nature of the imposture was now clear, or should have been, though the noises continued for a while, until other watchers caught the girl slipping a piece of wood into her bed.[47]

Once the truth was out, the eminent members of the examining committee were not praised for their clearheaded skepticism, but rather blamed for their foolish gullibility in thinking the whole affair worth investigating. Thus Johnson was attacked, as indeed Saunders Welch had warned him that he might be, for his credulity in believing that there could possibly be extrasensory sources for such noises. The most cutting attack came in the second book of Charles Churchill's poem *The Ghost,* which appeared on March 5.[48] In this amusing satire Johnson appears three times, once as "our lettered Polypheme" (referring to his near blindness), supporter of the plagiarist William Lauder; second as "Pomposo," importer of "crabbed foreign words" (doubtless an allusion to the *Dictionary*); and finally as the arrogant idol of so many lesser writers. Here Churchill pulls out the stops.

> Pomposo (insolent and loud,
> Vain idol of a *scribbling* crowd,
> Whose very name inspires an awe,
> Whose ev'ry word is Sense and Law,
> For what his Greatness hath decreed,
> Like Laws of PERSIA and of MEDE,
> Sacred thro' all the realm of *Wit,*
> Must never of Repeal admit;
> Who, cursing flatt'ry, is the tool
> Of ev'ry fawning flatt'ring fool;
> Who Wit with jealous eye surveys,
> And sickens at another's praise;
> Who, proudly seiz'd of *Learning's* throne,
> Now damns all Learning but his own;
> Who scorns those common wares to trade in,
> *Reas'ning, Convincing,* and *Persuading,*
> But makes each Sentence current pass
> With *Puppy, Coxcomb, Scoundrel, Ass;*
> For 'tis with *him* a certain rule,
> The Folly's prov'd, when he calls Fool;
> Who, to increase his native strength,
> Draws words, six syllables in length,
> With which, assisted with a frown
> By way of Club, he knocks us down;
> Who 'bove the Vulgar dares to rise,
> And sense of *Decency* defies,
> For this same *Decency* is made
> Only for Bunglers in the trade;

And, like the *Cobweb Laws,* is still
Broke thro' by *Great Ones* when they will)—
Pomposo, with *strong sense* supplied,
Supported, and confirmed by *Pride,*
His Comrades' terrors to beguile,
Grinn'd horribly a ghastly smile:
Features so horrid, were it light,
Would put the Devil himself to flight.

What could have aroused young Churchill to such animosity? In his first major satire, the *Rosciad* (1761), Churchill had been quite respectful of Johnson. But once he heard that Johnson was saying unflattering things about his poetry, he changed his stance. With *The Ghost* there came an opportunity to get revenge. How did Johnson react? According to one report, when told that Churchill had abused him "under the character of Pomposo," Johnson replied: "I always thought he was a shallow fellow and I think so still."[49] And the next year when talking to Boswell he contemptuously lashed out at Churchill. Boswell

said he was not a fair judge, as Churchill was a sort of enemy of his. "Sir," said he, "I am a very fair judge; because he turned my enemy when he found that I did not like his poetry. And, indeed, I have a better opinion of him now than I had at first, as he has shown more fertility than I expected. To be sure, he is a tree that cannot produce true fruit. He only bears crabs. But, Sir, a tree that produces a great many crabs is better than one which produces only a few crabs."[50]

Despite its exaggeration, the Pomposo portrait did catch many of Johnson's superficial mannerisms and weaknesses. It can be taken as a clever summing up of the anti-Johnsonian position. There were certainly others who felt the same way.

In the early 1760s in London there were obviously two entrenched camps made up of those who revered Johnson, despite his many weaknesses, and those who refused to do so and kept pointing out their reasons. Johnson, they felt, was unattractive physically, socially, intellectually. He was obviously very ugly, with his mottled skin and nervous quaverings. His manner was too pompous and eccentric, and his talk too dogmatic and bigoted. Overly opinionated and stubbornly holding to fixed positions which were often built on old prejudices, he would not accept new philosophic ideas. A strident mogul, he willingly accepted the adulation of fawning flatterers. And his literary style was too ponderous and formal, full of difficult long words and abstruse expressions. His ideas were often too general or too arcane, based on strict morality. How could anyone accept this crazy eccentric as a model?

On the other side were Johnson's friends and admirers who shut their eyes to various acknowledged weaknesses while stressing his kind heart and benevolent spirit, his deep commitment to Christianity and its moral demands, and his critical ability to get to the heart of human problems. Although at times he might appear ridiculous or crotchety, they found that basically he was a remarkable and inspiring man.[51]

One thing his admirers were agreed upon. Something had to be done to make his everyday life more comfortable and his financial situation less harassing.

CHAPTER XVI

Pensioner

For years Johnson's friends and admirers had been wondering what could be done to make his life a little easier. The constant pressure of financial needs may have forced him to do some writing that he would otherwise not have done, but it was becoming obvious that this was not the path to major creative works. What alternatives were there? Johnson had clearly shown that he was not one to accept favors from a wealthy patron. And so long as George II was on the throne a pension also seemed out of the question, even though Edmund Burke, when reviewing *Rasselas* in the 1759 issue of the *Annual Register,* closed with the sad observation that Johnson had "done so much for the improvement of our taste and our morals, and employed a great part of his life in an astonishing work for the fixing the language of this nation; whilst this nation, which admires his works, and profits by them, has done nothing for the author."[1]

Johnson in his *Dictionary* had made clear what he thought of the pension system as it functioned under Walpole and Newcastle. "Pension" he defined as "an allowance made to any one without an equivalent. In England it is generally understood to mean pay given to a state hireling for treason to his country." And "pensioner" had two meanings: (1) "one who is supported by an allowance paid at the will of another; a dependant," and (2) "a slave of state hired by a stipend to obey his master." To be sure, the infinitive "to pension" was defined simply as "to support by an arbitrary allowance," but even here the adjective "arbitrary" is pejorative. Among the quotations used to illustrate these meanings are two from Pope's satires. Johnson is clearly allying himself with the Opposition writers who scorned the cynical use of the system by George II's ministers.

There could be no mistaking Samuel Johnson's attitude toward pensions in 1755.

But with the accession of George III in the autumn of 1760, there was a new spirit abroad. Here was a young ruler, born and educated in England, who kept insisting that he was above party domination, with a chief minister, the Earl of Bute, who did not belong to the old Whig oligarchy. The time was ripe to push Johnson for a pension.

In the autumn of 1761 someone did something about it. From Cambridge a long and wordy anonymous letter was sent to the Earl of Bute, and was apparently delivered to the Earl's office in London by hand. On the outside was a note that this was for the minister's eyes alone.[2] The original letter still survives, though until recently it had never been carefully examined.[3]

Despite the fact that the writer has never met Johnson, and does not know any of his lordship's close associates, he insists that he is writing in a feigned hand to conceal his identity. Over and over he reiterates that he has no personal involvement in the suggestion, and is only making it for the reputation of England, to enhance his lordship's own reputation, and to save a worthy man from penury and want.

After a somewhat flowery beginning where he points out that England is now the happiest nation in the world, with the best of rulers, and the most liberty for individuals, he maintains that the one thing wanting to ensure national glory is some patronage for those who have "distinguished themselves in the literary way." And he points specifically to Samuel Johnson, a "truly great author," who nevertheless has been exposed to the "conflicts of indigence and want." Johnson has "not only immortalized as it were our language, but in every work that he has produced has done his utmost to the promotion of every moral and religious duty." Yet this virtuous man "still remains unpensioned, and left to procure himself a precarious subsistence by the bounty of booksellers."

The writer makes clear that he is well aware of a possible objection to any help for Johnson, a well-known Tory with reputed Jacobite sympathies, and tries to get around this difficulty by suggesting that "if it be objected that his political principles render him an unfit object of his majesty's favour, I would only say that he is to be the more pitied on this account, and that it may sometimes happen that our opinions however erroneous are not always in our own power." In addition, remembering the King's well-publicized plan to do away with party distinctions, he suggests that help for Johnson might be a way of accomplishing such a transformation.

The writer keeps emphasizing his admiration for Johnson as a truly great man, "though tarnished with some human failings," and points out

that others less worthy have been given pensions. His Majesty had conferred a pension of £200 on an Oxford biblical scholar, Benjamin Kenni-
cott, who was collating various ancient manuscripts. Without calling into
question such an award, the writer could not resist making an obvious
comparison:

> Yet what are the merits of this man compared to those of John-
> son? Will the world be in possession of any one undiscovered
> moral or religious truth, when he [Kennicott] has completed
> his scheme? But with respect to the other, I may venture to say
> that he hath done more by his writings to the advancement of
> real piety, and valuable learning than almost any other man
> now living.

How much better it is, the writer continues, to reward a worthy man while
he is living and not merely to pay empty tributes after his death. Then
comes a rather devious insinuation. If only Johnson could be given a pension of £200 or £300 a year it would "deliver this great author from every
fear of penury, and indigence, would fill his heart with gratitude, and at
the same time instigate him to show himself worthy of the royal favour by
every means in his power." Is the writer really suggesting that once given
financial support Johnson might even voluntarily come around to supporting the King in various ways? To be sure, he makes clear that he has
no illusions that Johnson could be hired to do any particular jobs. And
there follows a special kind of excuse and explanation.

> I am told that his political principles make him incapable of
> being in any place of trust, by incapacitating him from qualify-
> ing himself for any such office—but a pension my Lord requires
> no such performances—and my Lord it would seem but a just
> condescension to human infirmity that the man who endeav-
> oured in such a forcible manner to correct all our failings and
> errors should be excused one himself.

Having in this roundabout way made his chief point, the writer
apologizes profusely for keeping his lordship so long from his public business, expresses the hope that what he has said may not sound like the out-
pourings of a madman, and concludes with the claim that his only desire
has been to help a good man.

And so the long epistle ends. One wonders if the Earl ever had the
patience to read it through, or whether it had any influence whatever on
his later actions.

Who was the anonymous writer in Cambridge who claims never to have met either Johnson or Bute, who insists he is writing in a feigned hand, and sees so clearly all the difficulties? No one yet has come up with an acceptable answer. A young scholar named Richard Farmer, of Emmanuel College, Cambridge, has been suspected.[4] He was a friend of Thomas Percy, and he did meet Johnson four years later. But Farmer's handwriting is so completely different from that of the surviving letter that experts find it impossible to believe that he could have written it. Of course, one of his friends or an amanuensis could have done the actual writing. At Percy's suggestion, or with his advice, Farmer may have been responsible for the content. And there are other possibilities. For the moment the mystery is unsolved.

During the winter and spring of 1762 there was no progress, at least not with this proposal. Johnson continued his rather footloose existence. In his customary prayer on March 28 in memory of his wife, the usual goals were mentioned—his hope to avoid idleness, to return to his studies, to labor diligently, rise early, live temperately, read the Bible and go to church.[5] As in the past, after the prayer there seems to have been no sign of a major change.

He continued to be interested in other people's problems. Two letters in early June show this clearly—his message of farewell to George Staunton, who was emigrating to Guadaloupe, and his reply to a woman who had asked his help in securing the Archbishop of Canterbury's patronage in getting her son into the university.[6] Although Johnson declined to put any pressure on the Archbishop, he did talk to her son and wished him well. Undoubtedly during this period he was also helping Anna Williams with her plans to issue a subscription volume of her prose and verse. On July 8 Elizabeth Carter wrote to Elizabeth Montagu:

> Poor Mrs. Williams is endeavouring to get a subscription to some essays which are to be published next spring, in the hopes of being able to buy an annuity. She had this scheme some time ago, and then I hear you were so good as to procure her several subscribers. I am sure if it is in your power now to make any addition to the number, you will not need any solicitations from me.[7]

Johnson may have been amused to see, if he did, in the *London Evening Post* of July 1, 1762, a plagiarized and revised version of the poem "To Posterity" included in his anonymous *Marmor Norfolciense,* which had appeared back in 1739.[8] But, of course, his authorship of the original was still not widely known.

Although by July 1762 no headway had been made with the scheme for a pension, Johnson had been receiving much attention in print, a fact which may have kept encouraging his backers. Although Churchill's brutal satire in *The Ghost* hardly helped, there were other publications which did. In the *Universal Museum* for March there was a witty allegory concerning the state of literature at the Court of Parnassus, where Johnson appeared as one of the leaders of the intrepid veteran troops opposing the powers of Dullness. One of the courageous, experienced commanders, Johnson had the post of General, with Gray and Mason as colonels.[9]

Much more important, sometime in April there appeared a thirty-two-page pamphlet with the title *An Historical and Critical Account of the Lives and Writings of the Living Authors of Great Britain, Wherein their Respective Merits are Discussed with Candour and Impartiality,* by W. R.[10] It was reviewed in the May number of the *Critical Review.* William Rider, the author, may have known Johnson through contacts at the *Gentleman's Magazine.* In any event, Johnson comes out very well in the pamphlet. He appears in second place, just after an account of Edward Young, author of the very popular *Night Thoughts.* In the short account, which occupies only three pages, Rider is highly complimentary to Johnson, both as a writer and a person. There are constant references to him as a "genius," both "penetrating and sublime." "The sagacity of his criticisms sufficiently proves his penetration; the noble enthusiasm that runs through his allegorical and oriental compositions equally demonstrates his turn to the sublime."

As to Johnson's works, Rider has praise for his tragedy *Irene* and the *Rambler,* which "would be sufficient to immortalize his name" (indeed Rider tends to agree with critics who prefer the *Rambler* to Addison's *Spectator*); for the *Life of Savage* which is looked upon as "a masterpiece of biography"; and *Rasselas,* "a novel in the oriental way, a species of writing which is near of kin to poetry, and in which Mr. Johnson is allowed to surpass all English authors." Rider ends his series of encomiums with this final paragraph:

> Not contented with surpassing other men in genius, he makes it his study to surpass them in virtue, and all that humanity and that sincere attachment to religion, which shine through his writings, are equally conspicuous in his life. Though by no means in affluence, he is always ready to assist the indigent; and being of a truly philosophical disposition he is satisfied with a competency, though by the superiority of his talents he might have long since made a fortune.

Another pertinent comment came in the *Edinburgh Magazine* for May, where the statement is made that "the world has indeed been obliged

to Mr. Johnson for many admirable instructions," but with the qualifica-
tion that unfortunately Johnson's "abilities are contracted by the necessity of writing for money."[11] The implication is obvious. If only Johnson
were not under the continual pressure of having to stay alive, he might
produce more great pieces of literature.

By July something was in the wind. Johnson's friends had been
thinking of possible ways of putting pressure on those at the top, and
others became involved. Exactly what finally happened will probably
never be known. There are too many conflicting stories, none of them easy
to substantiate. And whether Johnson himself had any knowledge of what
was going on is also a mystery. Both Arthur Murphy and Thomas Sheridan
later claimed to have talked to him about the possibility,[12] though Johnson
may well have not taken their remarks seriously. Certainly he had no great
admiration for the Earl of Bute. James Elphinston claimed that once when
dining with Johnson, not long before the pension was given, he asked his
host why he so obviously disliked Bute. "Because," Johnson replied, "he
gave the King a wrong education. He had only taught him to *draw a
tree*."[13] Nevertheless, like most others of the day, Johnson had great hopes
of what the new King might do for the country.

Later writers, perhaps using *post hoc* reasoning, suggested that it was
the bad reputation produced by Bute's many grants to his Scottish supporters which gave his close associate Alexander Wedderburne the idea
that a pension for someone like Johnson, a well-known hater of the Scots,
might be a clever way to offset these sniping attacks. Surviving satirical
prints of the spring of 1762 show clearly that Bute's preference for his
northern followers was already a popular theme.[14] As a character in one
of the prints puts it, "I wish I had been born in a colder climate for I find
merit lies north." Moreover, in other prints which appeared somewhat
later the term "Scotch pensioners" is often used. Undoubtedly, the widespread dislike of some of Bute's recent actions had something to do with
the decision to reward the compiler of the English *Dictionary*. Thomas
Percy certainly thought so.[15]

If it was Wedderburne who astutely saw the possible value of such
an award, he also was clearly aware of some difficulties. He knew Johnson's
prejudices and his occasional violence. Whether Bute had ever shown him
the anonymous letter received the preceding autumn can never be established, but he may have. Wedderburne's way of proceeding suggests as
much. In any event, he moved cautiously and with great skill.

Once Bute and the King had agreed on the general idea, probably
sometime in early July, the sequence of events was something like this.
Because of Johnson's known independent spirit and occasional intransi-
gence, it was thought best to approach him carefully. Wedderburne him-

self preferred not to make the offer, for he feared that if Johnson were uncertain of just what was meant he might knock his visitor down with a folio, as he was said to have done to the bookseller Osborne. Thus, Wedderburne asked Arthur Murphy to be the emissary. At least so Murphy claims.[16]

From Murphy's account, written long afterward, on the weekend of July 16 to 18 he went to see Johnson in his chambers in Inner Temple Lane, and "by slow and studied approaches the message was disclosed. Johnson made a long pause; he asked if it was seriously intended? He fell into a profound meditation, and his own definition of a pensioner occurred to him." When Murphy insisted that Johnson certainly did not fit the well-known definition, Johnson suggested that they meet again the next day at the Mitre Tavern, at which time he would deliver his decision.

Johnson at once consulted Joshua Reynolds and other close friends, seeking their advice as to the propriety of accepting this royal favor, remembering his definitions in the *Dictionary* and his known anti-Hanoverian position. Reynolds told him that he could see no objection at all, since this was a reward for literary merit. The definitions were not applicable to his situation. Evidently Johnson did not hesitate any longer, and by Sunday, July 18, he had given up "all his scruples" and decided to accept the award. The next day, Monday, July 19, Murphy was at Johnson's chambers soon after nine o'clock in the morning, "got Johnson up and dressed in due time" (something of an achievement that early in the morning!), took him to see Wedderburne, who showed him the documents, and then conducted him to see the Earl of Bute. We can be sure of the date since Johnson mentions it in a letter to his stepdaughter, Lucy Porter, written the next Saturday.[17]

Happily, the meeting went off very well. Johnson expressed his sincere thanks for His Majesty's bounty, and insisted that he was highly honored. Bute behaved in a handsome manner, and twice repeated the point that the pension was being given Johnson "not for anything you are to do, but for what you have done." According to Charles Burney, Johnson told him that this was said in answer to a question which he himself had put, before formally accepting the intended bounty: "Pray, my Lord, what am I expected to do for this pension?"[18] Another version of just what the Earl said comes from Murphy, who phrased it this way: "No, Sir," said Lord Bute, "it is not offered to you for having dipped your pen in faction, nor with a *design* that you ever should."[19] From Johnson's point of view it was very clear that the pension was given as a reward for past labors, and not future political support. And Johnson's close friends all realized that this was true. But others were not so sure.

On Monday evening, after the interview, Johnson regaled Reynolds

Alex.ᵗ Mackenzie Inv.ᵗ et Sculp ·1762·

The HUNGRY MOB of SCRIBLERS and Etchers

If thine Enemy be hungry give him Bread to eat:
and if he be thirsty. give him water to drink Proverbs. 25. 21.

Let each Scribler that will ply his Needle or Quill
In Despite . of the Beadle or Gallows
And their Venom throw out all the Kingdom about
No Regard should be paid to such Fellows

Was a God to alight from Olimpus height
Or Pallas to Guide in this Nation
The hungry Tribe 'gainst her Rules would Subscribe
And endeavour to blacken her Station .

Then in Pit-y behold ; how they Scratch and they Scold
And Spew from their Airy Dominions .
Not any of Sense can sure take Offence !
Or be Bi-Asd by such weak Opinions !

If their snarling youd stop give the Hellhounds a Sop
Like Cerberus, that Infernal Growler .
They'l Riggle and bow ; and Praises bestow .
Tho' now they breathe nothing but Foul Air .

Verses in 1762 satirizing the world of political hacks.

and other friends with an account of what happened. The next day he
dispatched a formal letter of thanks to Bute for His Majesty's generosity.

> Bounty always receives part of its value from the manner in
> which it is bestowed; your Lordship's kindness includes every
> circumstance that can gratify delicacy, or enforce obligation.
> You have conferred your favours on a man who has neither
> alliance nor interest, who has not merited them by services,
> nor courted them by officiousness; you have spared him the
> shame of solicitation, and the anxiety of suspense.
>   What has been thus elegantly given, will, I hope, not be
> reproachfully enjoyed; I shall endeavour to give your Lordship
> the only recompense which generosity desires—the gratification
> of finding that your benefits are not improperly bestowed. . . .[20]

Public announcement in the newspapers came on Thursday, July 22, when
the *St. James's Chronicle* carried the statement, "His Majesty has been
graciously pleased to settle a pension of 300£ per annum on Mr. Samuel
Johnson, a gentleman well known in the literary world." Other papers
over the weekend repeated the same announcement.[21]

   As might have been expected, Johnson's friends and admirers applauded the decision; those who were on the other side politically, or who
disliked him personally, were shocked and were quick to point out the
inconsistency between Johnson's definitions of "pension" in his *Dictionary*
and his accepting one himself.

   The correspondences of the day and the local newspapers witness to
the variety of opinion. Even among provincials who had never met Johnson one could find enthusiastic admirers. For example, William Bewley,
a Norfolk surgeon, wrote to his friend Charles Burney on August 4:

> I rejoice at the prospect which the papers give us of Johnson's
> enjoying at last a decent independence in the eve of his days,
> in consequence of a pension from the crown. Does this bounty
> flow immediately from the throne?—*ex mero motu*? But I am
> arguing perhaps like the German doctors about the Golden
> Tooth. Does such a pension really exist?[22]

   And for clear evidence of the opposing reaction one has only to look
at the unpublished letters between Thomas Birch and Philip Yorke, a
staunch Whig of the old dispensation.[23] While Yorke was in the country
when Parliament was not in session, Birch every Saturday sent him a long
letter of London gossip and news. Thus on July 24, after complaining
about a recent royal present of £50 to John Kennedy, a Derbyshire clergy-

man who had dedicated to the King "an extravagant system of astronomical chronology deduced from the Old Testament, and which none but an Hutchinsonian can pretend to understand" (amusingly enough, Johnson had written the dedication for Kennedy!), Birch added: "Sam. Johnson likewise, who would lately scarce have owned the King's title, is now a royal pensioner with £300 a year. Monsignor Colbert was more delicate in his recommendations to Louis XIV of men of genius and learning than the great courtiers of more modern times." Two weeks later Birch commented again to his patron:

> Sam. Johnson's becoming a pensioner has occasioned his Dictionary to be turned to in the word *pension* thus defined by him: "an allowance made to any one without an equivalent. In England it is generally understood to mean pay given to a state-hireling for treason to his country." I do not know whether the acceptance of his pension obliges him to an oath to the government. If he now takes that oath, I know what to determine about the conscience of this *third Cato*.

Others, too, hit upon the obvious discrepancy, but it was not until some weeks later that sharp attacks began to appear in print. The most vigorous came in the radical opposition weekly, the *North Briton,* edited by John Wilkes and Charles Churchill. At the end of No. XI, which appeared on August 14, and which was largely given over to attacks on Bute and the periodical, *The Auditor,* which supported him, Wilkes adds a paragraph stirred up by Johnson's pension.

> I hope Johnson is a *writer of reputation,* because as a writer he has just got a pension of 300£ per annum. . . . I hope too that he is become a friend to this constitution and the family on the throne, now he is thus nobly provided for: but I know he has much to *unwrite,* more to *unsay,* before he will be forgiven by the true friends of the present illustrious family, for what he has been *writing* and *saying* for many years.[24]

Birch in his weekly letter to Yorke refers to the *Auditor* and Arthur Murphy, its editor, and then asks: "The *North Briton* of today not only attacks him [Murphy], but likewise Sam. Johnson, the new pensioner, who has been lately seen at Lord Bute's levee."[25]

But Wilkes's most vigorous and penetrating attack came the next week, in No. XII of August 21, which appeared while Johnson was down in Devonshire with Joshua Reynolds (if Johnson ever read through this issue, one can understand his later reluctance to dine with Wilkes). Because of the later and better-known attacks by his collaborator Charles Churchill, many people have assumed that Churchill was the author of this number of the *North Briton*, but Wilkes later confessed that it was his. Almost the entire number is centered on Johnson's pension, with numerous references to his *Dictionary* quotations, and an ironic suggestion as to Johnson's earlier position.

> Mr. Johnson's many writings in the cause of liberty, his steady attachment to the present Royal Family, his gentleman-like compliments to his Majesty's grandfather, and his decent treatment of the parliament, entitle him to a share of the royal bounty. It is a matter of astonishment that *no notice* has till now been taken of him by government for some of the most *extraordinary* productions, which appeared with the name of *Samuel Johnson*: a name sacred to *George and Liberty*.[26]

Birch refers to this issue in his weekly letter the same day, and it doubtless received much publicity.

It was stringent enough to draw strong protests from Johnson's defenders. The most detailed, as well as the most effective, defense came in an anonymous letter signed "A South Briton" which appeared in the *St. James's Chronicle* for September 2.[27] The editor of the newspaper printed it all, as an example of his willingness to give both sides of an argument, at the same time testifying to his belief that the writer was too severe in his rebuttal. In many ways it is an interesting piece, which deserves more critical examination, even if the author has never been identified.

It has certain resemblances to the other anonymous letter of the autumn before. Both letters begin and end in much the same way—starting with regret over the lack of recognition in the past of fine arts, literature, science, morality and religion, and ending with a disclaimer of any connection with Johnson. Thus "A South Briton" concludes: "P.S. I solemnly declare that I have not the least connection with Mr. Johnson. The indignation I conceived at seeing a man of such reputation and abilities abused by a little barking party-cur, was the sole cause of my troubling the public with this letter. Mr. Johnson himself knows nothing of it." In the main body the two letters are quite different in content—the earlier concentrating on Johnson's failings and merits and his need for financial help, the latter stressing the failings and corruption of the former administration. To be sure, Johnson's major works, the *Dictionary*, *Rambler* and *Idler* are mentioned—"performances held universally in the greatest esteem"—and the writer admits certain "disadvantages of person" in Johnson, but insists that "when I first heard . . . that a gratuity was conferred on him, I could not help breaking out into a rapture of praise, and blessing the royal hand that showed so worthy a regard to real learning and merit."

As to the definition of "pension" and other matters stressed by Wilkes in his damning attack, the writer suggests that in the next edition of the *Dictionary* Johnson merely add the following note:

> N.B. The above explanation was written in the reign of George the Second; since the accession of George the Third it bears an additional meaning, *viz* an annual reward from the Prince, &c. as above; and a reward given to learned men for merit, worth, and genius, &c., qualities little regarded at the time this Dictionary was first published.

As a defense of Johnson and as a vigorous reply to the editors of the *North Briton,* the "South Briton's" letter is very effective. Actually it contains one of the most devastating descriptions of ministerial chicanery and corruption under George II that one can find anywhere. With relentless severity the writer piles up the descriptions of his opponent's qualifications—corruption, jobbing, venality, contracting, electioneering, avarice and ambition, ignorance, extravagance, rapacity, dullness, malevolence, subtle artifices, conceit, and low cunning. These are the qualities which used to be rewarded.

Such a savage political attack would appear to rule out the possibility that it was written by the same hand which had recommended Johnson the year before for the pension, though Richard Farmer in Cambridge evidently showed some interest and was curious as to exactly what had happened.[28] Thomas Percy, when writing to his Emmanuel friend on October 9, passed on this piece of gossip:

> I have lately heard an account how Johnson came by his pension: it seems that Lord Bute had procured a pension of the same value for Hume: and some of his friends (my Lord Melcome [*sic*], say some) remonstrating, that to prevent an odium he ought [e]qually to distinguish English literati: he t[hought] it necessary to do this for one of the most eminent and at the same time most necessitous of them.[29]

A few days after the *St. James's Chronicle* defense, in the August *Gentleman's Magazine,* which came out early in September, Johnson's old friend and colleague John Hawkesworth, now acting as general editor of the periodical, in his usual section of excerpts from various other papers during the month, had only this to say about Wilkes's notorious piece: "The *North Briton,* No. XII, has thought fit to insult and vilify the highest characters, for encouraging literary merit without regard to party principles."[30] Birch in his weekly letter of September 4 commented:

> Hawkesworth, in the last Gentleman's Magazine, is angry, your Lordship sees, with the *North Briton* for animadverting upon the giving a pension to Sam. Johnson, which the candid and modest superintendent of that magazine styles *encouraging literary merit without regard to party principles,* a gentle expression for furious Jacobitism. A friend of Johnson's told me that when he mentioned to him the design of giving him a pension, he answered with a supercilious air, "if they offer me a small matter, I will not accept it."[31]

To which his patron answered from the country on September 7:

> I took notice of Hawkesworth's most indecent remark on the pension given to his fellow labourer in declamatory impertinence Johnson; and I presume from several symptoms in his collection that he flatters himself with the honour of standing next oars [the second available boat for hire] in the literary list. Both he and Smollett have changed their livery lately, and let them wear whose they will I shall have a most sovereign contempt for such hackney sycophants and scribblers.

The best known attack came in Churchill's third book of *The Ghost,* which appeared on Thursday, September 23. Johnson, as "Pomposo," had been derided in earlier parts of the poem for his supposed credulity in believing the Cock-Lane Ghost story and for other weaknesses. Now in the third part, which Birch in his letter of September 25 found inferior to the first two, Churchill lashed out at Pomposo for accepting a pension.

> How to all principles untrue,
> Nor fix'd to *old* Friends, nor to *New,*
> He damns the *Pension,* which he takes,
> And loves the Stuart he forsakes.[32]

In other political caricatures and prints, Johnson is usually seen fawning on Bute, with "300£ a year" attached to him somewhere. And in verse satires supporting the liberal Whig position "Pensioner Johnson" is rarely omitted. As a sample, there is an amusing later work entitled *The Theatres: A Poetical Dissection,* written supposedly by Sir Nicholas Nipclose, Baronet. After some hits at Johnson's *Irene,* "a turgid, tasteless tragic" work, and his egotism, "who, in his own opinion, sits supreme/ Whatever style he takes, whatever theme," the satirist continues:

> JOHNSON, who once, beneath a virtuous face,
> Gave venal pensioners to vile disgrace;
> JOHNSON, who since, more prudent grown, and old,
> Obeys the touch of all-converting gold;
> Of a court scribbler takes the paltry sphere,
> And damns his fame—for what?—three hundred pounds
> a year.[33]

How did Johnson take such obloquy? Did he answer his attackers? Not really. He was away in Devonshire until late in September, and if any of his friends ever showed him the newspaper controversy, or some of the later satires, he never reacted publicly, or seemed emotionally affected. Some years later when Boswell mentioned the "idle clamour" which had followed the announcement of his pension, Johnson said, with a smile, "I wish my pension were twice as large, that they might make twice as much noise."[34]

He would not answer such foolish lambasting. He had the Earl of Bute's definite assurance that the award had not been given him for future support, but solely for past writings, and he saw no reason to disbelieve him. In later editions of the *Dictionary* he never changed the definitions of "pension" and "pensioner." He had meant what he said, and thought his own case an exception.

But what about his later political pamphlets backing the King and his ministers? He wrote some of them in support of his friend Henry Thrale, a member of Parliament with whom he was living a large part of the time, and all of them represented his own frank opinion at the time.[35] He never thought of them as being his response to royal generosity.

Did Bute and his ministers think they had bought a possible political supporter, or at least silenced a potential antagonist? They obviously had no illusions as to Johnson's immediate open support. But there is some evidence which leads one to wonder. Both Boswell and Johnson were probably unaware that the pension was paid out of a royal fund which was labeled "Writers Political" in a list made up at the younger Pitt's request in August 1782 of "Private Pensions, and Secret Service Money" paid out by one of the secretaries of state or chief clerks of the treasury. Johnson's name appears in this "Private List" in the same column as a number of obvious, cheap political writers.[36]

It is quite true that a little over a year later, probably in October 1763, Charles Jenkinson, an influential member of the government, con-

Satirical print of 1763 in which quotations from Samuel Johnson's works are used.

sulted Johnson about negotiations then in progress concerning the Peace and left some important papers with him for his examination.[37] But Johnson did nothing about them, because two years later Jenkinson had to write to get them back. If any of the ministers may have had any illusions of getting practical help from the new pensioner, this episode must have shown how vain was this false hope.

There can be no doubt as to Johnson's genuine gratitude to the King and to the Earl of Bute for their generosity, though it is not easy to document just how he showed it. Arthur Murphy told an amusing story of an argument which Johnson had with Dr. William Rose, who had "contended for the pre-eminence of the Scotch writers." When Johnson exploded, Rose jokingly said he would name a Scottish writer whom Johnson must acknowledge as the best in the kingdom. "Who is that?" burst out Johnson. To which Rose replied, "The Earl of Bute, when he wrote an order for your pension." "There, Sir," Johnson replied, "you have me in the toil: to Lord Bute I must allow whatever praise you may claim for him."[38] But whether or not Johnson ever said this is not clear. When Boswell asked him if the story were true, Johnson said he had never heard it.

If the pension did not at once bring about a major change in his style of life, he was at least rescued from constant financial pressures and worries.

CHAPTER XVII

Trip to Devon

In AUGUST 1762, after the welcome news of the pension, Johnson was ready for some diversion outside London. Thus he gladly accepted the invitation of Joshua Reynolds to accompany him on a six-weeks' trip to Devon, a part of England that Johnson had never seen. He was in a particularly happy mood, and the tour proved a great success. Although not as famous as his later visit to the Hebrides with Boswell, or to Wales and Paris with the Thrales, the tour of Devon was one of Johnson's most delightful jaunts.

It is true that at the start Johnson was not wildly enthusiastic. In his long letter to Baretti in late July, after describing his visit to Lichfield the winter before, he added: "I think in a few weeks to try another excursion; though to what end?"[1] Significantly, he left the question unanswered, except for a series of moral reflections about man's habit of borrowing all his happiness from hope, which inevitably ends in disappointment. The author of *Rasselas* had not turned optimist overnight. Nevertheless, once he was on the road he was apparently in a jolly mood.

Although Johnson himself kept no records, Reynolds, by this time a busy and successful painter, had acquired the habit of keeping small engagement books, with meager notes of sittings, of social engagements, and of his own personal affairs. The one for 1762, which fortunately still survives, provides the basic chronology of the tour—the list of places they visited, and the names of people they met.[2] Moreover, quite a few of these people later recalled isolated incidents.

The two travelers set out from London on Monday, August 16, at two o'clock in the afternoon. Their first stop was Winchester, which they did not reach until eleven. Unfortunately, there is no reliable evidence as to how they traveled—whether in Reynolds's own private coach, or in a post chaise specially rented for the trip, or in the regular public conveyances. It is unlikely that Reynolds had his own coach this early, at least not the later flamboyant, rococo creation with panels painted with allegories of the seasons and wheels adorned with carved foliage and gilding.[3] Most likely the two took places in the regular cross-country stagecoaches, staying the night at the usual stopping places, at least until they reached the west country. Then they may well have rented vehicles for local trips around the countryside and often have been picked up by the coaches of people they were going to visit.

We have various descriptions of Johnson's normal behavior in a stagecoach. With his nearsightedness, there was not much pleasure in viewing the scenery. Instead, he usually passed the time reading some old familiar classic. Once he took along a copy of Euripides, another time Lucian, and another Pomponius Mela. Occasionally he would throw the book down, if struck by some remark made by one of the other travelers, and would pour forth "his knowledge and eloquence in a full stream, to the delight and astonishment of his auditors."[4] On one occasion he surprised his companions by a long dissertation on the digestive faculties of dogs. When the coach halted for a change of horses or for dinner Johnson might vehemently attack a stewed carp, or whatever was supplied, using his fingers.

Tuesday, the seventeenth, was spent in Winchester, where they appear to have had an engagement with somebody at eleven. They probably also saw an old friend, Joseph Warton, who had helped with the *Adventurer,* and who was now second master at Winchester School. The next day, the eighteenth, they set out from Winchester at 2:30, reaching Salisbury five hours later. Here also they spent a day seeing people and pictures, and on the nineteenth had a number of engagements. At eleven they were to see someone named Harris. It is natural at first to jump to the conclusion that this was James Harris, who lived in the Close. "Hermes" Harris, so-called because of the title of a pretentious volume of philosophical speculations which he had published in 1751, was never one of Johnson's favorites. In later years he definitely thought the man a prig.[5] But apparently they were to see another "Mr. Harris," merely to arrange plans for the next day.[6] There was no time for a formal call since they were due at Wilton, the home of Lord Pembroke, by twelve.

Whether any of the family was in residence at Wilton is not certain. Reynolds had painted Lord Pembroke and early in 1762 had been working on a portrait of his wife. But his lordship had recently run away with another woman, and he may not have been there to greet the visitors.[7]

The big house at Wilton stands low amongst rolling hills, with much water around it. One earlier traveler found the outside far from impressive, with a "regular old-fashioned front and irregular modern rear."[8] Boswell, years later, was greatly impressed by the "magnificence of the house" and was delighted by the way the Avon River had been channeled through the turf to make fine islands with tall cedars on them

Outside there was a superb Palladian bridge, and an Egyptian column; and inside there were numerous busts and pedestals, together with a number of handsome stone fireplaces, the work of Inigo Jones. What presumably drew Reynolds to the house—in addition to the desire to check the hanging of his own paintings—was the superb collection of portraits by Van Dyck, Lely, and others. While Reynolds critically viewed the pictures, we can imagine his companion drawing out some ancient folio from the shelves of the library and settling down to absorbed study.

After viewing Wilton in the afternoon, by six o'clock they had moved over to Longford Castle, the home of Lord Folkestone, where they were to spend the night. Here, too, it must have been the pictures which provided the chief attraction.

They left Longford Castle at 9:30 on Friday morning and drove twenty-seven miles to Blandford, and then nine more to Sturminster-Marshall, where they appear to have spent the night, visiting the Reverend John Harris.[9] By chance, we do know something about the rectory and its occupants. Harris, thirty-three years old at the time, an Etonian and King's College, Cambridge man, had for nine years been rector of Sturminster-Marshall, which was a "peculiar" in the gift of Eton College. Harris's mother had been a Dame of one of the houses occupied by schoolboys at Eton, and his sister Catharine succeeded her mother in this post. Many years later one of the boys in Catharine's house was Alexander Boswell, son of the biographer. In a postscript to a letter Sandie wrote to his father on July 7, 1791, the boy recorded a few anecdotes which he had heard from his Dame about the visit of Johnson and Reynolds to the Rev. John Harris in 1762.[10] It seems that Harris's house at that time, though still with a thatched roof, had sash windows. Johnson's first remark upon entering was: "Pull out the sashes or tile your house." To this Harris replied that he had no thought at present of doing either. But Johnson would not be diverted, and he blurted out, "Then it is quite inconsistent." The point of the story, of course, was that by the beginning of the eighteenth century the sash window was considered a sign of progress,[11] and Johnson thought that if one were to modernize he should not stop halfway.

Only a few miles from the church of Sturminster-Marshall, across a bridge over the Stour, is Kingston Lacy, the home of the Bankes family. It was natural that the visitors be taken there to see the pictures. Frances

Reynolds suggests that they went uninvited, or at least that the visit had not been planned ahead.[12] In any event, Mr. John Bankes courteously showed them through his apartments. Here there were fine portraits by Cornelius Jansen and Van Dyck, which the family had saved from the destruction of Corfe Castle during the Commonwealth. But it was the fine pictures by Sir Peter Lely which made the deepest impression on Reynolds. Indeed, he is reported to have said that he never fully appreciated the work of this artist until he saw the portraits of the Bankes family.

The trip through Kingston Hall had its amusing aspects. In the postscript to his father, Sandie Boswell added a few details recounted by his housemother. Mr. Bankes, when showing off one of his treasures, "desired Johnson to observe the fine trait of a picture," to which Johnson replied, "It is all one to me light or dark." Bankes then turned to Reynolds with a similar remark, only to receive the reply, "I can't hear what you say sir."[13] So goes the story, passed down in the Harris family, stressing the well-known physical weaknesses of the two travelers—nearsightedness and deafness. Reynolds later gave Boswell an account of the effect of Johnson's peculiar gesticulations on his host, and Boswell included the story in the *Life*.[14]

Frances Reynolds, who received the same anecdote from her brother, provides more details. For any stranger, or casual acquaintance, the experience of showing Johnson around one's house must have been something of a shock. His normal nervous twitchings were enough to cause astonishment, but at times he resorted to other unusual movements. In her later account, Frances Reynolds gives a detailed description of what these were like. When coming into a room he would sometimes perform strange maneuvers with his feet.

> Sometimes he would with great earnestness place his feet in a particular position, sometimes making his heels to touch, sometimes his toes, as if he was endeavouring to form a triangle, at least the two sides of one, and after having finished he would beat his sides, or the skirts of his coat, repeatedly with his hands, as if for joy that he had done his duty, and what was very extraordinary, after he had quitted the place, particularly at the entrance of a door, he would return to the same spot, evidently, I thought, from a scruple of conscience, and perform it all over again.[15]

Meanwhile the gestures of his hands were equally remarkable.

> . . . sometimes he would hold them up with some of his fingers bent, as if he had been seized with the cramp, and sometimes at

his breast in motion like those of a jockey on full speed; and often would he lift them up as high as he could stretch over his head for some minutes.

It was not only at the entrance of a door that Johnson might exhibit his gigantic straddles, for often this might occur in the middle of the room, as if he were trying to make the floor shake.

Evidently he startled Mr. Bankes, when they dropped in to see him, with some of these strange movements. As they were being shown the first apartment, Johnson

> began to exhibit his antics, stretching out his legs alternately as far as he could possibly stretch; at the same time pressing his foot on the floor as heavily as he could possibly press, as if endeavouring to smooth the carpet, or rather perhaps to rumple it, and every now and then collecting all his force, apparently to effect a concussion of the floor.

Bankes regarded him for some time in silent astonishment, but at last said that he believed his floor was firm. As Frances commented, this immediately made Johnson desist, "probably without making any reply. It would have been difficult indeed to frame an apology for such ridiculous manoeuvres."

From here the travelers moved on to Dorchester, dining there at four o'clock on Saturday, and through Bridport to Axminster. At ten on Sunday they set out for Exeter. Reynolds's scribblings in his notebook, unfortunately at this time made lightly in pencil, are not easy to decipher. All that is certain is that the travelers reached Exeter on Monday, the twenty-third, but only stopped overnight, for they were on their way to a reunion of the Reynolds family in Torrington. Consequently, all day Tuesday, the twenty-fourth—from ten in the morning to nine at night—they drove in a leisurely fashion across the country. Most likely they went through Crediton and Bow.[16] Although most of the way would have been through typical high-hedged roads (Donn's map of 1765 shows clearly that most were hedged), there were also some long stretches where they had beautiful views of the rolling west-country hills. The fields of grain this year were unusually fine. At least so London newspapers reported.[17] One traveler, indeed, described fields of beans many acres in extent, with plants eight and nine feet tall and full of pods. A perfect subject for a comprehensive remark by Johnson, had Boswell been his companion instead of Reynolds.

Two of Reynolds's sisters lived in Torrington—Elizabeth, the eldest, married to William Johnson; and Mary, the wife of John Palmer. Apparently Frances, who lived with her brother in London, was also there, so that the three sisters could vie with one another in showering attentions on the two travelers. Wednesday, the twenty-fifth, was spent with the Johnsons. Their host had tried various occupations—ironmonger, woollen draper—but had ambitions of becoming an active merchant. He had been mayor of Torrington in 1757 and was to be reelected to this post in 1764. In 1762 he was a bustling, ambitious man, whose future seemed assured. Unfortunately, later events always color our view of William Johnson, making it difficult ever to be quite fair to the man. Inevitably one tends to remember first his heavy borrowing from his successful brother-in-law— none of it ever paid back—his later bankruptcy, his pursuit of Sir Joshua in the courts, and most of all his desertion of his impoverished family to live openly in the same town with another woman.[18] But all this was far in the future. He appears to have been quite plausible, and even enlisted the help of Samuel Johnson in one of his schemes, something to do with marketing dried salmon, and Johnson made inquiries about its possibilities once he returned to London.[19]

Elizabeth, his wife—with a rather firm mouth and discontented expression in one of the portraits, but with a beautiful figure, so we are told —was a narrow-minded woman, restricted in her vision.[20] She later became a religious enthusiast and produced a learned explication of the Book of Ezekiel. Years later, Charlotte and Ann Burney labeled her as something of "a character" who thought no one could live in London without having a corrupt mind.[21] But this would have been after her long succession of troubles, enough to harden the gentlest character. In the Johnson house there were four children: Samuel, eight years old; William, almost seven; Elizabeth, five; and Richard, who was four.

Just where the William Johnson family was living in Torrington has never been definitely established. On the other hand, the handsome home of John Palmer, where the travelers went on Thursday, is still very much as it was then. Built in 1752, ten years earlier, it faced the churchyard across the road. Behind it were extensive gardens merging with green fields and hills beyond, with an elevated gazebo in the garden, where, according to later reports, Johnson retired to read. The house itself has style and distinction. One modern commentator describes it as a "most interesting example of brick work subordinated to a bold Palladian treatment of pilasters and cornices."[22] The central portion, which first catches one's eye, is balanced on either side with similar wings, with twin piers at the extremities of the railings.

The Palmer household was made up of John, the father, an attorney at law, solid, dependable, colorless, in contrast to his more daring and ambitious brother-in-law, William Johnson (yet Palmer, too, was mayor of Torrington three times, and his diary shows him to have been a devoted townsman); Mary his wife, sweet and affectionate, rather more feminine in the pictures than her elder sister Elizabeth, inherently a gifted writer, whose amusing *A Devonshire Dialogue* (in four parts) was published long afterward by one of her daughters; and five children.[23] They were Joseph, aged thirteen, later asked by Dr. Johnson for a prologue for Hoole's *Cleonice*, which was never used; Mary, to become Sir Joshua's heir, aged twelve; John, aged ten; Theophila (Offy), who was five in 1762; and Elizabeth, who was three. It was Offy who is supposed to have suggested the figure representing "comedy" in the well-known portrait of Garrick between tragedy and comedy.

Then there was Frances Reynolds, already a good friend of the author of the *Rambler,* and later to become one of his favorites. Long afterward one of her nieces made the claim that Frances could have married the ageing Dr. Johnson had she chosen to do so.[24] Certainly he was devoted to her, corrected her verses, came to her aid at various times of family stress. Well aware of her manifold weaknesses—Fanny Burney once described her as always living "in an habitual perplexity of mind and irresolution of conduct, which to herself was restlessly tormenting, and to all around her was teasingly wearisome"—Johnson still thought her goodness of heart and sweetness of temper enough to outweigh any such faults.[25] Like both her sisters she had definite literary gifts. Indeed, it is difficult not to describe more fully the three Reynolds sisters, so gifted yet so dissimilar, each producing a later published work characteristic of her own interests and temperament—Elizabeth on Ezekiel, Mary on comic country characters, and Frances on aesthetic taste.

There is no trustworthy evidence as to what happened during the Reynolds family gathering, with the great, lumbering dictionary-maker added to the group, although Frances in her later "Recollections" tells a number of stories, and there are in addition a few others which have come down through family tradition. Mary Palmer's great-grandson, for example, set down one of them.[26] Mary Palmer had invited in to meet the distinguished visitors the local schoolmaster, the Reverend George Wicky— a very intelligent and well-read man. When she broke in on Johnson's conversation with someone else to introduce the schoolmaster, Johnson, who may well have been a trifle annoyed, muttered aloud in a semi-absent manner, "Wicky—dicky—snicky—what a name!" and, turning on his heel, continued his talk with the other person. At least, that is the story. And it may have happened. Johnson always disliked people who interrupted unceremoniously what he was doing (witness Mrs. Thrale's later story of his rudeness to the young man, her nephew, who asked Johnson at Streatham if he should marry,[27] and any strange name or word could well have started a train of similar words in Johnson's mind. We have no more of the story, no mention of what happened later in the evening. If Johnson reacted typically, he must have later singled out the learned schoolmaster and had a talk with him. The trouble so often is that only Johnson's rudeness—what obviously startled at the time—is remembered, and not his accompanying act of conciliation.

Another family legend has it that during this visit Mrs. Palmer informed Johnson that there were to be pancakes for dinner, asking him at the same time if he liked them. Johnson replied, "Yes, Madam, but I never get enough of them." After such a pointed remark, Mrs. Palmer was determined that there should be no lack of pancakes, and Johnson devoured no fewer than thirteen.

Frances Reynolds tells of driving in a post chaise with Johnson past the churchyard of Wear, a village three miles from Torrington, just off the road to Bideford, where she had seen a striking monument put up by a widowed mother over the grave of her only child. As she was relating the tale with a multitude of melancholy circumstances, she heard her companion sobbing and saw tears in his eyes. Much affected by the experience, Frances described the whole incident in a long poem entitled "A Melancholy Tale," which some years later Johnson corrected, still much moved by the sentimental story.[28]

While in Torrington, Johnson willingly involved himself in a number of local problems.[29] He offered to exert his influence with the Bishop of Bristol to secure a pension for a local clergyman's widow, and to help find a suitable mistress for the local school (through Anna Williams he actually did later suggest a suitable candidate). And he promised to send a set of the *Idler* to a poetical clergyman who entertained him, Thomas Morrison of nearby Langtree. Some years later he was instrumental in getting Morrison's *Pindarick Ode on Painting* published.[30]

After three days of seeing relatives and their friends, Reynolds and his companion drove to Okehampton, where they stayed the night of the twenty-eighth. At nine o'clock on Sunday, the twenty-ninth, they set out for Plymouth, which they reached at six in the evening. Since Reynolds's first obligation was to pay his respects to his earlier patron and friend, Lord Edgcumbe, on Monday they took a boat over for a day at the beautiful house at Mount Edgcumbe.

One reason for his haste to get to Mount Edgcumbe may have been Reynolds's desire to see whether the 1761 portrait of Lord Edgcumbe and the recent one of his wife were properly hung. Moreover, he was eager to show Johnson what he must have considered one of the prize sights of the tour. Johnson later admitted the nobility of the prospect, what he could see of it, but characteristically insisted that it had one defect. At Mount Edgcumbe, he pointed out, "the sea is bounded by land on the other side, and if you have a fleet, you have also the ideas of there being a dockyard, etc., which are not agreeable."[31] Any general ideas of sublimity, he thought, were apt to be undermined by specific ideas of labor and discontent.

By Tuesday, the thirty-first, they were comfortably settled in St. Nicholas Yard in Plymouth at the home of Reynolds's old friend and schoolmate, Dr. John Mudge, which was to be their headquarters for the next three weeks. While they made expeditions around the neighborhood, at times staying the night at distant country houses, the Mudges' home was their base.

Who, then, was their host? The fourth and youngest son of the Reverend Zachariah Mudge, vicar of St. Andrews Church in Plymouth, John had been born in 1721 at Bideford, but had been educated by his father's good friend, Samuel Reynolds, at the Grammar School at Plympton, where he became the fast friend of his master's son, Joshua.[32] Deciding to become a physician, he became attached to the hospital at Plymouth. Having married early, he was for years in straitened circumstances, since his first wife had no fortune and rapidly presented him with a succession of children. But gradually his reputation grew, and he published various medical treatises, with the result that he eventually became a Fellow of the Royal Society. From all accounts he must have been a delightful person, a ready talker and most agreeable companion. Making friends easily, he knew also how to keep them. Natural and unaffected, cheerful, gentle and serene, he seems to have been universally admired. Family life obviously appealed to him, and his three wives gave him in all twenty children. In 1762 it was Jane, his second wife, who was hostess in the house in St. Nicholas Yard. Six months pregnant at the time, with a household of small children, Jane Mudge must have had her hands full with her famous guests. Nevertheless, she seems to have coped well with the situation, for there are no recorded complaints.

Jane Mudge fared better than did her mother-in-law, the wife of Zachariah Mudge, when the travelers came to call at the vicarage. The elder woman was of a thrifty disposition, even parsimonious in little things—so her own son thought—and Johnson's insatiable thirst was a sore trial to her. The inevitable explosion became a family legend. When one afternoon, after he had disposed of seventeen cups of tea, Johnson presented his cup to Mrs. Mudge for an eighteenth, she burst out with "What! Another, Dr. Johnson?" To which Johnson countered, "Madam, you are rude." It is quite possible that this episode was in Johnson's mind when he was dining many years later with Reynolds at Richard Cumberland's, and Sir Joshua had the temerity to point out the quantity of tea his friend was imbibing. This drew the retort, "Sir, I did not count your glasses of wine; why should you number my cups of tea?" Johnson, however, quickly turned to his hostess and added: "Madam, I must tell you

Mary Palmer and her sister, Frances Reynolds, painted by Frances Reynolds in 1759.

for your comfort, you have escaped much better than a certain lady did a while ago, upon whose patience I intruded greatly more than I have done on yours; but the lady asked me for no other purpose but to make a zany of me, and set me gabbling to a parcel of people I knew nothing of. So, Madam, I had my revenge of her, for I swallowed *five and twenty* cups of tea, and did not treat her with as many words."[33]

If Johnson was on somewhat strained terms with the vicar's wife, he had nothing but admiration for her husband. From all accounts the Reverend Zachariah Mudge, whom Reynolds had painted only a few months before, was a remarkable man. A native of Exeter, and at first a nonconformist, he was an undermaster in the school of Reynolds's grandfather. Here he became a close friend of Reynolds's father, Samuel, later headmaster of the Grammar School at Plympton. Thus there was a long tradition of association between the Mudge and Reynolds families. Eventually Zachariah conformed, took holy orders, and became an eloquent preacher, finally achieving one of the most valuable livings in the west of England, that of St. Andrew's in Plymouth. In 1739 he published a volume of sermons, and in 1744 a translation of the Psalms from the Hebrew. A ready conversationalist, he was also a deep philosophical thinker, whose ideas had a strong influence on his many acquaintances and friends. By the time Johnson and Reynolds came to Plymouth in 1762 he was evidently a high-churchman who looked deeply into the nature of things. He must have impressed Johnson greatly, for after his death Johnson composed a flattering account of him for the *London Chronicle,* embodying wholehearted admiration for his mind and character.[34]

According to Boswell, while the travelers were in Plymouth, Mudge "preached a sermon purposely that Johnson might hear him."[35] This was probably late in the visit, on September 19, where Reynolds left a blank in his list of social engagements. One may assume, too, that this was the occasion for another surviving anecdote of Johnson's brusque behavior.[36] Henry Tolcher, one of the senior magistrates of Plymouth, and an old friend of the Mudges, agreed to escort Johnson to the Alderman's seat in St. Andrews Church. Very proud of his companion, Tolcher tried to make the most of him, and not being "so religiously minded" as Johnson, he interrupted him during the service by several "trifling remarks." At this, according to the story, Johnson "at last became indignant, and rising up thundered out, 'I am surprised that an old man, and a magistrate, does not know how to conduct himself in the house of God.' " No doubt some stern rebuke was given, and not in a whisper, for Johnson could not have liked being distracted when his mind was on religious themes, but the "rising" and "thundering out" must surely represent the dramatic accretions of oral tradition.

It was to humor Mr. Tolcher, a "brisk young fellow" of seventy-four
—"full of life, full of talk, and full of enterprise," so Johnson described
him in a later letter[37]—that Johnson assumed a determined partisanship
in a local quarrel. Boswell relates the amusing story, as he had it from
Reynolds:

> Having observed that in consequence of the Dock-yard a new
> town had arisen about two miles off as a rival to the old; and
> knowing from his sagacity, and just observation of human na-
> ture, that it is certain if a man hates at all, he will hate his next
> neighbour; he concluded that this new and rising town could
> not but excite the envy and jealousy of the old, in which con-
> jecture he was very soon confirmed; he therefore set himself
> resolutely on the side of the old town, the *established* town, in
> which his lot was cast, considering it as a kind of duty to
> *stand by* it. He accordingly entered warmly into its interests,
> and upon every occasion talked of the *dockers,* as the inhabi-
> tants of the new town were called, as upstarts and aliens. Plym-
> outh is very plentifully supplied with water by a river brought
> into it from a great distance, which is so abundant that it runs
> to waste in the town. The Dock, or New-town, being totally
> destitute of water, petitioned Plymouth that a small portion of
> the conduit might be permitted to go to them, and this was now
> under consideration. Johnson, affecting to entertain the passions
> of the place, was violent in opposition; and half-laughing at
> himself for his pretended zeal, where he had no concern, ex-
> claimed, "No, no! I am against the *dockers*; I am a Plymouth-
> man. Rogues! Let them die of thirst. They shall not have a
> drop! "[38]

And Boswell later added a note: "A friend of mine once heard him during
this visit, exclaim with utmost vehemence, 'I *hate* a Docker.' " Actually
the story tells us more about his high good humor during the visit than
it does about any narrow partisanship, or bigoted opinions.

Dr. Mudge used to relate two other incidents which occurred during
Johnson's stay in his house, both illustrating Johnson's characteristic mixture of shrewd skepticism and deep curiosity about natural phenomena,
a combination which made a lasting impression on the scientifically-
minded physician. In the fantastic episode of the Cock-Lane Ghost, Johnson had shown clearly the same basic ambivalence—a rigid skepticism
about evidence, together with a willingness to conceive of the possibility
of the existence of powers or beings which lay outside the realm of man's
commonsense reason.

It seems that there was in Plymouth a Mr. Cookworthy, a Quaker and follower of Swedenborg, an eminent chemist who was convinced of his own power to discover metals underground by the use of a divining rod. Since he was particularly anxious to show Johnson his unusual powers, Dr. Mudge carefully buried in one part of his garden a large metal mortar as was used by druggists, and Cookworthy was called in to find it. As the venerable old man with white locks perambulated the garden with his rod, Johnson was seen to be "intently watching his progress." At last Cookworthy felt the power of the rod and determined the spot. But, alas, it was the wrong place, and Mudge triumphantly dug up the mortar from another part of the garden.

> The quickness of the Quaker at once endeavoured to account for the failure, and turning to his friend said, "Thou seest friend Mudge how this is." "I only see," replied Mudge, "you are mistaken, friend Cookworthy, in the supposed power of the rod." "Nay!" says Cookworthy, "it is bell metal; the mixture has destroyed the native metal, and therefore it would not assimilate."[39]

On another occasion Dr. Mudge happened to mention to Johnson a strange story told him by a friend of undoubted veracity, of a curious trial by fire which he had witnessed on the other side of the globe. Much interested, Johnson insisted on having it told to him by the actual person who had seen it. Thus the man was brought to the house and repeated the actual circumstances as he remembered them.

> In some part of the East Indies one of the natives was suspected of murder, and the mode taken to prove either his guilt or innocence was this. The suspected criminal was brought guarded, and his hands bound, to a public place prepared for the trial, where was a large fire, over which was a cauldron of melted lead: into this vessel of melted lead he was forced to dip his naked hand, which, if he was innocent of the supposed crime, it was concluded, would receive no injury from the burning metal; but if guilty, would be destroyed. All the officers of the English man-of-war then in the harbour, and of which the gentleman who related it was the purser, were present at this extraordinary manner of trial; and the gentleman averred that he distinctly saw the prisoner dip his hand into the melted lead, taking up some in his palm, and leisurely spilling it on the ground at his feet, without any apparent injury, or even pain to his hand. One of the English officers present had the curiosity to put a small stick, which he held in his hand, into the caul-

dron, and on taking it out again, found the part which had been immersed in the metal nearly consumed.[40]

Throughout, according to Mudge, Johnson listened to the narrative with much attention, and at the end "declared he would most willingly take a voyage to the East Indies, if he could be insured to be a witness to such a sight." James Northcote, who later recorded the story, could not help alluding to Johnson's "credulity" which made him a fit person to hear such a tale. But this is to miss the point. Johnson would not accept anyone's firsthand report of unusual occurrences, unless he was able himself to be on the spot and check all the evidence. While always keeping an open mind, he was not easily convinced.

Even from the very meager notebook entries it is evident that Reynolds wanted to show his friend the major sights of Devonshire, and to introduce him to the most important people. During their three weeks' stay in Plymouth they saw many visitors at the Mudges' and also took frequent trips into the country. Reynolds's notations are sometimes not too clear. Usually he put down places where they were to call, but sometimes the names may have referred to people who called on them. After all, he was not writing down historical facts, only notes to jog his own memory.

In some instances, there can be no doubt as to what is meant. From Thursday to Saturday, September 2 to 4, there are three entries: "Mr. Veal at Cofflet," then "Mr. Bastard," and again "Mr. Veal at Cofflet." From this it is obvious that they drove all the way out to see Veale at his home in Coffleet (now unhappily pulled down), then the next day went over to nearby Kitley to see the Bastard family, and returned to Coffleet for the third night. On Sunday the fifth they had an engagement with Dr. Vincent in Plymouth. Apparently this was their longest jaunt into the country, though there was another long trip out to Saltram for two days with the Parker family.

Other days were spent with friends closer by. Reynolds's terse entries give us only names—Dr. Vincent, Mr. Mangles, Mr. Robinson, Mr. Redstone, Mr. Hieren, Mr. Foot, Mr. Woolcomb, Dr. Blacket, Miss Howe, Mr. Dodge. There was a return visit to Mount Edgcumbe and a visit to the dockyard. Occasionally there is something more than the mere name, as, for example, "Mr. Mangles and supt at Mr. Lays" (perhaps a mistake for Ley—John Ley of the House of Commons). One day they picked up two guineas for subscriptions to Miss Williams's projected volume of poems.

The entry for Wednesday, September 8, documents a well-known account given by Boswell. One of the major objects of local pride was the new Eddystone Lighthouse, completed only a few years before, and situated some distance out in the harbor. The architect who had successfully built the handsome stone lighthouse, John Smeaton, sometimes called the father of English civil engineering, was an intimate friend of Dr. Mudge.[41] Obviously the new structure must have been much talked about in St. Nicholas Yard, particularly since it had just survived the worst storm in years, a tempest which had battered Plymouth on August 19, while the travelers were in Salisbury on their way down. Newspaper accounts at the time even compared this storm to the Lisbon earthquake for destructiveness, and there had been tremondous local damage. But the new lighthouse had survived without a blemish. There had been much doubt from the start about the feasibility of erecting a stone building at such an unprotected spot, where the power of the waves was greatest, so that this thorough test in the worst possible weather was a triumph for the supporters of Smeaton. Johnson's curiosity was naturally aroused. Indeed, the very day after the travelers reached Plymouth Reynolds had scribbled "Eddystone" in pencil in his notebook, perhaps indicating some talk of the local showplace. On that day a visit to a Mr. Lloyd was substituted, but plans for a close view of the lighthouse gradually matured. The Commissioner of the Dockyard, Sir Frederick Rogers, arranged to have a special yacht assigned to take the group out, and a week later the trip was actually made, through a harbor packed with ships of Sir Charles Hardy's fleet, ready to get under sail the next day. The magnificence of the Navy and all its adjuncts made a lasting impression on Johnson's mind. Indeed, there have been attempts to claim that he actually spent a night or two on one of the warships, but this is to confuse the 1762 visit with a later occasion at Portsmouth.[42] The weather was still too tempestuous, however, to allow a landing on the lighthouse, though they doubtless circled the structure, giving Johnson a good view of the graceful stone tower so familiar to present-day visitors to Plymouth Hoe. The fact that Boswell records Johnson's intense disappointment at not being able to land may be some indication of how strong the wind was.

At one large gathering, where there was something of a crowd, a young lad of fifteen stole up and reverently touched the skirt of Reynolds's coat. Little did Joshua Reynolds imagine that this boy, whom he probably did not even notice, would one day be his biographer. But for James Northcote it was a memorable day, and he carefully recorded the details long afterwards.[43]

What did they do on the other days? At least we may be sure that at the neighboring country houses there was plenty to eat and drink, and ample opportunity for leisurely talk. One day, according to Frances Reynolds, Johnson even ran a race. As he was sitting in the drawing room of one of the houses, looking out on a spacious lawn, somebody remarked that it was a proper place for a race. One of the young ladies present boasted that she could outrun anyone there, on which Johnson rose and said, "Madam, you cannot outrun me." Thus the challenge was accepted. At first, as the ill-assorted pair started running, the young lady had the advantage, for Johnson had on tight slippers too small for his feet. But he soon kicked them high into the air, and then, unencumbered, he left his adversary far behind. At last, as Miss Reynolds describes the incident, "having won the victory, he returned, leading her by the hand, with looks of high exultation and delight."[44]

This, like so many other of the anecdotes of the Devon trip, shows Johnson in cheerful spirits. He could even accept correction without a murmur. Readers of the *Life* are apt to forget that it was at this time, in the same country house where the race occurred, that his hostess, before a large company at dinner, had the temerity to ask, in a very audible voice, how he could have defined "pastern" in his *Dictionary* as the knee of a horse. To which she received the startling reply, "Ignorance, Madam, pure ignorance."[45] The complacent winner of an athletic event was in no mood to quibble or defend obvious mistakes.

Johnson even allowed himself, when in Devonshire, to make what was called an Irish "bull"—the only one which Boswell was able to authenticate. Once when the two travelers were out riding, Reynolds "complained that he had a very bad horse, for that even when going down hill he moved slowly step by step. 'Ay (said Johnson) and when he *goes* up hill he *stands still*.' "[46]

As might have been expected, Johnson astonished some of the natives by his enormous appetite. One day, when his host brought out every delicacy which his house afforded, Johnson, according to the story, devoured such a quantity of new honey and clotted Devonshire cream, besides drinking large portions of new cider, that his host became alarmed. Yet, as Northcote commented, the host was embarrassed between his fear for his guest's health and his fear of breaking through the rules of politeness by giving him a hint on the possible dangers involved. Wisely, he kept quiet, and there were no adverse consequences. The strength of Johnson's constitution, Northcote wrote,

> saved him from any unpleasant consequences which might have been expected; but his companion, Reynolds, was more discreet in his appetite, and was much better gratified by a present for his professional palate, which their host made him of a large jar of very old nut oil, grown fat by length of time, as it had belonged to an ancestor of the family. This prize Reynolds most eagerly took home with him in the carriage, regarding it as deserving of his own personal attention.[47]

Once Johnson even drank too much wine, and years later Reynolds described the incident to a friend. One night after supper Johnson put away three bottles of wine, "which affected his speech so much that he was unable to articulate a hard word which occurred in the course of his conversation." Having tried it three times and failing, he at last was successful, but then turning to his companion indicated that it was time to go to bed. It was, so Reynolds said, the only time in his life he had ever seen Johnson the least bit intoxicated.[48]

Modern critics tend to overstress Johnson's use of abstractions—his use of general terms and his failure to be specific.[49] Yet what often makes Johnson's phrases, whether written or spoken, so memorable is the concrete imagery he employed. A good example is the story related to Boswell by Dr. Amyat, a London physician, who chanced to be visiting at one of the Devonshire country houses when Johnson and Reynolds came to call. In order to amuse the visitors until dinner was ready, their host took them for a walk in the garden. The master of the house, thinking it proper to introduce something scientific into the conversation, asked Johnson if he was a botanist. "No, Sir, (answered Johnson) I am not a botanist; and, (alluding, no doubt, to his near sightedness) should I wish to become a botanist, I must first turn myself into a reptile."[50]

Just why a visit to Plympton was left to last is not clear. It was not from any lack of sentimental affection on Reynolds's part. All his life he retained a nostalgic feeling for his childhood haunts. Eighteen years later, in 1780, on another visit to Devonshire, when he was staying with the Parkers at Saltram, incidentally adding color to the blanched faces of his portraits of the family, his hostess wrote to her brother that Sir Joshua had gone to Plympton, in high spirits, pleased with the thoughts of looking "into every orchard and field that he remembered at school."[51] But in 1762, whatever the reason, it was not until Wednesday, September 22, that Reynolds took Johnson to see where he had been born and where he was educated.

There was much to show: his father's house, perhaps the actual room in which he was born; the great schoolroom, over 63 feet long and 26 feet in width, with a high coved ceiling, the room lighted by large perpendicular windows at the east and west ends, and squareheaded ones with granite mullions and transoms in the north and south walls. At the east end under the window stood elevated the master's desk, while over the entrance door in the center of the north wall was a small gallery, opening into an upper room. The plain walls and ceiling were whitewashed and relieved only by a rude cornice. Under the schoolroom, on the ground level, there was an open arcade or cloister, with a range of six granite columns with square capitals on the south side, separated by pointed arches. In wet weather this

made a convenient playground for the pupils. This cloister colonnade had
been the subject of one of Joshua's earliest known sketches.[52] In the center
of the north wall was the arched doorway, with solid oak door, leading to
the staircase up to the schoolroom. Although the school had been built in
1671, it was in 1715 that the Rev. Samuel Reynolds became Master, a post
he held until his death in 1746.

If Reynolds delighted in showing off the schoolroom and his father's
house, he was even more interested in reliving his own days of careless
youth, and once he slipped away from the rest of the party to pick up an
apple in an orchard which adjoined the school, and where, as a boy, he had
often stolen surreptitiously to pick fruit.[53]

In Plympton there was much more to be seen. High on a nearby hill
were the ruins of an ancient castle, and on the main street of the village was
the old guildhall, its columns extending out over the sidewalk. Here a few
years later Reynolds, then Sir Joshua, would be installed as mayor of the
town; and here would hang his self-portrait, which Farington tells us was
hurriedly painted for this purpose in a single day.

This was to be their last bit of Devon sightseeing, for the next day,
the twenty-third of September, they set out for home, reaching Exeter that
evening. From there on, no time was wasted. Now certainly in the fast
stagecoach, they reached Blandford the next night (69 miles), where they
stayed at The Crown, and Hartford Bridge the next (68 miles). They were
in London by two o'clock on Sunday, the twenty-sixth (36 miles), having
been away just six weeks.

For Reynolds it had been a welcome rest from his long days in his
studio, and also a chance to see family and boyhood friends. Much re-
freshed, he was back at work on Tuesday painting a portrait of the Duchess
of Douglas. For Johnson the trip was an opportunity to see more of a part
of England he did not know, and to widen his knowledge of life and manners. As Boswell stresses, the busy maritime existence at Plymouth, new
and fascinating, made a deep impression. The trip also added materially
to his wide circle of friends, especially the Mudges. (He became godfather
to the newest child born later in the autumn.) But most of all it cemented
his close relationship with Joshua Reynolds and his family. If they had
been good friends before, now they were intimates. And it brought Johnson into much closer contact with Reynolds's three sisters—to his "Dear
Renny," to Elizabeth, and to Mary, with their attractive children, notably
to young Samuel Johnson, and to Mary and Offy Palmer, of whom he
would see much in later years. Although it resulted in no great addition to
literature, as did his later journey to the western islands of Scotland, the
1762 trip to Devon had been a delightful interlude.

CHAPTER XVIII

Secure but Not Settled

WHEN JOHNSON RETURNED to London in late September 1762, he was in a happy mood. But he made no attempt to change his haphazard existence. Hawkins realistically, if ponderously, describes it this way:

> Johnson was now at ease in his circumstances: he wanted his usual motive to impel him to the exertion of his talents, necessity, and he sunk into indolence. Whoever called in on him at about midday found him and Levet at breakfast, Johnson in dishabille, as just risen from bed, and Levet filling out tea for himself and his patron alternately, no conversation passing between them. All that visited him at these hours were welcome. A night's rest, and breakfast, seldom failed to refresh and fit him for discourse, and whoever withdrew went too soon. His invitations to dinners abroad were numerous, and he seldom balked them. At evening parties, where were no cards, he very often made one, and from these, when once engaged, most unwillingly retired.
>
> In the relaxation of mind, which almost anyone might have foreseen would follow the grant of his pension, he made little account of that lapse of time on which, in many of his papers, he so severely moralizes. And though he was so exact an observer of the passing minutes as frequently, after his coming from church, to note in his diary how many the service took up in reading, and the sermon in preaching, he seemed to forget how many years had passed since he had begun to take in subscriptions for his edition of Shakespeare. Such a torpor had seized his faculties as not all the remonstrances of his friends

were able to cure; applied to some minds, they would have burned like caustics, but Johnson felt them not; to other objects he was sufficiently attentive, as I shall presently show.[1]

For the most part Johnson's friends accepted his way of life as unalterable. Yet they did exert pressure on him to complete one project which had become crucial. The third part of Charles Churchill's satiric poem *The Ghost,* which was published a few days before Johnson's return from Devon, in addition to making slurs at Pomposo's recent pension, contained a keen thrust at his long delay in completing the edition of Shakespeare.

> He for *Subscribers* baits his hook,
> And takes their cash—but where's the Book?
> No matter where—*Wise* Fear, we know,
> Forbids the robbing of a Foe,
> But what, to serve our private ends,
> Forbids the cheating of our Friends?[2]

Churchill certainly put his finger on a very sore spot, one which annoyed Johnson's supporters tremendously. Indeed, many of them had been worrying about this for a long time. Baretti, in Milan, recounted a series of his own recent disappointments in a long letter which was probably waiting for Johnson on his return to the city, and then added:

> I am informed that you continue to live on in idleness, and that you have not finished your Shakespeare. This, my Johnson, is blamable, very blamable. Yet I dare not fall too hard upon you. I cannot conquer my stubborn love as you cannot conquer your idleness. . . .[3]

A way would have to be found to get the edition completed.

Hawkins later insisted that after Churchill's suggestion of dishonesty on Johnson's part, various people "took the alarm, and, by all the arts of reasoning and persuasion, laboured to convince him" that his "credit was at stake."[4] Hawkins added that Reynolds and others of his friends "contrived to entangle him by a wager, or some other pecuniary engagement, to perform his task by a certain time." And so Johnson did begin to undertake special reading connected with the annotation of the plays, and requested advice from many of his friends about certain difficult passages. Garrick carried messages back and forth to Hawkins in Twickenham, and various other friends sent in notes.

Of course, we have no way of knowing just how the wagers were phrased, or how they were meant to function—if they actually existed. Whatever was worked out did finally succeed, though it took a long time. It was not until almost three years later that the Shakespeare edition finally appeared, but Churchill's jabs and the continuing nudges of various friends undoubtedly played a part.

There was always some shrinkage in Johnson's immediate circle of friends. Bathurst, whom he had loved dearly, died in Havana. Samuel Richardson also was gone. And a quarrel was developing with Thomas Sheridan, who may have played some part in negotiating for the pension. When Sheridan, too, was given a pension (only two hundred pounds), and began work on a rival dictionary, Johnson was upset. There is a story (whether true or not has never been proved) that when Johnson heard of Sheridan's pension he blurted out: "What, have they given *him* a pension? Then it is time for me to give up *mine!*" Then realizing how unfair he had been, he added: "However, I am glad that Mr. Sheridan has a pension, for he is a very good man."[5] Unfortunately Sheridan heard about Johnson's explosion and never forgave him. From that time on he refused ever to visit Johnson or to have any further association with him. His resentment could not be assuaged, even though Johnson tried in vain to restore their friendship. As one writer later commented, Johnson "made frequent overtures for a renewal of that intimacy which had formerly subsisted between him and Sheridan, but they were most ungraciously repelled." One day, when Johnson had agreed to dine with the publisher Dilly, Sheridan, who had also been invited, "left the house immediately upon hearing into whose company he was about to be ushered." Johnson knew how to forgive rude explosions, but others found it more difficult.

Johnson's frankness and candor are shown in a number of incidents which occurred probably about this time. A story was later told by a daughter of the Dean of Ossory about one occasion when Johnson spent a day or two in the country with the Dean and his family. They went to see the neighboring house of a rich merchant, who, "all bows and smiles," seemed delighted to show off his rarities. One of these he described to Johnson as "*Vesuvius* Caesar."[6] When the Dean's daughter could not suppress a titter, Johnson turned around and "to the discomfiture of the merchant and herself, sternly rebuked her aloud, 'What is the child laughing at? Ignorance is a subject for pity—not for laughter.'"

And there is the story of how, when a person who was dining with him "endeavoured to make his court to him by laughing immoderately at everything he said," Johnson bore it as long as he could, but finally, when "the impertinent ha! ha!" became intolerable, he turned to his guest and said, "Pray, Sir, what is the matter? I hope I have not said anything that *you* can comprehend."[7]

Innumerable comments concerned Johnson and tea—how many cups he drank at one sitting, and what he said about his love of the beverage.[8] What was the cause of this abnormal tea drinking? George Irwin has suggested that it was a kind of neurotic compulsion—an unconscious identification with his mother, who had often complained about not being able to obtain tea because of the unsympathetic, penny-pinching attitude of her husband.[9] Whatever the cause, if drinking tea was more than a social habit, it was an inevitable ritual when visiting friends.

His tea drinking also came to be associated in some people's minds with his convulsive physical ailments. Later, a tale was told about how, when he was having tea with a number of ladies, his hostess, who was particularly proud of her possessions, had brought out her finest set of china.[10] Eager to begin, and needing a lump of sugar, Johnson "without permission put his finger and thumb into the sugar-dish, tumbling the contents over, till he met with a piece of the proper size." All the while his hostess had kept her eye fixed on him, and "deeming his conduct a great breach of decorum," she ordered the servant to change the sugar dish. Johnson, though "apparently attentive only to his tea," noticed what had occurred and "as soon as he had emptied the cup, put it together with the saucer under the fire-place, with due care, however, not to break them." When his hostess demanded the reason why he had treated her in such a rude fashion, he replied: "Why, my dear Madam, I was alarmed with the idea that whatever I touched was thereby contaminated, and impressed with anxious desire to contribute towards your felicity, I removed the object so defiled from your presence with all possible expedition." Although his reply brought a smile to the rest of the company, it failed to mollify the lady.

Johnson's violent gesticulations led to another amusing anecdote, later told by Samuel Whyte. This happened at the home of Mrs. Sheridan's elder brother, a surgeon who lived at the bottom of Beaufort Buildings. Johnson was often invited there "in a snug way with the family party." At dinner once, when dessert was still on the table and the ladies had not yet withdrawn, his hostess, Mrs. Chamberlaine

> had moved a little back from the table, and was carelessly dangling her foot backwards and forwards as she sat, enjoying "the feast of reason and the flow of soul." Johnson, the while, in a moment of abstraction, was convulsively working his hand up and down, which the lady observing, she roguishly edged her foot within his reach, and, as might partly have been expected, Johnson clenched hold of it, and drew off her shoe; she started, and hastily exclaimed, "O fie! Mr. Johnson!" The company at first knew not what to make of it: but one of them,

perceiving the joke, tittered. Johnson, not improbably aware of
the trick, apologized. "Nay, Madam, recollect yourself; I know
not that I have justly incurred your rebuke; the emotion was
involuntary, and the action not intentionally rude."

Throughout the autumn, Johnson was presumably doing some work
on the Shakespeare, but apparently not much else. In late November the
two-volume edition of Du Fresnoy's *Chronological Tables of Universal
History, Sacred and Profane Ecclesiastical and Civil; from the Creation of
the World, to the Year One Thousand Seven Hundred and Forty-three,*
translated into English by Thomas Flloyd, appeared.[11] For this Johnson
had written a one-paragraph preface, and probably revised the dedication
to the Earl of Pomfret. In advertising the work in *Lloyd's Evening Post*
on November 19 the publishers had included the statement: "Recommended by Samuel Johnson."

Then in December or early January Johnson made some changes in
another work, John Kennedy's *A Complete System of Astronomical Chronology Unfolding the Scriptures.* Having known Kennedy, Rector of
Bradley in Derbyshire, and his wife for many years, Johnson had willingly
written the dedication to the King for this work, which had finally been
scheduled for publication late in 1762. But when he read proofs, or first
versions of the printed text, Johnson was disappointed by the conclusion
and offered to supply something better. His offer was accepted, and the last
page of text was canceled and a new one substituted. All this took time,
and though 1762 remained on the title page, the work was not published
until March 29, 1763, with Johnson's paragraph at the end. Whether it
was worth this delay is for the reader to judge. Here is the way Johnson
summed up Kennedy's arguments:

> Thus have I endeavoured to free religion and history from the
> darkness and difficulties of a disputed and uncertain chronol-
> ogy; from difficulties which have appeared insuperable, and
> darkness which no luminary of learning has hitherto been able
> to dissipate. I have established the truth of the Mosaical ac-
> count, by evidence which no transcription can corrupt, no
> negligence can lose, and no interest can pervert. I have shown
> that the universe bears witness to the inspiration of its his-
> torian, by the revolution of its orbs, and the succession of its
> seasons; *that the stars in their courses fight against* incredulity,
> that the works of God give hourly confirmation to the *law,* the
> *prophets,* and the *gospel,* of which *one day telleth another, and
> one night certifieth another*; and that the validity of the sacred
> writings never can be denied, while the moon shall increase
> and wane, and the sun shall know his going down.

In the spring of 1763 Johnson wrote a superb dedication to the new Queen for John Hoole's translation of Tasso's *Jerusalem Delivered,* and a short account of George Graham's *Telemachus* for the *Critical Review.*[12] According to the going rates at the time, Johnson would have been paid only about ten shillings for the latter. But with his pension, he was no longer in desperate need.

Memories of his pleasant trip through Devon remained vivid, and he did not forget all the promises he had made in Torrington and Plymouth. His letter to Frances Reynolds on December 21, 1762, shows how involved he was with the possibility of becoming godfather to Dr. Mudge's son, of securing a pension for the clergyman's widow, helping Reynolds's brother-in-law, William Johnson, with his speculation in salmon, and finding a new helper for the school in Torrington.

> If Mr. Mudge should make the offer you mention, I shall certainly comply with it, but I cannot offer myself unasked. I am much pleased to find myself so much esteemed by a man whom I so much esteem.
>
> Mr. Tolcher is here; full of life, full of talk, and full of enterprise. To see brisk young fellows of seventy-four is very pleasing to those who begin to suspect themselves of growing old.
>
> You may tell at Torrington that whatever they may think, I have not forgot Mrs. Johnson's widow nor school, Mr. Johnson's salmon, nor Dr. Morrison's Idlers. For the widow I shall apply very soon to the Bishop of Bristol who is now sick. The salmon I cannot yet learn any hope of making into a profitable scheme, for where I have enquired which was where I think the information very faithful I was told that dried salmon may be bought in London for a penny a pound; but I shall not yet drop the search.
>
> For the school, a sister of Miss Carwurthen's has offered herself to Miss Williams, who sent her to Mr. Reynolds, where the business seems to have stopped. Miss Williams thinks her well qualified and I am told she is a woman of elegant manners and of a lady-like appearance. Mr. Reynolds must be written to, for, as she knows more of him than of me, she will probably choose rather to treat with him.
>
> Dr. Morrison's book shall be sent to him with my sincere acknowledgments of all his civilities.[13]

If Johnson was sometimes slow in fulfilling rash promises, he did not ignore them.

The same day he wrote another long letter to Baretti in Milan, full of advice and news of their mutual friends. Once these two epistles were off his mind, he went up to Oxford for the holidays, hoping to free himself from a harsh cough which had sometimes been violent. Thus he was not able to go to Christmas dinner at Tom Davies's, where he had been invited and where he would have met an engaging young Scot named James Boswell. That meeting would have to wait.[14]

With all the controversy connected with his pension, Johnson continued to receive much publicity, and during the early months of 1763 he was often mentioned in the newspapers.[15] In the *St. James's Chronicle* of January 15 there was a letter from "Fitz Henriques" complaining that the papers gave lists of deaths, marriages, church preferments, but not of those who resigned from the government or had been turned out or in. The writer also suggested a further category for pensions. In ironic fashion he provided examples for his four categories: "Resigned," "Turned out," "Turned In," and "Pensions." In the last there was the following:

	£
"Mr. A.B. per Ann.	300
B.C.	500
C.D.	200
Mr. Sheridan	200
Mr. S. Johnson	300
Cum multis aliis[16]	

In the same newspaper on January 27, 1763, there appeared some verses with the title "CLASSICUS, a Literary Character." The author, who signed himself Mellifont, has never been identified. "Classicus" appears to have been based largely on Johnson's characteristics, and many readers undoubtedly made the association.

> In Classicus we always see
> An Author of Celebrity,
> Master of Arts—of Learning too,
> In literature excell'd by few;
> But wants one Art—the Art to hide
> Th' Emotions of scholastic Pride,
> Which make him with contemptuous Frown
> On Half the letter'd World look down.
> When Classicus, with all his Might,
> Dogmatic as the Stagyrite,
> In Conversation over-bears,
> And puts on self-sufficient Airs,
> His literary Lustre fades;
> For Pride the brightest Parts degrades.
> By frequent Disappointments sour'd,
> And acrimonious Thoughts devour'd,
> With much Acerbity he writes,

And in keen Satire most delights.
O'er all his Views of Life he throws
A Gloom, and dwells upon its Woes:
We therefore from his Works arise,
Too smartly tax'd for being wise;
For, while we to his Truths assent,
We pay—what most we want—Content.
      On serious Themes he chiefly shines,
And happily his Words combines;
With proper Pomp his Periods roll,
And his Sense penetrates the Soul;
But on a hum'rous Subject—there
You see the Gambols of a Bear.
      Sometimes, with Periods of a Mile,
He apes the Ciceronian Style;
But often fails by that to please,
For want of Tully's graceful Ease.
      In general, his Diction's good,
And generally understood;
But sometimes five-feet Words offend
Ears, which to Harmony attend;
And readers of the softer Sex,
With their enormous Length perplex.
For instance now—Con-ca-te-na-tion
Gives many a pretty Mouth Vexation,
Which can, with Ease, a Charm express,
As well as any Part of Dress.
      However, Classicus, with all
His Faults, is an Original;
And has, the wicked Wits must own,
In spite of all their Wagg'ry shown,
In various Parts of Composition,
Genius, Taste, Fire, and Erudition.[17]

Among the miscellaneous references a few deserve mention. In the *St. James's Chronicle* of February 19 Johnson was included in lists of those recently attacked by the *Auditor* and *North Briton,* and these were reprinted in the *Caledonian Mercury* (Edinburgh) and the periodical *Political Controversy.* In the March *British Magazine* appeared a letter about "new fangled" spelling in which the writer recommended the quotations in Johnson's *Dictionary* as proper authority for spelling. In April the forty-fourth number of Wilkes's *North Briton* referred to "Pensioner Johnson" (repeated in various other newspapers); and in the *Public Advertiser* for April 11 a letter signed "W. A." to Lord Bute, with the title "A New North Briton," included attacks on Johnson for accepting the pension and for his use of difficult words. In the May 21 *London Chronicle* appeared the interesting proposal that Wilkes's animosity toward Johnson could be traced to the definition of "distiller" in the *Dictionary*—"one who makes and sells pernicious and inflammatory spirits." Since Wilkes's father had been a distiller, he felt it was his duty to be revenged. This piece was also often reprinted.[18] How many of these Johnson saw, or in what way he reacted, is not clear. Probably he accepted the publicity, favorable and unfavorable, merely as part of his career as a literary man.

During these years Johnson showed a keen interest in the education of the children of his close friends, advising them constantly and helping them in every way he could. Francis Newbery, the son of the publisher John Newbery, is one example. When Francis attended the Merchant Taylors' School he lived with his parents in St. Paul's Churchyard. Since Johnson paid frequent visits to his father there, he saw the boy often and kept putting pressure on him to work hard at his studies. On one occasion Johnson, upon noticing a violin hanging on the wall of the parlor of the Newbery home, asked Mrs. Newbery to whom it belonged. When she replied that it was "Frank's," Johnson firmly addressed the boy: "Young man, give the fiddle to the first beggar man you meet, or you will never be a scholar." Frank, one might add, did not take this advice seriously, and later admitted that he had been more attracted to the violin than to books. But he did go to Oxford, doubtless with Johnson's help, for he entered Trinity College under Thomas Warton. Later when he became a businessman, his adviser heartily approved and they remained good friends. In his autobiography Francis Newbery tells a number of stories about Johnson.[19]

Another boy with whom Johnson had even closer ties was George Strahan, his printer's son. In October 1762, on the advice of Thomas Warton, Johnson helped young Strahan to get into Henry Bright's school in Abingdon, Berkshire. In his letter to the Master, Henry Bright, Johnson described his "young friend" as one who, after working in a shop for a number of years, had been seized with a desire for scholarship, for studying the learned languages, and entering the university as soon as he could. Johnson hoped that the strength of the youth's resolution would enable him to make up quickly for what he had lost. He had as a person "uncommon purity of manners and gentleness of temper."[20] Fortunately the recommendation was successful and young Strahan was accepted at the Abingdon School. Though told that it would be six or seven years before he could qualify for a degree, young Strahan refused to be overawed and became a serious student.

From a few encouraging letters Johnson wrote to him early the next year we can glimpse something of the affectionate relationship between the student and his fatherly adviser. In February Johnson urged George to read widely and not merely to do required lessons. The more books he looked into for his own entertainment, the better acquainted he would be with varieties of style. Over a month later Johnson wrote again.

> You did not very soon answer my letter, and therefore cannot complain that I make no great haste to answer yours. I am well enough satisfied with the proficiency that you make, and hope that you will not relax the vigour of your diligence. I hope you begin now to see that all is possible which was professed. Learning is a wide field, but six years spent in close application are a long time; and I am still of opinion that if you continue to consider knowledge as the most pleasing and desirable of all acquisitions, and do not suffer your course to be interrupted, you may take your degrees not only without deficiency, but with great distinction.
>
> You must still continue to write Latin. This is the most difficult part, indeed the only part that is very difficult of your undertaking. If you can exemplify the rules of syntax, I know not whether it will be worth while to trouble yourself with any more translations. You will more increase your number of words, and advance your skill in phraseology, by making a short theme or two every day; and when you have construed properly a stated number of verses, it will be pleasing to go from reading to composition, and from composition to reading. But do not be very particular about method; any method will do if there be but diligence. Let me know, if you please, once a week what you are doing.

One very much doubts that George complied with the request for such frequent reports, but he did keep his adviser up-to-date. On April 16 Johnson wrote again:

> Your account of your proficiency is more nearly equal, I find, to my expectation than to your own. You are angry that a theme on which you took so much pains was at last a kind of English Latin; what could you expect more? If at the end of seven years you write good Latin, you will excel most of your contemporaries. Scribendo disces scribere; it is only by writing ill that you can attain to write well. Be but diligent and constant, and make no doubt of success.

Then came advice as to how long to spend reading Cicero's *De Officiis* and other works.

> I hope you read by the way at loose hours other books though you do not mention them, for no time is to be lost, and what can be done with a Master is but a small part of the whole.

> I would have you now and then try at some English verses.
> When you find that you have mistaken any thing review the
> passage carefully and settle it in your mind.

After this the correspondence gradually became less regular or urgent. No doubt Johnson saw George when he was in London, and in October 1764 he was successful in getting the young man into University College at Oxford, with a small scholarship. Looking further ahead, George later did receive his M.A. at Oxford and became Vicar of St. Mary's, Islington. It was he who brought out the first slightly bowdlerized edition of Johnson's prayers after his death.[21]

Another young student whom Johnson tried to help in a desultory way was Jeremy Bentham. This brilliant prodigy entered Queen's College, Oxford, at the age of twelve, and on the death of George II in the autumn of 1760 wrote a Latin ode which attracted some attention. According to one account, it was shown to Johnson by John Hawkins.[22] Whether Jeremy ever met Johnson is uncertain, though they may at times have been in the same room. Bentham later claimed to have gone to the Mitre Tavern to hear Johnson talk. In the spring of 1763, however, the two did become involved in a strange connection. Oxford University decided to devote its 1763 Encaenia to the celebration of the Peace of Paris, which had been concluded in February. Young Bentham, who was to receive his bachelor's degree at that time, decided to try for a place as one of the Encaenia speakers, planning to write a Latin poem on some subject connected with the Peace. At first he thought the demilitarization of Dunkirk might do, but then asked others for advice. At some time, probably in April, his father, Zachariah Bentham, asked Johnson for his opinion. What would be the best topic for his son to choose in order to attain some notice in Oxford? On May 6 young Bentham sent a letter to his father.

> I have fixed upon the Havannah for the subject of my verses:
> I have settled my plan and have made some progress in the
> execution of it; with all due deference to the respectable opin-
> ion of Mr. Johnson, I must own, the conquest of North America
> did not suggest to me any thoughts whereon to lay the founda-
> tion of a copy of verses; I think I could better execute a pro-
> saical narration, and excuse me, Sir, if I likewise take the liberty
> to say that I am no better able to find matter on the subject of
> the Manillas.[23]

It is easy to see why Jeremy refused to accept Johnson's suggestion of the conquest of North America. The successful capture of Havana, which had occurred in August the year before, was much less controversial. Young Bentham set to work and was able to send a portion of his poem up to London to be shown to his "learned adviser." There were always some risks involved in submitting a work to Johnson. Once when Isaac Hawkins Browne asked his opinion of a poem on the immortality of the soul, the manuscript mysteriously disappeared. The author and Johnson had to put together a new version. And the only advice for one lady was the suggestion that she throw her tragedy into the fire![24] With Bentham the trouble was delay. If Johnson immediately looked at what the elder Bentham showed him, he did nothing about it. Eventually, he did write down a long sheet of comments, corrections, and suggestions, but he was so slow in getting the sheet to Jeremy that the young man had already produced a final copy without benefit of Johnson's criticisms.

A subsequent letter to his father tells the sad story.

> I am sorry to acquaint you that I have not succeeded; upon my not receiving Mr. Johnson's criticisms on Saturday, I was obliged to give my verses up to Mr. Jefferson as they were, and tell him how the matter stood; upon which he thought it was best to stay until the next day before he carried them up, in expectation of my receiving them then, as I did, but when they came, they did not answer our expectations; we expected Mr. Johnson would have altered the mistakes as well as pointed them out, especially as we had so little time before us; however, I corrected them myself as well as I could. On Monday there was a final meeting to determine who should be speakers but Mr. Jefferson was so dissatisfied with my verses that I almost question whether he gave them up.[25]

Thus the young man failed, and probably never forgave what he thought was the older man's dilatory procedure. Indeed, in later life Bentham never spoke of Johnson with enthusiasm.

In the spring of 1763 the fifty-three-year-old Samuel Johnson was slowly moving out of his most productive period. The great decade of the 1750s, when much of his most memorable work had appeared—the *Rambler* and *Idler*, the *Dictionary*, the work for the *Literary Magazine*, and *Rasselas*—was behind him. With no more financial worries, and his wife and mother dead, he faced the last stage in his remarkable career. Talk was becoming increasingly important to him. About the middle of May something happened that was to affect his reputation in succeeding centuries.

On the morning of May 16, 1763, Johnson had no idea that this was to be one of the most significant days of his life. He probably arose at the usual late hour, sipped his tea, and vaguely thought about what he might do for the rest of the day. Elsewhere in London a twenty-two-year-old Scot also had no inkling how momentous a day lay ahead of him.[26] "Jamie"

Boswell had come to London the previous November, planning to secure a commission in the Foot Guards, and throughout the winter had met many interesting people, had seen a lot, and had frequently associated with streetwalkers and prostitutes, with a resulting long siege of gonorrhea. Because of continuing pressure from his father, the laird of Auchinleck, he had given up his idea of an army career, and instead now planned to study law. But what interested him most was describing whatever happened to him with vivid and dramatic skill. One might almost say that nothing was of much importance to Boswell until it became a part of his daily journal. Particularly he enjoyed recording colorful phrases from the conversation of various people he met.

At this time Boswell had a habit of jotting down lists of what he intended to do during the day, along with exhortations to himself to behave properly. For May 16 his list began:

> Send breeches mend by barber's boy. You are now on good plan. Breakfast neat today, toast, rolls, and butter, easily and not too laughable. Then Love's and get money, or finish journal. Keep plan in mind and be in earnest. Keep in this fine frame, and be directed by Temple. At night see Pringle. . . .[27]

There was no mention of his having tea with the bookseller Tom Davies and his wife, at his shop in Russell Street, Covent Garden. The important event in store for him this day was unexpected and unrehearsed. But in his journal written shortly afterward he set down an accurate account of what happened.

Davies had originally been an actor, but had left the stage, along with his beautiful wife, when cruelly attacked by Charles Churchill in his first satire, *The Rosciad*.[28] Although Davies had a pompous manner, he was a frank and generous friend and an entertaining companion. Johnson often dropped into his bookshop for relaxed talk, as he did this day. As Boswell describes the meeting:

> I drank tea at Davies's in Russell Street, and about seven came in the great Mr. Samuel Johnson, whom I have so long wished to see. Mr. Davies introduced me to him. As I knew his mortal antipathy at the Scotch, I cried to Davies, "Don't tell where I come from." However, he said, "From Scotland." "Mr. Johnson," said I, "indeed I come from Scotland, but I cannot help it." "Sir," replied he, "that, I find, is what a very great many of your countrymen cannot help." Mr. Johnson is a man of a most dreadful appearance. He is a very big man, is troubled with sore eyes, the palsy, and the king's evil. He is very slovenly in his dress and speaks with a most uncouth voice. Yet his great knowledge and strength of expression command vast respect

and render him very excellent company. He has great humour and is a worthy man. But his dogmatical roughness of manners is disagreeable. I shall mark what I remember of his conversation.

Fortunately for us, Boswell did just that. But not at once.

The close friendship developed slowly. It was over a week before Boswell decided to call on Johnson in his rooms in Inner Temple Lane, where he found his host living in "literary state," and "very solemn and very slovenly."[29] Johnson received him courteously and twice pressed him to stay when he made a move to depart. When he was leaving, Boswell begged Johnson to call upon him some evening in his lodgings. Actually it was almost three weeks before they met again, at which time Johnson asked his new friend why he had not called oftener.

Six days later they happened to dine in the same room at Clifton's Chop House in Butcher's Row, and then spent the evening together at the Mitre. At last the intimacy began to develop, when Boswell told him the whole story of his life. From this time on they saw each other every few days, with Boswell dropping in at Inner Temple Lane, or meeting Johnson at the Mitre. In his journal the remarks of Johnson began to occupy more and more space. To be sure, the young Scot at times found recording the older man's conversation difficult. "It requires more parts than I am master of even to retain that strength of sentiment and perspicuity of expression for which he is remarkable." But he was determined to do what he could. "I shall just do my best and relate as much as I can."

Increasingly Boswell found this new relationship entertaining and absorbing, and was able to forget Johnson's disagreeable eccentricities. On July 14, after an evening at the Mitre Boswell wrote in his journal: "I take pleasure in recording every little circumstance about so great a man as Mr. Johnson."

During late July and early August they were together every day or so. Once they took a boat trip to Greenwich, and when Boswell finally left London to study law in the Netherlands and travel around the Continent, Johnson went all the way to Harwich to see him off.

As Boswell recorded, Johnson

walked down with me to the beach, where we embraced and parted with tenderness, and engaged to correspond by letters. I said, "I hope, Sir, you will not forget me in my absence." JOHNSON. "Nay, Sir, it is more likely you should forget me than I should forget you." As the vessel put out to sea, I kept my eyes upon him for a considerable time while he remained rolling his majestic frame in his usual manner; and at last I perceived him walk back into the town, and he disappeared.[30]

It would be two years and a half before the "majestic frame" and memorable conversation of "Dictionary Johnson" would appear again in Boswell's journals.

To end this account of Johnson's middle years with the beginning of his friendship with Boswell is not to imply that 1763 was a turning point. Johnson continued his rather disordered existence, disturbed by insomnia and increasing worry about his own mental state. Indeed, the next few years included some of the lowest points of his life. So the momentous meeting of these two men did not alter their lives immediately, but rather was a portent of the future.

Looking ahead, we can see that it was another person, also over thirty years younger than Johnson, who helped rescue Johnson from these recurring despondent periods. This was Hester Thrale, wife of a well-to-do brewer, mother of many children, and a bright, entertaining talker. After being introduced to Johnson in January 1765, the Thrales at once began to invite him to their home. In 1766, when they saw how morbidly depressed he had become, they took him out to their country estate at Streatham for the whole summer, gradually nursing him back to health. From then on, he spent about half his time living with the Thrales at Southwark and Streatham. The well-run and well-staffed household, with children all about, and with some attempt at regular hours, apparently calmed Johnson's nerves. As Walter Jackson Bate convincingly points out, after the dramatic turn for the better during the summer at Streatham, Johnson continued to improve.[31] His insomnia, which had bothered him for many years, began to disappear, and his whole mental pattern changed.

During these later years, for part of the time at least, Johnson could escape the quarrels and weird posturings of members of his changing household near Fleet Street. Whenever he wished, he could enjoy the regular everyday life of an intelligent, affluent household, with constant attention from Hester Thrale. To be sure, this, too, came to an end in the early 1780s, but for some eighteen years it provided the balance and sanity which Johnson badly needed.[32]

The relaxed and witty Johnson so marvelously described by Boswell in the *Life* was the result in part of the kindly care given him by the Thrales. With Mrs. Thrale as confidante and helper, and with "Jamie" Boswell setting down for posterity the best of his conversation, Samuel Johnson was to take his place as one of the greatest writers and personalities of all literary history. But those who read and reread Johnson's own works cherish the memory of this remarkable man chiefly for his wisdom and for the rich legacy of his writing.

SHORT TITLES

DNB	*Dictionary of National Biography*
ECS	*Eighteenth-Century Studies*
ELH	*English Literary History*
HLQ	*Huntington Library Quarterly*
JEGP	*Journal of English and Germanic Philology*
JNL	*Johnsonian News Letter*
MLN	*Modern Language Notes*
MLQ	*Modern Language Quarterly*
N&Q	*Notes and Queries*
PBSA	*Papers of the Bibliographical Society of America*
PMLA	*Publications of the Modern Language Association of America*
PQ	*Philological Quarterly*
RES	*Review of English Studies*
SAQ	*South Atlantic Quarterly*
SEL	*Studies in English Literature 1500–1900*
SP	*Studies in Philology*

Bate—W. Jackson Bate, *Samuel Johnson* (New York: Harcourt Brace Jovanovich, 1977).

Bibliography—William P. Courtney and David Nichol Smith, *A Bibliography of Samuel Johnson* (Oxford: Clarendon Press, 1915).

B.L.—British Library, London.

Brack and Kelley—*The Early Biographies of Samuel Johnson*, ed. O M Brack, Jr., and Robert E. Kelley (Iowa City: University of Iowa Press, 1974).

Clifford and Greene—James L. Clifford and Donald J. Greene, *Samuel Johnson: A Survey and Bibliography of Critical Studies* (Minneapolis: University of Minnesota Press, 1970).

Diaries, Prayers, and Annals—*Samuel Johnson: Diaries, Prayers, and Annals*, edited by E. L. McAdam, Jr., with Donald and Mary Hyde, vol. I of the Yale Edition of the Works of Samuel Johnson (New Haven: Yale University Press, 1958).

Gent. Mag.—*Gentleman's Magazine*, London.

Greene, *Political Writings*—*Samuel Johnson: Political Writings*, ed. Donald J. Greene, vol. x of the Yale Edition of the Works of Samuel Johnson (New Haven: Yale University Press, 1977).

Greene, *Politics*—Donald J. Greene, *The Politics of Samuel Johnson* (New Haven: Yale University Press, 1960).

Hawkins—Sir John Hawkins, *The Life of Samuel Johnson, LL.D.*, 2d ed. (London, 1787).

Hazen—Allen T. Hazen, *Samuel Johnson's Prefaces & Dedications* (New Haven: Yale University Press, 1937).

Johns. Misc.—*Johnsonian Miscellanies*, ed. G. B. Hill, 2 vols. (Oxford, 1897).

Letters—*The Letters of Samuel Johnson*, ed. R. W. Chapman, 3 vols. (Oxford: Clarendon Press, 1952).

Life—*Boswell's Life of Johnson*, ed. G. B. Hill, revised and enlarged by L. F. Powell, 6 vols. (Oxford: Clarendon Press, 1934, 1950; 2d ed., v and vi, 1964).

Poems—*Samuel Johnson: Poems*, edited by E. L. McAdam, Jr. with George Milne, vol. VI of the Yale Edition of the Works of Samuel Johnson (New Haven: Yale University Press, 1964).

Thraliana—*Thraliana: The Diary of Mrs. Hester Lynch Thrale (Later Mrs. Piozzi) 1776–1809*, ed. Katharine C. Balderston, 2 vols. (Oxford: Clarendon Press, 1942; 2d. ed., 1951).

Waingrow—*The Correspondence and Other Papers of James Boswell Relating to the Making of the Life of Johnson*, edited by Marshall Waingrow, vol. 2 of the Research Edition of the Private Papers of James Boswell (New York: McGraw-Hill, 1969).

Works—*The Works of Samuel Johnson, LL.D.*, 11 volumes (Oxford, 1825).

Yale Boswell Papers—Unprinted manuscripts from the collection of James Boswell now in the Library of Yale University.

YSJ—James L. Clifford, *Young Sam Johnson* (New York: McGraw-Hill, 1955), *Young Samuel Johnson* (London: Heinemann, 1955).

NOTES

CHAPTER I: The New Playwright

1 *General Advertiser,* Feb. 6, 1749, and other papers. The title of the play had been changed to avoid a mix-up with earlier plays on the same subject. On February 9 the newspapers announced the publication of another play with the title *Mahomet and Palmira* by a "Gentleman of Wadham College" (James Miller), which had appeared some years earlier, perhaps hoping to deceive the public into thinking that this was the text of the current play. Actually *Irene: A Tragedy,* by "Mr. Samuel Johnson," was published by Dodsley on the sixteenth.

2 See newspapers for Feb. 6, 1749, and *The London Stage, 1660–1800,* Part 4, ed. G. W. Stone, Jr. (Carbondale, Ill.: So. Illinois University Press, 1967), I, pp. 95–96.

3 Entry in Latin in Birch's diary (B. L. Add. MS. 4478c).

4 *Life,* I, 196, 538, 197–198, n. 5, and 538.

5 *Life,* I, 200; v, 364. For Johnson's earlier life see *YSJ.*

6 For general surveys of the background of the play see D. Nichol Smith, *Samuel Johnson's Irene* (Oxford: Clarendon Press, 1929); Bertrand H. Bronson, "Johnson's 'Irene': Variations on a Tragic Theme," in *Johnson and Boswell: Three Essays* (University of California Publications in English, III, No. 9, 1944); Berna Moran, "The Irene Story and Dr. Johnson's Sources," *MLN,* LXXI (February 1956), 87–91; and James Gray, "*Mahomet and Irene:* More Tragedy than Triumph," *The Humanities Association Review,* XXVII (Fall 1976), 421–440, XXVIII (Winter 1977), 65–87. It was Peter Garrick who first put the Knolles book (*The General History of the Turks,* 1603) in Johnson's hands.

7 Victoria and Albert Museum, 48.E.6, Forster 457 (letter of Jan. 12, 1749).

8 Dutton Cook, "*Irene* at Drury Lane," *Once a Week,* v (Dec. 7, 1861), 651–656, etc. Also *The London Stage, 1660–1800,* Part 4, vol. I, pp. 97–98. For Yonge see Greene, *Political Writings,* p. 179, n. 1.

9 Joseph Cradock, *Literary and Miscellaneous Memoirs* (London, 1828), I, 240.

10 Samples of lines left out were included in the February 1749 number of *Gent. Mag.*, p. 80. See note 29 below. Thomas Davies in his *Memoirs of the Life of Garrick* (London, 1780) says Garrick first suggested the strangling (I, 128).

11 *Life*, I, 538.

12 *A Criticism on Mahomet and Irene in a Letter to the Author* (London, 1749), pp. 5–6.

13 B. L. Egerton MS. 2185 (Press 524H), ff. 5–6.

14 *Life*, I, 196; Waingrow, p. 22.

15 *Gent. Mag.*, XIX (February 1749), 85; *Poems*, pp. 111–112.

16 *Life*, I, 197–198, n. 5.

17 See Smith, *Samuel Johnson's Irene* (see note 6), p. 19; Diary of Richard Cross, see *London Stage* (note 2), Pt. 4, I, 95–98.

18 *General Advertiser*, Feb. 8, 1749.

19 *Life*, I, 198, n. 2.

20 See note 6.

21 William Shaw, *Memoirs of Samuel Johnson* (London, 1785), p. 86; Brack and Kelley, p. 159.

22 *The Works of Aaron Hill* (London, 1753), II, 355 (Feb. 5, 1749).

23 The letter is unsigned and merely dated Kent, Feb. 17.

24 *Letters Written by the Late Right Honourable Lady Luxborough to William Shenstone* (London, 1775), from Barrells, Mar. 23, 1749. See also his letter to her of March 22.

25 XVIII (February 1749), 91; also in *Universal Magazine*, IV, 89–90.

26 Davies, *Life of David Garrick*, vol. I, chap. 12.

27 See note 12.

28 See Robert F. Metzdorf, "A Newly Recovered Criticism of Johnson's *Irene*," *Harvard Library Bulletin*, IV (Spring 1950), 265–268.

29 *Gent. Mag.*, XIX (February 1749), 76–81, signed H. H. Probably by John Hawkesworth.

30 B.L. Egerton MS. 2185 (Press 524H), ff. 9–10.

31 B.L. Add. MS. 39,312 (P55/13360), letter dated Jan. 17, 1786. Yet see Johnson's remarks in the *Preface* to Shakespeare (Vol. VII, p. 63, of Yale Edition).

32 *Life*, IV, 5; I, 199.

33 H. L. Piozzi, *Letters to and from the Late Samuel Johnson* (London, 1788), II, 386–387. Most of the originals are in the John Rylands Library, MS 538.

34 *General Advertiser*, Feb. 18, 1749.

35 *Johns. Misc.*, II, 318.

36 *Life*, I, 200–201, etc.

37 Robert Anderson, *The Life of Samuel Johnson*, 3d ed. (Edinburgh, 1815), p. 128.

38 *Letters*, I, 30 (No. 24).

CHAPTER II: Life in Gough Square in 1749

1 See *YSJ*, pp. 293–294. I am indebted to the present custodian, Miss Margaret Eliot, for her help in describing the house. For published descriptions see *Johnson's House: Gough Square* (1967), the present guide to the house; H. Clifford-Smith, "Dr. Johnson's House," *Apollo*, LII (November and December 1950), 136–140, 165–168; and other works listed in section 7 of Clifford and Greene (see Cue Titles).

2 *The Works of Thomas Carlyle*, ed. H. D. Traill, Centenary Edition (London, 1896–1899), XXVIII, pp. 113–114, n. 1.

3 *Life*, I, 328–330.

4 *YSJ*, pp. 151–172, etc.

5 Much of what follows was first printed in my article "Some Aspects of London Life in the Mid-18th Century," in *City & Society in the 18th Century*, ed. Paul Fritz and David Williams (Toronto: Hakkert, 1973), pp. 19–38. See also Oliver Brackett, "The Interior of the House," *Johnson's England*, ed. A. S. Turberville (London: Oxford University Press, 1933), II, 130–131, etc.

6 See Dorothy George, *London Life in the Eighteenth Century* (London: Kegan Paul, 1925), p. 103; and Lawrence Wright, *Clean and Decent: The Fascinating History of the Bathroom and the Water Closet* (New York: Viking, 1960), pp. 62–63, 93–94. Also Sir D'Arcy Power, "Medicine" in *Johnson's England* (note 5), II, 277.

7 "Night" from "The Four Times of the Day," 1738. See also G. M. Trevelyan, *England Social History* (1942), pp. 437–438, cited in Wright, *Clean and Decent*, p. 76.

8 Dorothy George, pp. 352–353. John Gwynn in his *Essay on Improvements* (1750), listed ordure lying in the streets as one of the worst nuisances of the day; see George Rudé, *Hanoverian London, 1714–1808* (Berkeley: University of California Press, 1971), p. 135.

9 "Directions to Servants," *Prose Writings of Jonathan Swift*, ed. Herbert Davis, vol. XIII (Oxford: Blackwell, 1959), pp. 53, 60–61.

10 Marjorie Quennell and C. B. Quennell, *A History of Everyday Things in England* (London: Batsford, 1933), vol. III, pp. 90–91.

11 I owe this information to the late F. W. Hilles, who sent me a copy of Haydon's marginal comments made in vol. I of the *Works of Sir Joshua Reynolds*, 3d ed. (1801), p. xcviii ff. This was Haydon's copy and is now at Yale Uni-

versity. See Hilles, "Reynolds among the Romantics," *Literary Theory and Structure: Essays in Honor of William K. Wimsatt,* ed. F. Brady, J. Palmer, and M. Price (New Haven, Conn.: Yale, 1973), pp. 267–283.

12 *The Diary of Samuel Pepys,* ed. Robert Latham and William Matthews (Berkeley: University of California Press, 1970–), vol. I, p. 269 (Oct. 20, 1660); p. 304 (Nov. 29).

13 S. Stevens Hellyer, *The Plumber and Sanitary Houses* (London, 1877), p. 2.

14 *The Diary of Samuel Pepys,* vol. V, p. 129 (Apr. 21, 1664).

15 *A Frenchman in England 1784,* translated by S. C. Roberts (New York: Macmillan, 1933), pp. 30–31. Also W. S. Lewis, *Three Tours Through England in the Years 1748, 1776, 1797* (New Haven, Conn.: Yale, 1941), p. 60.

16 Pierre-J. Grosley, *A Tour to London,* trans. Thomas Nugent (London, 1772), I, 151.

17 *Boswell's Journal of a Tour to the Hebrides with Samuel Johnson: Now First Published from the Original Manuscript,* ed. F. A. Pottle and C. H. Bennett (New York: Viking, 1936), pp. 291–292; rev. ed., New York: McGraw-Hill, 1961.

18 *Letters of Lord Chesterfield,* ed. Bonamy Dobrée (London: Eyre & Spottiswoode, 1932), III, 1066–1067 (Dec. 11, 1747).

19 Quoted through the kindness of W. S. Lewis, who has a copy. See also Richard Graves's Preface to his translation of the *Galateo* (1774) of Giovanni de la Casa.

20 See p. 200.

21 I am greatly indebted to G. R. H. Cooper and others at the Guildhall Library for their help in securing the following information.

22 See *Life,* I, 328–329, etc.

23 James A. Cochrane, *Dr. Johnson's Printer* (Cambridge, Mass.: Harvard, 1964), pp. 23–29, etc.

24 Guildhall, No. 3428.

25 Charles P. Moritz, *Travels, Chiefly on Foot Through Several Parts of England in 1782,* entry for June 5, 1782. See Roland Bartel, *Johnson's London* (Boston: Heath, 1956), p. 15.

26 See Esmond S. de Beer, "The Early History of London Street-Lighting," *History,* n.s. XXV (March 1941), 311–324. Also *N&Q,* July 5, 1941, pp. 4–8.

27 From a letter to me from de Beer of Sept. 4, 1972.

28 Guildhall Library, No. 3430.

29 For a later summary of some of the statutes see *Gent. Mag.,* XXIII (October 1753), 472–473.

30 *Works,* X, pp. 239–240; first published in *Gent. Mag.,* XII (April 1742), 179 (debate of Feb. 24, 1740/41). There were other vivid vignettes of life in

London in Johnson's "Debates"; for example, that on the Gin Bill (February 1743).

31 *Whitehall Evening Post,* Jan. 14–17, 1749.

32 *Penny London Post, or Morning Advertiser,* Jan. 4–6, 1749.

33 *Daily Advertiser,* Nov. 6, 1749.

34 *Daily Advertiser,* Apr. 3, 1750.

35 *Daily Advertiser,* Feb. 6, 1750. See also Feb. 15 and May 18, 1750.

36 *Whitehall Evening Post,* Feb. 21–23, 1749.

37 John Riely, "The Hours of the Georgian Day," *History Today,* May 1974, pp. 307–314. I owe much of my information to Riely.

38 *The Early Diary of Frances Burney,* ed. Annie R. Ellis (London: G. Bell and Sons, 1907), I, 15 (July 17, 1768).

39 *Letters,* I, 30 (No. 24).

40 P. 31 (No. 25).

41 *YSJ,* pp. 311–312.

42 *Johns. Misc.,* II, 173–174. Originally from *European Magazine,* October 1799.

43 *Life,* I, 238; *YSJ,* p. 314; Bate, pp. 236–238, 262.

44 See *YSJ,* pp. 314–316. Labeled by Boswell "Tacenda" (things to be kept silent), he never used the evidence. It will be included by Irma Lustig and F. A. Pottle in the forthcoming volume of the Yale Edition of Boswell's journal, published by McGraw-Hill.

45 *Diaries, Prayers, and Annals,* pp. 27, 89, 90, 100, etc. The symbol "M" may, to be sure, have different meanings. Yet on Jan. 3, 1766, the entry "Strongly tempted in a dream to M" is certainly suggestive. In a letter to me of Oct. 1, 1969, George Irwin, author of *Samuel Johnson: A Personality in Conflict* (Auckland: Auckland University Press, 1971) wrote that he had little doubt that the "M" which appears in Johnson's diary during 1765 "stands for masturbat, masturbare."

CHAPTER III: The Ivy Lane Club and a Few Old Friends

1 *Life,* I, 190. A full account of the later Club was written by the late James M. Osborn, using many surviving documents. It should appear in print soon. A version of what follows appears in *Evidence in Literary Scholarship: Essays in Memory of James Marshall Osborn* (Oxford: Clarendon Press, 1979), 197–213.

2 See Hawkins, p. 219 ff. Hawkins digresses a good deal, and only if out of the main discussion do I document quotations. When not documented, they come from Hawkins's main account.

3 In Derbyshire Record Office, Matlock (D239, pp. 14–15), a volume of anecdotes of the life of Sarah Perrin, who married William Fitzherbert. She was the daughter of William and Frances Perrin. Her sister, Mary, who attended Mrs. Hawkesworth's School, died in 1756 at the age of thirteen. I quote with the permission of Sir John FitzHerbert of Tissington Hall, the present owner of the manuscript.

4 The standard authority is Bertram H. Davis, *A Proof of Eminence: The Life of Sir John Hawkins* (Bloomington: Indiana University Press, 1973). See also Davis's "Dr. Johnson and Sir John Hawkins: A Friendship of Four Decades," *SAQ*, LXXIV (Spring 1975), 212–223.

5 *Diary and Letters of Madame D'Arblay*, ed. A. Dobson (1904–1905), I, 58–59.

6 Information obtained from Bertram H. Davis.

7 See bound copy of *Gentleman's Magazine* for 1747, facing general title page. Figures identified in *Gent. Mag.*, n.s. XLVII (1857), 284.

8 A complete account of Hawkesworth is being prepared by John L. Abbott of the University of Connecticut at Storrs.

9 John Nichols, *Literary Anecdotes* (London, 1812), IX, 500–502.

10 See *Life*, I, 317, n. 1, 212, n. 3, 330, n. 3, 243, etc.

11 Hawkins, p. 276. Michael Marcuse believes that this occurred at the gathering on Tuesday, Dec. 5, 1749. Lauder's *Essay on Milton's Use and Imitation of the Moderns*, the work referred to, was published on December 14.

12 Arthur Murphy (*Johns. Misc.*, I, 390).

13 From her *Anecdotes* (*Johns. Misc.*, I, 158, 204).

14 Lewis M. Knapp, *Tobias Smollett: Doctor of Men and Manners* (Princeton, N.J.: Princeton University Press, 1949), pp. 80–82. McGhie received his A.B. and M.D. at Edinburgh, the latter in 1746. He did not receive his appointment to Guy's Hospital until early 1754, and he died June 7, 1756. Arthur Sherbo suggests that McGhie helped translate some of the mottoes for the *Adventurer*. See *Samuel Johnson: Editor of Shakespeare* (Urbana: University of Illinois Press, 1956), pp. 148–149.

15 Salter had been prebendary of Norwich and archdeacon of Norfolk. It is claimed that he later retired to a boarding house kept by Mrs. Hawkesworth in Bromley, Kent (*DNB*). He was living in Bromley, not with the Hawkesworths, in June 1752. We know this from a reference in the diary of John Loveday (information sent to me by Mrs. Sarah Markham).

16 See *Life*, I, 191, n. 5.

17 *Life*, IV, 10–11; Waingrow, pp. 269, 362–363, etc. For various information concerning Dyer, see *DNB*; Edward Peacock, *Index to English Speaking Students Who Have Graduated at Leyden University* (London, 1883), p. 32; *Letters*, III, 18 (No. 835.1); James Prior, *Life of Edmond Malone* (London, 1860), pp. 419–426; *Public Advertiser*, Sept. 17, 1772.

18 Hawkins, pp. 222, 414, etc.

19 Nichols, *Literary Anecdotes* (see note 9), VI, 266, from a statement by Richard Gough.

20 See also account of Dyer in *DNB*.

21 *N&Q*, 2d ser., IX, 261; Prior, *Life of Edmond Malone* (note 17), pp. 419–426; *Life,* IV, 11, n. 1.

22 *Life,* I, 363, n. 3.

23 See account in *DNB*.

24 Hawkins, p. 318. The story is not explicitly connected with the meetings of the Ivy Lane Club but probably occurred then.

25 Hawkins, p. 250.

26 I am indebted to Duncan Isles of the University College of Wales at Aberystwyth for details concerning the life of Charlotte Lennox. The most accurate summary of her career may be found in his "The Lennox Collection," *Harvard Library Bulletin,* XVIII (October 1970), pp. 326–328. See also P. Séjourné, *The Mystery of Charlotte Lennox* (Aix-en-Provence: Editions Ophrys, 1967).

27 "Memoirs of Charlotte Lennox," *Edinburgh Weekly Magazine,* LVIII (1783), p. 34.

28 See Miriam R. Small, *Charlotte Ramsay Lennox* (New Haven, Conn.: Yale, 1935), pp. 27, 28.

29 See Walpole's letter to George Montagu of Sept. 3, 1748. *Horace Walpole's Correspondence with George Montagu,* ed. W. S. Lewis and Ralph S. Brown (New Haven, Conn.: Yale, 1941), I, 74.

30 See Dobson (ed.), *Diary* (note 5), I, 86.

31 See "Memoir of Mrs. Lennox," *Lady's Monthly Museum,* XIV (June 1813), pp. 313–315. Cited also in Séjourné (see note 26), pp. 20–21.

32 *Gent. Mag.,* XIX (June 1749), 278; XX (November 1750), 518–519; XXI (January 1751), 35; etc.

33 Hawkins, pp. 286–287.

34 James Marshall and Marie-Louise Osborn Collection, Beinecke Library, Yale University, from the Hayley Papers.

35 Thomas Taylor, *A Life of John Taylor* (ca. 1910), p. 18.

36 An annotation in Baretti's copy of the 1788 *Letters to and from Samuel Johnson,* II, 384 (now in British Library), *Life,* III, 507.

37 Waingrow, p. 185.

38 B.L. Egerton MS. 3700 B; Barrett Collection, vol. XIII, ff. 1–9.

39 *Dr. Campbell's Diary of a Visit to England in 1775,* ed. J. L. Clifford (New York: Macmillan, 1947), p. 69. See also *The Private Papers of James Boswell from Malahide Castle in the Collection of Lieut.-Col. Ralph H. Isham,* ed. Geoffrey Scott and Frederick A. Pottle, 18 vols. (privately printed, 1928–1934), X, 173.

CHAPTER IV: Lexicographer at Work

1 *Life,* I, 187. In the early stages someone named Stockton may also have been involved. See *Letters,* I, 30 (No. 23.3). For an earlier description of the process see *YSJ,* pp. 291–304.

2 Thomas's doctoral dissertation at the University of Wales in Cardiff (1974) is entitled "A Bibliographical and Critical Analysis of Johnson's *Dictionary* with Special Reference to Twentieth Century Scholarship." In the surviving thirteen works (18 vols.) used by Johnson, Thomas was able to see over 27,000 marked words in quotations, of which over 17,000 were used in the *Dictionary*. See also his articles in *Transactions* (Lichfield Johnson Society), December 1974; *JNL,* March 1973, pp. 6–7; and his "Dr. Johnson's Amanuenses: The Men Behind the Man," (address delivered at Lexicography Conference, Indiana State University Terre Haute, 1975).

3 This is Thomas's theory.

4 First edition.

5 See Gwin J. Kolb and Ruth A. Kolb, "The Selection and Use of the Illustrative Quotations in Dr. Johnson's *Dictionary,*" *New Aspects of Lexicography,* ed. Howard D. Weinbrot (Carbondale: Southern Illinois University Press, 1972), pp. 61–72.

6 Thomas dissertation (note 2), p. 138.

7 The Kolbs (note 5, pp. 68–71) examine these and other examples.

8 *Letters,* I, 42 (No. 39), probably late in 1751.

9 *Gent. Mag.,* LXIX² (Supplement 1799), 1171–1172, letter signed W. N. Final slips were probably made using post paper, which when folded twice allowed pages of 7 × 9 inches. When quotations were copied in double columns and later cut into slips, the resulting dimensions of some surviving slips seem to fit this procedure, with a width of between 3¾ and 4¼ inches.

10 *Boswell's Note Book 1776–1777* (London: H. Milford, 1925), pp. 1–2; *YSJ,* p. 295.

11 Hyde MS. J. D. Fleeman, *Preliminary Handlist of Documents and Manuscripts of Samuel Johnson* (Oxford: Oxford Bibliographical Society Occasional Pub. no. 2, 1967), No. 35.

12 See note 9 and *Life,* I, 536.

13 Isaac D'Israeli, *Curiosities of Literature* (London, 1866), I, 305. See Greene in *JNL,* XXI (September 1961), 11.

14 *Life,* I, 187; Waingrow, p. 167.

15 Mrs. Piozzi's letter to her daughters of Apr. 27, 1796, is now at Bowood.

16 See Thomas dissertation (note 2), p. 27. See also manuscripts in the Hyde collection.

17 *Life,* I, 187, and *DNB.*

18 Greater London Record Office (Middlesex) MJ/SR/2938. Recog. 68. Martin and Ruthe Battestin gave me the details. See also *Life*, II, 173–174. Mary Peyton was later discharged. For Peyton see also *Life*, II, 155, 379.

19 B.L. Add. MS. 35,397, f. 140.

20 Vol. XIX, 65–66; and Sherbo, *PQ*, XXXI (January 1952), 91–93.

21 Sotheby sale catalogue, June 7, 1855. I owe this information to Mary Hyde. See also *YSJ*, p. 356, n. 46.

22 Francis Grose, *The Olio* (London, 1793), p. 161.

23 *Letters*, I, 41 (No. 38).

24 *Letters*, I, 40–41 (No. 37). It was essential that copy be set and proof be corrected quickly. Printers did not have enough type to allow leisurely handling of proofs or printing. For Johnson's procedures I depend on Thomas (see note 2) and on James H. Sledd and Gwin J. Kolb, *Dr. Johnson's Dictionary* (Chicago: University of Chicago Press, 1955), pp. 227–230.

25 See note 9.

26 See note 22.

27 *Letters*, I, 38–39 (No. 35).

28 *Diaries, Prayers, and Annals*, p. 50. The process was slow. According to Strahan's ledgers, 70 sheets were in print by December 1750, 50 more by May 1752, and a further 100 by October 1753.

29 See Greene, *RES*, n.s. III (April 1952), 158–161; Gwin Kolb, *SEL*, I (Summer 1961), 77–95; Arthur Sherbo, *Johnsonian Studies* (Cairo), ed. Magdi Wahba (1962), 133–159; etc.

30 See my account, more fully annotated, in *PQ*, LIV (Winter 1975), 342–356. Michael Marcuse has completed a thorough discussion of the Lauder affair in five articles, which are cited later.

31 For an account of Lauder see A. H. Millar, *Blackwood's Edinburgh Magazine*, CLXVI (September 1899), 381–396; the short biography by Sidney Lee in *DNB*; and other works listed in n. 1 of my essay mentioned in note 30.

32 [Andrew Henderson], *Furius* [1748], pp. 4–6, 13, etc. There was a reissue in 1754, apparently.

33 For example, see Grant McColley, *Paradise Lost: An Account of Its Growth and Major Origins* (Chicago: Packard, 1940); and Watson Kirkconnell, *The Celestial Cycle* (Toronto: University of Toronto Press, 1952); and Michael Marcuse, "Miltonoklastes: The Lauder Affair Reconsidered," *Eighteenth Century Life*, IV, 4 (June 1978), 86–91.

34 A copy of the original *Proposals*, four octavo leaves, bound in with later pamphlets concerned with Lauder, is in the British Library (11822). Johnson's piece here appears in its original form.

35 Hawkins, pp. 274–276. See also Michael Lort in *Gent. Mag.*, LXI (May 1791), pp. 432–433. For Boswell's attempt to defend Johnson see *Life*, I, 229–231; Arthur Murphy's in *Johns. Misc.*, I, 394–395. See also *YSJ*, p. 36.

36 See note 30. *Zoilomastix* appeared in the autumn of 1747. For *Furius* see note 32.

37 See p. 33 in Chap. III, and n. 9 in my piece listed in note 30. Also Michael Marcuse, "The Pre-publication History of William Lauder's *Essay on Milton's Use and Imitation of the Moderns in* His *Paradise Lost,*" PBSA, LXXII (1978), 35–57. Malone's copy of the essay is in the Bodleian Library (G.P. 334[1]), and Malone underscored all of Lauder's interpolated lines. I owe my knowledge of this to David Fleeman.

38 Marcuse thinks that Johnson may have written the address to the public in these *Proposals.* See his "The Lauder Controversy and the Jacobite Cause," *Studies in Burke and His Time,* XVIII (Fall 1977), 40–41. The ascription has not yet been generally accepted.

39 John Nichols, in *Anecdotes* (see Chap. III, n. 9), VI, 182, insists that the Rev. John Bowle of Idmiston was the first to detect Lauder's forgeries and suggested the clue to Douglas. Douglas acknowledged this. In the later "Autobiography of Sylvanus Urban," *Gent. Mag.,* March 1857, pp. 289–290, the claim is made that it was the Reverend Richard Richardson of Epping who was first, but he was denied space in the magazine and thus was deprived of "the fair honour he might have acquired as the bold slinger who slew the Philistine." See Marcuse, " 'The Scourge of Imposters, the Terror of Quacks': John Douglas and the Exposé of William Lauder," *HLQ,* XLII, 3 (Summer 1979).

40 *Gent. Mag.,* XX (December 1750), 536.

41 B.L. Add. MS. 35,397, f. 321.

42 Hazen, p. 79. The title page has 1751, but it was announced for publication on November 26, 1750, and some copies may have been available earlier.

43 *Milton Vindicated,* p. 77. Later Johnson and Douglas were involved in the exposure of two other frauds. See p. 257 and D. J. Greene, *RES,* n.s. VII (October 1956), 381–382.

44 Hazen, p. 79. The November *Gent. Mag.,* which appeared early in December, along with the notice of the appearance of Douglas's work, carried the statement that Lauder had acknowledged the forgeries and interpolations (p. 535).

45 "A New Preface by the Booksellers," p. ii. See Hazen, p. 79. The "New Postscript" is dated Jan. 2, 1950/51. A few copies have survived.

46 Seen at the National Archives in London in 1958. The present Lord Lichfield has given me permission to quote from the letter.

47 *A Series of Letters between Mrs. Elizabeth Carter and Miss Catherine Talbot,* ed. Montagu Pennington, 2 vols. (London, 1808), I, 372.

48 IV, 97–106. The name of the reviewer is given in Benjamin C. Nangle, *The Monthly Review: First Series 1749–1789* (Oxford: Clarendon Press, 1934), p. 91).

49 XIII (February 1751), 78.

50 Donald J. Greene, "Some Notes on Johnson and the *Gentleman's Magazine*," *PMLA*, LXXIV (March 1959), 84. And Michael Marcuse, "The *Gentleman's Magazine* and the Lauder/Milton Controversy," *Bulletin of Research in the Humanities* (formerly *BNYPL*), LXXX (1978) LXXXI, 2 (Summer 1978), 179–209.

51 *Gent. Mag.*, XX (December 1750), 535–536.

52 Probably around January 4. Included in *Works* (Oxford, 1825), vol. v, p. 282.

53 *Life*, I, 228–229.

54 Hawkins, p. 277. See also Anderson's *Life of Johnson* (3d ed., 1815), pp. 136–137; "The Autobiography of Sylvanus Urban" (see note 39), p. 290; and *Blackwood's*, CLXVI (September 1899), 395.

55 London, 1754, pp. 3–5. See also Hawkins, p. 281.

56 Malone (see note 37) commented: "This Postscript, contradicting almost every word of what Dr. Johnson had written for him and he has himself subscribed, shows Lauder to have been the most impudent and contemptible fellow that ever lived."

57 The pamphlet was published Mar. 20, 1751 (*Daily Advertiser*).

58 B.L. Add. MS. 4312, f. 465 (Mar. 15, 1751). See also letter to Richard Mead, April 9, 1751 (MSS. & Archives Div., New York Public Library). It was published in John Nichols, *Illustrations* (London, 1822), IV, 428–430.

59 R. Reece, *N&Q*, Jan. 22, 1870, pp. 83–85; and Millar (see note 31) p. 396.

60 Murphy (*Johns. Misc.*, I, 398); Nichols, *Anecdotes* (see Chap. III, note 9), II, 551.

CHAPTER V: The Rambler

1 *Diaries, Prayers, and Annals*, pp. 42–43.

2 For a recent account see George S. Rousseau, "The London Earthquakes of 1750," *Journal of World History*, XI, No. 3 (1968), pp. 436–451. See also Carter-Talbot Letters (Chap. IV, note 47), I, 219 ff.

3 *London Magazine*, XIX (March 1750), 138. See also *Gent. Mag.* for February and March.

4 *Johns. Misc.*, I, 391.

5 *Life*, I, 202.

6 H. L. Piozzi, *British Synonymy* (London, 1794), II, 358; and *Life*, III, 411.

7 For general information about *The Rambler* see W. J. Bate's "Introduction" (pp. xxi–xlii) to the authoritative Yale Johnson Edition, vols. III–V (New Haven, Conn.: Yale, 1969). Also his *Samuel Johnson*, pp. 289–317.

8 B.L. Add. MS. 35,399, f. 190 (Birch to Yorke, Oct. 25, 1760).

9   *Johns. Misc.,* II, 414

10 *An Account of the Life of Dr. Samuel Johnson,* ed. Richard Wright (London, 1805), p. 80.

11 *Life,* I, 205–207.

12 See *YSJ,* pp. 318–319.

13 Hawkins, p. 381.

14 *Diaries, Prayers and Annals,* p. 43.

15 *The Correspondence of Samuel Richardson,* ed. Anna Laetitia Barbauld (London, 1804), I, 168–170 (Cave to Richardson, Aug. 23, 1750).

16 *Selected Letters of Samuel Richardson,* ed. John Carroll (Oxford: Clarendon Press, 1964), p. 165. Also in Barbauld, I, 165.

17 Richardson's *Correspondence* (note 15), I, 168.

18 *Selected Letters* (note 16), p. 247 (Oct. 4, 1753).

19 *Selected Letters,* p. 249 (Richardson to Lady Bradshaigh, Dec. 8, 1753).

20 *Bibliography,* p. 26; Hawkins, p. 269; and Murphy (*Johns. Misc.,* I, 393). Evidently there were usually unsold copies of the original issues and their availability was noticed in the advertisements.

21 "The Contemporary Distribution of Johnson's *Rambler,*" *ECS,* II (December 1968), 155–171. The *Halifax Gazette* in Nova Scotia reprinted excerpts from some *Ramblers.*

22 See my "Some Problems of Johnson's Obscure Middle Years," *Johnson, Boswell and Their Circle: Essays Presented to L. F. Powell* (New York: Oxford University Press, 1965), pp. 107–108. Then, as now, copy for notices of this sort may well have had to be in hand some time before news items or editorial material.

23 All quotations, etc., from issues of *The Rambler* come from the Yale Johnson Edition. See Roy Wiles, "The Periodical Essay," in *English Symposium Papers* (State University of New York/Fredonia, 1972), 10–12.

24 *Life,* I, 210.

25 See note 16 above.

26 William Shaw's *Memoirs of Dr. Johnson* (London, 1785), pp. 89–91 (Brack and Kelley, p. 160).

27 *Life,* I, 208–209.

28 xx (July 1750), 324.

29 Reprinted in *Gent. Mag.,* xx (October 1750), 465.

30 Ibid. Part of this was also included in the November *Magazine of Magazines,* p. 372.

31 Hagley MSS., vol. II, 143. I owe this to Edward Ruhe.

32 Richardson's *Correspondence* (note 15), I, 168–170; *Memoirs of the Life of Mrs. Elizabeth Carter,* ed. Montagu Pennington (London, 1808), I, 146.

33 Bedford County Record Office, Lady Lucas Collection. L30/9A/5. Secured from Martin and Ruthe Battestin. The writer's husband later became the second Earl of Hardwicke.

34 This and the following quotations can be found in *Letters between Mrs. Elizabeth Carter and Miss Catherine Talbot* (see Chap. IV, note 47), vol. I, p. 348 ff.

35 *Johns. Misc.,* I, 178.

36 See A. T. Elder, "Irony and Humor in the *Rambler*," *University of Toronto Quart.*, xxx (October 1960), 57–71.

37 See Bate's Introduction to vol. III of the Yale Johnson Edition, and *Thraliana*, I, 162.

38 Edward A. Bloom, "Symbolic Names in Johnson's Periodical Essays," *MLQ,* xiii (December 1952), 333–352.

39 W. J. Bate, *The Achievement of Samuel Johnson* (New York: Oxford University Press, 1955), p. 93. See also his *Samuel Johnson* (1977), chaps. 17, 18.

40 See Chap. IV, p. 60; *Poems,* pp. 239–240.

41 *Letters,* I, 32–33 (Letter No. 27). Advertising had begun as early as March 19. There had also been notices in the *General Advertiser* for March 3, 5. On March 6 the publication of the prologue was announced.

42 See note 40 and letter of Birch to Yorke, of Nov. 17, 1750 (B.L. Add. MS. 35,397, f. 321).

43 *Poems,* p. 241.

44 See note 41 (No. 28) and Duncan Isles, "The Lennox Collection," *Harvard Library Bulletin,* xviii (October 1970), 334–335.

45 B.L. Add. MS., 35,397, f. 306 (Oct. 20, 1750).

46 See J. D Fleeman, "The Revenue of a Writer: Samuel Johnson's Literary Earnings," *Studies in the Book Trade in Honour of Graham Pollard* (Oxford: Oxford Bibliographical Society, 1975), p. 213, and other evidence.

CHAPTER VI: The Last of Tetty

1 *Letters,* I, 36 (No. 32). See also Nos. 33 and 34.

2 *R. B. Adam Library* (1929), III, 172, with facsimile. Now in the Hyde collection.

3 *Bibliography,* p. 38; Greene, *Politics,* pp. 30–32; *Works,* VI, 413–428.

4 *Letters,* I, 35–36 (No. 31), Mar. 9, 1751.

5 See Duncan Isles, "The Lennox Collection," *Harvard Library Bulletin,* xviii (October 1970), 317–344; xix (January, April, October 1971), 36–60, 165–186, 416–433.

6 See Dobson (ed.) (Chap. III, note 5), I, 86.

7 Isles, "The Lennox Collection," October 1970, pp. 335, 336–342; October
   1971, pp. 432–433. Charlotte's letter of Feb. 3, 1752 is in the Chicago Historical Society Library.

8 Hazen, pp. 94–98, and *General Advertiser*, Mar. 13, 1752.

9 Miriam R. Small, *Charlotte Ramsay Lennox* (New Haven, Conn.: Yale, 1935),
   pp. 77–82; Hazen, pp. 94–98. Duncan Isles (see, in note 5, XVIII, p. 341) will
   not accept the usual explanation that Johnson wrote "the second-last
   chapter either wholly or in part."

10 *Letters*, I, 39 (No. 36). Chapman thinks Orrery the recipient, but T. C. Duncan
   Eaves conclusively proves that it was Richardson. See *PMLA*, LXXXV (September 1960), 379–380.

11 *Letters*, III, 268. See Paul J. Korshin, "Johnson and the Earl of Orrery," *Eighteenth-Century Studies in Honor of Donald F. Hyde*, ed. W. H. Bond
   (New York: Grolier Club, 1970), pp. 32–34. I rely on Korshin for what
   follows concerning Orrery.

12 *The Orrery Papers*, ed. Countess of Cork and Orrery (1903), II, 100.

13 For details about Williams's life see *Gent. Mag.*, LVII (December 1787), Supplement, 1157–1159; John Nichols, *Literary Anecdotes* (see Chap. III, note
   9), II, 179–180; *DNB*; and E. G. R. Taylor, "A Reward for the Longitude,"
   The Mariner's Mirror, XLV (February 1959), 59–66. Quotations are from
   Taylor and Nichols.

14 Taylor, p. 63.

15 *Gent. Mag.*, LVII (September 1787), 757–759; (December), 1041–1043; *Letters*,
   I, 433–442.

16 T. C. Duncan Eaves (see note 10) and his *Samuel Richardson: A Biography*
   (with B. Kimpel) (Oxford: Clarendon Press, 1971), p. 333.

17 Isles (note 5), October 1970, p. 336. *Rambler* (Yale Edition), IV, 158.

18 *Letters*, I, 39 (No. 36). See note 10.

19 *Daily Advertiser*, Dec. 17 and 19. On Jan. 30, 1752, there appeared a notice
   "Next Saturday will be published" and finally on Saturday, February 1,
   came "This day are published" (repeated February 3, 4, etc.).

20 *Letters*, I, 38–39 (No. 35). See earlier, p. 56.

21 Isles (note 5), October 1970, p. 343.

22 Now in the possession of Sir Geoffrey Harmsworth, who kindly allowed me to
   examine the copies. To be sure, the name may possibly have been written
   by Johnson.

23 *Letters*, I, 42–43 (No. 40). But he did not pay off the mortgage until over five
   years later.

24 See *Letters*, I, 45 (No. 42.2), where he apologizes for not doing what he had
   promised in the earlier letter. Then see account of final settlement in June
   1757.

25 *Thraliana*, p. 178. See also A. L. Reade, *Johnsonian Gleanings,* II vols. (privately printed, 1909–1952), VI, 27, 28, 118; and Shaw in Brack and Kelley, p. 165.

26 *Life,* I, 238; *Letters,* I, 43 (Nos. 41 and 42); and Waingrow, pp. 166, 523, 276, etc.

27 Hawkins, p. 314.

28 I owe this information to John L. Abbott (see Chap. III, note 8).

29 Brack and Kelly, pp. 75, 274; *Life,* I, 241–242; John L. Abbott, in *ECS,* III (1970), 345–346, etc.

30 The law requiring burial in wool was passed in 1678. See also *Life,* I, 237, 540; *Diaries, Prayers, and Annals,* pp. 44–47. Muriel H. Hughes, Hon. Parish Archivist at Bromley, has provided me with much of the evidence which follows. The spelling of the name "Deneuen" is not clear.

31 *Letters,* III, 181 (No. 975). Johnson's memory is obviously hazy since he misdates the year. See also p. 247 (No. 1032).

32 *Letters to and from Samuel Johnson,* ed. H. L. Piozzi (London, 1788), II, 384–385.

33 See Murphy, *Johns. Misc.,* I, 476. The sermon first appeared in *Sermons on Different Subjects Left for Publication by John Taylor, LL.D.,* published by the Reverend Samuel Hayes (London, 1789), II, Sermon 12. Included in the edition of Johnson's *Sermons,* ed. Jean H. Hagstrum and James Gray, vol. XIV in the Yale Johnson Edition.

34 Susan M. Radcliffe, *Sir Joshua's Nephew* (London: J. Murray, 1930), pp. 86–88.

35 Waingrow, pp. 163–169.

36 Hawkins, p. 323, and sources mentioned in note 13, etc.

37 See A. L. Reade, *Francis Barber: The Doctor's Negro Servant* (vol. II of *Johnsonian Gleanings* [1912]); and Waingrow, pp. 39, 164–165, 268, 293, 335–336.

38 Hawkins, p. 316.

39 Shaw in Brack and Kelley, p. 165.

40 J. D. Fleeman, *Handlist* (Chap. IV, note 11), No. 49.

41 *Diaries, Prayers, and Annals,* pp. 44–47. See also Irwin, *Samuel Johnson* (Chap. II, note 45), pp. 100–101.

42 *Diaries, Prayers, and Annals,* p. 44; Waingrow, p. 294, n. 6; *Life,* I, 237.

CHAPTER VII: The Widower and the Adventurer

1 *The R. B. Adam Library Relating to Dr. Samuel Johnson and His Era* (London and New York: Oxford University Press, 1929), III, 54–55 (Apr. 29, 1752).

2 Duncan Isles, "The Lennox Collection," *Harvard University Library Bulletin,* XVIII (October 1970), 343–344, and XIX (January 1971), 36–37.

3 *Letters*, I, 44–45 (No. 42.1).

4 *Letters*, I, 45 (No. 42.2). See also pp. 36–37 (letter 32.1, which really was written in 1757).

5 B.L. Add. MS. 35,398, f. 84v.

6 *Gent. Mag*, xxII (August 1752), 387. As John Abbott will point out in his forthcoming life of Hawkesworth, Hawkesworth was doing most of the miscellaneous writing for the magazine at this time.

7 Hawkins, pp. 320–321. According to Hawkins, Johnson quizzed the "miserable females" about "their course of life, the history of their seduction, and the chances of reclaiming them." See *Ramblers* Nos. 102 and 170–171.

8 *Universal Magazine*, cxI (October 1802), 234. The most authoritative account so far of the periodical is David Fairer, "Authorship Problems in *The Adventurer*," *RES*, n.s. xxv (May 1974), 137–151. For additional details see L. F. Powell, Introduction, *Samuel Johnson: The Idler and The Adventurer*, vol. 2 of Yale Johnson Edition (New Haven, Conn.: Yale, 1963), pp. 323–338; Arthur Sherbo, *Samuel Johnson, Editor of Shakespeare* (Urbana: University of Illinois Press, 1956), pp. 145–174; Philip M. Griffith, "The Authorship of the Papers Signed 'A' in Hawkesworth's *Adventurer*," *Tulane Studies in English*, xII (1962), 63–70; and Victor J. Lams, Jr., "The 'A' Papers in *The Adventurer*: Bonnell Thornton, Not Dr. Bathurst, Their Author," *SP*, LxIV (January 1967), 83–96.

9 Sherbo (note 8), p. 148.

10 *Life*, I, 253, n. 2; also Fairer (note 8), p. 144, n. 1.

11 *Letters*, I, 48 (Letter 46).

12 B.L. Sloan MS. 4316, f. 168 (no date).

13 Memoir of Thornton prefixed to later edition of the *Connoisseur* (1803).

14 Percy to Shenstone, September 1760 (*The Percy Letters*, ed. Cleanth Brooks and A. F. Falconer [New Haven, Conn.: Yale, 1977], p. 70).

15 Lams (note 8), pp. 95, 88.

16 *Gent. Mag.*, xxII (November 1752), 521–525.

17 B.L. Add. MS. 35,398, f. 109.

18 *Letters between Elizabeth Carter and Catherine Talbot* (see Chap. Iv, note 47), I, 395, II, 1–2, etc.

19 B.L., Add. MS. 42,560, ff. 24–25.

20 There were advertisements in the *London Evening Post* for January 23 and in the *Daily Advertiser* for February 3, 10, 17, 24, and March 10, 1753, and in other papers.

21 Carter (note 18), II, 2, etc.

22 Fairer (note 8), pp. 142–144.

23 Fairer, pp. 144–146.

24 *Letters,* I, 47–48 (No. 46).

25 Samuel Richardson to Lady Bradshaigh, Oct. 9, 1754; Victoria and Albert Museum, Forster Collection 457 (48 E.5).

26 B.L. Add. MS. 42,560, f. 28; and f. 26 (J. Warton to T. Warton, postmarked May 28)

27 Fairer, pp. 137–139.

28 *Life,* I, 254.

29 Letter of Hill Boothby to Johnson dated Feb. 16, 1754. In hers of Dec. 4, 1753, she had asked if he sometimes wrote an *Adventurer.* He evidently told her the secret, and in February she commented that "I shall seek for letter T, that I may read with *redoubled* pleasure." *An Account of the Life of Dr. Samuel Johnson (including letters of Hill Boothby)* (London, 1805), pp. 42, 47–48.

30 Fairer, p. 147.

31 Bodleian MS. Don. c.75, ff. 36–37. I owe this information to David Fairer, p. 144.

32 Fairer, p. 139; *Willis's Current Notes,* February 1857, p. 14. Original letter now in the Hyde collection.

33 *Letters between Elizabeth Carter and Catherine Talbot* (see Chap. IV, note 47), II, 161–164, 172.

34 *Jackson's Oxford Journal,* Apr. 6, 1754. Sherbo (note 8, pp. 149–150) suggests that William McGhie, another member of the Ivy Lane Club, helped with the translations of the mottoes.

35 Victoria and Albert Museum, Forster Collection 457, 48.E.5; Richardson's reply is dated May 30.

36 *Diaries, Prayers, and Annals,* pp. 49–50. See also pp. 50–54.

37 See Donald and Mary Hyde, *Dr. Johnson's Second Wife* (privately printed, Princeton, N.J., 1953).

38 *Dr. Campbell's Diary of a Visit to England in 1775,* ed. J. L. Clifford (New York: Macmillan, 1947), p. 68. Boswell, in his Journal, also records this, though not in as full detail (*Private Papers* [Chap. III, note 39], X, 173).

39 *Diaries, Prayers, and Annals,* p. 50 (Apr. 3, 1753). He had left room for a Preface and "Grammar and History," not yet begun.

40 *Letters,* I, 49–50 (No. 48). See also Vedder M. Gilbert, "The Altercations of Thomas Edwards with Samuel Johnson," *JEGP,* LI (July 1952), 326–335.

41 *Letters,* I, 48–49 (No. 47), and Isles (note 2), XIX (January 1971), 36–38.

42 Isles, p. 38, and Hazen, pp. 104–110.

43 Isles, pp. 38–39, and n. 56.

44 *Life,* I, 146–147.

45 *Posthumous Works of Mrs. Chapone* (London, 1807), I, 72–74.

46 A. D. McKillop, *Samuel Richardson: Printer and Novelist* (Chapel Hill: University of North Carolina Press, 1936), p. 188.

47 *Letters*, I, 50 (No. 49). T. C. Duncan Eaves, "Dr. Johnson's Letters to Richardson," *PMLA*, LXXV (September 1960), 377–378.

48 *Letters*, I, 54 (No. 51.1).

49 *Letters*, I, 59–60 (No. 56).

CHAPTER VIII: The Harmless Drudge

1 *Diaries, Prayers, and Annals*, p. 50.

2 Eugene Thomas's dissertation (see Chap. IV, note 1) is my authority for Johnson's amanuenses. See also Waingrow, p. 167.

3 See Arthur Sherbo, *PQ*, XXXI (October 1952), 372–382, and *ECS*, VII (Fall 1973), 18–39; and Gwin J. Kolb and Ruth A. Kolb, in *New Aspects of Lexicography*, ed. H. Weinbrot (Carbondale: Southern Illinois University Press, 1972), pp. 61–72. See also my Preface to a forthcoming facsimile reprint of the fourth edition to be produced by the Librairie du Liban in Beirut, Lebanon.

4 *Boswell's London Journal*, ed. F. A. Pottle (New York: McGraw-Hill, 1950), p. 332 (Aug. 2, 1763).

5 J. D. Fleeman, "Johnson's Literary Earnings" (see Chap. V, note 46), p. 213.

6 Strahan's ledgers make this clear.

7 *Letters*, I, 56 (No. 53). For an account of a sheet of notes made by Johnson for the "Grammar" see David Fleeman in *Bodleian Library Record*, VII (December 1964), 205–210.

8 *Life*, I, 271–275. The exact length of Johnson's stay in Oxford is not clear. Usually it is described as "five weeks," but from entries in a diary now at Trinity College (see note 26) it would appear to have been slightly shorter.

9 *"Sufflamina"*—from Ben Jonson's famous critique of Shakespeare. "Cabiri"—beneficent Greek nature deities.

10 *Life*, I, 276, note 2; and Oliver F. Sigworth, *William Collins* (New York: Twayne, 1965), p. 47.

11 *Poems by the Late George Monck Berkeley* (London, 1797), pp. ccl–ccliii. See also *JNL*, June 1951, pp. 11–12.

12 *Letters*, I, 55–56 (No. 52).

13 B.L. Add. MS. 35,398, f. 214v.

14 Murphy, *Johns. Misc.*, I, 407–408; Piozzi's *Anecdotes (Johns. Misc.)*, I, 306; *Life*, I, 356; C. B. Bradford, *PQ*, XVIII (July 1939), 318–320.

15 E. L. McAdam, Jr., *Dr. Johnson and the English Law* (Syracuse, N.Y.: Syracuse University Press, 1951).

16 *Letters,* I, 57 (No. 54).

17 The dating of this visit to London comes from the surviving account book of the elder Langton. I am indebted to J. C. P. Langton of Tinwell, Lincolnshire, for allowing me to consult the documents. See also C. N. Fifer, "Dr. Johnson and Bennet Langton," *JEGP,* LIV (October 1955), 504–506.

18 *Life,* I, 247.

19 H. D. Best, *Johns. Misc.,* II, 390.

20 Laetitia Matilda Hawkins, *Memoirs, Anecdotes, Facts, and Opinions* (London, 1824), I, 288–289, 148, etc.

21 *Life,* IV, 28.

22 For a complete account of this episode see my "Johnson and Foreign Visitors to London: Baretti and Others," in *Eighteenth Century Studies Presented to Arthur M. Wilson,* ed. Peter Gay (Hanover, N.H.: University Press of New England, 1972), pp. 99–115. Specific sources are given there.

23 See Chap. III, note 26. As the first volume of Mrs. Lennox's *Shakespeare Illustrated,* including six translations from the Italian, appeared in May 1753, it may be safe to assume that Johnson met Baretti some time late in 1752 or early 1753. Years later, when giving testimony at Baretti's trial for murder, Johnson estimated "1753 or 1754," but the earlier date appears more likely. See Hazen, p. 104, and Lacy Collison-Morley, *Giuseppe Baretti* (London: J. Murray, 1909), p. 82.

24 In the Hyde collection at Four Oaks Farm, near Somerville, N.J., there are four manuscript letters by Baretti, three to Croker and the fourth apparently to Huggins, all at least partly connected with this episode. I am indebted to Mrs. Donald Hyde for permission to quote from these manuscripts.

25 See Collison-Morley, pp. 90–93. The letter in the original Italian may be found in Giuseppe Baretti, *Epistolario,* ed. Luigi Piccioni (Bari, 1936), I, 100–107.

26 I owe this information to David Fairer, Lecturer in English at the University of Leeds. The few loose leaves of the diary are in the Trinity Warton papers. The ascription to Holloway comes through his election as Chaplain to Aleppo. Though not conclusive, the identification seems from Fairer's evidence to be fairly certain.

27 *Letters,* I, 442–445 (Nos. 53.1 and 53.2).

28 B.L. Add. MS. 42,560, f. 37 (Apr. 28, 1755).

29 See Miriam R. Small, *Charlotte Ramsay Lennox* (New Haven, Conn.: Yale, 1935), pp. 18, 157–163. Baretti's ode was found in Italy by Capt. Frank L. Pleadwell.

30 *Life,* I, 287–288.

31 *Letters,* I, 58–61, 63–68 (Nos. 55, 56, 57, 58, 59, 60), and one from Wise to Warton on Dec. 14 (Wooll, ed., *Biographical Memoirs of the Late Revd.*

Joseph Warton (London, 1806), p. 228); also Nos. 61, 62, 63, 64, 65. *Jackson's Oxford Journal* for Saturday, March 1, announced, "Last week this university conferred the degree of Master of Arts, by diploma, on Mr. Samuel Johnson, the learned and ingenious author of the Rambler, and of that celebrated and judicious work, a Dictionary of the English Language, with which literature will speedily be enriched." This was six weeks before publication.

32 For full accounts of the episode see *Life*, I, 256–67; Waingrow, pp. 21–22, 24–25, 60–62, 234–35; Murphy (*Johns. Misc.*, I, 405–406, etc.). Although they did not know it, Johnson and Chesterfield were distantly related by marriage: Chesterfield's younger brother was married to Johnson's cousin's wife's great-niece. See A. L. Reade, *Johnsonian Gleanings*, 11 vols. (privately printed, 1909–1952), III, 152; *YSJ*, p. 304.

33 See *Original Letters, from Richard Baxter, Matthew Prior, Bolingbroke . . . &c,* ed. Rebecca Warner (London, 1817), 202–205.

34 See Paul Korshin, "The Johnson-Chesterfield Relationship: A New Hypothesis," *PMLA*, LXXXV (March 1970), 247–259; and comments by Jacob Leed and Korshin in *Studies in Burke and His Time,* XII (Fall 1970), 1677–1690, XII (Winter 1971), 1804–1811; XIII (Fall 1971), 2011–2015.

35 *Life,* I, 256–257, 264–265; Waingrow, p. 24.

36 *Letters,* I, 64–65 (No. 61).

37 Roger Lonsdale, *Dr. Charles Burney: A Literary Biography* (New York: Oxford, 1965), pp. 46–47. For Burney's later view of the *Dictionary,* see p. 50.

38 *Letters,* I, 68–69 (No. 67).

39 See James H. Sledd and Gwin J. Kolb, *Dr. Johnson's Dictionary* (Chicago: University of Chicago Press, 1955), pp. 110, 230.

40 J. A. Cochrane, *Dr. Johnson's Printer: The Life of William Strahan* (Cambridge: Harvard, 1964), chap. 3. It was reprinted immediately in weekly parts.

CHAPTER IX: The *Dictionary*

1 *Daily Advertiser,* Apr. 16, 1755, and repeated on April 17, 18, 21, 22, etc. The *Monthly Review* for April, p. 324, states that the work was published on April 15.

2 *Gent. Mag.,* XXV, 147–151. I owe the identification of the reviewer to John Abbott.

3 *Monthly Review,* XII (April 1755), 292–324. Benjamin C. Nangle in *The Monthly Review, First Series, 1749–1789, Indexes of Contributors and Articles* (Oxford: Clarendon Press, 1934) identifies the reviewer.

4 *Edinburgh Review,* No. 1 (January-June 1755), pp. 61–73. Reviewer identified by a handwritten annotation in a copy.

5 *Life,* I, 300–301. "Forty" refers to the number of members of the French Academy.

6 *Life,* I, 285. B.L. Add. MS. 4310, ff. 307, 309. Typical high praise may also be found in Charles Burney's later comment that Johnson's *Dictionary* was "not yet equalled in any language" (Lonsdale, *Dr. Charles Burney* [see Chap. VIII, note 37], p. 50).

7 *Biographical Memoirs of the Late Revd. Joseph Warton,* ed. John Wooll (London, 1806), pp. 230–231.

8 B.L. Add. MS. 42,560, ff. 40, 41.

9 "The Letter Book of Thomas Edwards" in the Bodleian Library, pp. 208–211. Letters sent from Turrick. See Vedder M. Gilbert, *JEGP,* LI (July 1952), 326–335.

10 Donald J. Greene, *Samuel Johnson* (New York: Twayne, 1970), p. 181.

11 *Life,* I, 293, 378; *Johns. Misc.,* II, 404, 390.

12 Samuel Whyte, *Miscellanea Nova* (Dublin, 1800), pp. 50–51, and Maurice J. Quinlan, "Samuel Whyte's Anecdotes about Dr. Johnson," *Dartmouth College Library Bulletin,* V (January 1963), 58.

13 *Letters between Elizabeth Carter and Catherine Talbot* (see Chap. IV, note 47), II, 214. From St. Paul's, Feb. 24, 1756.

14 Supposedly first printed in the *Public Advertiser* (date uncertain). Joel Gold suggests it may have been in May 1756. See letters to Wilkes in B.M. Add MS. 30,867, f. 117. No copy of the original number has been found. A reprint was sent me by Herman Liebert of Yale. See also *Life,* I, 300. For a suggestion as to Johnson's source see Jacob Leed, *PBSA,* LIV (1960), 101–110.

15 *Life,* I, 295, n. 9. Quotations from a copy received from the Custom and Excise Library, City Gate House, Finsbury Square, London.

16 From a copy sent to me with no indication of the present whereabouts of the original. The letter was sent from near Navan to Rev. Robert Maxwell at Grays in Sussex.

17 *Ancient Scottish Poems* (London, 1786), II, 403. Edited by John Pinkerton. Reprinted in a letter signed "O. G. G." (Octavius Graham Gilchrist) in *Gent. Mag.,* LXX (April 1800), 335–336.

18 P. B. Gove, "Notes on Serialization and Competitive Publishing," *Proceedings of the Oxford Bibliographical Society,* V (1940), 305–322. The first number of the second edition came out on June 14.

19 For a description of the octavo see *Bibliography,* p. 62. See also Greene, *Samuel Johnson* (note 10), p. 177.

20 See Arthur Sherbo, "Dr. Johnson's Revision of His *Dictionary,*" *PQ,* XXXI (October 1952), 372–382, and his "1773: The Year of Revision," *ECS,* VII (Fall 1973), 18–39; Gwin J. Kolb and Ruth A. Kolb, in *New Aspects of Lexicography,* ed. Howard D. Weinbrot (Carbondale: Southern Illinois

University Press, 1972), pp. 61–72; and my Preface to a facsimile reprint of the fourth edition being printed in Beirut, Lebanon.

21 See James H. Sledd and Gwin J. Kolb, *Dr. Johnson's Dictionary* (Chicago: University of Chicago Press, 1955), chaps. 1 and 5.

22 James T. Callender, *The Deformities of Johnson* (Edinburgh, 1782). Callender also has severe criticism of Johnson in *A Critical Review of the Works of Samuel Johnson* (London, 1783), pp. 55–64.

23 For various modern evaluations see: Sledd and Kolb, *Dr. Johnson's Dictionary*; W. K. Wimsatt, *Day of the Leopards* (New Haven, Conn.: Yale, 1976), pp. 162–180; and Howard D. Weinbrot (ed.), *New Aspects of Lexicography* (note 20), pp. 61–116.

24 *On Heroes, Hero Worship,* Lecture 5, "The Hero as Man of Letters."

25 B.L. Add. MS. 32,325, ff. 143–144; correspondence of Edward Lye.

CHAPTER X: Still the Hack

1 *Weekly Entertainer,* v (Apr. 25, 1785), 392; see also *Johns. Misc.,* I, 406; Bate, pp. 242–243, etc.

2 *Letters,* I, 71–74 (Nos. 70, 71, 71.1, 72, and 73).

3 *YSJ,* p. 20. George Irwin, *Samuel Johnson* (see Chap. II, note 45), p. 90.

4 *YSJ,* pp. 226–227, 317; also Robert Bracey, "Dr. Johnson and Miss Hill Boothby," *Blackfriars,* XIII (April 1932), 223–230.

5 *Johns. Misc.,* I, 257.

6 *Life,* I, 244–246.

7 John Rylands Library, English MS. 556. See *The French Journals of Mrs. Thrale and Doctor Johnson,* ed. Moses Tyson and Henry Guppy (1932), pp. 44–46, and *Thraliana,* I, 579, n. 4.

8 *Letters,* I, 74–75 (No. 74). Chapman identifies the recipient as Charlotte, but from other evidence I think it was Frances Cotterell. The original letter, now in the Hyde collection, contains no indication as to the first name of Miss Cotterell. It may have been about this time that Johnson met Joshua Reynolds at Frances Cotterell's. F. W. Hilles, in *Portraits by Sir Joshua Reynolds* (New York: McGraw-Hill, 1952), p. 62, guesses that they did not meet until 1756, but I think the preceding year more likely.

9 *Johns. Misc.,* II, 261. First published by Croker.

10 See note 7, *French Journals,* p. 46. See also *Life,* I, 246.

11 *Johns. Misc.,* I, 408–409.

12 *Diaries, Prayers, and Annals,* pp. 56–57. See also pp. 57–58. Johnson did instruct young Francis Barber, his servant.

13 *Letters,* I, 75–76 (Nos. 74.1, 75, 75.1).

14 *Johns. Misc.*, I, 414. In the *Diary of Benjamin Robert Haydon*, ed. W. B. Pope Cambridge: Harvard, 1963), vol. v, entry for May 25, 1841, there is the statement: "Johnson after his Dictionary passed two years doing little. Sir Joshua thought his mind would not recover. This was nothing but the over relaxation of the string after constant tension."

15 John Wilson Croker's edition of *Boswell's Life of Johnson* (London, 1831), I, 227.

16 *Life*, I, 301–302; E. G. R. Taylor, "A Reward for the Longitude," *Mariner's Mirror*, XLV (February 1959), 59–66, (November), 339–341; Bodleian Library 4° BS. 729; B.L. Add. MS. 48,802A (listed as "Mr Williams by Mr Sam. Johnson"). Williams's *Account* was published in 1755.

17 *Life*, IV, 246, 525–526.

18 *Bibliography*, pp. 72–74; Hazen, pp. 12–15; 110–116, 148–151, 198–200, 247–248.

19 See suggestions by Donald Greene in *RES*, n.s. III (April 1952), 158–161, and *PMLA*, LXXIV (March 1959), 75–84; and Arthur Sherbo in *Johnsonian Studies*, ed. Magdi Wahba (Cairo, 1962; dist. Oxford University Press), pp. 133–159. For the Williams obituary see Taylor (note 16), p. 59, and Bodleian 4° BS 729.

20 See James Gray, *Johnson's Sermons: A Study* (Oxford: Clarendon Press, 1972), pp. 8–9; *Life*, III, 507, and v, 67; Waingrow, pp. 250–255.

21 B.L. Add. MS. 35,400, f. 268 (May 3, 1765). No further supporting evidence has ever been found.

22 *The Yale Edition of Horace Walpole's Correspondence*, vol. 37 (New Haven, Conn., 1974), p. 416.

23 Brack and Kelley, p. 105; Wm. Cooke, *The Life of Samuel Johnson, LL.D.* (London: G. Kearsley, 1785), p. 34.

24 *Johns. Misc.*, I, 412; Hazen, pp. 198–200.

25 *Letters*, I, 78 (No. 77), and pp. 78–79 (No. 78). Chapman reprints all Johnson's letters to Miss Boothby. The winter of 1755–1756 was described in the newspapers as extraordinary for wind and cold.

26 Mary C. Hyde, "Not in Chapman," *Johnson, Boswell and Their Circle: Essays Presented to L. F. Powell* (New York: Oxford University Press, 1965), p. 306.

27 *Letters*, I, 80–81 (No. 79). See also Nos. 78, 80, 81, 82, 84. For Johnson and orange peel see *Life*, II, 330–331; IV, 204–205.

28 Irwin (see note 3), p. 105–108.

29 *Johns. Misc.*, I, 257.

30 *Diaries, Prayers, and Annals*, pp. 59–60.

31 *Letters*, I, 83–86 (Nos. 85, 87, 88, 89), and letter of Catherine Talbot to Elizabeth Carter, Feb. 24, 1756. (See Chap. IV, note 47). The list of names described on pp. 156–157 may have been made at this time.

32 *Letters*, I, 86 (No. 90).

33 *Letters*, I, 89 (No. 94). See also letter No. 90, misdated by Chapman (I, 86). The endorser's "Feb." was probably a slip. See *Letters*, I, 426.

34 *Life*, I, 304, and n. 1 from 303. *Johns. Misc.*, II, 323 (anecdotes by George (Steevens).

35 Hawkins, p. 360; Robert Anderson's *Life of Samuel Johnson*, 3d ed. (Edinburgh, 1815), p. 255.

36 See Arthur Sherbo, *Christopher Smart: Scholar of the University* (East Lansing: Michigan State University Press, 1967), pp. 39–40, 68–71, 101–111, and Edward A. Bloom, *Samuel Johnson in Grub Street* (Providence, R.I.: Brown University Press, 1957). A copy of the contract was discovered in 1928.

37 Hawkins, p. 351; *Life*, I, 306–307; Greene, *Political Writings*, pp. 116–125.

38 Bloom, p. 124.

39 *Life*, II, 345.

CHAPTER XI: Speaking His Mind—*The Literary Magazine*

1 *Letters*, I, 90–91 (No. 96). On April 8 Dodsley wrote to Warton: "Your Essay is published . . . You have surely not kept your secret: Johnson mentioned it to Mr. Hitch as yours . . ." Wooll (Chap. IX, note 7), p. 237. For some details in this chapter I am indebted to Michael Selkin of the University of Maine.

2 Waingrow, pp. 23–24. Maty ended his connection with the *Journal Brittannique* in late 1755.

3 *Life*, I, 285, 543.

4 Now in the William Salt Library, Stafford, Staffordshire (S 630, vol. 1). The scrap may merely be a list of engagements or of people to see. Some words are very difficult to read. White could have been his servant, Mrs. White.

5 Much of what follows was first printed in my "Samuel Johnson and the Seven Years' War," *Lex et Scientia*, II (April–September 1975), 72–88. See also Donald J. Greene, "Johnson's Contributions to the *Literary Magazine*," *RES*, n.s. VII (October 1956), 367–392; his "Samuel Johnson and the Great War for Empire," in *English Writers of the Eighteenth Century*, ed. J. H. Middendorf (New York: Columbia, 1971), pp. 37–65; and *Political Writings*, pp. 126–183. See also *Bibliography*, pp. 75–77, and Edward A. Bloom, *Samuel Johnson in Grub Street* (Providence, R.I.: Brown University Press, 1957), pp. 89–112, etc. Donald Eddy of Cornell University is completing a book on the *Literary Magazine*. Quotations are from the Bodleian Library copy, available on microfilm.

6 *Letters*, I, 92–93 (No. 98.1).

7 *YSJ*, pp. 281–284.

8 *Life*, I, 545; Septimus Rivington, *The Publishing Family of Rivington* (1919), pp. 65–66.

9 Hawkins, p. 362.

10 *Johnson on Shakespeare*, ed. Arthur Sherbo (1968), I, 51–58 (vol. VII of the Yale Edition).

11 *Letters*, I, 91 (No. 97).

12 *Richardson's Correspondence* (1804), III, 136 (July 12, 1756).

13 Warton Papers, Trinity College, Oxford. The names of all twelve subscribers are on the list.

14 See, for example, the Greene and Bloom references in note 5.

15 Duncan Isles, "The Lennox Collection," *Harvard Library Bulletin*, XIX (January 1971), 44–47.

16 Ibid., p. 46, n. 82. Johnson did do a flattering review for the *Literary Magazine*, which appeared in the October number.

17 See Greene, *Political Writings*, p. 127, and *RES* (see note 5), pp. 380–383; and Bloom, p. 102.

18 For example, the *New Yorker* magazine used it to begin its "Talk of the Town" section in the issue of March 24, 1973. See also Greene, *Political Writings*, pp. 184–196.

19 Greene, *RES*, pp. 374–376, and Greene, *Politics*, p. 268. The main part of the piece was taken from John Armstrong's *History of Minorca* (London, 1740), but the latter portion may have been written by Johnson. See Greene in *English Writers* (note 5), pp. 49–52.

20 Strong support for the war with France may be found in later numbers. For example, see No. 8, pp. 398–399, 409–411.

21 See Greene, (note 4), *RES*, pp. 390–391; *Politics*, p. 269; *English Writers*, p. 43.

22 See Arthur Sherbo, *New Essays by Arthur Murphy* (East Lansing: Michigan State University Press, 1973), pp. 186, 99–100.

23 Greene, *Political Writings*, pp. 197–212. See also pp. 213–260.

24 *Letters*, I, 93–94 (No. 99.1).

25 Benjamin Victor, *Original Letters* (London, 1776), I, 287.

26 *Letters*, I, 77 (No. 75.2).

27 *YSJ*, pp. 241–242.

28 *Letters*, I, 86 (note for No. 91), and problems of dating other letters.

29 In Johnson's view of Hanway, in the *Literary Magazine* for May 1757. See Ruth K. McClure, "Johnson's Criticism of the Foundling Hospital and Its Consequences," *RES*, n.s. XXVII (February 1976), 17–26; and John Brownlow, *History and Objects of the Foundling Hospital* (3d ed., 1865), p. 10.

30 In his answer to Hanway in the June number of *The Literary Magazine*. See McClure (note 29), p. 21.

31 *Letters*, I, 441–442 (not numbered).

32 *Letters*, I, 100–101 (No. 106.1).

33 F. W. Hilles, *Portraits by Sir Joshua Reynolds* (New York: McGraw-Hill, 1952), pp. 62–63.

34 Unfortunately Reynolds's pocket book in which he noted all his engagements for 1756 has been lost, so that we cannot be certain when the sittings took place, but, according to Hilles, the portrait was completed by early 1757.

35 *Some Account of the Life and Writings of Mrs. Trimmer* (London, 1814), I, 8–9. (See also *JNL*, March 1963, pp. 11–12). I owe my knowledge of this to Donald Greene. The incident must have taken place shortly after 1755, when the Kirbys came to London.

36 *Life*, III, 222–223 and A. L. Reade, *Johnsonian Gleanings*, IV, 112.

37 *Life*, I, 239, note 1; *Johnsonian Gleanings*, II, 11–12.

38 *Letters*, I, 94 (No. 100).

39 *Harvard Library Bulletin*, XIX (January 1971), 49, n. 93. There is no evidence to show just when Frank returned.

40 *Life*, I, 317; Hazen, pp. 11–32; and *Works*, V, 207.

41 *Bibliography*, p. 78; Hazen, pp. 15–16, 116–125.

42 Boswell's *Journal of A Tour to the Hebrides* (original manuscript), ed. F. A. Pottle and C. H. Bennett (New York: Viking Press, 1936), pp. 234–235; *Life*, V, 269. Dating of the episode is possible from a letter of Young to Richardson on February 24, 1757, indicating that he planned to visit him the following Monday in order to read to him the "amended" "Conjectures." See Henry Pettit's edition of Young's *Letters* (Oxford: Clarendon Press, 1971), p. 452.

43 See note 15.

44 *Life*, I, 320.

45 *Life*, III, 20, 471–472 and I, 242, n. 1. Bathurst's letters may be found in Thomas Harwood, *The History and Antiquities of Lichfield* (London, 1806), pp. 451–452.

46 Hawkins, p. 350; *Letters*, I, 102 (No. 108).

47 *Diaries, Prayers, and Annals*, p. 63.

48 See Donald Greene, *Samuel Johnson* (New York: Twayne, 1970), pp. 128–132, etc. The most recent discussion is Richard B. Schwartz, *Samuel Johnson and the Problem of Evil* (Madison: University of Wisconsin Press, 1975). In B.L. Add. MS. 5873, pp. 5152, there are some interesting references to Jenyns and the review in William Cole's notes. Cole refers to Johnson as having "the Direction of this Magazine."

49 John Wilson Croker (ed.), *Boswell's Life of Johnson*, 2d ed. (London, 1876), p. 106, n. 1. For Boswell's reply see *Life*, I, 316, n. 2.

50 See Ruth McClure's account of the whole episode (note 29).

51 *London Chronicle*, June 16–18. Wilkie there called the allegations "groundless," but he did not give Johnson's name.

52 *Literary Magazine,* No. 13 (May 1757), p. 177.

53 John Nichols in his *Anecdotes* (II, 554) mentions Faden. When recounting a visit he had paid to Johnson, during his last days in the autumn of 1784, Nichols added: "Before I quitted him he asked whether any of the family of Faden the printer were living. Being told that the geographer near Charing Cross was Faden's son, he said, after a pause, "I borrowed a guinea of his father near thirty years ago; be so good as to take this, and pay it for me.""

54 *Gent. Mag.,* XXVII (November 1757), 527; LV² (October 1785), 764–765; Greene, *Political Writings,* pp. 261–265.

CHAPTER XII: *The Idler*

1 Hyde Collection; reproduced in *The R. B. Adam Library* (see Chap. VII, note 1), III, 198. There is nothing on the manuscript to indicate the recipient.

2 *Letters,* I, 36–37 (No. 32.1). Chapman wrongly places this in 1751. Other evidence makes 1757 conclusive.

3 A. L. Reade, *Johnsonian Gleanings,* IV, 8–9.

4 B. H. Bronson, "Introduction," *Johnson on Shakespeare,* vol. VII of the Yale Johnson Edition (1968), p. xvi. Other details concerning early progress with the edition come from this authority.

5 *Letters,* I, 102–103 (No. 109).

6 B.L. Add. MS. 28, 221, f. 5v (*The Percy Letters,* ed. Brooks and Falconer [see Chap. VII, note 14], p. 2); *Letters,* I, 104 (No. 112).

7 *Letters,* I, 105 (No. 113). To Burney, Mar. 8, 1758. Also No. 109.

8 *Diaries, Prayers, and Annals,* pp. 63–64.

9 *Letters,* I, 103–104 (No. 111). Perhaps to Warton or Chambers.

10 See note 6. Johnson later had sixteen volumes of the *Acta* in his library. See Donald Greene, *Samuel Johnson's Library: An Annotated Guide* (Victoria, B.C.: English Literary Studies, University of Victoria, 1975), pp. 25–26.

11 Duncan Isles, "The Lennox Collection," *Harvard Library Bulletin,* XIX (January 1971), 47–49; Hazen, pp. 142–146; E. L. McAdam, Jr., "Dr. Johnson and Saunders Welch's *Proposals,*" *RES,* n.s. IV (October 1953), 337–345; and Waingrow, pp. 6–7. Donald Greene believes that he dictated a speech on the Rochefort Expedition (*Political Writings,* pp. 261–265).

12 *Life,* III, 8–9.

13 *Letters,* I, 105 (No. 112.1).

14 See L. F. Powell, Introduction, *Idler and Adventurer,* vol. II of Yale Johnson Edition, pp. xv–xxiii (1963).

15 Hazen, pp. 205–213.

16 J. D. Fleeman, "Johnson's Literary Earnings" (see Chap. V, note 46), p. 214.

17 *Life*, I, 331. And see Charles Welsh, *A Bookseller of the Last Century* (London, 1885), p. 37.

18 *Johns. Misc.*, II, 215–216.

19 Introduction, *Idler and Adventurer*, p. xxii. Issue of Jan. 20, 1759.

20 *Universal Chronicle*, April 29–May 6, 1758. Dated May 1. I owe knowledge of this to Helen Louise McGuffie.

21 Ending of *Idler* 5. See pages 16–19 in Yale Edition.

22 See Greene, *Political Writings*, pp. 266–277.

23 *Life*, I, 328–330; also Roger Lonsdale, *Dr. Charles Burney* (New York: Oxford University Press, 1965), pp. 51–52.

24 *Life*, I, 328, n. 1.

25 *Town and Country Magazine*, VII (March 1775), 116. Repeated in numerous other papers such as the *London Packet*, the *Morning Chronicle*, and the *Weekly Magazine* (see McGuffie [Chap. XIII, note 19]).

26 Waingrow, p. 90.

27 For all the following details I am indebted to J. G. Woodward, G. R. H. Cooper, and others at the Guildhall Library. "Impropriate" meant in lay hands and "augmentation" meant additional to tithes.

28 Shown in Land Tax records, etc. Also *Life*, I, 350, n. 3.

29 *Letters*, I, 108–109 (No. 115).

30 Nichols, *Illustrations* (see Chap. IV, note 58), VII, 259. Later letter of July 20, 1758, is now in the Hyde collection.

31 *Letters*, I, 112–113 (No. 116.1).

32 For accounts of this performance see Ralph Straus, *Robert Dodsley* (London: John Lane, 1910), chap. x; and James Gray, "'More Blood than Brains': Robert Dodsley and the *Cleone* Affair," *Dalhousie Review*, LIV (Summer 1974), 207–227, and his "A Fresh Look at Dr. Johnson as Theatre Goer," *English Studies in Canada*, II (Spring 1976), 49, etc.

33 Straus, *Robert Dodsley*, pp. 202–203.

34 *Letters*, I, 114 (No. 117).

35 See Gray, *Dalhousie Review* (note 32), pp. 217–219, etc.

36 James Prior, *Life of Edmund Burke* (Philadelphia, 1825), p. 68; and Donald C. Bryant, *Edmund Burke and His Literary Friends* (St. Louis: Washington University Press, 1939), p. 16.

CHAPTER XIII: *Rasselas*

1 *Letters*, I, 113–115 (No. 117). Letters about this time to his mother and to Lucy Porter can be found in pp. 117–122 (Nos. 118, 119, 120, 121, 122, 123, 125, 126, 126.1, 127, 128, 129, 130).

2 George Irwin, *Samuel Johnson: A Personality in Conflict* (Auckland, N.Z.: Auckland University Press, 1971), pp. 107–113, etc.

3 *Life*, I, 341. Hester Mulso later commented in a letter to Elizabeth Carter, "they say he wrote it in three mornings." *Posthumous Works of Mrs. Chapone* (London, 1807), I, 110.

4 See *YSJ*, pp. 126, 145; *Ramblers*, Nos. 38, 65, 120, 186–187, 190, 204–205, etc. For background, see Mary Lascelles, "*Rasselas* Reconsidered," *Essays and Studies* (The English Association), 1951, pp. 37–52.

5 *Letters*, I, 117–118 (No. 124). For a detailed evaluation of the letter and its problems, see Gwin J. Kolb, "Johnson's 'Little Pompadour': A Textual Crux and a Hypothesis," *Restoration and Eighteenth-Century Literature: Essays in Honor of Alan Dugald McKillop* (Chicago: University of Chicago Press, 1963), pp. 125–142.

6 Brack and Kelley, pp. 109, 170, 236, and 279. (Cooke, Shaw, anonymous, and Harrison [?]).

7 *Diaries, Prayers, and Annals*, pp. 66–67. Sarah Johnson probably died on Sunday, January 21, or possibly on Saturday, the twentieth.

8 *The Idler and the Adventurer*, ed. W. J. Bate, John M. Bullitt, and L. F. Powell (New Haven, Conn.: Yale, 1963), pp. 128–131. Dated Saturday, Jan. 27, 1759.

9 Percy Diary, B.L. Add. MS. 32,336, ff. 19–21. I owe knowledge of these entries to Bertram H. Davis.

10 *Letters*, I, 122 (No. 130). See p. 200 concerning his move from Gough Square.

11 J. D. Fleeman, "Johnson's Literary Earnings," (Chap. v, note 46), p. 214; and *Life*, I, 350, n. 3.

12 See note 5. Kolb is editing *Rasselas* for the Yale Johnson Edition. Whether Johnson ever did the translation mentioned in the next paragraph is uncertain.

13 See Donald D. Eddy, "The Publication Date of the First Edition of *Rasselas*," *N&Q*, January 1962, pp. 21–22.

14 *Gent. Mag.*, XXIX (April 1759), 184–186; *London Magazine*, XXVIII (May 1759), 258–262; *Monthly Review*, XX (May 1759), 428–437. The reviewer in the last is identified in B. Nangle, *The Monthly Review, First Series, 1749–1789* (Oxford: Clarendon Press, 1934), p. 180.

15 *Lloyd's Evening Post and British Chronicle*, No. 280 (May 2–4, 1759), p. 428. Hawkesworth's remarks from the *Gent. Mag.* preceded the poem. An interesting later reaction came in a letter and poem by a supposed servant maid in Warwickshire, which appeared in the *London Chronicle* for Dec. 26–29, 1761, and was reprinted in the *Royal Magazine*, VI (January 1762), 9–10 and in other places.

16 *Critical Review*, VII (April 1759), 372–375.

17 See note 14. For Ruffhead see account in the *DNB*.

18 J. D. Fleeman (note 11), and Oliver Farrar Emerson, "The Text of Johnson's *Rasselas*," *Anglia*, XXII (December 1899), 499–509. Emerson is sure Johnson was responsible for the many changes.

19 For a list of all these see Helen Louise McGuffie, *Samuel Johnson in the British Press, 1749–1784* (New York: Garland, 1976), pp. 20–21.

20 *Annual Register* (1759), pp. 477–479.

21 *The Posthumous Works of Mrs. Chapone* (1807), pp. 108–111.

22 C. R. Tracy, "Democritus Arise! A Study of Dr. Johnson's Humor," *Yale Review*, XXXIX (Winter 1950), 294–310. See also Alvin Whitley, "The Comedy of *Rasselas*," *ELH*, XXIII (March 1956), 48–70, and Emrys Jones, "The Artistic Form of *Rasselas*," *RES*, n.s. XVIII (November 1967), 387–401; and Gwin J. Kolb, "The Structure of Rasselas," *PMLA*, LXVI (September 1951), 698–717.

23 See *Bicentenary Essays on Rasselas*, collected by Magdi Wahba, Supplement to *Cairo Studies in English* (Cairo: S.O.P. Press, 1959).

24 For example, see Richard B. Hovey, "Dr. Samuel Johnson, Psychiatrist," *MLQ*, XV (December 1954), 321–335; Nicholas Joost, "Whispers of Fancy; or, the Meaning of *Rasselas*," *Modern Age*, I (Fall, 1957), 166–173; Kathleen M. Grange, "Dr. Samuel Johnson's Account of a Schizophrenic Illness in *Rasselas*," *Medical History*, VI (April 1962), 162–169, 291; Kenneth T. Reed, "This Tasteless Tranquility: A Freudian Note on Johnson's *Rasselas*," *Literature and Psychology*, XIX (1969), 61–62.

25 See my article "Some Remarks on *Candide* and *Rasselas*," *Cairo Studies in English*, ed. Magdi Wahba (1959), pp. 7–14. Some of what follows first appeared there.

26 Joseph Wood Krutch, *Samuel Johnson* (New York: Holt, 1944), p. 182.

27 See William Kenney, "Johnson's *Rasselas* after Two Centuries," *Boston University Studies in English*, III (Summer 1957), 88–96.

28 Quoted by Kenney.

29 Frederick M. Link, "*Rasselas* and the Quest for Happiness," *Boston University Studies in English*, III (Summer 1957), 121–123. See also Bate, pp. 337–341.

30 *New Statesman*, XXV (Sept. 5, 1925), 571–572.

CHAPTER XIV: Struggling to Keep Alive

1 *Letters*, I, 123 (Nos. 132.2 and 132.1). David Fairer tells me that the period from January to December 1759 is the blankest of all in the Warton papers at Trinity. On this visit Johnson may have stayed with Robert Vansittart.

2 *Gent. Mag.*, XXIX (July 1759), 342.

3 *Life*, III, 245.

4 A. L. Reade, *Francis Barber: The Doctor's Negro Servant*, vol. II of *Johnsonian Gleanings* (privately printed, 1912), pp. 12–14; *Life*, I, 350.

5 *Letters*, I, 124 (No. 132.3).

6 *Life*, I, 349–350; Waingrow, p. 165.

7 Frank was officially discharged August 8, 1760, but told Boswell that he did not leave the Navy until "three days before George II died" (Waingrow, p. 165), which was on Oct. 25, 1760.

8 *European Magazine*, xxx (September 1796), 161.

9 See Hazen, pp. 89–94, and Isles, "Lennox Collection" (see Chap. III, note 26), pp. 327 and XIX, 53.

10 Hazen, pp. 216–237; Donald Greene, *Politics*, pp. 270–271.

11 *Life*, I, 351–352; Hawkins, pp. 373–377; Works (1825), V, 303–310.

12 For a fuller account of what follows see my "Johnson and the Society of Artists," in *The Augustan Milieu: Essays Presented to Louis A. Landa*, ed. H. K. Miller, Eric Rothstein, and G. S. Rousseau (Oxford: Clarendon Press, 1970), pp. 333–348. I quote from the original minutes with the permission of the President and Council of the Royal Academy of Arts. Early portions were printed in the *Walpole Society*, vol. VI (1918).

13 *Life*, II, 139; "Dr. Johnson and His Friends at the Society of Arts," *Journal of the Society of Arts*, XLVII (Oct. 12, 1900), 829–831; and John L. Abbott, "Dr. Johnson and the Society," *Journal of the Royal Society for the Encouragement of Arts &c.*, cxv (April-May 1967), 395–400, 486–491. See also F. R. Lewis, in *TLS*, June 25, 1938, p. 433.

14 *Life*, II, 139–140, n. 1.

15 Abbott (note 13), p. 397.

16 I owe this information to Mr. David Allan, Curator-Librarian of the Royal Society of Arts of London.

17 Just what the "good offices" had been is not completely clear.

18 The "Address" also appeared in the *Daily Advertiser* for Monday, Jan. 12, 1761, p. 1. In the *London Gazette* for Jan. 31–Feb. 3 appeared an address from the Society for the Encouragement of Arts, etc., but there is no evidence that Johnson had anything to do with it.

19 *Life*, I, 352; *Bibliography*, p. 99, etc.

20 Yale Boswell Papers, Cat. No. M 148. A copy was sent to Garrick in a letter of Sept. 10, 1772 (Cat. No. L 560), requesting corrections and additions. In this list no mention is made of where the piece had been published, although items above and below do carry such information. See also *Life*, III, 321. I am deeply indebted to Mrs. Marion Pottle, who has searched through all the Boswell Papers and sent me what is relevant to this matter. Three other manuscript lists of Johnson's works made by Boswell may be found in Cat. M. 147, Cat. M. 149, and in L 1095. For Boswell's explanation of his use of asterisk and dagger in ascribing Johnson's writings, see *Life*, I, 112, n. 4.

21 The address stirred up an anonymous set of verses in the *London Evening Post,* of Jan. 10–13 and the *Public Advertiser* of Jan. 14. See *Anecdotes of Painting in England 1760–1795 . . . Collected by Horace Walpole,* vol. v, edited by F. W. Hilles and Philip Daghlian (New Haven, Conn.: Yale University Press, 1937), pp. 1–3.

22 Abbott (note 13), pp. 488–490.

23 *Life,* ii, 364–365 (Apr. 18, 1775). Also Boswell Papers at Yale.

24 *Letters,* i, 134 (No. 138).

25 Arieh Sachs, *Passionate Intelligence: Imagination and Reason in the Works of Samuel Johnson* (Baltimore: Johns Hopkins, 1967), p. 3. See also John C. Riely, in *ECS,* iii (Spring 1970), 389–397.

26 James Harrison (?) suggests as much. Brack and Kelley, p. 273.

27 For a complete account see Maurice J. Quinlan, "Dr. Franklin Meets Dr. Johnson," *Pennsylvania Magazine of History and Biography,* lxxiii (January 1949), 34–44.

28 See my "Johnson and Foreign Visitors to London: Baretti and Others," in *Eighteenth Century Studies Presented to Arthur M. Wilson,* ed. Peter Gay (Hanover, N.H.: University Press of New England, 1972), pp. 111–112; and J. Torbarina, "The Meeting of Boskovič with Dr. Johnson," *Studia Romanica et Anglica Zagrabiensia,* No. 13–14 (July–December 1962), 3–12; *Life,* ii, 125, 406; iii, 318; *Johns. Misc.,* i, 416–417.

29 See my "Some Problems of Johnson's Obscure Middle Years," in *Johnson, Boswell and Their Circle: Essays Presented to L. F. Powell* (New York: Oxford University Press, 1965), pp. 101–106. The unpublished Hollis diary is now in the Houghton Library of Harvard University.

30 See Hollis diary entries of Dec. 17 and 21, 1761, and Jan. 3, 1762. When Johnson refused, Hawkesworth produced a version which Hollis found unacceptable.

31 Greene, *Political Writings,* pp. 285–289.

32 Frank D. MacKinnon, "Dr. Johnson and the Temple," *Cornhill Mag.,* n.s. lvii (October 1924), 465–477 (a paper read at the Johnson Club Mar. 21, 1924); *Life,* i, 350, 546; iii, 535.

33 *Life,* i, 350, n. 1; Waingrow, p. 165.

34 John Nichols, *Illustrations* (London, 1831), vi, 147–148.

35 *Johns. Misc.,* ii, 400. This was in 1764.

36 *Life,* i, 350, n. 3.

37 *Diaries, Prayers, and Annals,* p. 71.

38 *Life,* v, 284. See also *Life,* iii, 306, and i, 468–469.

39 *Life,* ii, 118–119.

40 Hawkins, p. 382.

41 See Charles Ryskamp, *Johnson & Cowper* (privately printed for the Johnsonians, 1965).

42 *Life*, IV, 134.

43 *Johns. Misc.*, II, 401.

44 See note 34.

45 *Life*, I, 250–251.

46 B.L. Add. MS. 35,399, f. 190v.

47 *Diaries, Prayers, and Annals*, pp. 73–74; David Fleeman, "Some Notes on Johnson's Prayers and Meditations," *RES*, n.s. XIX (May 1968), 174.

CHAPTER XV: Friend and Talker

1 *Life*, I, 421. Full accounts of Miss Williams may be found in the *European Mag.* XXXV (October 1799), 225–227 and Nichols, *Literary Anecdotes* (Chap. III, note 9), II, 179–181. Percy in his notes recorded that when Johnson was in Inner Temple Lane, "he lived alone; but went to drink tea with Mrs. Williams" (Ms. Percy d.11 f. 13v).

2 "An Account of Mr. John Ellis," *European Mag.*, XXI (January and February 1792), 3–5, 125–128; *Life*, III, 21.

3 *Life*, III, 21.

4 *Life*, III, 443–449; IV, 187, 274. For useful summations see Frederick M. Smith, *Some Friends of Doctor Johnson* (London: Hartley, 1931) and A. R. Winnet in *The New Rambler*, Spring 1971, pp. 6–17. Also letters of Thomas Birch to Yorke, Aug. 27, 1757, and May 14, 1763 (B.L. Add. MS. 35,398 and 35,400).

5 Howard H. Dunbar, *The Dramatic Career of Arthur Murphy* (New York: Oxford University Press, 1946), pp. 75–76.

6 B.L. Add. MS. 35,399, f. 191r.

7 *Works of Arthur Murphy* (London, 1786), VII, 3–12.

8 *Critical Review*, X (October 1760), 319–320.

9 *Life*, II, 374–375.

10 *The Universal Magazine*, CXI (October 1802), 237.

11 R. Freeman, *Kentish Poets* (1821), II, 191–192.

12 *The Library*, I (June 1761), 158.

13 *Gent. Mag.*, LII (January 1782), 19.

14 *Johns. Misc.*, II, 298. For recent important summations see John L. Abbott in *ECS*, III (1970), 339–350, and in *The New Rambler*, Autumn 1971, pp. 2–21.

15 In a letter of Birch to Lord Hardwicke, June 13, 1765. (B.L. Add. MS. 35,400). See also *Miscellaneous Works of Oliver Goldsmith* (London, 1801), I, 62–

63, and Bertram H. Davis, in *Transactions of the Lichfield Johnson Society*, 1976, p. 22.

16 Arthur Friedman, *Collected Works of Oliver Goldsmith* (New York: Oxford University Press, 1966), IV, 4–7. There are various versions of the story.

17 Thomas Tyers, *A Biographical Sketch of Dr. Samuel Johnson* (London, 1785). See Brack and Kelley, p. 79

18 Ibid., pp. 79–80.

19 See John H. Middendorf, "Dr. Johnson and Adam Smith," *PQ*, XL (April 1961), 281–296. Middendorf thinks this particular argument occurred at this time, though the dating cannot be documented.

20 *Letters*, I, 130 (No. 135).

21 Murphy's review of Hawkins, *Monthly Review*, LXXVI (May 1787), 374.

22 *Life*, II, 95.

23 *Life*, II, 299.

24 *Life*, II, 154–155; III, 69–70.

25 Arthur Sherbo, "Anecdotes by Mrs. LeNoir," *Durham University Journal*, LVII (June 1965), 168.

26 *Life*, I, 242.

27 Few copies of the first edition survive. With the help of Arthur Friedman I quote from the one in the British Library. It was reviewed in the *Critical Review*, X (April 1761), 291–293; *Gent. Mag.*, XXXI (March 1761), 136, etc.

28 I am indebted to Bertram H. Davis for much help with the Percy diaries which are in the British Library (Add. MS. 32,336). See also *Letters*, I, 127, 130 (Nos. 134.2 and 136).

29 Percy to Shenstone, May 22, 1761, in *The Percy Letters*, ed. Cleanth Brooks and A. F. Falconer (New Haven, Conn.: Yale, 1977), p. 96.

30 See Robert Anderson, *Life of Samuel Johnson*, 3d ed. (Edinburgh, 1815), p. 279.

31 Percy to Warton, May 28, 1761 (B.L. Add. MS. 42,560, f. 69.)

32 *Letters*, I, 132–135 (No. 138).

33 B.L. Add. MS. 35,399, f. 245 (Aug. 22, 1761).

34 B.L. Add. MS. 42,560, f. 89v (from Birmingham Mar. 29, 1762).

35 J. D. Fleeman, "Johnson's Literary Earnings," (Chap. V, note 46), p. 214. A reviewer in the *Critical Review*, XII (December 1761), 481, commented that Johnson, when he was writing the essays, was "never less *idle*." A total of 1500 copies were printed, selling for 5s. sewed, or 6s. bound.

36 For Johnson's publications during this period see *Bibliography*, pp. 99–100; Hazen, 19–23; 41–42, 98–102; 200–205.

37 Hazen, p. 100.

38 Greene, *Political Writings*, pp. 290–300; Hazen, pp. 38–42.

39 Hazen, p. 42; Greene, p. 293.

40 Hazen, p. 20.

41 *London Chronicle,* Oct. 22, 1761. The reason given for the delay was to digest some materials communicated by many learned gentlemen.

42 Again see my account in *The Augustan Milieu* (Chap. xiv, note 12), pp. 344–348. I relied heavily on the advice of the late F. W. Hilles.

43 Text from Hazen, pp. 204–205.

44 *Letters,* i, 139 (No. 142, July 20, 1762).

45 The best general summary of the affair is Douglas Grant, *The Cock Lane Ghost* (London: Macmillan, 1965). See also *Life,* i, 22, 407; iii, 268.

46 Text is taken from the *St. James's Chronicle,* Jan. 30–Feb. 2, 1762. It also appeared in the *London Chronicle,* February 2; *Daily Advertiser,* February 3, *Public Advertiser,* February 3, and other papers. Also in *Gent. Mag.,* xxxii (February 1762), 81. See also letter from Aldrich to Douglas (B.L. Egerton, 2182, f. 27).

47 Grant (note 45), p. 76.

48 Ibid., pp. 102–104.

49 *Johns. Misc.,* ii, 9.

50 *Boswell's London Journal,* ed. F. A. Pottle (New York: McGraw-Hill, 1950), p. 287. The version in *Life,* i, 418–419 is slightly different.

51 For a highly complimentary summation from someone not a close associate of Johnson see Tobias Smollett's evaluation in his *Continuation of the Complete History of England* (*Public Advertiser,* Oct. 8, 1761, p. 2, and *Scots Mag.,* xxiii, December 1761, 678).

CHAPTER XVI: Pensioner

1 ii (1759), 479. For a somewhat longer version of what follows see my "Problems of Johnson's Middle Years—the 1762 Pension," in *Studies in the Eighteenth Century III,* ed. R. F. Brissenden and J. C. Eade (Canberra: Australian National University Press, 1976), pp. 1–19.

2 B.L. Add. MS. 36,796, p. 248. In the "Register of Correspondence" of the Earl of Bute from 1739 to 1762, for Nov. 15, 1761, there is listed "Anonymous to the Earl of Bute Recommends Mr. Sam. Johnson to the notice of His Majesty as being worthy of a pension."

3 I owe my knowledge of this to Catherine Armet, and quote from it with the permission of the present Marquess of Bute. There is also a copy in the Boswell Papers at Yale (MS. Yale C 3182). The letter is dated Nov. 15, 1761.

4 See my essay (see note 1), pp. 8–10 and nn. 12–18.

5 *Diaries, Prayers, and Annals,* pp. 74–75.

6 *Letters,* i, 136–138 (Nos. 140 and 141).

7 *Letters from Mrs. Elizabeth Carter, to Mrs. Montagu,* ed. Montagu Pennington (London, 1817), I, 164.

8 I owe my knowledge of this to Helen Louise McGuffie. See also *YSJ,* pp. 213–215.

9 *Universal Museum,* March 1762, pp. 158–161.

10 See Brack and Kelley, pp. 1–3. A facsimile of the original piece with an introduction by O M Brack is available as publication No. 163 of the Augustan Reprint Society (1974). *Critical Review,* XIII (May 1762), 441–442.

11 *Edinburgh Magazine,* May 1762, pp. 222–225.

12 *Life,* I, 374.

13 William Shaw, in Brack and Kelley, p. 171.

14 See the *Catalogue of Prints and Drawings in the British Museum, Division I: Political and Personal Satires,* ed. F. G. Stephens (London, 1883). Vol. IV: No. 3843, "The State Ballance"; No. 3865, "Britannia guided by Justice &c.c.c."; and later ones—No. 3844, "The Hungry Mob of Scribblers and Etchers" (conjecturally dated May 26, 1762, but must be after July, since Johnson is included); No. 3885, "A Wonderful Sight"; No. 3979, "John a Boot's Asses"; and No. 4068, "The Irish Stubble alia[s] Bubble Goose."

15 B.L. Add. MS. 28,222, f. 4.

16 *Johns. Misc.,* I, 417–419. See also *Life,* I, 374.

17 *Letters,* I, 141 (No. 144).

18 *Life,* I, 375, n. 1.

19 *Johns. Misc.,* I, 418. Also *Life,* I, 429.

20 *Letters,* I, 140–141 (No. 143).

21 *St. James's Chronicle,* July 20–22, 1762; *Public Advertiser,* July 23; *London Evening Post,* July 22–24; *Gloucester Journal,* July 26, etc.

22 I owe this information to Roger Lonsdale. The letter is in the James M. Osborn Collection at Yale. Another example is a letter to Thomas Percy from his friend Edward Blakeway on July 31, 1762, now in the Northamptonshire Record Office (X 1079/ E (S) 1206, f. 42). Blakeway writes: "I most heartily congratulate you upon your friend Mr. Johnson's honorable pension. I have not lately seen a piece of news that has given me so much pleasure." I know of this through Bertram H. Davis. Percy may somehow have been involved in the process.

23 B.L. Add. MS. 35,399, ff. 307 and 319 (Aug. 7, 1762).

24 Quoted by George Nobbe, *The North Briton* (1939), p. 74. If Shaw is to be believed (*Memoirs,* pp. 116–117), Johnson did read this and remembered it years later. See Joel J. Gold, "John Wilkes and the Writings of 'Pensioner Johnson,'" *Studies in Burke and His Time,* XVIII (1977), 85–98.

25 B.L. Add. MS. 35,399, f. 323 (Aug. 14, 1762). Also f. 332.

26 See Nobbe, *North Briton,* pp. 75, 83–84.

27 Issue of Aug. 31–Sept. 2. The *St. James's Chronicle* had reprinted *The North Briton, No.* XII, in its issue of August 19–21, pp. 3–4.

28 It does not sound like Farmer. However, John Shebbeare is a possibility.

29 B.L. Add. MS., 28,222, f. 4. See also note 22.

30 *Gent. Mag.,* XXXII (August 1762), 379.

31 B.L. Add. MS. 35,399, f. 344, 346, and 361. Yorke was styled Viscount Royston before he succeeded to the Earldom of Hardwicke; hence Birch addresses him as "your Lordship."

32 *The Poetical Works of Charles Churchill,* ed. Douglas Grant (New York: Oxford University Press, 1956), p. 127.

33 London, 1772, p. 30 (perhaps by Francis Gentleman). In Edward Burnaby Greene's "The Laureat" (1765), in *Poetical Essays* (1772), p. 273, occur the lines:

> These the stern Johnson eye'd, and stalk'd along,
> The huge Colossus o'er an abject throng.
> This hand, with conscious joy a PENSION bore,
> And grasp'd the idol, which it loath'd before.

For some of the satirical prints, see especially "The Hungry Mob of Scribblers and Etchers" and "John a Boot's Asses," *Catalogue of Prints and Drawings* (IV, 3844 and 3979).

34 *Life,* I, 429, n. 2.

35 See my *Hester Lynch Piozzi (Mrs. Thrale),* 2d ed., rev. (Oxford: Clarendon Press, 1968), p. 74. Also Donald Greene, *Politics,* pp. 203, 319, etc.

36 Public Record Office, 30/8/229. pt. 1; in the Chatham Papers. I acknowledge help from Arthur Sherbo, Paul Korshin, and Donald Greene here.

37 See *The Jenkinson Papers, 1760–1766,* ed. Ninetta S. Jucker (New York: Macmillan, 1949), pp. 390–391, 203. The Peace mentioned is the Peace of Paris.

38 Murphy, *Johns. Misc.,* I, 419; also *Life,* IV, 168, n. 1 and 509.

CHAPTER XVII: Trip to Devon

1 *Letters,* I, 139 (No. 142). For an earlier version of what follows see my "Johnson's Trip to Devon in 1762," *Eighteenth-Century Studies in Honor of Donald F. Hyde,* ed. W. H. Bond (New York: Grolier Club, 1970), pp. 3–28. I am especially indebted to the late F. W. Hilles of Yale, and to Dr. John Edgcumbe of Exmouth, a great-great-great-grandson of Reynolds's sister Mary, for valuable help in retracing this trip.

2 Reynolds's engagement book for 1762 is at the Royal Academy of Arts in London. I am indebted to the Academy for permission to use the material.

3 Derek Hudson, *Sir Joshua Reynolds* (London: Bles, 1958), p. 77, suggests that Reynolds's spectacular coach was not acquired until at least two years later.

4 *Johns. Misc.,* II, 405; *Life,* I, 465, IV, 311.

5 *Life,* III, 245.

6 In Reynolds's engagement book, under the date Aug. 2, 1762, two weeks before the journey began, there is a note, in an unidentified hand, "Mr. Harris at Sturminster Marshall near Blandford Dorset, Grayhound Inn Blandford." For further details, see my earlier account (cited in note 1).

7 See letters of Horace Walpole to George Montague and to Horace Mann in the Yale Edition (Montague, II, 14, 52; Mann, VI, 33). None of the family may have been in residence in August 1762.

8 B.L. Add. MS. 47,989 (748A), Stephen Martin Leake's Letter Book (1726), pp. 49–50; *Boswell: The Ominous Years,* ed. Charles Ryskamp and F. A. Pottle (New York: McGraw-Hill, 1963), pp. 154–156. Boswell's visit was in 1775. An enthusiastic description of Wilton appeared in the *Royal Magazine,* June 1761, pp. 289–291. Johnson may have seen this.

9 See note 6.

10 Yale Boswell Papers, Cat. C252.

11 See B. Sprague Allen, *Tides in English Taste* (Cambridge, Mass.: Harvard, 1937), I, 52.

12 *Johns. Misc.,* II, 275.

13 See note 10.

14 *Life,* I, 145.

15 The original manuscript versions of Frances Reynolds's "Recollections of Dr. Johnson" are now in the Hyde Collection. Hill combined passages from early and late versions in *Johns. Misc.,* II, 274–275.

16 Dr. John Edgcumbe, from studying old maps, suggests this was their route.

17 *St. James's Chronicle,* Sept. 18, 1762.

18 *Sir Joshua's Nephew,* ed. Susan Radcliffe (1930). The original letters upon which this is based are now in the possession of Mr. W. R. van Straubenzee, M.B.E., M.P., of Wokingham, Berks.

19 *Letters,* I, 144–145 (No. 146).

20 *Sir Joshua's Nephew,* p. 222 ff.

21 B.L. Egerton, MS. 3700B, f. 28v. For help in describing the Johnson and Palmer families I owe much to Joyce Hemlow.

22 A. E. Richardson and C. Lovett Gill, *Regional Architecture of the West of England* (London: E. Benn, 1924), pp. 98–99, 101.

23 *The Devonshire Dialogue* was first printed in three parts by J. F. Palmer in 1837, and in four parts by Offy (Mrs. Gwatkin) in 1839, the latter being the more complete, authentic version.

24 *Sir Joshua's Nephew,* p. 111.

25 Frances d'Arblay, *Memoirs of Dr. Burney* (London, 1832), I, 332.

26 Sir Robert Edgcumbe, *The Parentage and Kinsfolk of Sir Joshua Reynolds* (London: Chiswick Press, 1901), p. 23. He is responsible also for the other anecdote concerning the pancakes.

27 H. L. Piozzi, *Anecdotes of Samuel Johnson* (*Johns. Misc.*, I, 213).

28 *Johns. Misc.*, II, 279. The monument cannot be found in the Wear churchyard today.

29 *Letters,* I, 144–145 (No. 146) to Frances Reynolds, Dec. 21, 1762.

30 Thomas Morrison, *A Pindarick Ode on Painting* (1767), Preface by F. W. Hilles and a biographical introduction by J. T. Kirkwood (Augustan Reprint Society, No. 37, 1952).

31 *Boswell's Tour to the Hebrides,* ed. F. A. Pottle and C. H. Bennett (New York: Viking Press, 1936), p. 74 (the original version).

32 For the Mudges see *Mudge Memoirs,* ed. S. R. Flint (Truro, 1883). While visiting the Mudges, Reynolds and Johnson measured their apartments for pictures, and at various times Reynolds painted members of the family. Unfortunately, Dr. Mudge lost a number of letters from Johnson written in 1762 after the visit. See his letter to Boswell, Nov. 13, 1787 (Yale Cat C. 2061).

33 *Memoirs of Richard Cumberland* (London, 1807), I, 357–358; *Life,* I, 313.

34 *London Chronicle,* May 2, 1769, p. 410.

35 *Life,* I, 378.

36 *Mudge Memoirs,* pp. 14–15.

37 *Letters,* I, 144 (No. 146). For Tolcher's part in the local quarrel, see *Johns. Misc.,* II, 419.

38 *Life,* I, 379. See also *Johns. Misc.,* II, 419.

39 *Mudge Memoirs,* pp. 84–85.

40 James Northcote, *Life of Sir Joshua Reynolds* (2d ed., 1818), I, 116–118.

41 See *Life,* I, 377–378, and *Mudge Memoirs,* p. 87. See also London newspapers. For Sir Charles Hardy's fleet see *St. James's Chronicle,* September 16. From a surviving plaque it appears that Capt. Rogers, later Sir Frederick, 4th Bt., a naval officer, was Commissioner from 1753 to 1775.

42 *Autobiography of Cornelia Knight* (London, 1861), I, 16.

43 Northcote (note 40), p. 116.

44 *Johns. Misc.,* II, 278.

45 *Life,* I, 293, 378.

46 *Life,* IV, 322.

47 *Northcote,* p. 118.

48 *Life,* I, 379, n. 2.

49 See Donald J. Greene, " 'Pictures to the Mind': Johnson and Imagery," in

Johnson, Boswell and Their Circle: Essays Presented to L. F. Powell (New York: Oxford University Press, 1965), pp. 137–158.

50 *Life*, I, 377, n. 2. For a discussion of other anecdotes which appear to be unreliable see my earlier account (note 1), p. 26.

51 B.L. Add. MS. 48,218, f. 58v. (letter from Anne Robinson, Saltram, Sept. 12, 1780).

52 William Cotton, *Some Account of the Ancient Borough Town of Plympton St. Maurice* (London, 1859), pp. 29–30.

53 *The Farington Diary* (London: Hutchinson & Co., 1925), v, 282 (Oct. 10, 1809).

CHAPTER XVIII: Secure but not Settled

1 Hawkins, pp. 435–436.

2 *The Poetical Works of Charles Churchill*, ed. Douglas Grant (New York: Oxford University Press, 1956), p. 126, lines 801–806.

3 Alan T. McKenzie, "Two Letters from Giuseppe Baretti to Samuel Johnson," *PMLA*, LXXXVI (March 1971), 220.

4 Hawkins, p. 440.

5 Alicia LeFanu, *Memoirs of the Life and Writings of Mrs. Frances Sheridan* (1824), 324–327.

6 *Johns. Misc.*, II, 408.

7 *Morning Post and Daily Advertiser*, Jan. 19, 1781, p. 2.

8 *Farington Diary*, II, 107 (June 13, 1803); *Johns. Misc.*, II, 76.

9 Letter from Irwin, Oct. 17, 1969. *Diaries, Prayers, and Annals*, p. 10.

10 *Memoirs of James Lackington* (new ed., 1792), pp. 433–435, and Maurice Quinlan, "Samuel Whyte's Anecdotes about Dr. Johnson," *Dartmouth College Library Bulletin*, January 1963, pp. 62–63; and Croker (1876), p. 439, n. 3.

11 Hazen, pp. 84–89. See also pp. 74–77. He refused to contribute to a new publication, *The Universal Museum*. See John G. Gazley, *The Life of Arthur Young* (Philadelphia: American Philosophical Society, 1973), p. 12.

12 Hazen, pp. 62–66; Fleeman (see Chap. v, note 46), pp. 215, 226.

13 *Letters*, I, 144–145 (No. 146) (see Chap. XVII above), and pp. 145–147 (No. 147). For an explanation of the various references see R. W. Chapman's notes.

14 *Boswell's London Journal*, ed. F. A. Pottle (New York: McGraw-Hill, 1950), p. 105.

15 Helen Louise McGuffie, *Samuel Johnson in the British Press, 1749–1784* (New York: Garland, 1976).

16 Added, too, was a fifth category, "Swops."

17 Mellifont had contributed a poem in the January 15 number.

18 Repeated in the *Caledonian Mercury* (Edinburgh) May 23; *Political Controversy*, May 30; *Public Advertiser*, June 4, etc.

19 From a microfilm of Francis Newbery's autobiography now in the University of Reading Library. See also Charles Welsh, *A Bookseller of the Last Century* (London, 1885), pp. 126–127, etc.

20 *Letters*, I, 142 (No. 144.1). Also letters Nos. 148, 149, 151, 155.

21 See J. A. Cochrane, *Dr. Johnson's Printer: The Life of William Strahan* (Cambridge, Mass.: Harvard, 1964), pp. 153–157, and Hawkins, pp. 583–587.

22 The most important discussion of this whole episode is Paul J. Korshin, "Dr. Johnson and Jeremy Bentham: An Unnoticed Relationship," *Modern Philology*, LXX (August 1972), 38–45. See in particular p. 39. See also *The Works of Jeremy Bentham*, ed. John Bowring (Edinburgh, 1853), X, 41, 124.

23 Korshin, pp. 41–42, and *The Correspondence of Jeremy Bentham*, ed. T. L. S. Sprigge (New York: Oxford University Press, 1968), I, 72.

24 J. Cradock's *Literary Memoirs* (London, 1828), IV, 332; *Johns. Misc.*, II, 192; *Memoirs of Hannah More* (3d ed., 1835), I, 200–201. See also *Life*, II, 51, 195, etc.

25 See notes 22 and 23; Korshin, p. 42; *Correspondence*, I, 79.

26 *Boswell's London Journal* (see note 14), pp. 259–261.

27 Ibid., pp. 259–260, and 10–16.

28 *Life*, I, 390–391; III, 223; and Peter Steese, "Boswell 'Walking upon Ashes,' " *English Symposium Papers*, No. 1 (1970). Boswell revised his account a good deal when preparing it for the *Life*, taking out some of the original shock.

29 *London Journal*, p. 267 ff.

30 *Boswell in Holland*, ed. F. A. Pottle (New York: McGraw-Hill, 1952), p. 2; and Pottle's *James Boswell: The Earlier Years* (New York: McGraw-Hill, 1966), pp. 121–122.

31 Bate, pp. 411–412, 414–417, 421, etc.

32 For some of the details see my *Hester Lynch Piozzi (Mrs. Thrale)* (Oxford: Clarendon Press, 1941, 1952); and Mary Hyde, *The Thrales of Streatham Park* (Cambridge, Mass.: Harvard, 1977).

INDEX

A SELECTIVE INDEX of persons, places, and subjects. Not all places, streets, classical authors, or authorities cited have been indexed. Citations of the following merely as authority for anecdotes and other information are not indexed: Thomas Birch, James Boswell, Charles Burney, Elizabeth Carter, Sir John Hawkins, Arthur Murphy, Thomas Percy, and Frances Reynolds. Maiden, and sometimes later married, names of women are given in parentheses.